# Fractional Calculus—Theory and Applications

# Fractional Calculus—Theory and Applications

Editor

**Jorge E. Macías Díaz**

MDPI • Basel • Beijing • Wuhan • Barcelona • Belgrade • Manchester • Tokyo • Cluj • Tianjin

*Editor*
Jorge E. Macías Díaz
Tallinn University
Estonia
Universidad Autónoma de
Aguascalientes
Mexico

*Editorial Office*
MDPI
St. Alban-Anlage 66
4052 Basel, Switzerland

This is a reprint of articles from the Special Issue published online in the open access journal *Axioms* (ISSN 2075-1680) (available at: https://www.mdpi.com/journal/axioms/special_issues/fractional_calculus_theory).

For citation purposes, cite each article independently as indicated on the article page online and as indicated below:

LastName, A.A.; LastName, B.B.; LastName, C.C. Article Title. *Journal Name* **Year**, *Volume Number*, Page Range.

**ISBN 978-3-0365-3262-2 (Hbk)**
**ISBN 978-3-0365-3263-9 (PDF)**

# Contents

# About the Editor

**Jorge E. Macías-Díaz** is a full-time professor at the Autonomous University of Aguascalientes (UAA), where he carries out teaching, research, outreach and administration activities, and a visiting associate professor at Tallinn University, Estonia. His work is internationally recognized for his contributions to the numerical analysis of partial differential equations, which have been the basis for the development of new results and techniques in the area. His articles focus on the rigorous analysis of numerical techniques and their efficient computational implementation. He was the first investigator to employ the fractional version of the discrete energy method for fractional hyperbolic systems, which has been subsequently used by other scholars to propose and analyze new computational methodologies.

He has 223 articles published or accepted in journals, 198 of them in Science Citation Index journals and more than a third in Q1 journals. He is one of the most active reviewers and editors in Mexico (Publons). He has been a reviewer for more than 150 journals; an editor of *Applied Numerical Mathematics* (Elsevier), the *International Journal of Computer Mathematics* (Taylor & Francis), *Open Physics* (De Gruyter), *Advances in Mathematical Physics* (Hindawi), *Axioms* (MDPI), and *Computational and Applied Mathematics* (Wiley); a guest editor for several Special Issues in the *Journal of Computational and Applied Mathematics* (Elsevier) and *Discrete Dynamics in Nature and Society* (Hindawi); and an evaluator of several national and foreign research proposals.

*axioms*

MDPI

*Editorial*

# Fractional Calculus—Theory and Applications

**Jorge E. Macías-Díaz [1,2]**

1 Department of Mathematics and Didactics of Mathematics, School of Digital Technologies, Tallinn University, 10120 Tallinn, Estonia; jorgmd@tlu.ee or jemacias@correo.uaa.mx; Tel.: +52-449-9108400

2 Departamento de Matemáticas y Física, Universidad Autónoma de Aguascalientes, Avenida Universidad 940, Ciudad Universitaria, Aguascalientes 20130, Mexico

**Citation:** Macías-Díaz, J.E. Fractional Calculus—Theory and Applications. *Axioms* **2022**, *11*, 43. https://doi.org/10.3390/axioms11020043

Received: 19 January 2022
Accepted: 20 January 2022
Published: 22 January 2022



In recent years, fractional calculus has witnessed tremendous progress in various areas of sciences and mathematics. On one hand, new definitions of fractional derivatives and integrals have appeared in recent years, extending the classical definitions in some sense or another. Moreover, the rigorous analysis of the functional properties of these new definitions has been an active area of research in mathematical analysis. Systems considering differential equations with fractional-order operators have been investigated rigorously from the analytical and numerical points of view, and potential applications have been proposed in the sciences and in technology. The purpose of this Special Issue is to serve as a specialized forum for the dissemination of recent progress in the theory of fractional calculus and its potential applications. We invite authors to submit high-quality reports on the analysis of fractional-order differential/integral equations, the analysis of new definitions of fractional derivatives, numerical methods for fractional-order equations, and applications to physical systems governed by fractional differential equations, among other interesting topics of research.

The present Special Issue includes 10 articles, which cover the following topics.

- Fractional-order differential/integral equations.
- Existence and regularity of solutions.
- Numerical methods for fractional equations.
- Analysis of convergence and stability.
- Applications to science and technology.

In one of the articles published in this Special Issue [1], the authors considered a fractional-order system of malaria pestilence. The stability of the model at equilibrium points was investigated by applying the Jacobian matrix technique. The contribution of the basic reproduction number, $R_0$, in the infection dynamics and stability analysis was elucidated. The results indicated that the given system is locally asymptotically stable at the disease-free steady-state solution when $R_0 < 1$. A similar result was obtained for the endemic equilibrium when $R_0 > 1$. The underlying system showed global stability at both steady states. The fractional-order system was then converted into a stochastic model. For a more realistic study of the disease dynamics, the non-parametric perturbation version of the stochastic epidemic model was developed and studied numerically. The general stochastic fractional Euler method, the Runge–Kutta method, and a proposed numerical method were applied to solve the model. The standard techniques failed to preserve the positivity property of the continuous system. Meanwhile, the proposed stochastic fractional nonstandard finite-difference method preserved the positivity. For the boundedness of the nonstandard finite-difference scheme, a result was established. All the analytical results were verified by numerical simulations.

The article [2] is devoted to studying GPU-based modeling for a parallel fractional-order derivative model of the spiral-plate heat exchanger. As pointed out by the authors, a spiral-plate heat exchanger with two fluids is a compact plant that only requires a small space and is excellent in high heat-transfer efficiency. However, the spiral-plate heat exchanger is a nonlinear plant with uncertainties, considering the difference between the heat fluid, the heated fluid, and other complex factors. The fractional-order derivation model is more accurate than the traditional integer-order model. In this paper, a parallel fractional order derivation model was proposed by considering the merit of the graphics processing unit (GPU). Then, the parallel fractional-order derivation model for the spiral-plate heat exchanger was constructed. Simulations show the relationships between the output temperature of heated fluid and the orders of fractional-order derivatives with two directional fluids impacted by complex factors, namely, the volume flow rate in hot fluid and the volume flow rate in cold fluid, respectively.

In turn, a forecasting of the economic growth of the Group of Seven (G7) via a fractional-order gradient descent approach was investigated in [3]. More concretely, this work established a model of economic growth for all G7 countries from 1973 to 2016, in which the gross domestic product (GDP) is related to land area, arable land, population, school attendance, gross capital formation, exports of goods and services, general government, final consumer spending and broad money. The fractional-order gradient descent and integer-order gradient descent were used to estimate the model parameters to fit the GDP and forecast GDP from 2017 to 2019. The results showed that the convergence rate of the fractional-order gradient descent is faster and has a better fitting accuracy and prediction effect.

In [4], the authors studied the approximate and analytic solutions of the time-fractional intermediate diffusion wave equation associated with the Fokker–Planck operator. More precisely, the time-fractional wave equation associated with the space-fractional Fokker–Planck operator and with the time-fractional-damped term were studied in this work. The concept of the Green function was implemented to drive the analytic solution of the three-term time-fractional equation. The explicit expressions for the green function of the three-term time-fractional wave equation with constant coefficients was also studied for two physical and biological models. The explicit analytic solutions for the two studied models were expressed in terms of the Weber, hypergeometric, exponential, and Mittag–Leffler functions. The relation to the diffusion equation was given therein. The asymptotic behaviors of the Mittag–Leffler function, the hypergeometric function, and the exponential functions were compared numerically. The Grünwald–Letnikov scheme was then used to derive the approximate difference schemes of the Caputo time-fractional operator and the Feller–Riesz space-fractional operator. The explicit difference scheme was numerically studied, and the simulations of the approximate solutions were plotted for different values of the fractional orders.

On the other hand, the authors of [5] reported on some new fractional estimates of inequalities for LR-$p$-convex interval-valued functions by means of pseudo order relation. Interval analysis provides tools to deal with data uncertainty. In general, interval analysis is typically used to deal with the models whose data are composed of inaccuracies that may occur from certain kinds of measurements. In this context, both the inclusion relation ($\subseteq$) and the pseudo-order relation ($\leq_p$) are two different concepts. By using the latter relation, the authors introduce the new class of nonconvex functions known as LR-$p$-convex interval-valued functions (LR-$p$-convex-IVFs). With the help of this relation, they establish a strong relationship between LR-$p$-convex-IVFs and Hermite–Hadamard-type inequalities (HH-type inequalities) via the Katugampola fractional integral operator. The results include a wide class of new and known inequalities for LR-$p$-convex-IVFs and their variant forms as special cases. Useful examples that demonstrate the applicability of the theory proposed in this study were given in that study.

Sequential Riemann–Liouville and Hadamard–Caputo fractional differential systems with nonlocal coupled fractional integral boundary conditions were studied in [6]. In that work, the authors investigated the existence of solutions for a fractional differential system that contains mixed Riemann–Liouville and Hadamard–Caputo fractional derivatives, complemented with nonlocal coupled fractional integral boundary conditions. They derived necessary conditions for the existence and uniqueness of solutions of those system by using standard fixed-point theorems, such as Banach contraction mapping principle and the

Leray–Schauder alternative. Numerical examples illustrating the theoretical results were also presented.

In [7], a numerical method for solving a fractional diffusion-wave and nonlinear Fredholm and Volterra integral equations with zero absolute error was presented. The method was based on Euler wavelet approximation and matrix inversion of $M \times M$ collocation points. The proposed equations were presented based on the Caputo fractional derivative, and the authors reduced the resulting system to a system of algebraic equations by implementing the Gaussian quadrature discretization. The reduced system was generated via the truncated Euler wavelet expansion. Several examples with known exact solutions were solved with zero absolute error. This method was also applied to the Fredholm and Volterra nonlinear integral equations and achieved the desired absolute error for all tested examples. The new numerical scheme is appealing in terms of its efficiency and accuracy in the field of numerical approximation.

On the other hand, some non-instantaneous impulsive boundary-value problems containing Caputo fractional derivatives of a function with respect to another function as well as Riemann–Stieltjes fractional integral boundary conditions were considered in [8]. In that work, the authors studied existence and uniqueness results for a new class of boundary-value problems consisting of non-instantaneous impulses and Caputo fractional derivative of a function with respect to another function, supplemented with Riemann–Stieltjes fractional integral boundary conditions. The existence of a unique solution was obtained via Banach's contraction mapping principle, while an existence result is established by using Leray–Schauder nonlinear alternative. Examples illustrating the main results were also constructed.

In article [9], the authors considered a retarded linear fractional differential system with distributed delays and Caputo-type derivatives of incommensurate orders. For this system, several a priori estimates for the solutions, applying the two traditional approaches (Gronwall's inequality and integral representations of the solutions) were obtained. As an application of the obtained estimates, different sufficient conditions that guarantee finite-time stability of the solutions were established. A comparison of the obtained different conditions was made with respect to the estimates and norms used.

Finally, a fractional coupled hybrid Sturm–Liouville differential equation with a multi-point boundary coupled hybrid condition was presented in [10]. It is worth recalling here that the Sturm–Liouville differential equation is an important tool for physics, applied mathematics, and other fields of engineering and science and has wide applications in quantum mechanics, classical mechanics, and wave phenomena. In this paper, the authors investigated the coupled hybrid version of the Sturm–Liouville differential equation. They studied the existence of solutions for the coupled hybrid Sturm–Liouville differential equation with multi-point boundary-coupled hybrid condition. Furthermore, they investigated the existence of solutions for the coupled hybrid Sturm–Liouville differential equation with an integral boundary coupled hybrid condition. To close that work, the authors gave an application and some examples to illustrate their results.

**Funding:** The editor wishes to acknowledge the financial support from the National Council for Science and Technology of Mexico (CONACYT) through grant A1-S-45928.

**Conflicts of Interest:** The editor declares no potential conflict of interest.

## References

1. Ahmed, N.; Macías-Díaz, J.E.; Raza, A.; Baleanu, D.; Rafiq, M.; Iqbal, Z.; Ahmad, M.O. Design, Analysis and Comparison of a Nonstandard Computational Method for the Solution of a General Stochastic Fractional Epidemic Model. *Axioms* **2022**, *11*, 10. [CrossRef]
2. Dong, G.; Deng, M. GPU Based Modelling and Analysis for Parallel Fractional Order Derivative Model of the Spiral-Plate Heat Exchanger. *Axioms* **2021**, *10*, 344. [CrossRef]
3. Wang, X.; Fečkan, M.; Wang, J. Forecasting Economic Growth of the Group of Seven via Fractional-Order Gradient Descent Approach. *Axioms* **2021**, *10*, 257. [CrossRef]

4. Abdel-Rehim, E.A. The Approximate and Analytic Solutions of the Time-Fractional Intermediate Diffusion Wave Equation Associated with the Fokker–Planck Operator and Applications. *Axioms* **2021**, *10*, 230. [CrossRef]
5. Khan, M.B.; Mohammed, P.O.; Noor, M.A.; Baleanu, D.; Guirao, J.L.G. Some new fractional estimates of inequalities for LR-p-convex interval-valued functions by means of pseudo order relation. *Axioms* **2021**, *10*, 175. [CrossRef]
6. Kiataramkul, C.; Yukunthorn, W.; Ntouyas, S.K.; Tariboon, J. Sequential Riemann–Liouville and Hadamard–Caputo fractional differential systems with nonlocal coupled fractional integral boundary conditions. *Axioms* **2021**, *10*, 174. [CrossRef]
7. Mohammad, M.; Trounev, A.; Alshbool, M. A novel numerical method for solving fractional diffusion-wave and nonlinear Fredholm and Volterra integral equations with zero absolute error. *Axioms* **2021**, *10*, 165. [CrossRef]
8. Asawasamrit, S.; Thadang, Y.; Ntouyas, S.K.; Tariboon, J. Non-Instantaneous Impulsive Boundary Value Problems Containing Caputo Fractional Derivative of a Function with Respect to Another Function and Riemann–Stieltjes Fractional Integral Boundary Conditions. *Axioms* **2021**, *10*, 130. [CrossRef]
9. Kiskinov, H.; Veselinova, M.; Madamlieva, E.; Zahariev, A. A Comparison of a Priori Estimates of the Solutions of a Linear Fractional System with Distributed Delays and Application to the Stability Analysis. *Axioms* **2021**, *10*, 75. [CrossRef]
10. Paknazar, M.; De La Sen, M. Fractional Coupled Hybrid Sturm–Liouville Differential Equation with Multi-Point Boundary Coupled Hybrid Condition. *Axioms* **2021**, *10*, 65. [CrossRef]

axioms

MDPI

Article

# Fractional Coupled Hybrid Sturm–Liouville Differential Equation with Multi-Point Boundary Coupled Hybrid Condition

**Mohadeseh Paknazar [1,†] and Manuel De La Sen [2,*,†]**

1 Department of Mathemathics Educations, Farhangian University, 1417466191 Tehran, Iran; m.paknazar@cfu.ac.ir
2 Institute of Reasearch and Development of Processes, University of Basque Country, 48940 Leioa, Spain
* Correspondence: manuel.delasen@ehu.eus
† These authors contributed equally to this work.

**Abstract:** The Sturm–Liouville differential equation is an important tool for physics, applied mathematics, and other fields of engineering and science and has wide applications in quantum mechanics, classical mechanics, and wave phenomena. In this paper, we investigate the coupled hybrid version of the Sturm–Liouville differential equation. Indeed, we study the existence of solutions for the coupled hybrid Sturm–Liouville differential equation with multi-point boundary coupled hybrid condition. Furthermore, we study the existence of solutions for the coupled hybrid Sturm–Liouville differential equation with an integral boundary coupled hybrid condition. We give an application and some examples to illustrate our results.

**Keywords:** Caputo fractional derivative; fractional differential equations; hybrid differential equations; coupled hybrid Sturm–Liouville differential equation; multi-point boundary coupled hybrid condition; integral boundary coupled hybrid condition; dhage type fixed point theorem

**MSC:** 34A08; 47H10

**Citation:** Paknazar, M.; De La Sen, M. Fractional Coupled Hybrid Sturm–Liouville Differential Equation with Multi-Point Boundary Coupled Hybrid Condition. *Axioms* **2021**, *10*, 65. https://doi.org/10.3390/axioms10020065

Academic Editor: Jorge E. Macías Díaz

Received: 9 March 2021
Accepted: 14 April 2021
Published: 16 April 2021

**Publisher's Note:** MDPI stays neutral with regard to jurisdictional claims in published maps and institutional affiliations.



## 1. Introduction and Preliminaries

Various papers have been published on fractional differential equations (FDEs) (see, e.g., in [1–6]). Over the years, hybrid fractional differential equations have attracted much attention. There have been many works on the hybrid differential equations, and we refer the readers to the papers in [7–17] and the references therein. During the history of mathematics, an important framework of problems called Sturm–Liouville differential equations has been in the spotlight of the mathematicians of applied mathematics and engineering; scientists of physics, quantum mechanics, and classical mechanics; and certain phenomena; for some examples see in [18,19] and the list of references of these papers. In such a manner, it is important that mathematicians design complicated and more general abstract mathematical models of procedures in the format of applicable fractional Sturm–Liouville differential equations, see in [20–22].

In 2011, Zhao et al. [15] investigated the following fractional hybrid differential equation involving Riemann–Liouville differential operators of order $0 < \alpha < 1$,

$$\begin{cases} D_c^{\alpha}\left(\dfrac{u(t)}{g(t,u(t))}\right) = f(t,u(t)),\ t \in I = [0,1] \\ u(0) = 0 \end{cases} \tag{1}$$

where $g \in C(I \times \mathbb{R}, \mathbb{R} \setminus \{0\})$ and $f \in C(I \times \mathbb{R}, \mathbb{R})$.

In 2019, El-Sayed et al. [23] investigated the following fractional Sturm–Liouville differential equation:

$$D_c^{\alpha}(p(t)u'(t)) + q(t)u(t) = h(t)f(u(t)),\ t \in I$$

with multi-point boundary hybrid condition

$$\begin{cases} u'(0) = 0, \\ \sum_{i=1}^{m} \xi_i u(a_i) = \nu \sum_{j=1}^{n} \eta_j u(b_j), \end{cases} \tag{2}$$

where $\alpha \in (0,1]$, $D_c^{\alpha}$ denotes the Caputo fractional derivative and $p \in C(I,\mathbb{R})$, $q(t)$, and $h(t)$ are absolutely continuous functions on $I = [0,T]$, $T < \infty$ with $p(t) \neq 0$ for all $t \in I$, $f : \mathbb{R} \to \mathbb{R}$ is defined and differentiable on the interval $I$, $0 \leq a_1 < a_2 < \ldots < a_m < c$, $d \leq b_1 < b_2 < \ldots < b_n < T$, $c < d$ and $\xi_i$, $\eta_j$ and $\nu \in \mathbb{R}$.

Motivated by the above results, we study the following fractional coupled hybrid Sturm–Liouville differential equation:

$$D_c^{\alpha}\left[p(t)D_c^{\beta}\left(\frac{u(t) - \zeta_1(t,u(t))}{\zeta_2(t,u(t))}\right) - k(t,u(t))\right] + q(t)u(t) = h(t)f(u(t)),$$

with multi-point boundary coupled hybrid condition

$$\begin{cases} D_c^{\beta}\left(\dfrac{u(t) - \zeta_1(t,u(t))}{\zeta_2(t,u(t))}\right)_{t=0} = k(0,u(0)), \\ \sum_{i=1}^{m} \xi_i \left(\dfrac{u(a_i) - \zeta_1(a_i,u(a_i))}{\zeta_2(a_i,u(a_i))}\right) = \nu \sum\limits_{j=1}^{n} \eta_j \left(\dfrac{u(b_j) - \zeta_1(b_j,u(b_j))}{\zeta_2(b_j,u(b_j))}\right), \end{cases}$$

Motivated by the above results, we study the following fractional coupled hybrid Sturm–Liouville differential equation:

$$D_c^{\alpha}\left[p(t)D_c^{\beta}\left(\frac{u(t) - \zeta_1(t,u(t))}{\zeta_2(t,u(t))}\right) - k(t,u(t))\right] + q(t)u(t) = h(t)f(u(t)),$$

with multi-point boundary coupled hybrid condition

$$\begin{cases} D_c^{\beta}\left(\dfrac{u(t) - \zeta_1(t,u(t))}{\zeta_2(t,u(t))}\right)_{t=0} = k(0,u(0)), \\ \sum_{i=1}^{m} \xi_i \left(\dfrac{u(a_i) - \zeta_1(a_i,u(a_i))}{\zeta_2(a_i,u(a_i))}\right) = \nu \sum\limits_{j=1}^{n} \eta_j \left(\dfrac{u(b_j) - \zeta_1(b_j,u(b_j))}{\zeta_2(b_j,u(b_j))}\right), \end{cases}$$

where $\alpha, \beta \in (0,1]$, $D_c^{\alpha}$ and $D_c^{\beta}$ denote the Caputo fractional derivative, $p \in C(I,\mathbb{R})$ and $q(t)$ and $h(t)$ are absolutely continuous functions on $I = [0,1]$, with $p(t) \neq 0$ for all $t \in I$, $\zeta_2(.,.) \in C(I \times \mathbb{R}, \mathbb{R} \setminus \{0\})$, $\zeta_1(.,.) \in C(I \times \mathbb{R}, \mathbb{R})$, $f(u(t)) : \mathbb{R} \to \mathbb{R}$ is defined on the interval $I$, $0 \leq a_1 < a_2 < \ldots < a_m < c$, $d \leq b_1 < b_2 < \ldots < b_n < 1$, $c < d$ and $\xi_i$, $\eta_j$ and $\nu \in \mathbb{R}$. Moreover, we study the existence of solutions for the coupled hybrid Sturm–Liouville differential equation with integral boundary coupled hybrid condition. We give an application and some examples to illustrate our results.

Define a supremum norm $\|.\|$ in $E = C(I,\mathbb{R})$ by $\|u\| = \sup_{t \in I} |u(t)|$, and a multiplication in $E$ by $(xy)(t) = x(t)y(t)$ for all $x, y \in E$. Evidently, $E$ is a Banach algebra with respect to above supremum norm and the multiplication in it; also notice that $\|u\|_{L_1} = \int_0^1 |u(s)|ds$ is the norm in $L_1[0,1]$.

It is well known that the Riemann–Liouville fractional integral of order $\alpha$ of a function $f$ is defined by $I^\alpha f(t) = \frac{1}{\Gamma(\alpha)} \int_0^t (t-s)^{\alpha-1} f(s)ds (\alpha > 0)$ and the Caputo derivative of order $\alpha$ for a function $f$ is defined by

$$D_c^\alpha f(t) = \frac{1}{\Gamma(n-\alpha)} \int_0^t \frac{f^{(n)}(s)}{(t-s)^{\alpha-n+1}} ds$$

where $n = [\alpha] + 1$ (for more details on Riemann–Liouville fractional integral and Caputo derivative see in [2,4,5]).

**Definition 1.** *Let $\alpha, \beta \in \mathbb{R}^+$. We have*

*(i)* $I^\alpha : L_1 \to L_1$ *and* $\lim_{\alpha \to 1} I^\alpha f(t) = I^1 f(t) = \int_0^t f(s)ds$.

*(ii)* $I^\alpha I^\beta f(t) = I^{\alpha+\beta} f(t)$.

*(iii) If $f(t)$ is absolutely continuous on $I$, then* $\lim_{\alpha \to 1} D_c^\alpha f(t) = Df(t)$ *and*

$$DI^\alpha f(t) = \frac{t^{\alpha-1}}{\Gamma(\alpha)} f(0) + I^\alpha Df(t), \ \alpha > 0.$$

*(iv)* $I^\alpha t^\gamma = \frac{\Gamma(\gamma+1) t^{\alpha+\gamma}}{\Gamma(\alpha+\gamma+1)}, \gamma > -1$.

The following hybrid fixed point result for three operators, due to Dhage [24], plays a key role in our first main theorem.

**Lemma 1.** *Let $S$ be a closed convex, bounded, and nonempty subset of a Banach algebra $E$ and let $\mathcal{A}, \mathcal{C} : E \to E$ and $\mathcal{B} : S \to E$ be three operators such that*

*(a) $\mathcal{A}$ and $\mathcal{C}$ is Lipschitzian with a Lipschitz constant $\delta$ and $\rho$, respectively;*

*(b) $\mathcal{B}$ are compact and continuous;*

*(c) $u = \mathcal{A}u\mathcal{B}v + \mathcal{C}u \ \Rightarrow \ u \in S$ for all $v \in S$;*

*(d) $\delta M + \rho < 1$ where $M = \|\mathcal{B}(S)\| = \sup_{z \in S} \|\mathcal{B}(z)\|$.*

*Then, the operator equation $u = \mathcal{A}u\mathcal{B}u + \mathcal{C}u$ has a solution in $S$.*

## 2. Main Results

In this section, we take into account the existence and uniqueness of solution for the following fractional coupled hybrid Sturm–Liouville differential equation:

$$D_c^\alpha \left[ p(t) D_c^\beta \left( \frac{u(t) - \zeta_1(t, u(t))}{\zeta_2(t, u(t))} \right) - k(t, u(t)) \right] + q(t)u(t) = h(t) f(u(t)), \tag{3}$$

with multi-point boundary coupled hybrid condition

$$\begin{cases} D_c^\beta \left( \frac{u(t) - \zeta_1(t, u(t))}{\zeta_2(t, u(t))} \right)_{t=0} = k(0, u(0)), \\ \sum_{i=1}^m \xi_i \left( \frac{u(a_i) - \zeta_1(a_i, u(a_i))}{\zeta_2(a_i, u(a_i))} \right) = \nu \sum_{j=1}^n \eta_j \left( \frac{u(b_j) - \zeta_1(b_j, u(b_j))}{\zeta_2(b_j, u(b_j))} \right), \end{cases} \tag{4}$$

where $\alpha, \beta \in (0,1]$, $D_c^\alpha$ and $D_c^\beta$ denote the Caputo fractional derivative, $p \in C(I, \mathbb{R})$ and $q(t)$ and $h(t)$ are absolutely continuous functions on $I = [0,1]$, with $p(t) \neq 0$ for all $t \in I$, $\zeta_2(.,.) \in C(I \times \mathbb{R}, \mathbb{R} \setminus \{0\})$, $\zeta_1(.,.) \in C(I \times \mathbb{R}, \mathbb{R})$, $f(u(t)) : \mathbb{R} \to \mathbb{R}$ is defined on $I$, $0 \le a_1 < a_2 < \ldots < a_m < c$, $d \le b_1 < b_2 < \ldots < b_n < 1$, $c < d$ and $\xi_i$, $\eta_j$ and $\nu \in \mathbb{R}$, under the following hypotheses.

$(D_1)$ The function $f(u(t)) : \mathbb{R} \to \mathbb{R}$ is defined on the interval $I$, $\frac{\partial f}{\partial u}$ is bounded on $I$ with $|\frac{\partial f}{\partial u}| \le \mathcal{K}$ and $f(u(t))$ is differentiable in $(0,1)$, right-differentiable at 0 and left-differentiable at 1.

$(D_2)$ The function $p \in C(I, \mathbb{R})$ with $p(t) \neq 0$ for all $t \in I$, $\inf_{t \in I} |p(t)| = p$. Furthermore, $q(t)$ and $h(t)$ are absolutely continuous functions on $I$.

$(D_3)$ The function $g : I \times \mathbb{R} \to \mathbb{R} \setminus \{0\}$ is continuous in its two variables, and there exists a function $\mu(t) \ge 0$ $(\forall t \in I)$ such that

$$|\zeta_2(t,x) - \zeta_2(t,y)| \le \mu(t)|x-y|$$

for all $(t,x,y) \in I \times \mathbb{R} \times \mathbb{R}$.

$(D_4)$ Two functions $f, k : I \times \mathbb{R} \to \mathbb{R}$ are continuous in their two variables, and there are two functions $\tilde{\mu}(t), \mu^*(t) \ge 0$ $(\forall t \in I)$ such that

$$|\zeta_1(t,x) - \zeta_1(t,y)| \le \tilde{\mu}(t)|x-y|$$

and

$$|k(t,x) - k(t,y)| \le \mu^*(t)|x-y|$$

for all $(t,x,y) \in I \times \mathbb{R} \times \mathbb{R}$, respectively.

$(D_5)$ There exists a number $r > 0$ such that

$$r \ge \frac{g_0\Theta + \zeta_1^*}{1 - \|\mu\|\Theta - \|\tilde{\mu}\|} \text{ and } \|\mu\|\Theta + \|\tilde{\mu}\| < 1,$$

where

$$\Theta = \frac{1}{p\Gamma(\alpha+\beta+1)}[E(\sum_{i=1}^{m} |\xi_i| + |\nu| \sum_{j=1}^{n} |\eta_j|) + 1][(\|q\| + \mathcal{K}\|h\| + \frac{\Gamma(\alpha+\beta+1)\|\mu^*\|}{\Gamma(\beta+1)})r$$
$$+ \mathcal{M}\|h\| + \frac{\Gamma(\alpha+\beta+1)k_0}{\Gamma(\beta+1)}],$$

$\zeta_1^* = \sup_{t \in I} \zeta_1(t,0)$, $\zeta_2^* = \sup_{t \in I} \zeta_2(t,0)$, $\mathcal{M} = f(0)$, $k_0 = \sup_{t \in I} k(t,0)$ and $E = \dfrac{1}{\sum_{i=1}^{m} \xi_i - \nu \sum_{j=1}^{n} \eta_j}$ where $\sum_{i=1}^{m} \xi_i - \nu \sum_{j=1}^{n} \eta_j \neq 0$.

**Definition 2.** *We say $D_c^\beta$ has the quotient-property with respect to $u_1, u_2 \in L_1(I, \mathbb{R}))$ with $u_2 \neq 0$, if $D_c^\beta(\frac{u_1(t)}{u_2(t)}) = \dfrac{u_2(t) D_c^\beta(u_1(t)) - u_1(t) D_c^\beta(u_2(t))}{(u_2(t))^2}$.*

We will use the following condition:

$(\mathcal{B}^*)$ $D_c^\beta$ has the quotient-property with respect to $\zeta_1(t, u(t))$ and $\zeta_2(t, u(t))$, and

$$D_c^\beta(\zeta_1(t,u(t)), D_c^\beta(\zeta_2(t,u(t)) \in C(I,\mathbb{R}) \ (\forall u \in C(I,\mathbb{R})).$$

**Lemma 2.** *Assume that the hypotheses $(D_1)$–$(D_2)$ are satisfied. Then, the problem (3) and (4) is equivalent to the integral equation*

$$\begin{aligned} u(t) = \zeta_2(t,u(t)) \Big[ & E\Big(\sum_{i=1}^{m} \xi_i Au(a_i) - \nu \sum_{j=1}^{n} \eta_j Au(b_j) + \nu \sum_{j=1}^{n} \eta_j Bu(b_j) \\ & - \sum_{i=1}^{m} \xi_i Bu(a_i)\Big) + \nu \sum_{j=1}^{n} \eta_j Cu(b_j) - \sum_{i=1}^{m} \xi_i Cu(a_i)) - Au(t) + Bu(t) + Cu(t) \Big] \\ & + \zeta_1(t,u(t)). \end{aligned} \tag{5}$$

*where* $Au(t) = I^{\beta}\Big(\frac{1}{p(t)}I^{\alpha}(q(t)u(t))\Big)$, $Bu(t) = I^{\beta}\Big(\frac{1}{p(t)}I^{\alpha}(h(t)f(u(t)))\Big)$, $C(t) = I^{\beta}\Big(\frac{1}{p(t)}k(t,u(t))\Big)$ *and* $E = \dfrac{1}{\sum_{i=1}^{m}\xi_i - \nu\sum_{j=1}^{n}\eta_j}$. *Moreover,*

- $D_c^{\beta}\left(\dfrac{u(t)-\zeta_1(t,u(t))}{\zeta_2(t,u(t))}\right) \in C(I,\mathbb{R})$;
- *if* $(\mathcal{B}^*)$ *holds, then* $D_c^{\beta}(u(t)) \in C(I,\mathbb{R})$;
- $\dfrac{d}{dt}\left[D_c^{\beta}\left(\dfrac{u(t)-\zeta_1(t,u(t))}{\zeta_2(t,u(t))}\right) - k(t,u(t))\right] \in L_1[0,1]$.

**Proof.** Equation (3) can be written as

$$I^{1-\alpha}\left(\frac{d}{dt}\left[p(t)D_c^{\beta}\left(\frac{u(t)-\zeta_1(t,u(t))}{\zeta_2(t,u(t))}\right) - k(t,u(t))\right]\right) = -q(t)u(t) + h(t)f(u(t)).$$

Operating by $I^{\alpha}$ on both sides, we get

$$I^{1}\left(\frac{d}{dt}\left[p(t)D_c^{\beta}\left(\frac{u(t)-\zeta_1(t,u(t))}{\zeta_2(t,u(t))}\right) - k(t,u(t))\right]\right) = -I^{\alpha}(q(t)u(t)) + I^{\alpha}(h(t)f(u(t))).$$

Consequently,

$$p(t)D_c^{\beta}\left(\frac{u(t)-\zeta_1(t,u(t))}{\zeta_2(t,u(t))}\right) - k(t,u(t)) - p(0)D_c^{\beta}\left(\frac{u(t)-\zeta_1(t,u(t))}{\zeta_2(t,u(t))}\right)_{t=0} + k(0,u(0))$$
$$= -I^{\alpha}(q(t)u(t)) + I^{\alpha}(h(t)f(u(t))).$$

As $D_c^{\beta}\left(\dfrac{u(t)-\zeta_1(t,u(t))}{\zeta_2(t,u(t))}\right)_{t=0} = k(0,u(0))$, we have

$$p(t)D_c^{\beta}\left(\frac{u(t)-\zeta_1(t,u(t))}{\zeta_2(t,u(t))}\right) - k(t,u(t)) = -I^{\alpha}(q(t)u(t)) + I^{\alpha}(h(t)f(u(t))).$$

and so

$$D_c^{\beta}\left(\frac{u(t)-\zeta_1(t,u(t))}{\zeta_2(t,u(t))}\right) = -\frac{1}{p(t)}I^{\alpha}(q(t)u(t)) + \frac{1}{p(t)}I^{\alpha}(h(t)f(u(t))) + \frac{1}{p(t)}k(t,u(t)). \quad (6)$$

The above equation can be written as

$$I^{1-\beta}\frac{d}{dt}\left(\frac{u(t)-\zeta_1(t,u(t))}{\zeta_2(t,u(t))}\right) = -\frac{1}{p(t)}I^{\alpha}(q(t)u(t)) + \frac{1}{p(t)}I^{\alpha}(h(t)f(u(t))) + \frac{1}{p(t)}k(t,u(t)).$$

Operating by $I^{\beta}$ on both sides, we obtain

$$I^{1}\frac{d}{dt}\left(\frac{u(t)-\zeta_1(t,u(t))}{\zeta_2(t,u(t))}\right) = -I^{\beta}\left(\frac{1}{p(t)}I^{\alpha}(q(t)u(t))\right) + I^{\beta}\left(\frac{1}{p(t)}I^{\alpha}(h(t)f(u(t)))\right)$$
$$+ I^{\beta}\left(\frac{1}{p(t)}k(t,u(t))\right).$$

Therefore, we can obtain

$$\begin{aligned}\frac{u(t)-\zeta_1(t,u(t))}{\zeta_2(t,u(t))}-\ell &= -I^{\beta}\Big(\frac{1}{p(t)}I^{\alpha}(q(t)u(t))\Big)+I^{\beta}\Big(\frac{1}{p(t)}I^{\alpha}(h(t)f(u(t)))\Big)\\ &+I^{\beta}\Big(\frac{1}{p(t)}k(t,u(t))\Big) = -Au(t)+Bu(t)+Cu(t).\end{aligned} \tag{7}$$

where $\ell = \dfrac{u(0)-f(0,u(0))}{g(0,u(0))}$. Now, we get

$$\sum_{i=1}^{m}\xi_i\Big(\frac{u(a_i)-\zeta_1(t,u(a_i))}{\zeta_2(t,u(a_i))}\Big)-\sum_{i=1}^{m}\xi_i\ell = -\sum_{i=1}^{m}\xi_i Au(a_i)+\sum_{i=1}^{m}\xi_i Bu(a_i)+\sum_{i=1}^{m}\xi_i Cu(a_i). \tag{8}$$

and

$$\begin{aligned}\nu\sum_{j=1}^{n}\eta_j\Big(\frac{u(b_j)-\zeta_1(b_j,u(b_j))}{\zeta_2(b_j,u(b_j))}\Big)-\nu\sum_{j=1}^{n}\eta_j\ell &= -\nu\sum_{j=1}^{n}\eta_j Au(b_j)+\nu\sum_{j=1}^{n}\eta_j Bu(b_j)\\ &+\nu\sum_{j=1}^{n}\eta_j Cu(b_j).\end{aligned} \tag{9}$$

On subtracting (8) from (9) and applying

$$\sum_{i=1}^{m}\xi_i\Big(\frac{u(a_i)-\zeta_1(a_i,u(a_i))}{\zeta_2(a_i,u(a_i))}\Big) = \nu\sum_{j=1}^{n}\eta_j\Big(\frac{u(b_j)-\zeta_1(b_j,u(b_j))}{\zeta_2(b_j,u(b_j))}\Big),$$

we deduce that

$$\begin{aligned}\ell = E\Big(&\sum_{i=1}^{m}\xi_i Au(a_i)-\nu\sum_{j=1}^{n}\eta_j Au(b_j)+\nu\sum_{j=1}^{n}\eta_j Bu(b_j)-\sum_{i=1}^{m}\xi_i Bu(a_i)\\ &+\nu\sum_{j=1}^{n}\eta_j Cu(b_j)-\sum_{i=1}^{m}\xi_i Cu(a_i)\Big)\end{aligned}$$

where $E = \dfrac{1}{\sum_{i=1}^{m}\xi_i-\nu\sum_{j=1}^{n}\eta_j}$. Therefore, by substituting the value of $\ell$ in (7), we get

$$\begin{aligned}u(t) = \zeta_2(t,u(t))\Big[&E\Big(\sum_{i=1}^{m}\xi_i Au(a_i)-\nu\sum_{j=1}^{n}\eta_j Au(b_j)+\nu\sum_{j=1}^{n}\eta_j Bu(b_j)\\ &-\sum_{i=1}^{m}\xi_i Bu(a_i)\Big)+\nu\sum_{j=1}^{n}\eta_j Cu(b_j)-\sum_{i=1}^{m}\xi_i Cu(a_i)\Big)-Au(t)+Bu(t)+Cu(t)\Big]+\zeta_1(t,u(t)).\end{aligned}$$

Conversely, to complete the equivalence between integral Equation (5) and the problem (3) and (4), we have from (6)

$$\begin{aligned}D_c^{\beta}\Big(\frac{u(t)-\zeta_1(t,u(t))}{\zeta_2(t,u(t))}\Big) &= -\frac{1}{p(t)}I^{\alpha}(q(t)u(t))+\frac{1}{p(t)}I^{\alpha}(h(t)f(u(t)))\\ &+\frac{1}{p(t)}k(t,u(t))\in C([0,1]).\end{aligned} \tag{10}$$

and so

$$\frac{d}{dt}\Big[p(t)D_c^{\beta}\Big(\frac{u(t)-\zeta_1(t,u(t))}{\zeta_2(t,u(t))}\Big)-k(t,u(t))\Big] = -\frac{d}{dt}I^{\alpha}(q(t)u(t))+\frac{d}{dt}I^{\alpha}(h(t)f(u(t)))$$

Operating by $I^{1-\alpha}$ on both sides, we obtain

$$I^{1-\alpha}\frac{d}{dt}\left[p(t)D_c^{\beta}\left(\frac{u(t)-\zeta_1(t,u(t))}{\zeta_2(t,u(t))}\right)-k(t,u(t))\right]=-I^{1-\alpha}\frac{d}{dt}I^{\alpha}(q(t)u(t))$$
$$+I^{1-\alpha}\frac{d}{dt}I^{\alpha}(h(t)f(u(t)))$$

Now, by using the definition of Caputo derivative and (iii), we get

$$\begin{aligned}D^{\alpha}&\left[p(t)D_c^{\beta}\left(\frac{u(t)-\zeta_1(t,u(t))}{\zeta_2(t,u(t))}\right)-k(t,u(t))\right]\\&=-I^{1-\alpha}I^{\alpha}\frac{d}{dt}(q(t)u(t))+I^{1-\alpha}I^{\alpha}\frac{d}{dt}(h(t)f(u(t)))\\&-I^{1-\alpha}\frac{t^{\alpha-1}}{\Gamma(\alpha)}q(0)u(0)+I^{1-\alpha}\frac{t^{\alpha-1}}{\Gamma(\alpha)}h(0)f(u(0)),\end{aligned}$$

and then by applying (ii) and (iv), we have

$$\begin{aligned}D^{\alpha}\left[p(t)D_c^{\beta}\left(\frac{u(t)-\zeta_1(t,u(t))}{\zeta_2(t,u(t))}\right)-k(t,u(t))\right]&=-I^{1}\frac{d}{dt}(q(t)u(t))+I^{1}\frac{d}{dt}(h(t)f(u(t)))\\&-q(0)u(0)+h(0)f(u(0))\\&=-q(t)u(t)+h(t)f(u(t)).\end{aligned}$$

and so we get (3). Clearly, from (6), we can get

$$D_c^{\beta}\left(\frac{u(t)-\zeta_1(t,u(t))}{\zeta_2(t,u(t))}\right)_{t=0}=k(0,u(0)).$$

Moreover, by using a simple computation and (5), we can obtain

$$\sum_{i=1}^{m}\xi_i\left(\frac{u(a_i)-\zeta_1(a_i,u(a_i))}{\zeta_2(a_i,u(a_i))}\right)=\nu\sum_{j=1}^{n}\eta_j\left(\frac{u(b_j)-\zeta_1(b_j,u(b_j))}{\zeta_2(b_j,u(b_j))}\right).$$

Now, assume that $(B^*)$ holds. From (10), we know that

$$\mathcal{H}(t):=D_c^{\beta}\left(\frac{u(t)-\zeta_1(t,u(t))}{\zeta_2(t,u(t))}\right)\in C(I,\mathbb{R}).$$

Then,

$$\begin{aligned}\mathcal{H}(t)&=D_c^{\beta}\left(\frac{u(t)-\zeta_1(t,u(t))}{\zeta_2(t,u(t))}\right)\\&=\frac{\zeta_2(t,u(t))D_c^{\beta}(u(t)-\zeta_1(t,u(t)))-(u(t)-\zeta_1(t,u(t)))D_c^{\beta}(\zeta_2(t,u(t)))}{(\zeta_2(t,u(t)))^2},\end{aligned}$$

and so

$$\begin{aligned}\mathcal{H}(t)&=D_c^{\beta}\left(\frac{u(t)-\zeta_1(t,u(t))}{\zeta_2(t,u(t))}\right)\\&=\frac{\zeta_2(t,u(t))D_c^{\beta}(u(t)-\zeta_1(t,u(t)))-(u(t)-\zeta_1(t,u(t)))D_c^{\beta}(\zeta_2(t,u(t)))}{(\zeta_2(t,u(t)))^2}\\&=\frac{\zeta_2(t,u(t))D_c^{\beta}(u(t))-\zeta_2(t,u(t))D_c^{\beta}(\zeta_1(t,u(t)))-(u(t)-\zeta_1(t,u(t)))D_c^{\beta}(\zeta_2(t,u(t)))}{(\zeta_2(t,u(t)))^2}\\&=\frac{D_c^{\beta}(u(t))}{\zeta_2(t,u(t))}-\frac{\zeta_2(t,u(t))D_c^{\beta}(\zeta_1(t,u(t)))+(u(t)-\zeta_1(t,u(t)))D_c^{\beta}(\zeta_2(t,u(t)))}{(\zeta_2(t,u(t)))^2}.\end{aligned}$$

Therefore, we have

$$
\begin{aligned}
&D_c^{\beta}(u(t))\\
&=\zeta_2(t,u(t))\left(\mathcal{H}(t)+\frac{\zeta_2(t,u(t))D_c^{\beta}(\zeta_1(t,u(t)))+(u(t)-\zeta_1(t,u(t)))D_c^{\beta}(\zeta_2(t,u(t)))}{(\zeta_2(t,u(t)))^2}\right)\\
&\in C(I,\mathbb{R}).
\end{aligned}
$$

Let us prove that $\frac{d}{dt}\left[D_c^{\beta}\left(\frac{u(t)-\zeta_1(t,u(t))}{\zeta_2(t,u(t))}\right)-k(t,u(t))\right]\in L_1[0,1]$. From (6) and (iii) of Definition 1 we have

$$
\begin{aligned}
\frac{d}{dt}\left[D_c^{\beta}\left(\frac{u(t)-\zeta_1(t,u(t))}{\zeta_2(t,u(t))}\right)-k(t,u(t))\right] &= \frac{d}{dt}\left(\frac{1}{p(t)}I^{\alpha}(-q(t)u(t)+h(t)f(u(t)))\right)\\
&=-\frac{p'(t)}{p^2(t)}I^{\alpha}(-q(t)u(t)+h(t)f(u(t)))\\
&+\frac{1}{p(t)}I^{\alpha}\frac{d}{dt}(-q(t)u(t)+h(t)f(u(t)))\\
&+\frac{1}{p(t)}\frac{t^{\alpha-1}}{\Gamma(\alpha)}(q(0)u(0)+h(0)f(u(0))).
\end{aligned}
$$

Now, we can write

$$
\begin{aligned}
&\left|\frac{d}{dt}\left[D_c^{\beta}\left(\frac{u(t)-\zeta_1(t,u(t))}{\zeta_2(t,u(t))}\right)-k(t,u(t))\right]\right|\\
&\qquad\le\frac{|p'(t)|}{|p^2(t)|}\int_0^t\frac{(t-s)^{\alpha-1}}{\Gamma(\alpha)}(|q(s)||u(s)|+|h(s)||f(u(s))|)ds\\
&\qquad+\frac{1}{|p(t)|}\int_0^t\frac{(t-s)^{\alpha-1}}{\Gamma(\alpha)}\Big(|q'(s)||u(s)|+|q(s)||u'(s)|\\
&\qquad+|h'(s)|f(u(s))|+|h(s)||\frac{\partial f(u(s))}{\partial u}||u'(s)|\Big)ds\\
&\qquad+\frac{1}{|p(t)|}\frac{t^{\alpha-1}}{\Gamma(\alpha)}(|q(0)||u(0)|+|h(0)||f(u(0))|).
\end{aligned}
$$

Therefore,

$$
\begin{aligned}
&\int_0^1\left|\frac{d}{dt}\left[D_c^{\beta}\left(\frac{u(t)-\zeta_1(t,u(t))}{\zeta_2(t,u(t))}\right)-k(t,u(t))\right]\right|dt\\
&\le\int_0^1\frac{|p'(t)|}{|p^2(t)|}\int_0^t\frac{(t-s)^{\alpha-1}}{\Gamma(\alpha)}(|q(s)||u(s)|\\
&+|h(s)||f(u(s))|)dsdt+\int_0^1\frac{1}{|p(t)|}\int_0^t\frac{(t-s)^{\alpha-1}}{\Gamma(\alpha)}\Big(|q'(s)||u(s)|+|q(s)||u'(s)|\\
&+|h'(s)|f(u(s))|+|h(s)||\frac{\partial f(u(s))}{\partial u}||u'(s)|\Big)dsdt\\
&+(|q(0)||u(0)|+|h(0)||f(u(0))|)\int_0^1\frac{1}{|p(t)|}\frac{t^{\alpha-1}}{\Gamma(\alpha)}dt.
\end{aligned}
$$

Notice that

$$\begin{aligned}
&\int_0^1 \frac{|p'(t)|}{|p^2(t)|}\int_0^t \frac{(t-s)^{\alpha-1}}{\Gamma(\alpha)}(|q(s)||u(s)|+|h(s)||f(u(s))|)dsdt \\
&= \int_0^1 (|q(s)||u(s)|+|h(s)||f(u(s))|)ds\int_s^1 \frac{|p'(t)|}{|p^2(t)|}\frac{(t-s)^{\alpha-1}}{\Gamma(\alpha)}dt \\
&\le (\|q(s)\|\|u(s)\|+\|h(s)\|\|f(u(s))\|)\frac{\|p'\|}{p^2\Gamma(\alpha+1)},
\end{aligned}$$

$$\begin{aligned}
&\int_0^1 \frac{1}{|p(t)|}\int_0^t \frac{(t-s)^{\alpha-1}}{\Gamma(\alpha)}\Big(|q'(s)||u(s)|+|q(s)||u'(s)|+|h'(s)|f(u(s))| \\
&+|h(s)||\frac{\partial f(u(s))}{\partial u}||u'(s)|\Big)dsdt \\
&\le \Big(\|q'\|_{L_1}\|u\|+\|q\|\|u'\|+\|h'\|_{L_1}\|f\|+\mathcal{K}\|h\|\|u'\|\Big)\frac{1}{p\Gamma(\alpha+1)},
\end{aligned}$$

and

$$\begin{aligned}
&\int_0^1 \frac{1}{|p(t)|}\frac{t^{\alpha-1}}{\Gamma(\alpha)}(|q(0)||u(0)|+|h(0)||f(u(0))|)dt \\
&\qquad\le \frac{1}{p\Gamma(\alpha+1)}(|q(0)||u(0)|+|h(0)||f(u(0))|).
\end{aligned}$$

Then, we can obtain

$$\begin{aligned}
&\int_0^1 \left|\frac{d}{dt}\left[D_c^\beta\left(\frac{u(t)-\zeta_1(t,u(t))}{\zeta_2(t,u(t))}\right)-k(t,u(t))\right]\right|dt \\
&\le (\|q(s)\|\|u(s)\|+\|h(s)\|\|f(u(s))\|)\frac{\|p'\|}{p^2\Gamma(\alpha+1)} \\
&+\Big(\|q'\|_{L_1}\|u\|+\|q\|\|u'\|+\|h'\|_{L_1}\|f\|+\mathcal{K}\|h\|\|u'\|\Big)\frac{1}{p\Gamma(\alpha+1)} \\
&+\frac{1}{p\Gamma(\alpha+1)}(|q(0)||u(0)|+|h(0)||f(u(0))|).
\end{aligned}$$

That is, $\frac{d}{dt}\left[D_c^\beta\left(\frac{u(t)-\zeta_1(t,u(t))}{\zeta_2(t,u(t))}\right)-k(t,u(t))\right]\in L_1[0,1]$. This completes the proof. □

**Lemma 3.** *Assume that the hypotheses $(D_1)$–$(D_5)$ are satisfied. Let $|u(t)|\le r$ for all $t\in I$,*
$Au(t)=I^\beta\Big(\frac{1}{p(t)}I^\alpha(q(t)u(t))\Big)$,
$Bu(t)=I^\beta\Big(\frac{1}{p(t)}I^\alpha(h(t)f(u(t)))\Big)$ *and* $C(t)=I^\beta\Big(\frac{1}{p(t)}k(t,u(t))\Big)$. *Then,*

*(i)* $|Au(t)|\le L_1$, $|Bu(t)|\le L_2$ *and* $|Cu(t)|\le L_3$ *for all $t\in I$ where* $L_1=\frac{\|q\|}{p\Gamma(\alpha+\beta+1)}r$, $L_2=\frac{\mathcal{K}\|h\|}{p\Gamma(\alpha+\beta+1)}r+\frac{\mathcal{M}\|h\|}{p\Gamma(\alpha+\beta+1)}$ *and* $L_3=\frac{\|\mu^*\|}{p\Gamma(\beta+1)}r+\frac{k_0}{p\Gamma(\beta+1)}$.

*(ii)* *for $t_1,t_2\in I$ with $t_1<t_2$,*

$$|Au(t_1)-Au(t_2)|\le \frac{\|q\|r}{p\Gamma(\alpha+1)\Gamma(\beta+1)}\Big[|t_2^\beta-t_1^\beta-(t_2-t_1)^\beta|+(t_2-t_1)^\beta\Big],$$

$$|Bu(t_1)-Bu(t_2)|\le \frac{\|h\|(\mathcal{K}r+\mathcal{M})}{p\Gamma(\alpha+1)\Gamma(\beta+1)}\Big[|t_2^\beta-t_1^\beta-(t_2-t_1)^\beta|+(t_2-t_1)^\beta\Big].$$

*and*

$$|Cu(t_1) - Cu(t_2)| \leq \frac{(\|\mu^*\|r + k_0)}{p\Gamma(\beta+1)}\left[|t_2^\beta - t_1^\beta - (t_2-t_1)^\beta| + (t_2-t_1)^\beta\right].$$

**Proof.** $(i)$ Assume that $|u(t)| \leq r$ for all $t \in I$. Then, we can write

$$\begin{aligned}
|Au(t)| &= |I^\beta\Big(\frac{1}{p(s)}I^\alpha(q(s)u(s))\Big)| \\
&= |\frac{1}{\Gamma(\alpha)\Gamma(\beta)}\int_0^t \frac{(t-s)^{\beta-1}}{p(s)}\Big(\int_0^s (s-\tau)^{\alpha-1}q(\tau)u(\tau)d\tau\Big)ds| \\
&\leq \frac{1}{\Gamma(\alpha)\Gamma(\beta)}\int_0^t \frac{(t-s)^{\beta-1}}{|p(s)|}\Big(\int_0^s (s-\tau)^{\alpha-1}|q(\tau)||u(\tau)|d\tau\Big)ds \\
&\leq \frac{r\|q\|}{p\Gamma(\alpha)\Gamma(\beta)}\int_0^t (t-s)^{\beta-1}\Big(\int_0^s (s-\tau)^{\alpha-1}d\tau\Big)ds \\
&= \frac{r\|q\|}{p\Gamma(\alpha+1)\Gamma(\beta)}\int_0^t s^\alpha(t-s)^{\beta-1}ds \\
&\leq \frac{r\|q\|}{p\Gamma(\alpha+1)\Gamma(\beta)}\int_0^1 s^\alpha(1-s)^{\beta-1}ds
\end{aligned}$$

On the other hand, $\mathbf{B}(\alpha+1,\beta) = \int_0^1 s^\alpha(1-s)^{\beta-1}ds = \frac{\Gamma(\alpha+1)\Gamma(\beta)}{\Gamma(\alpha+\beta+1)}$ (where $\mathbf{B}$ is the beta function). Thus,

$$|Au(t)| \leq \frac{\|q\|}{p\Gamma(\alpha+\beta+1)}r$$

for all $t \in I$.

Let $|u(t)| \leq r$ for all $t \in I$ and $\mathcal{M} = f(0)$. At first, notice that

$$\begin{aligned}
|f(u(t))| = |f(u) - f(0) + f(0)| &\leq \mathcal{K}|u| + \mathcal{M} \\
&\leq \mathcal{K}r + \mathcal{M}.
\end{aligned}$$

Therefore, we have

$$\begin{aligned}
|Bu(t)| &= |I^\beta\Big(\frac{1}{p(s)}I^\alpha(h(s)f(u(s)))\Big)| \\
&= |\frac{1}{\Gamma(\alpha)\Gamma(\beta)}\int_0^t \frac{(t-s)^{\beta-1}}{p(s)}\Big(\int_0^s (s-\tau)^{\alpha-1}h(\tau)f(u(\tau))d\tau\Big)ds| \\
&\leq \frac{1}{\Gamma(\alpha)\Gamma(\beta)}\int_0^t \frac{(t-s)^{\beta-1}}{|p(s)|}\Big(\int_0^s (s-\tau)^{\alpha-1}|h(\tau)||f(u(\tau))|d\tau\Big)ds \\
&\leq \frac{(\mathcal{K}r + \mathcal{M})\|h\|}{p\Gamma(\alpha)\Gamma(\beta)}\int_0^t (t-s)^{\beta-1}\Big(\int_0^s (s-\tau)^{\alpha-1}d\tau\Big)ds \\
&= \frac{\mathcal{K}\|h\|}{p\Gamma(\alpha+\beta+1)}r + \frac{\mathcal{M}\|h\|}{p\Gamma(\alpha+\beta+1)}.
\end{aligned}$$

Similarly, we can prove that

$$|C(t)| \leq \frac{\|\mu^*\|}{p\Gamma(\beta+1)}r + \frac{k_0}{p\Gamma(\beta+1)}.$$

$(ii)$ Let $t_1, t_2 \in I$ with $t_1 < t_2$. Thus,

$$|Au(t_1) - Au(t_2)| = \frac{1}{\Gamma(\beta)}\left| \int_0^{t_1} \frac{(t_1-s)^{\beta-1}}{p(s)} I^\alpha(q(s)u(s))ds - \int_0^{t_2} \frac{(t_2-s)^{\beta-1}}{p(s)} I^\alpha(q(s)u(s))ds \right|$$

$$= \frac{1}{\Gamma(\beta)}\left| \int_0^{t_1} \frac{(t_1-s)^{\beta-1} - (t_2-s)^{\beta-1}}{p(s)} I^\alpha(q(s)u(s))ds \right.$$

$$\left. - \int_{t_1}^{t_2} \frac{(t_2-s)^{\beta-1}}{p(s)} I^\alpha(q(s)u(s))ds \right|$$

$$\leq \frac{1}{\Gamma(\beta)}\left[ \int_0^{t_1} \frac{|(t_1-s)^{\beta-1} - (t_2-s)^{\beta-1}|}{p(s)} |I^\alpha(q(s)u(s))|ds \right.$$

$$\left. + \int_{t_1}^{t_2} \frac{(t_2-s)^{\beta-1}}{p(s)} |I^\alpha(q(s)u(s))|ds \right]$$

Now, as $|I^\alpha(q(s)u(s))| \leq \|q\| r I^\alpha(1) = \frac{\|q\| r s^\alpha}{\Gamma(\alpha+1)} \leq \frac{\|q\| r}{\Gamma(\alpha+1)}$, then

$$|Au(t_1) - Au(t_2)| \leq \frac{\|q\| r}{p\Gamma(\alpha+1)\Gamma(\beta)} \left[ \int_0^{t_1} |(t_1-s)^{\beta-1} - (t_2-s)^{\beta-1}| ds + \int_{t_1}^{t_2} (t_2-s)^{\beta-1} ds \right]$$

$$= \frac{\|q\| r}{p\Gamma(\alpha+1)\Gamma(\beta+1)} \left[ |t_2^\beta - t_1^\beta - (t_2-t_1)^\beta| + (t_2-t_1)^\beta \right].$$

Similarly, we have

$$|Bu(t_1) - Bu(t_2)| \leq \frac{\|h\|(\mathcal{K}r + \mathcal{M})}{p\Gamma(\alpha+1)\Gamma(\beta+1)} \left[ |t_2^\beta - t_1^\beta - (t_2-t_1)^\beta| + (t_2-t_1)^\beta \right]$$

and

$$|Cu(t_1) - Cu(t_2)| \leq \frac{(\|\mu^*\| r + k_0)}{p\Gamma(\beta+1)} \left[ |t_2^\beta - t_1^\beta - (t_2-t_1)^\beta| + (t_2-t_1)^\beta \right].$$

□

Now, we are ready to state and prove our main theorem.

**Theorem 1.** *Let the hypotheses* $(D_1)$*–*$(D_5)$ *be satisfied. Then, the coupled hybrid Sturm–Liouville differential Equation (3) with multi-point boundary hybrid condition (4) has a unique solution* $u \in C[I, \mathbb{R}]$. *Furthermore, if* $(\mathcal{B}^*)$ *holds, then* $D_c^\beta(u(t)) \in C(I, \mathbb{R})$.

**Proof.** Let $E = C(I, \mathbb{R})$. From $(D_5)$, we know that there exists a number $r > 0$ such that

$$r \geq \frac{\zeta_2^*\Theta + \zeta_1^*}{1 - \|\mu\|\Theta - \|\tilde{\mu}\|} \text{ and } \|\mu\|\Theta + \|\tilde{\mu}\| < 1,$$

where

$$\Theta = \frac{1}{p\Gamma(\alpha+\beta+1)}[E(\sum_{i=1}^{m} |\xi_i| + |\nu| \sum_{j=1}^{n} |\eta_j|) + 1][(\|q\| + \mathcal{K}\|h\| + \frac{\Gamma(\alpha+\beta+1)\|\mu^*\|}{\Gamma(\beta+1)})r$$

$$+ \mathcal{M}\|h\| + \frac{\Gamma(\alpha+\beta+1)k_0}{\Gamma(\beta+1)}],$$

$\zeta_1^* = \sup_{t\in I} \zeta_1(t,0)$, $\zeta_2^* = \sup_{t\in I} \zeta_2(t,0)$, $k_0 = \sup_{t\in I} k(t,0)$ and $\mathcal{M} = f(0)$. Define a subset $S_r$ of $E$ defined by

$$S_r = \{u \in E : \ \|u\| \leq r\}.$$

Clearly, $S_r$ is a closed, convex, and bounded subset of $E$. From Lemma 2, we know that the problems in (3) and (4) are equivalent to the equation

$$u(t) = \zeta_2(t,u(t))\Big[E\big(\sum_{i=1}^{m}\xi_i Au(a_i) - \nu\sum_{j=1}^{n}\eta_j Au(b_j) + \nu\sum_{j=1}^{n}\eta_j Bu(b_j) - \sum_{i=1}^{m}\xi_i Bu(a_i)\big) + \nu\sum_{j=1}^{n}\eta_j Cu(b_j) - \sum_{i=1}^{m}\xi_i Cu(a_i)\big) - Au(t) + Bu(t) + Cu(t)\Big] + \zeta_1(t,u(t)),\ t\in I. \tag{11}$$

Define three operators $\mathcal{A},\mathcal{C} : E \to E$ and $\mathcal{B} : S_r \to E$ by

$$\mathcal{A}u(t) = \zeta_2(t,u(t)),\ t\in I,$$

$$\mathcal{B}u(t) = E\big(\sum_{i=1}^{m}\xi_i Au(a_i) - \nu\sum_{j=1}^{n}\eta_j Au(b_j) + \nu\sum_{j=1}^{n}\eta_j Bu(b_j) - \sum_{i=1}^{m}\xi_i Bu(a_i)\big) + \nu\sum_{j=1}^{n}\eta_j Cu(b_j) - \sum_{i=1}^{m}\xi_i Cu(a_i)\big) - Au(t) + Bu(t) + Cu(t),\ t\in I,$$

and

$$\mathcal{C}u(t) = \zeta_1(t,u(t)),\ t\in I.$$

Now, the integral Equation (11) can be written as

$$u(t) = \mathcal{A}u(t)\mathcal{B}u(t) + \mathcal{C}u(t),\ t\in I.$$

In the following steps, we will show that the operators $\mathcal{A}$, $\mathcal{B}$, and $\mathcal{C}$ satisfy all the conditions of Lemma 1.

**Step 1:** In this step, we show that $\mathcal{A}$ and $\mathcal{C}$ are Lipschitzian on $E$. Let $u,v\in E$, then by $(D_3)$, we have

$$|\mathcal{A}u(t) - \mathcal{A}v(t)| = |\zeta_2(t,u) - \zeta_2(t,v)| \le \mu(t)|u(t) - v(t)|$$

for all $t\in I$. Taking the supremum over $t$, we get

$$\|\mathcal{A}u - \mathcal{A}v\| \le \|\mu\|\|u - v\|.$$

Similarly, by applying $(D_3)$, we can obtain

$$\|\mathcal{C}u - \mathcal{C}v\| \le \|\tilde{\mu}\|\|u - v\|.$$

That is, $\mathcal{A}$ and $\mathcal{C}$ are Lipschitzian with Lipschitz constants $\|\mu\|$ and $\|\tilde{\mu}\|$, respectively.

**Step 2:** We show that $\mathcal{B}$ is compact and continuous operator on $S_r$ into $E$. At first, we show that $\mathcal{B}$ is continuous on $S_r$. Let $\{u_n\}$ be a sequence in $S_r$ converging to a point $u\in S_r$. Then, by the Lebesgue dominated convergence theorem,

$$\lim_{n\to\infty}\mathcal{B}u_n(t) = \lim_{n\to\infty}[E(\sum_{i=1}^{m}\xi_i Au_n(a_i) - \nu\sum_{j=1}^{n}\eta_j Au_n(b_j) + \nu\sum_{j=1}^{n}\eta_j Bu_n(b_j) - \sum_{i=1}^{m}\xi_i Bu_n(a_i)$$
$$+ \nu\sum_{j=1}^{n}\eta_j Cu_n(b_j) - \sum_{i=1}^{m}\xi_i Cu_n(a_i)) - Au_n(t) + Bu_n(t) + Cu_n(t)]$$
$$= E(\sum_{i=1}^{m}\xi_i A(\lim_{n\to\infty}u_n(a_i)) - \nu\sum_{j=1}^{n}\eta_j A(\lim_{n\to\infty}u_n(b_j)) + \nu\sum_{j=1}^{n}\eta_j B(\lim_{n\to\infty}u_n(b_j))$$
$$-\sum_{i=1}^{m}\xi_i B(\lim_{n\to\infty}u_n(a_i)) + \nu\sum_{j=1}^{n}\eta_j C(\lim_{n\to\infty}u_n(b_j)) - \sum_{i=1}^{m}\xi_i C(\lim_{n\to\infty}u_n(a_i)))$$
$$- A(\lim_{n\to\infty}u_n(t)) + B(\lim_{n\to\infty}u_n(t)) + C(\lim_{n\to\infty}u_n(t))$$
$$= E(\sum_{i=1}^{m}\xi_i Au(a_i) - \nu\sum_{j=1}^{n}\eta_j Au(b_j) + \nu\sum_{j=1}^{n}\eta_j Bu(b_j)$$
$$-\sum_{i=1}^{m}\xi_i Bu(a_i) + \nu\sum_{j=1}^{n}\eta_j Cu(b_j) - \sum_{i=1}^{m}\xi_i Cu(a_i)) - Au(t) + Bu(t) + Cu(t)$$
$$= \mathcal{B}u(t)$$

for all $t \in I$. That is, $\mathcal{B}$ is a continuous operator on $S_r$.

Next, we will show that the set $\mathcal{B}(S_r)$ is a uniformly bounded in $S_r$. For any $u \in S_r$, by using Lemma 3 (i), we have

$$|\mathcal{B}u(t)| \le |E|(\sum_{i=1}^{m}|\xi_i||Au(a_i)| + |\nu|\sum_{j=1}^{n}|\eta_j||Au(b_j)|$$
$$+ |\nu|\sum_{j=1}^{n}|\eta_j||Bu(b_j)| + \sum_{i=1}^{m}|\xi_i||Bu(a_i)| + |\nu|\sum_{j=1}^{n}|\eta_j||Cu(b_j)| + \sum_{i=1}^{m}|\xi_i||Cu(a_i)|)$$
$$+ |Au(t)| + |Bu(t)| + |Cu(t)|$$
$$\le |E|\sum_{i=1}^{m}|\xi_i|L_1 + |E||\nu|\sum_{j=1}^{n}|\eta_j|L_1 + |E||\nu|\sum_{j=1}^{n}|\eta_j|L_2 + |E|\sum_{i=1}^{m}|\xi_i|L_2$$
$$+ |E||\nu|\sum_{j=1}^{n}|\eta_j|L_3 + |E|\sum_{i=1}^{m}|\xi_i|L_3 + L_1 + L_2 + L_3$$
$$= [|E|(\sum_{i=1}^{m}|\xi_i| + |\nu|\sum_{j=1}^{n}|\eta_j|) + 1]L_1 + [|E|(\sum_{i=1}^{m}|\xi_i| + |\nu|\sum_{j=1}^{n}|\eta_j|) + 1]L_2$$
$$+ [|E|(\sum_{i=1}^{m}|\xi_i| + |\nu|\sum_{j=1}^{n}|\eta_j|) + 1]L_3$$
$$= [|E|(\sum_{i=1}^{m}|\xi_i| + |\nu|\sum_{j=1}^{n}|\eta_j|) + 1][L_1 + L_2 + L_3]$$

Now, as

$$L_1 + L_2 + L_3$$
$$= \frac{\|q\|}{p\Gamma(\alpha+\beta+1)}r + \frac{\mathcal{K}\|h\|}{p\Gamma(\alpha+\beta+1)}r + \frac{\|\mu^*\|}{p\Gamma(\beta+1)}r + \frac{\mathcal{M}\|h\|}{p\Gamma(\alpha+\beta+1)} + \frac{k_0}{p\Gamma(\beta+1)}$$
$$= \frac{1}{p\Gamma(\alpha+\beta+1)}[(\|q\| + \mathcal{K}\|h\| + \frac{\Gamma(\alpha+\beta+1)\|\mu^*\|}{\Gamma(\beta+1)})r + \mathcal{M}\|h\| + \frac{\Gamma(\alpha+\beta+1)k_0}{\Gamma(\beta+1)}],$$

then we get

$$|\mathcal{B}u(t)| \leq \frac{1}{p\Gamma(\alpha+\beta+1)}[E(\sum_{i=1}^{m}|\xi_i| + |\nu|\sum_{j=1}^{n}|\eta_j|) + 1][(\|q\| + \mathcal{K}\|h\| + \frac{\Gamma(\alpha+\beta+1)\|\mu^*\|}{\Gamma(\beta+1)})r + \mathcal{M}\|h\| + \frac{\Gamma(\alpha+\beta+1)k_0}{\Gamma(\beta+1)}] = \Theta$$

Taking supremum over t,

$$\|\mathcal{B}u\| \leq \Theta$$

for all $u \in S_r$. This shows that $\mathcal{B}$ is uniformly bounded on $S_r$.

Now, we show that $\mathcal{B}(S_r)$ is an equi-continuous set in $E$. Let $t_1, t_2 \in I$ with $t_< t_2$. Then, for any $u \in S_r$, by applying Lemma 3 (ii), we have

$$\begin{aligned}
|\mathcal{B}u(t_1) - \mathcal{B}u(t_2)| &= | - Au(t_1) + Au(t_2) + Bu(t_1) - Bu(t_2) + Cu(t_1) - Cu(t_2)| \\
&\leq |Au(t_1) - Au(t_2)| + |Bu(t_1) - Bu(t_2)| + |Cu(t_1) - Cu(t_2)| \\
&\leq \frac{\|q\|r}{p\Gamma(\alpha+1)\Gamma(\beta+1)}\left[|t_2^{\beta} - t_1^{\beta} - (t_2-t_1)^{\beta}| + (t_2-t_1)^{\beta}\right] \\
&+ \frac{\|h\|(\mathcal{K}r + \mathcal{M})}{p\Gamma(\alpha+1)\Gamma(\beta+1)}\left[|t_2^{\beta} - t_1^{\beta} - (t_2-t_1)^{\beta}| + (t_2-t_1)^{\beta}\right] \\
&+ \frac{(\|\mu^*\|r + k_0)}{p\Gamma(\beta+1)}\left[|t_2^{\beta} - t_1^{\beta} - (t_2-t_1)^{\beta}| + (t_2-t_1)^{\beta}\right]
\end{aligned}$$

Then, for $\varepsilon > 0$, there exist $\delta > 0$ such that

$$|t_1 - t_2| < \delta \implies |\mathcal{B}(t_1) - \mathcal{B}(t_2)| < \varepsilon,$$

for all $t_1, t_2 \in I$ and for all $u \in S_r$. This shows that $\mathcal{B}(S_r)$ is an equi-continuous set in $E$. Therefore, we proved that the set $\mathcal{B}(S_r)$ is uniformly bounded and equi-continuous set in $E$. Then, $\mathcal{B}(S_r)$ is compact by Arzela–Ascoli Theorem. As a consequence, $\mathcal{B}(S_r)$ is a completely continuous operator on $S_r$.

**Step 3:** Let $u \in E$ and $v \in S_r$ be two given elements such that $u = \mathcal{A}u\mathcal{B}v + \mathcal{C}u$. Then, we get

$$\begin{aligned}
|u(t)| &\leq |\mathcal{A}u(t)||\mathcal{B}v(t)| + |\mathcal{C}u(t)| \\
&\leq \Theta|\zeta_2(t, u(t))| + |\zeta_1(t, u(t))| \\
&= \Theta|\zeta_2(t, u(t)) - \zeta_2(t, 0) + \zeta_2(t, 0)| + |\zeta_1(t, u(t)) - \zeta_1(t, 0) + \zeta_1(t, 0)| \\
&\leq \Theta(\|\mu\||u(t)| + \zeta_2^*) + \|\tilde{\mu}\||u(t)| + \zeta_1^*,
\end{aligned}$$

and so

$$|u(t)| \leq \frac{\zeta_2^*\Theta + \zeta_1^*}{1 - \|\mu\|\Theta - \|\tilde{\mu}\|} \leq r.$$

Taking the supremum over t, we get

$$\|u\| \leq r.$$

**Step 4:** Finally, we prove that $\delta M + \rho < 1$. As $M = \|\mathcal{B}(S_r)\| = \sup_{u \in S_r}\{\sup_{t \in I}|\mathcal{B}u(t)|\} \leq \Theta$, we have

$$\|\mu\|M + \|\tilde{\mu}\| \leq \|\mu\|\Theta + \|\tilde{\mu}\| < 1,$$

where $\delta = \|\mu\|$ and $\rho = \|\tilde{\mu}\|$. Therefore, all conditions of Lemma 1 hold and the operator equation $u = \mathcal{A}u\mathcal{B}u + \mathcal{C}u$ has a solution in $S_r$. Thus, the problem (3) and (4) has a solution $u \in C(I, \mathbb{R})$. □

**Example 1.** *Let us consider the following fractional couple hybrid Sturm–Liouville differential equation:*

$$D_c^{\frac{4}{5}}\left(1000\sqrt{e^t+t^2}D_c^{\frac{9}{10}}(\frac{u(t)-\zeta_1(t,u(t))}{\zeta_2(t,u(t))})-k(t,u(t))\right)+e^{-t}\cos^2(t)u(t) \\ = e^{-\frac{t}{1+t}}\tan^{-1}(u(t)+1),\ t\in I \tag{12}$$

*with boundary values*

$$\begin{cases} D_c^{\frac{9}{10}}(\frac{u(t)-\zeta_2(t,u(t))}{\zeta_2(t,u(t))})_{t=0}=\frac{1}{240}u(0),\ t\in I=[0,1] \\ \Sigma_{i=1}^2\frac{1}{4i}(\frac{u(\frac{1}{\pi^i})-\zeta_1(\frac{1}{\pi^i},u(\frac{1}{\pi^i}))}{\zeta_2(\frac{1}{\pi^i},u(\frac{1}{\pi^i}))})=\frac{1}{3}\sum_{j=1}^{3}\frac{1}{2^j}(\frac{u(\frac{1}{e^j})-\zeta_1(\frac{1}{e^j},u(\frac{1}{e^j}))}{\zeta_2(\frac{1}{e^j},u(\frac{1}{e^j}))}), \end{cases} \tag{13}$$

*where*

$$\zeta_1(t,u(t))=\frac{e^{-t}}{300}(u(t)+e^{-\pi t})+\frac{1}{300+\ln(t^2+t+1)}$$

$$\zeta_2(t,u(t))=\frac{\cos^2(\pi t)}{(500+\ln(1+e^{\pi t+1}))}\frac{|u(t)|}{1+|u(t)|}+e^{-\sin^2(\pi t)}$$

*and*

$$k(t,u(t))=\frac{e^{-t}}{100}u(t)+e^{-t^2}.$$

*In this case, we take* $\alpha=\frac{4}{5}$, $\beta=\frac{9}{10}$, $r=0.1$, $\zeta_1=\frac{1}{4}$, $\zeta_2=\frac{1}{8}$, $\eta_1=\frac{1}{2}$, $\eta_2=\frac{1}{4}$, $\eta_3=\frac{1}{8}$, $\nu=\frac{1}{3}$, $p(t)=1000\sqrt{e^t+t^2}$, $q(t)=e^{-t}\cos^2(t)$, $h(t)=e^{-\frac{t}{1+t}}$, $f(u(t))=\tan^{-1}(u(t)+1)$. *Therefore,* $|\frac{\partial f(u)}{\partial u}|\leq 1=\mathcal{K}$, $\mathcal{M}=\frac{\pi}{4}$, $p=1000$, $\|q\|=1$, $\|h\|=1$. *Further,*

$$|\zeta_1(t,u(t))-\zeta_1(t,v(t))|\leq\frac{e^{-t}}{300}|u(t)-v(t)|,$$

$$\begin{aligned}|\zeta_2(t,u(t))-\zeta_2(t,v(t))| &= \frac{\cos^2(\pi t)}{(500+\ln(1+e^{\pi t+1}))}\frac{||u(t)|-|v(t)||}{(1+|u(t)|)(1+|v(t)|)} \\ &\leq \frac{\cos^2(\pi t)}{(500+\ln(1+e^{\pi t+1}))}|u(t)-v(t)|\end{aligned}$$

*and*

$$|k(t,u(t))-k(t,v(t))|\leq\frac{e^{-t}}{100}|u(t)-v(t)|.$$

*Then,* $\zeta_1^*=\sup_{t\in I}\zeta_1(t,0)=\frac{1}{150}$, $\zeta_2^*=\sup_{t\in I}\zeta_2(t,0)=1$, $k_0=\sup_{t\in I}k(t,0)=1$, $\|\mu\|=\frac{1}{500+\ln(1+e)}$, $\|\mu^*\|=\frac{1}{100}$ *and* $\|\tilde{\mu}\|=\frac{1}{300}$. *Furthermore,* $\sum_{i=1}^2\frac{1}{4i}-\frac{1}{3}\sum_{j=1}^3\frac{1}{2^j}=\frac{3}{8}-\frac{7}{24}=\frac{1}{12}\neq 0$, *and so* $E=12$. *Then,*

$$\begin{aligned}\Theta &= \frac{1}{p\Gamma(\alpha+\beta+1)}[|E|(\sum_{i=1}^{m}|\zeta_i|+|\nu|\sum_{j=1}^{n}|\eta_j|)+1][(\|q\|+\mathcal{K}\|h\|+\frac{\Gamma(\alpha+\beta+1)\|\mu^*\|}{\Gamma(\beta+1)})r \\ &+\mathcal{M}\|h\|+\frac{\Gamma(\alpha+\beta+1)k_0}{\Gamma(\beta+1)}] \\ &\approx \frac{1}{1000\Gamma(2.7)}[12(\sum_{i=1}^{2}\frac{1}{4i}+\frac{1}{3}\sum_{j=1}^{3}\frac{1}{2^j})+1][1.807699588+\frac{\pi}{4}]\approx 0.0151084953\end{aligned}$$

*and so*

$$r = 0.1 \geq 0.0218486492 \approx \frac{\zeta_2^*\Theta + \zeta_1^*}{1 - \|\mu\|\Theta - \|\tilde{\mu}\|}$$

*and*

$$\|\mu\|\Theta + \|\tilde{\mu}\| \approx 0.0033634712 < 1,$$

*As all the conditions of Theorem 1 be satisfied, the problems (12) and (13) have a solution.*

**Example 2.** *Let us consider the following fractional couple hybrid Sturm–Liouville differential equation:*

$$D_c^{\frac{1}{2}}\left(5^{\frac{4}{1+t^2}} D_c^{\frac{1}{3}}\left(\frac{u(t) - \zeta_1(t,u(t))}{\zeta_2(t,u(t))}\right) - k(t,u(t))\right) + 2^{|\sin x|}u(t) = \cot^{-1}\left(\frac{1}{2}u(t)\right),\ t \in I \quad (14)$$

*with boundary values*

$$\begin{cases} D_c^{\frac{1}{3}}\left(\frac{u(t) - \zeta_2(t,u(t))}{\zeta_2(t,u(t))}\right)_{t=0} = \frac{1}{240}u(0),\ t \in I = [0,1] \\ \sum_{i=1}^{2}\frac{i}{2}\left(\frac{u(10^i) - \zeta_1(10^i,u(10^i))}{\zeta_2(10^i,u(10^i))}\right) = -2\sum_{j=1}^{2}\frac{(-1)^j}{j+2}\left(\frac{u(13^j) - \zeta_1(13^j,u(13^j))}{\zeta_2(13^j,u(13^j))}\right), \end{cases} \quad (15)$$

*where*

$$\zeta_1(t,u(t)) = 7^{t-1}\left(1 + 6^{\frac{-9}{1+2t}}u(t)\right) - \frac{76t}{77}$$

$$\zeta_2(t,u(t)) = \frac{8}{30 + \ln(1+t)}e^{-t^2-t^3}u(t) + \frac{1}{20}\cos\left(\frac{\pi}{1+t^2}\right)$$

*and*

$$k(t,u(t)) = \frac{u(t)}{(2+t)(5+3t)(6+7t)(4+9t)} + \sinh(\ln(2)t^5).$$

*Now, we put* $\alpha = \frac{1}{2}$, $\beta = \frac{1}{3}$, $r = 0.9$, $\xi_1 = 1$, $\xi_2 = \frac{1}{2}$, $\eta_1 = -\frac{1}{3}$, $\eta_2 = \frac{1}{4}$, $\nu = -2$, $p(t) = 5^{\frac{4}{1+t^2}}$, $q(t) = 2^{|\sin x|}$, $h(t) = 1$, $f(u(t)) = \cot^{-1}(\frac{1}{2}u(t))$. *Hence,* $|\frac{\partial f(u)}{\partial u}| \leq \frac{1}{2} = \mathcal{K}$, $\mathcal{M} = \frac{\pi}{2}$, $p = 625$, $\|q\| = 2$, $\|h\| = 1$, $\zeta_1^* = \frac{1}{77}$, $\zeta_2^* = \frac{1}{20}$, $k_0 = \frac{3}{4}$, $\|\mu\| = \frac{30}{8}$, $\|\mu^*\| = \frac{1}{240}$, $\|\tilde{\mu}\| = \frac{1}{216}$, $\sum_{i=1}^{2}\frac{i}{2} - \nu\sum_{j=1}^{2}\frac{(-1)^j}{j+2} = \frac{4}{3} \neq 0$ *and* $E = \frac{3}{4}$. *Therefore,* $\Theta \approx 0.0235484505$. *Then, we have*

$$r = 0.9 \geq 0.0564209808 \approx \frac{\zeta_2^*\Theta + \zeta_1^*}{1 - \|\mu\|\Theta - \|\tilde{\mu}\|}$$

*and*

$$\|\mu\|\Theta + \|\tilde{\mu}\| \approx 0.0047386502 < 1,$$

*That is, all the conditions of Theorem 1 hold and the problem (14) and (15) has a solution.*

If in Theorem 1, we take $\zeta_1(t,w) = k(t,w) = \zeta_2(t,w) - 1 = 0$ for all $t \in I$ and $w \in \mathbb{R}$, we have the following Corollary.

**Corollary 1.** *Let the hypotheses* $(D_1)$–$(D_2)$ *be satisfied. Assume that*

$$\frac{1}{p\Gamma(\alpha+\beta+1)}\left[|E|\left(\sum_{i=1}^{m}|\xi_i| + |\nu|\sum_{j=1}^{n}|\eta_j|\right) + 1\right](\|q\| + \mathcal{K}\|h\|) < 1,$$

*where* $E = \dfrac{1}{\sum_{i=1}^{m}\xi_i - \nu\sum_{j=1}^{n}\eta_j}$ *and* $\sum_{i=1}^{m}\xi_i - \nu\sum_{j=1}^{n}\eta_j \neq 0$. *Then, the fractional Sturm–Liouville differential problem*

$$\begin{cases} D_c^{\alpha}[p(t)D_c^{\beta}(u(t))] + q(t)u(t) = h(t)f(u(t)),\ t \in I \\ D_c^{\beta}(u(t)))_{t=0} = 0, \\ \sum_{i=1}^{m}\xi_i u(a_i) = \nu\sum_{j=1}^{n}\eta_j u(b_j), \end{cases} \tag{16}$$

*has a solution* $u \in C(I,\mathbb{R})$ *if and only if* $u$ *solves the integral equation*

$$u(t) = E(\sum_{i=1}^{m}\xi_i Au(a_i) - \nu\sum_{j=1}^{n}\eta_j Au(b_j) + \nu\sum_{j=1}^{n}\eta_j Bu(b_j)$$
$$-\sum_{i=1}^{m}\xi_i Bu(a_i)) - Au(t) + Bu(t).$$

*Therefore,* $D_c^{\beta}(u(t)) \in C(I,\mathbb{R})$.

## 3. Continuous Dependence

The following result will be useful in this section (in fact it is a special case of Theorem 1 with $\zeta_2(t,x) = 1$ for all $t \in I$ and $x \in \mathbb{R}$).

**Corollary 2.** *Let the hypotheses* $(D_1)$, $(D_2)$, *and* $(D_4)$ *be satisfied. Assume that there exists a number* $r > 0$ *such that*

$$r > \frac{\Theta + \zeta_1^*}{1 - \|\tilde{\mu}\|} \text{ and } \|\tilde{\mu}\| < 1,$$

*where*

$$\Theta = \frac{1}{p\Gamma(\alpha+\beta+1)}[E(\sum_{i=1}^{m}|\xi_i| + |\nu|\sum_{j=1}^{n}|\eta_j|) + 1][(\|q\| + \mathcal{K}\|h\| + \frac{\Gamma(\alpha+\beta+1)\|\mu^*\|}{\Gamma(\beta+1)})r$$
$$+\mathcal{M}\|h\| + \frac{\Gamma(\alpha+\beta+1)k_0}{\Gamma(\beta+1)}],$$

$\zeta_1^* = \sup_{t\in I}\zeta_1(t,0)$, $k_0 = \sup_{t\in I}|k(t,0)|$, $\mathcal{M} = f(0)$ *and* $E = \dfrac{1}{\sum_{i=1}^{m}\xi_i - \nu\sum_{j=1}^{n}\eta_j}$ *where* $\sum_{i=1}^{m}\xi_i - \nu\sum_{j=1}^{n}\eta_j \neq 0$. *Then, the fractional couple hybrid Sturm–Liouville differential equation*

$$D_c^{\alpha}\left[p(t)D_c^{\beta}(u(t) - \zeta_1(t,u(t))) - k(t,u(t))\right] + q(t)u(t) = h(t)f(u(t)),\ t \in I \tag{17}$$

*with multi-point boundary couple hybrid condition*

$$\begin{cases} D_c^{\beta}\left(u(t) - \zeta_1(t,u(t))\right)_{t=0} = k(0,u(0)), \\ \sum_{i=1}^{m}\xi_i(u(a_i) - \zeta_1(a_i,u(a_i))) = \nu\sum_{j=1}^{n}\eta_j(u(b_j) - \zeta_1(b_j,u(b_j))), \end{cases} \tag{18}$$

*has a solution $u \in C(I,\mathbb{R})$ if and only if $u$ solves the integral equation*

$$\begin{aligned} u(t) = {} & E\Big(\sum_{i=1}^{m}\xi_i Au(a_i) - \nu\sum_{j=1}^{n}\eta_j Au(b_j) + \nu\sum_{j=1}^{n}\eta_j Bu(b_j) \\ & - \sum_{i=1}^{m}\xi_i Bu(a_i)\Big) + \nu\sum_{j=1}^{n}\eta_j Cu(b_j) - \sum_{i=1}^{m}\xi_i Cu(a_i)\Big) \\ & - Au(t) + Bu(t) + Cu(t) + \zeta_1(t,u(t)). \end{aligned} \tag{19}$$

*Furthermore, $D_c^{\beta}(u(t)) \in C(I,\mathbb{R})$.*

In this section, we will investigate continuous dependence (on the coefficients $\xi_i$ and $\eta_j$ of the multi-point boundary couple hybrid condition) of the solution of the fractional couple hybrid Sturm–Liouville differential Equation (17) with multi-point boundary couple hybrid condition (18). The main Theorem of this section generalizes Theorem 3.2 in [23] and Theorem 5 in [8].

First, we give the following Definition.

**Definition 3.** *The solution of the fractional couple hybrid Sturm–Liouville differential Equation (17) is continuously dependent on the data $\xi_i$ and $\eta_j$ if for every $\epsilon > 0$, there exist $\delta_1(\epsilon)$ and $\delta_2(\epsilon)$, such that for any two solutions $u(t)$ and $\tilde{u}(t)$ of (17) with the initial data (18) and*

$$\begin{cases} D_c^{\beta}\Big(\tilde{u}(t) - \zeta_1(t,\tilde{u}(t))\Big)_{t=0} = k(0,\tilde{u}(0)), \\ \sum_{i=1}^{m}\tilde{\xi}_i(\tilde{u}(a_i) - \zeta_1(a_i,\tilde{u}(a_i)) = \nu\sum_{j=1}^{n}\tilde{\eta}_j(\tilde{u}(b_j) - \zeta_1(b_j,\tilde{u}(b_j))), \end{cases} \tag{20}$$

*respectively, one has $\sum_{i=1}^{m}|\xi_i - \tilde{\xi}_i| < \delta_1$ and $\sum_{j=1}^{n}|\eta_j - \tilde{\eta}_j| < \delta_2$, then $\|u - \tilde{u}\| < \epsilon$ for all $t \in I$.*

**Theorem 2.** *Assume that the assertions of Corollary (21) are satisfied. Then, the solution of the fractional couple hybrid Sturm–Liouville differential problem (17) and (18) is continuously dependent on the coefficients $\xi_i$ and $\eta_j$ of the multi-point boundary couple hybrid condition.*

**Proof.** Assume that $u$ is a solution of the fractional couple hybrid Sturm–Liouville differential problem (17) and (18) and that

$$\begin{aligned} \tilde{u}(t) = {} & \tilde{E}\sum_{i=1}^{m}\tilde{\xi}_i A\tilde{u}(a_i) - \nu\tilde{E}\sum_{j=1}^{n}\tilde{\eta}_j A\tilde{u}(b_j) + \nu\tilde{E}\sum_{j=1}^{n}\tilde{\eta}_j B\tilde{u}(b_j) - \tilde{E}\sum_{i=1}^{m}\tilde{\xi}_i B\tilde{u}(a_i)) \\ & + \nu\tilde{E}\sum_{j=1}^{n}\tilde{\eta}_j C\tilde{u}(b_j) - \tilde{E}\sum_{i=1}^{m}\tilde{\xi}_i C\tilde{u}(a_i) - A\tilde{u}(t) + B\tilde{u}(t) + C\tilde{u}(t) + \zeta_1(t,\tilde{u}(t)) \end{aligned}$$

is a solution of the fractional couple hybrid Sturm-Liouville differential Equation (17) with the multi-point boundary couple hybrid condition (18). Therefore,

$$\begin{aligned} |\tilde{u}(t) - u(t)| \le {} & |\tilde{E}\sum_{i=1}^{m}\tilde{\xi}_i A\tilde{u}(a_i) - E\sum_{i=1}^{m}\xi_i Au(a_i)| + |\nu\tilde{E}\sum_{j=1}^{n}\tilde{\eta}_j A\tilde{u}(b_j) - \nu E\sum_{j=1}^{n}\eta_j Au(b_j)| \\ & + |\nu\tilde{E}\sum_{j=1}^{n}\tilde{\eta}_j B\tilde{u}(b_j) - \nu E\sum_{j=1}^{n}\eta_j Bu(b_j)| + |\tilde{E}\sum_{i=1}^{m}\tilde{\xi}_i B\tilde{u}(a_i) - E\sum_{i=1}^{m}\xi_i Bu(a_i)| \\ & + |\nu\tilde{E}\sum_{j=1}^{n}\tilde{\eta}_j C\tilde{u}(b_j) - \nu E\sum_{j=1}^{n}\eta_j Cu(b_j)| + |\tilde{E}\sum_{i=1}^{m}\tilde{\xi}_i C\tilde{u}(a_i) - E\sum_{i=1}^{m}\xi_i Cu(a_i)| \\ & + |A\tilde{u}(t) - Au(t)| + |B\tilde{u}(t) - Bu(t)| + |C\tilde{u}(t) - Cu(t)| + |\zeta_1(t,\tilde{u}(t)) - \zeta_1(t,u(t))|. \end{aligned} \tag{21}$$

On the other hand,

$$
\begin{aligned}
&|E\sum_{i=1}^{m}\xi_i Au(a_i) - \tilde{E}\sum_{i=1}^{m}\tilde{\xi}_i A\tilde{u}(a_i)| = |E\sum_{i=1}^{m}\xi_i Au(a_i) - E\sum_{i=1}^{m}\xi_i A\tilde{u}(a_i)\\
&+ E\sum_{i=1}^{m}\xi_i A\tilde{u}(a_i) - E\sum_{i=1}^{m}\tilde{\xi}_i A\tilde{u}(a_i) + E\sum_{i=1}^{m}\tilde{\xi}_i A\tilde{u}(a_i) - \tilde{E}\sum_{i=1}^{m}\tilde{\xi}_i A\tilde{u}(a_i)|\\
&\leq |E|\sum_{i=1}^{m}|\xi_i||A(u(a_i) - \tilde{u}(a_i))| + |E|\sum_{i=1}^{m}|\xi_i - \tilde{\xi}_i||A\tilde{u}(a_i)| + |E - \tilde{E}|\sum_{i=1}^{m}|\tilde{\xi}_i||A\tilde{u}(a_i)|\\
&\leq |E\sum_{i=1}^{m}\xi_i Au(a_i) - \tilde{E}\sum_{i=1}^{m}\tilde{\xi}_i A\tilde{u}(a_i)|\\
&\leq \frac{\|q\||E|\sum_{i=1}^{m}|\xi_i|}{p\Gamma(\alpha+\beta+1)}\|u-\tilde{u}\| + \frac{\|q\||E|\|\tilde{u}\|}{p\Gamma(\alpha+\beta+1)}\sum_{i=1}^{m}|\xi_i - \tilde{\xi}_i|\\
&+ \frac{\|q\|\|\tilde{u}\|\sum_{i=1}^{m}|\tilde{\xi}_i||E||\tilde{E}|}{p\Gamma(\alpha+\beta+1)}(\sum_{i=1}^{m}|\xi_i - \tilde{\xi}_i| + |\nu|\sum_{j=1}^{n}|\eta_j - \tilde{\eta}_j|).
\end{aligned}
$$

AS $\sum_{i=1}^{m}|\xi_i - \tilde{\xi}_i| < \delta_1$ and $\sum_{j=1}^{n}|\eta_j - \tilde{\eta}_j| < \delta_2$, then

$$
\begin{aligned}
&|E\sum_{i=1}^{m}\xi_i Au(a_i) - \tilde{E}\sum_{i=1}^{m}\tilde{\xi}_i A\tilde{u}(a_i)| \leq \frac{\|q\||E|\sum_{i=1}^{m}|\xi_i|}{p\Gamma(\alpha+\beta+1)}\|u-\tilde{u}\| + \frac{\|q\||E|\|\tilde{u}\|}{p\Gamma(\alpha+\beta+1)}\delta_1\\
&+ \frac{\|q\|\|\tilde{u}\|\sum_{i=1}^{m}|\tilde{\xi}_i||E||\tilde{E}|}{p\Gamma(\alpha+\beta+1)}(\delta_1 + |\nu|\delta_2).
\end{aligned}
$$

Similarly,

$$
\begin{aligned}
&|\nu E\sum_{j=1}^{n}\eta_j Au(b_j) - \nu\tilde{E}\sum_{j=1}^{n}\tilde{\eta}_j A\tilde{u}(b_j)| \leq |\nu||E|\sum_{j=1}^{n}|\eta_j||A(u(b_j) - \tilde{u}(b_j))|\\
&+ |\nu||E|\sum_{j=1}^{n}|\eta_j - \tilde{\eta}_j||A\tilde{u}(b_j)| + |\nu||E - \tilde{E}|\sum_{j=1}^{n}|\tilde{\eta}_j||A\tilde{u}(b_j)|\\
&\leq \frac{\|q\||E||\nu|\sum_{i=1}^{m}|\eta_i|}{p\Gamma(\alpha+\beta+1)}\|u-\tilde{u}\| + \frac{\|q\||E||\nu|\|\tilde{u}\|}{p\Gamma(\alpha+\beta+1)}\delta_2\\
&+ \frac{\|q\|\|\tilde{u}\||\nu|\sum_{i=1}^{m}|\tilde{\eta}_i||E||\tilde{E}|}{p\Gamma(\alpha+\beta+1)}(\delta_1 + |\nu|\delta_2),
\end{aligned}
$$

and so

$$
\begin{aligned}
&|E\sum_{i=1}^{m}\xi_i Au(a_i) - \tilde{E}\sum_{i=1}^{m}\tilde{\xi}_i A\tilde{u}(a_i)| + |\nu E\sum_{j=1}^{n}\eta_j Au(b_j) - \nu\tilde{E}\sum_{j=1}^{n}\tilde{\eta}_j A\tilde{u}(b_j)|\\
&\leq \frac{\|q\||E|(\sum_{i=1}^{m}|\xi_i| + |\nu|\sum_{i=1}^{m}|\eta_i|)}{p\Gamma(\alpha+\beta+1)}\|u-\tilde{u}\| + \Omega_1(\delta_1 + |\nu|\delta_2)
\end{aligned}
\tag{22}
$$

where

$$
\Omega_1 = \frac{\|q\||E|\|\tilde{u}\|}{p\Gamma(\alpha+\beta+1)} + \frac{\|q\|\|\tilde{u}\|\sum_{i=1}^{m}|\tilde{\xi}_i||E||\tilde{E}|}{p\Gamma(\alpha+\beta+1)} + \frac{\|q\|\|\tilde{u}\||\nu|\sum_{i=1}^{m}|\tilde{\eta}_i||E||\tilde{E}|}{p\Gamma(\alpha+\beta+1)}
$$

Furthermore,

$$
\begin{aligned}
&|\nu E\sum_{j=1}^{n}\eta_j Bu(b_j)-\nu\tilde{E}\sum_{j=1}^{n}\tilde{\eta}_j B\tilde{u}(b_j)|\leq|\nu||E|\sum_{j=1}^{n}|\eta_j||B(u(b_j)-\tilde{u}(b_j))|\\
&+|\nu||E|\sum_{j=1}^{n}|\eta_j-\tilde{\eta}_j|B\tilde{u}(b_j)|+|\nu||E-\tilde{E}|\sum_{j=1}^{n}|\tilde{\eta}_j||B\tilde{u}(b_j)|\\
&\leq\frac{\mathcal{K}\|h\||\nu||E|\sum_{j=1}^{n}|\eta_j|}{p\Gamma(\alpha+\beta+1)}\|u-\tilde{u}\|+\frac{(\mathcal{K}\|\tilde{u}\|+\mathcal{M})\|h\||\nu||E|}{p\Gamma(\alpha+\beta+1)}\delta_2\\
&+\frac{(\mathcal{K}\|\tilde{u}\|+\mathcal{M})\|h\||\nu|\sum_{j=1}^{n}|\tilde{\eta}_j||E||\tilde{E}|}{p\Gamma(\alpha+\beta+1)}(\delta_1+|\nu|\delta_2).
\end{aligned}
$$

Similarly,

$$
\begin{aligned}
&|E\sum_{i=1}^{m}\xi_i Bu(a_i)-\tilde{E}\sum_{i=1}^{m}\tilde{\xi}_i B\tilde{u}(a_i)|\leq|E|\sum_{i=1}^{m}|\xi_i||B(u(a_i)-\tilde{u}(a_i))|+|E|\sum_{i=1}^{m}|\xi_i-\tilde{\xi}_i||B\tilde{u}(a_i)|\\
&+|E-\tilde{E}|\sum_{i=1}^{m}\tilde{\xi}_i B\tilde{u}(a_i)\leq\frac{\mathcal{K}\|h\||E|\sum_{j=1}^{n}|\xi_j|}{p\Gamma(\alpha+\beta+1)}\|u-\tilde{u}\|+\frac{(\mathcal{K}\|\tilde{u}\|+\mathcal{M})\|h\||E|}{p\Gamma(\alpha+\beta+1)}\delta_1\\
&+\frac{(\mathcal{K}\|\tilde{u}\|+\mathcal{M})\|h\|\sum_{j=1}^{n}|\tilde{\xi}_j||E||\tilde{E}|}{p\Gamma(\alpha+\beta+1)}(\delta_1+|\nu|\delta_2).
\end{aligned}
$$

and then

$$
\begin{aligned}
&|\nu E\sum_{j=1}^{n}\eta_j Bu(b_j)-\nu\tilde{E}\sum_{j=1}^{n}\tilde{\eta}_j B\tilde{u}(b_j)|+|E\sum_{i=1}^{m}\xi_i Bu(a_i)-\tilde{E}\sum_{i=1}^{m}\tilde{\xi}_i B\tilde{u}(a_i)|\\
&\leq\frac{\mathcal{K}\|h\||E|(\sum_{i=1}^{m}|\xi_i|+|\nu|\sum_{j=1}^{n}|\eta_j|)}{p\Gamma(\alpha+\beta+1)}\|u-\tilde{u}\|+\Omega_2(\delta_1+|\nu|\delta_2)
\end{aligned}
\tag{23}
$$

where

$$
\begin{aligned}
\Omega_2=&\frac{(\mathcal{K}\|\tilde{u}\|+\mathcal{M})\|h\||E|}{p\Gamma(\alpha+\beta+1)}+\frac{(\mathcal{K}\|\tilde{u}\|+\mathcal{M})\|h\||\nu|\sum_{j=1}^{n}|\tilde{\eta}_j||E||\tilde{E}|}{p\Gamma(\alpha+\beta+1)}\\
&+\frac{(\mathcal{K}\|\tilde{u}\|+\mathcal{M})\|h\|\sum_{j=1}^{n}|\tilde{\xi}_j||E||\tilde{E}|}{p\Gamma(\alpha+\beta+1)}
\end{aligned}
$$

Further,

$$
\begin{aligned}
&|\nu\tilde{E}\sum_{j=1}^{n}\tilde{\eta}_j C\tilde{u}(b_j)-\nu E\sum_{j=1}^{n}\eta_j Cu(b_j)|\\
&\leq|\nu||E|\sum_{j=1}^{n}|\eta_j||C(u(b_j)-\tilde{u}(b_j))|+|\nu||E|\sum_{j=1}^{n}|\eta_j-\tilde{\eta}_j||C\tilde{u}(b_j)|+|\nu||E-\tilde{E}|\sum_{j=1}^{n}|\tilde{\eta}_j||C\tilde{u}(b_j)|\\
&\leq\frac{\|\mu^*\||\nu||E|\sum_{j=1}^{n}|\eta_j|}{p\Gamma(\beta+1)}\|u-\tilde{u}\|+\frac{(\|\mu^*\|\|\tilde{u}\|+k_0)|\nu||E|}{p\Gamma(\beta+1)}\delta_2\\
&+\frac{(\|\mu^*\|\|\tilde{u}\|+k_0)|\nu|\sum_{j=1}^{n}|\tilde{\eta}_j||E||\tilde{E}|}{p\Gamma(\beta+1)}(\delta_1+|\nu|\delta_2).
\end{aligned}
$$

Similarly,

$$|\tilde{E}\sum_{i=1}^{m}\tilde{\xi}_iC\tilde{u}(a_i)-E\sum_{i=1}^{m}\xi_iCu(a_i)|\le\frac{\|\mu^*\||E|\sum_{j=1}^{n}|\xi_j|}{p\Gamma(\beta+1)}\|u-\tilde{u}\|+\frac{(\|\mu^*\|\|\tilde{u}\|+k_0)|E|}{p\Gamma(\beta+1)}\delta_1$$
$$+\frac{(\|\mu^*\|\|\tilde{u}\|+k_0)\sum_{j=1}^{n}|\tilde{\xi}_j||E||\tilde{E}|}{p\Gamma(\beta+1)}(\delta_1+|\nu|\delta_2).$$

and so

$$\begin{aligned}&|\nu\tilde{E}\sum_{j=1}^{n}\tilde{\eta}_jC\tilde{u}(b_j)-\nu E\sum_{j=1}^{n}\eta_jCu(b_j)|+|\tilde{E}\sum_{i=1}^{m}\tilde{\xi}_iC\tilde{u}(a_i)-E\sum_{i=1}^{m}\xi_iCu(a_i)|\\&\le\frac{\|\mu^*\||E|(\sum_{j=1}^{n}|\xi_j|+|\nu|\sum_{j=1}^{n}|\eta_j|)}{p\Gamma(\beta+1)}\|u-\tilde{u}\|+\Omega_3(\delta_1+|\nu|\delta_2)\end{aligned}\tag{24}$$

where

$$\Omega_3=\frac{(\|\mu^*\|\|\tilde{u}\|+k_0)|E|}{p\Gamma(\beta+1)}+\frac{(\|\mu^*\|\|\tilde{u}\|+k_0)\sum_{j=1}^{n}|\tilde{\xi}_j||E||\tilde{E}|}{p\Gamma(\beta+1)}$$
$$+\frac{(\|\mu^*\|\|\tilde{u}\|+k_0)\sum_{j=1}^{n}|\tilde{\xi}_j||E||\tilde{E}|}{p\Gamma(\beta+1)}$$

At last we have

$$\begin{aligned}&|A\tilde{u}(t)-Au(t)|\le\frac{\|q\|}{p\Gamma(\alpha+\beta+1)}\|u-\tilde{u}\|,\\&|B\tilde{u}(t)-Bu(t)|\le\frac{\mathcal{K}\|h\|}{p\Gamma(\alpha+\beta+1)}\|u-\tilde{u}\|,\\&|C\tilde{u}(t)-Cu(t)|\le\frac{\|\mu^*\|}{p\Gamma(\beta+1)}\|u-\tilde{u}\|,\\&|\zeta_1(t,\tilde{u}(t))-\zeta_1(t,u(t))|\le\|\tilde{\mu}\|\|u-\tilde{u}\|.\end{aligned}\tag{25}$$

Thus, from (21)–(25), we have

$$\|u-\tilde{u}\|\le(\Omega^*+\|\tilde{\mu}\|)\|u-\tilde{u}\|+(\Omega_1+\Omega_2+\Omega_3)(\delta_1+|\nu|\delta_2)$$

where $\Omega^*=\frac{1}{p\Gamma(\alpha+\beta+1)}[E(\sum_{i=1}^{m}|\xi_i|+|\nu|\sum_{j=1}^{n}|\eta_j|)+1](\|q\|+\mathcal{K}\|h\|+\frac{\Gamma(\alpha+\beta+1)\|\mu^*\|}{\Gamma(\beta+1)})$. That is,

$$(1-\Omega^*-\|\tilde{\mu}\|)\|u-\tilde{u}\|\le(\Omega_1+\Omega_2+\Omega_3)(\delta_1+|\nu|\delta_2).\tag{26}$$

From our hypotheses, we know that

$$r>\frac{\Theta+\zeta_1^*}{1-\|\tilde{\mu}\|},\ \|\tilde{\mu}\|<1\text{ and}$$

$$\Theta=\frac{1}{p\Gamma(\alpha+\beta+1)}[E(\sum_{i=1}^{m}|\xi_i|+|\nu|\sum_{j=1}^{n}|\eta_j|)+1][(\|q\|+\mathcal{K}\|h\|+\frac{\Gamma(\alpha+\beta+1)\|\mu^*\|}{\Gamma(\beta+1)})r$$
$$+\mathcal{M}\|h\|+\frac{\Gamma(\alpha+\beta+1)k_0}{\Gamma(\beta+1)}]=\Omega^*r+\Omega_0^*$$

where

$$\Omega_0^*=\frac{1}{p\Gamma(\alpha+\beta+1)}[E(\sum_{i=1}^{m}|\xi_i|+|\nu|\sum_{j=1}^{n}|\eta_j|)+1][\mathcal{M}\|h\|+\frac{\Gamma(\alpha+\beta+1)k_0}{\Gamma(\beta+1)}].$$

Therefore,

$$r > \frac{\Theta + \zeta_1^*}{1 - \|\tilde{\mu}\|} = \frac{\Omega^* r + \Omega_0^* + \zeta_1^*}{1 - \|\tilde{\mu}\|},$$

and so

$$(1 - \|\tilde{\mu}\|)r > \Omega^* r + \Omega_0^* + \zeta_1^*.$$

Then, $\Omega^* r < (1 - \|\tilde{\mu}\|)r$. Since $r > 0$, thus $0 < 1 - \Omega^* - \|\tilde{\mu}\|$. Thus, from (26), we obtain

$$\|u - \tilde{u}\| \leq \epsilon = (1 - \Theta - \|\tilde{\mu}\|)^{-1}(\Omega_1 + \Omega_2 + \Omega_3)(\delta_1 + |\nu|\delta_2).$$

That is, we proved that for every $\epsilon > 0$, there exist $\delta_1(\epsilon)$ and $\delta_2(\epsilon)$ such that $\sum_{i=1}^{m} |\xi_i - \tilde{\xi}_i| < \delta_1$ and $\sum_{j=1}^{n} |\eta_j - \tilde{\eta}_j| < \delta_2$, then $\|u - \tilde{u}\| < \epsilon$. □

## 4. Fractional Couple Hybrid Sturm–Liouville Differential Equation with Integral Boundary Hybrid Condition

In this section, we deduce some fractional couple hybrid Sturm–Liouville differential equation via integral boundary conditions.

**Theorem 3.** *Let the hypotheses $(D_1)$–$(D_4)$ be satisfied. Let a number $r > 0$ exist such that*

$$r \geq \frac{\zeta_2^* \Theta + \zeta_1^*}{1 - \|\mu\|\Theta - \|\tilde{\mu}\|} \text{ and } \|\mu\|\Theta + \|\tilde{\mu}\| < 1, \tag{27}$$

*where*

$$\Theta = \frac{1}{p\Gamma(\alpha+\beta+1)}\Big[\frac{\varpi(c) - \varpi(a) + |\nu|(v(e) - v(d))}{|\varpi(c) - \varpi(a) - \nu(v(e) - v(d))|} + 1\Big][(\|q\| + \mathcal{K}\|h\| + \frac{\Gamma(\alpha+\beta+1)\|\mu^*\|}{\Gamma(\beta+1)})r + \mathcal{M}\|h\| + \frac{\Gamma(\alpha+\beta+1)k_0}{\Gamma(\beta+1)}],$$

*$\varpi(c) - \varpi(a) \neq \nu(v(e) - v(d))$, $\varpi(\theta)$ and $v(\theta)$ are increasing functions and the integrals are meant in the Riemann–Stieltjes sense for $0 \leq a < c \leq d < e \leq 1$. Then, there exists a solution $u \in C(I, \mathbb{R})$ of the fractional couple hybrid Sturm–Liouville differential problem:*

$$\begin{cases} D_c^\alpha\Big[p(t) D_c^\beta\Big(\frac{u(t) - \zeta_1(t, u(t))}{\zeta_2(t, u(t))}\Big) - k(t, u(t))\Big] + q(t)u(t) = h(t)f(u(t)), \\ D_c^\beta\Big(\frac{u(t) - \zeta_1(t, u(t))}{\zeta_2(t, u(t))}\Big)_{t=0} = k(0, u(0)), \\ \int_a^c \Big(\frac{u(\theta) - \zeta_1(\theta, u(\theta))}{\zeta_2(\theta, u(\theta))}\Big) d\varpi(\theta) = \nu \int_d^e \Big(\frac{u(\theta) - \zeta_1(\theta, u(\theta))}{\zeta_2(\theta, u(\theta))}\Big) dv(\theta), \end{cases} \tag{28}$$

*and u solves (28) if and only if u solves the integral equation*

$$\begin{aligned} u(t) = &\zeta_2(t, u(t))\left[\frac{1}{\varpi(c) - \varpi(a) - \nu(v(e) - v(d))}\left(\int_a^c Au(\theta)d\varpi(\theta)\right.\right. \\ &- \nu\int_d^e Au(\theta)dv(\theta) + \nu\int_d^e Bu(\theta)dv(\theta) - \int_a^c Bu(\theta)d\varpi(\theta) \\ &+ \nu\int_d^e Cu(\theta)dv(\theta) - \left.\int_a^c Cu(\theta)d\varpi(\theta)\right) \\ &\left. - Au(t) + Bu(t) + Cu(t)\right] + \zeta_1(t, u(t)). \end{aligned} \tag{29}$$

*Furthermore, if* $(\mathcal{B}^*)$ *holds, then* $D_c^\beta(u(t)) \in C(I, \mathbb{R})$.

**Proof.** Let $u$ be a solution of the problem (3) and (4). Assume that $\xi_i = \varpi(t_i) - \varpi(t_{i-1})$, $a_i \in (t_{i-1}, t_i)$, $0 \le a = t_0 < t_1 < t_2 < \ldots < t_m = c$, $\eta_j = v(\tau_j) - v(\tau_{j-1})$, $b_j \in (\tau_{j-1}, \tau_j)$ and $d = \tau_0 < \tau_1 < \ldots < \tau_n = e \le 1$. Thus, the multi-point boundary hybrid condition (4) will be

$$\sum_{i=1}^{m}(\varpi(t_i) - \varpi(t_{i-1}))\left(\frac{u(a_i) - \zeta_1(a_i, u(a_i))}{\zeta_2(a_i, u(a_i))}\right) = \nu\sum_{j=1}^{n}(v(\tau_j) - v(\tau_{j-1}))\left(\frac{u(b_j) - \zeta_1(b_j, u(b_j))}{\zeta_2(b_j, u(b_j))}\right),$$

As the solution $u$ of (3) and (4) is continuous, we have

$$\begin{aligned} &\lim_{m\to\infty}\sum_{i=1}^{m}(\varpi(t_i) - \varpi(t_{i-1}))\left(\frac{u(a_i) - \zeta_1(a_i, u(a_i))}{\zeta_2(a_i, u(a_i))}\right) \\ &= \nu\lim_{n\to\infty}\sum_{j=1}^{n}(v(\tau_j) - v(\tau_{j-1}))\left(\frac{u(b_j) - \zeta_1(b_j, u(b_j))}{\zeta_2(b_j, u(b_j))}\right), \end{aligned}$$

or equivalently

$$\int_a^c\left(\frac{u(\theta) - \zeta_1(\theta, u(\theta))}{\zeta_2(\theta, u(\theta))}\right)d\varpi(\theta) = \nu\int_d^e\left(\frac{u(\theta) - \zeta_1(\theta, u(\theta))}{\zeta_2(\theta, u(\theta))}\right)dv(\theta).$$

Now, from the continuity of the solution $u$ in (5), we can obtain

$$\begin{aligned} u(t) = &\zeta_2(t, u(t))\left[\frac{1}{\sum_{i=1}^{\infty}\xi_i - \nu\sum_{j=1}^{\infty}\eta_j}\left(\lim_{m\to\infty}\sum_{i=1}^{m}(\varpi(t_i) - \varpi(t_{i-1}))Au(a_i)\right.\right. \\ &- \nu\lim_{n\to\infty}\sum_{j=1}^{n}(v(\tau_j) - v(\tau_{j-1}))Au(b_j) + \nu\lim_{n\to\infty}\sum_{j=1}^{n}(v(\tau_j) - v(\tau_{j-1}))Bu(b_j) \\ &- \lim_{m\to\infty}\sum_{i=1}^{m}(\varpi(t_i) - \varpi(t_{i-1}))Bu(a_i)) + \nu\lim_{n\to\infty}\sum_{j=1}^{n}(v(\tau_j) - v(\tau_{j-1}))Cu(b_j) \\ &\left. - \lim_{m\to\infty}\sum_{i=1}^{m}(\varpi(t_i) - \varpi(t_{i-1}))Cu(a_i)) - Au(t) + Bu(t) + Cu(t)\right] + \zeta_1(t, u(t)) \\ = &\zeta_2(t, u(t))\left[\frac{1}{\varpi(c) - \varpi(a) - \nu(v(e) - v(d))}\left(\int_a^c Au(\theta)d\varpi(\theta) - \nu\int_d^e Au(\theta)dv(\theta)\right.\right. \\ &+ \nu\int_d^e Bu(\theta)dv(\theta) - \int_a^c Bu(\theta)d\varpi(\theta) + \nu\int_d^e Cu(\theta)dv(\theta) - \left.\int_a^c Cu(\theta)d\varpi(\theta)\right) \\ &\left. - Au(t) + Bu(t) + Cu(t)\right] + \zeta_1(t, u(t)). \end{aligned}$$

and clearly $u \in C(I, \mathbb{R})$ solves the problem (28) if and only if solves (29). Similarly, by taking $\xi_i = \varpi(t_i) - \varpi(t_{i-1})$ and $\eta_j = v(\tau_j) - v(\tau_{j-1})$ and $m, n \to \infty$ in $(D_5)$, we get (27). □

**Example 3.** *Consider the fractional couple hybrid Sturm–Liouville differential problem*

$$\begin{cases} D_c^{\frac{4}{5}}\left(\ln(e^{100}+t)D_c^{\frac{2}{3}}\left(\dfrac{u(t)-\frac{\sin t}{60}(\frac{1}{70}u(t)+3)}{\frac{t}{200}|u(t)|+\frac{2+\ln(1+t)}{1+\ln(1+t)}}\right)-u(t)\right)+\dfrac{1}{400(1+t^2)}u(t) \\ = \cos^3(t)\tanh(u(t)) \\ D_c^{\frac{2}{3}}\left(\dfrac{u(t)-\frac{\sin t}{60}(\frac{1}{70}u(t)+3)}{\frac{t}{200}|u(t)|+\frac{2+\ln(1+t)}{1+\ln(1+t)}}\right)_{t=0}=u(0), \\ \int_0^{\frac{1}{3}}\left(\dfrac{u(\theta)-\frac{\sin\theta}{60}(\frac{1}{70}u(\theta)+3)}{\frac{t}{200}|u(\theta)|+\frac{2+\ln(1+\theta)}{1+\ln(1+\theta)}}\right)d(3\theta+1) \\ = \frac{1}{300}\int_{\frac{1}{2}}^{1}\left(\dfrac{u(\theta)-\frac{\sin\theta}{60}(\frac{1}{40}u(\theta)+3)}{\frac{t}{200}|u(\theta)|+\frac{2+\ln(1+\theta)}{1+\ln(1+\theta)}}\right)d(\theta^2), \end{cases} \tag{30}$$

*In this case, we take* $\alpha = \frac{4}{5}$, $\beta = \frac{2}{3}$, $r = 1$, $\nu = \frac{1}{300}$, $\varpi(\theta) = 3\theta + 1$, $v(\theta) = \theta^2$, $p(t) = \ln(e^{100} + t)$, $q(t) = \frac{1}{400(1+t^2)}$, $h(t) = \cos^3(t)$, $f(u(t)) = \tanh(u(t))$, $\zeta_1(t, u(t)) = \frac{\sin t}{60}(\frac{1}{70}u(t) + 3)$, $\zeta_2(t, u(t)) = \frac{t}{200}|u(t)| + \frac{2+\ln(1+t)}{1+\ln(1+t)}$ *and* $k(t, u(t)) = u(t)$. *Therefore* $\mathcal{K} = 1$, $\mathcal{M} = 0$, $p = 100$, $\|q\| = \frac{1}{400}$, $\|h\| = 1$, $\varpi(0) = 1$, $\varpi(\frac{1}{3}) = 2$, $v(\frac{1}{2}) = \frac{1}{4}$, $v(1) = 1$. *Also*

$$|\zeta_2(t, u(t)) - \zeta_2(t, v(t))| \leq \frac{t}{200}|u(t) - v(t)|,$$

$$|\zeta_1(t, u(t)) - \zeta_1(t, v(t))| \leq \frac{\sin t}{4200}|u(t) - v(t)|$$

*and* $|\zeta_2(t, u(t)) - \zeta_2(t, v(t))| \leq |u(t) - v(t)|$. *Then,* $\|\mu\| = \frac{1}{200}$, $\|\tilde{\mu}\| = \frac{1}{4200}$, $\|\mu^*\| = 1$ $\zeta_2^* = 2$, $\zeta_1^* = \frac{1}{20}$ *and* $k_0 = 0$. *Thus,*

$$\varpi(\frac{1}{3}) - \varpi(0) = 1 \neq \frac{1}{400} = \nu(v(1) - v(\frac{1}{2})) \text{ and } \Theta \approx 0.0468369692,$$

$$r = 1 \geq 0.1437418248 \approx \frac{\zeta_2^*\Theta + \zeta_1^*}{1 - \|\mu\|\Theta - \|\tilde{\mu}\|}$$

*and*

$$\|\mu\|\Theta + \|\tilde{\mu}\| \approx 0.0004722801 < 1,$$

*Then, all the conditions of Theorem 3 are satisfied and the problem (30) has a solution.*

**Corollary 3.** *Let the hypotheses* $(D_1)$*–*$(D_2)$ *be satisfied. Let*

$$\frac{1}{p\Gamma(\alpha+\beta+1)}[\frac{\varpi(c) - \varpi(a) + |\nu|(v(e) - v(d))}{|\varpi(c) - \varpi(a) - \nu(v(e) - v(d))|} + 1](\|q\| + \mathcal{K}\|h\|) < 1,$$

*where* $\varpi(c) - \varpi(a) \neq \nu(v(e) - v(d))$, $\varpi(\theta)$ *and* $v(\theta)$ *are increasing functions, and the integrals are meant in the Riemann–Stieltjes sense for* $0 \leq a < c \leq d < e \leq 1$. *Then, there exists a solution* $u \in C(I, \mathbb{R})$ *of the fractional couple hybrid Sturm–Liouville differential problem:*

$$\begin{cases} D_c^{\alpha}\left[p(t)D_c^{\beta}(u(t))\right] + q(t)u(t) = h(t)f(u(t)), \\ D_c^{\beta}(u(t))_{t=0} = 0, \\ \int_a^c u(\theta)d\varpi(\theta) = \nu \int_d^e u(\theta)dv(\theta), \end{cases} \tag{31}$$

*and u solves* (31) *if and only if u solves the integral equation*

$$u(t) = \frac{1}{\varpi(c) - \varpi(a) - \nu(v(e) - v(d))}\Big(\int_a^c Au(\theta)d\varpi(\theta) - \nu\int_d^e Au(\theta)dv(\theta)$$
$$+\nu\int_d^e Bu(\theta)dv(\theta) - \int_a^c Bu(\theta)d\varpi(\theta)\Big) - Au(t) + Bu(t).$$

*Furthermore,* $D_c^{\beta}(u(t)) \in C(I, \mathbb{R})$.

## 5. Conclusions

Scientists utilize various Sturm–Lioville equations for modeling various phenomena and processes. This variety factor in investigating complicates the fractional Sturm-Lioville equations and boosts scientists' ability for exact modelings of more phenomena. This methods will lead scientists to make advanced software which help them to allow more cost-free testing and less material consumption. In this paper, we investigate a coupled hybrid version of the Sturm–Liouville differential equation. Indeed, we study the existence of solutions for the coupled hybrid Sturm–Liouville differential equation with multi-point boundary coupled hybrid condition. Furthermore, we study the existence of solutions for the coupled hybrid Sturm–Liouville differential equation with integral boundary coupled hybrid condition. We give an application and some examples to illustrate our results.

**Author Contributions:** The authors M.P. and M.D.L.S. contributed equally to this work. Both authors have read and agreed to the published version of the manuscript.

**Funding:** This research has been supported by the Basque Government through Grant IT207-19 and by the Spanish Government and European Commission through Grant RTI2018-094336-B-I00 (MCIU/AEI/FEDER, UE).

**Acknowledgments:** The authors thank the anonymous referees for their helpful comments.

**Conflicts of Interest:** The authors declare no conflict of interest.

## References

1. Allahviranloo, T.; Noeiaghdam, Z.; Noeiaghdam, S.; Salahshour,S.; Nieto, J.J. A Fuzzy Method for Solving Fuzzy Fractional Differential Equations Based on the Generalized Fuzzy Taylor Expansion. *Mathematics* **2020**, *8*, 2166. [CrossRef]
2. Kilbas, A.A.; Srivastava, H.M.; Trujillo, J.J. *Theory and Applications of Fractional Differential Equations*; North-Holland Mathematics Studies; Elsevier: Amsterdam, The Netherlands, 2006.
3. Miller, K.S.; Ross, B. *An Introduction to Fractional Calculus and Fractional Differential Equations*; Wiley: New York, NY, USA, 1993.
4. Podlubny, I. *Fractional Differential Equations*; Academic Press: New York, NY, USA, 1999.
5. Samko, S.G.; Kilbas, A.A.; Marichev, O.I. *Fractional Integrals and Derivatives: Theory and Applications*; Gordon and Breach: Yverdon, Switzerland, 1993.
6. Noeiaghdam, S.; Sidorov, D. Caputo-Fabrizio Fractional Derivative to Solve the Fractional Model of Energy Supply-Demand System. *Math. Model. Engine. Prob.* **2020**, *7*, 359–367.
7. Ahmad, B.; Ntouyas, S.K.; Tariboon, J. A nonlocal hybrid boundary value problem of Caputo fractional integro-differential equations. *Acta Math. Sci.* **2016**, *36*, 1631–1640. [CrossRef]

8. Charandab, Z.Z.; Rezapour, S.H.; Etefagh, M. On fractional hybrid version of the Sturm-Liouville equation. *Adv. Differ. Equ.* **2020**, *2020*, 301. [CrossRef]
9. Derbazi, C.H.; Hammouche, H.; Benchohra, M.; Zhou, Y. Fractional hybrid differential equations with three-point boundary hybrid conditions. *Adv. Differ. Equ.* **2019**, *2019*, 125. [CrossRef]
10. Herzallah, A.E.M.; Baleanu, D. On Fractional Order Hybrid Differential Equations. *Abstr. Appl. Anal.* **2014**, *2014*, 389386. [CrossRef]
11. Hilal, K.; Kajouni, A. Boundary value problems for hybrid differential equations with fractional order. *Adv. Differ. Equ.* **2015**, *2015*, 183. [CrossRef]
12. Sitho, S.; Ntouyas, S.K.; Tariboon, J. Existence results for hybrid fractional integro-differential equations. *Bound. Value Probl.* **2015**, *2015*, 113. [CrossRef]
13. Sun, S.; Zhao, Y.; Han, Z.; Lin, Y. The existence of solutions for boundary value problem of fractional hybrid differential equations. *Commun. Nonlinear Sci. Numer. Simulat.* **2012**, *17*, 4961–4967. [CrossRef]
14. Ullah, Z.; Ali, A.; Khan, R.A.; Iqbal, M. Existence results to a class of hybrid fractional differential equations. *Matrix Sci. Math.* **2018**, *1*, 13–17. [CrossRef]
15. Zhao, Y.; Sun, S.; Han, Z.; Li, Q. Theory of fractional hybrid differential equations. *Comput. Math. Appl.* **2011**, *62*, 1312–1324. [CrossRef]
16. Zhao, Y.; Wang, Y. Existence of solutions to boundary value problem of a class of nonlinear fractional differential equations. *Adv. Differ. Equ.* **2014**, *2014*, 174. [CrossRef]
17. Mahmudov, N.; Matar, M. Existence of mild solutions for hybrid differential equations with arbitrary fractional order. *TWMS J. Pure Appl. Math.* **2017**, *8*, 160–169.
18. Joannopoulos, J.D.; Johnson, S.G.; Winnn, J.N.; Meade, R.D. *Photonic Crystals: Molding the Flow of Light*, 2nd ed.; Princeton University Press: Princeton, NJ, USA, 2008.
19. Teschl, G. Mathematical Methods in Quantum Mechanics: With Applications to Schrödinger Operators. In *Graduate Studies in Mathematics*; American Mathematical Society: Providence, RI, USA, 2009; Volume 99.
20. Abbas, S.; Benchohra, M.; N'Guérékata, G.M. *Topics in Fractional Differential Equations*; Springer: New York, NY, USA, 2012.
21. Ashrafyan, Y. A new kind of uniqueness theorems for inverse Sturm-Liouville problems. *Bound. Value Probl.* **2017**, *2017*, 79. [CrossRef]
22. Liu, Y.; He, T.; Shi, H. Three positive solutions of Sturm-Liouville boundary value problems for fractional differential equations. *Differ. Equ. Appl.* **2013**, *5*, 127–152. [CrossRef]
23. EL-Sayed, A.M.A.; Gaafar, F.M. Existence and uniqueness of solution for Sturm–Liouville fractional differential equation with multi-point boundary condition via Caputo derivative. *Adv. Differ. Equ.* **2019**, *2019*, 46. [CrossRef]
24. Dhage, B.C. A fixed point theorem in Banach algebras with applications to functional integral equations. *Kyungpook Math. J.* **2004**, *44*, 145–155.

*axioms*

*Article*

# A Comparison of a Priori Estimates of the Solutions of a Linear Fractional System with Distributed Delays and Application to the Stability Analysis

**Hristo Kiskinov *, Magdalena Veselinova, Ekaterina Madamlieva and Andrey Zahariev**

Faculty of Mathematics and Informatics, University of Plovdiv, 4000 Plovdiv, Bulgaria; veselinova@uni-plovdiv.bg (M.V.); ekaterinaa.b.m@gmail.com (E.M.); zandrey@uni-plovdiv.bg (A.Z.)
* Correspondence: kiskinov@uni-plovdiv.bg

**Abstract:** In this article, we consider a retarded linear fractional differential system with distributed delays and Caputo type derivatives of incommensurate orders. For this system, several a priori estimates for the solutions, applying the two traditional approaches—by the use of the Gronwall's inequality and by the use of integral representations of the solutions are obtained. As application of the obtained estimates, different sufficient conditions which guaranty finite-time stability of the solutions are established. A comparison of the obtained different conditions in respect to the used estimates and norms is made.

**Keywords:** Caputo fractional derivative; linear fractional system; distributed delay; finite time stability

**MSC:** 34A08; 34A30; 26A33; 34A12

**Citation:** Kiskinov, H.; Veselinova, M.; Madamlieva, E.; Zahariev, A. A Comparison of a Priori Estimates of the Solutions of a Linear Fractional System with Distributed Delays and Application to the Stability Analysis. *Axioms* **2021**, *10*, 75. https://doi.org/10.3390/axioms10020075

Academic Editor: Jorge E. Macías Díaz

Received: 31 March 2021
Accepted: 21 April 2021
Published: 27 April 2021



## 1. Introduction.

As a highly applicable mathematical tool to study models of real-world phenomena, fractional calculus theory attracts a lot of attention. For a deep understanding of the fractional calculus theory and fractional differential equations, we recommend the monographs [1,2]. The distributed order fractional differential equations are treated in [3], and for an application-oriented exposition see [4]. The impulsive functional differential equations and some applications are considered in [5]. Some new ideas for efficient schemes for numerical solving of fractional differential problems can be found, for example, in [6,7].

Fractional differential equations with delay generally speaking are more complicated in comparison with the integer order differential equations with delay. This is conditioned such that a distinguishing feature of the fractional differential equations with delay is that the evolution of the processes described by such equations depends on the past history inspired from two independent sources. The first of them is the impact condition of the delays and the other one the impact condition from the availability of Volterra type integral in the definitions of the fractional derivatives, i.e., the memory of the fractional derivative.

It is well known that the classical stability concepts (Lyapunov type stabilities) are devoted to study the asymptotical properties of the solutions of differential systems over an infinite time interval. It is well known that the theme of the stability of the solutions of fractional differential equations and/or systems (ordinary or with delay) is an "evergreen" theme for research. Furthermore, the wide appearance of the aftereffect to regard it as a universal property of the surrounding world, is a serious reason to consider mathematical models with delay and fractional derivatives. This explains why a lot of papers are devoted to different aspects of this problem. A very good overview of the stability of the fractional differential systems is given in the comprehensive survey [8]. From the recent works we refer also to [9–18].

However, in many practical cases is more important to study the solution behaviors in some specified (finite) time interval, where larger values of the state variables are not admissible. Moreover, many authors made the observation that a system could be stable, but it can own unacceptable transient outputs. Such a situation from an engineering point of view leads to these types of analysis being useless. This is a reason to study not only Lyapunov type stabilities but also to study the boundedness of the solutions defined over a finite time interval, i.e., the finite-time stability (FTS). As far as we know the first work concerning the FTS is written by Kamenkov [19] in the year 1953. A historical overview of this theme can be obtained from the survey of Dorato [20]. Concerning the more recent works devoted to the different approaches to study the finite-time stability, we refer to the works [21–30].

The aim of our work, motivated by remarkable works [24–27], is twofold. First, we obtain a priori estimates using the two most popular approaches and then compare the precisions of the obtained via them estimates. Second, as an application, we apply these estimates to investigate the finite-time stability of fractional differential systems with Caputo type derivatives in the case of incommensurate fractional orders and distributed delays.

The paper is organized as follows. In Section 2, we recall the definitions of Riemann–Liouville and Caputo fractional derivatives. In the same section is the statement of the problem, as well as some necessary definitions and preliminary results used later. Section 3 is devoted to obtaining a priori estimates of the solutions of nonautonomous fractional differential systems with Caputo type derivatives of incommensurate orders with distributed delays via Gronwall inequality. In Section 4 for the solutions of the same systems we obtain a priori estimates using the approach based on their integral representations obtained in [31]. In Section 5 as application of the proved estimates we obtain sufficient conditions for finite-time stability of the considered systems. Some examples and comments are given in Section 5 and in Section 6 we present conclusions about the two main approaches analyzed in the previous sections.

## 2. Preliminaries and Problem Statement

For the reader convenience, below we recall the definitions of Riemann-Liouville and Caputo fractional derivatives. For details and properties we refer to [1–3].

Let $\alpha \in (0,1)$ be an arbitrary number and denote by $L_1^{loc}(\mathbb{R},\mathbb{R})$ the linear space of all locally Lebesgue integrable functions $f : \mathbb{R} \to \mathbb{R}$. Then for $a \in \mathbb{R}, f \in L_1^{loc}(\mathbb{R},\mathbb{R})$ and each $t > a$ the definitions of the left-sided fractional integral operator, the left side Riemann–Liouville and Caputo fractional derivatives of order $\alpha$ with lower limit (terminal) $a$ are given below (see [1]):

$$(D_{a+}^{-\alpha} f)(t) = \frac{1}{\Gamma(\alpha)} \int_a^t (t-s)^{\alpha-1} f(s)\mathrm{d}s,$$

$${}_{RL}D_{a+}^{\alpha} f(t) = \frac{\mathrm{d}}{\mathrm{d}t}(D_{a+}^{-(1-\alpha)} f(t));$$

$${}_{C}D_{a+}^{\alpha} f(t) = {}_{RL}D_{a+}^{\alpha}[f(s) - f(a)](t);$$

Everywhere below the following notations will be used: $\mathbb{R}_+ = (0,\infty), \bar{\mathbb{R}}_+ = [0,\infty)$, $J_T = [0,T], T \in \mathbb{R}_+, \langle n \rangle = \{1,2,\ldots,n\}, \langle n \rangle_0 = \langle n \rangle \cup \{0\}, n \in \mathbb{N}, I, \Theta \in \mathbb{R}^{n\times n}$ denote the identity and zero matrix respectively, $I^k, k \in \langle n \rangle$ denotes the $k$-th column of the identity matrix and $\mathbf{0} \in \mathbb{R}^n$ is the zero element.

For $\beta = (\beta_1,\ldots,\beta_n), \beta_k \in [-1,1], k \in \langle n \rangle, Y(t) = (y^1(t),\ldots,y^n(t))^T : \mathbb{R}_+ \to \mathbb{R}^n$ we use the notations $I_\beta(Y(t)) = \mathrm{diag}((y_1(t))^{\beta_1},\ldots,(y_n(t))^{\beta_n})$, for $W(t) = \{w_{kj}(t)\}_{k,j=1}^n : \bar{\mathbb{R}}_+ \to \mathbb{R}^{n\times n}, W(t) \in L_1^{loc}(\bar{\mathbb{R}}_+,\mathbb{R}^{n\times n})$ and is locally bounded, we note for every fixed $t \in \bar{\mathbb{R}}_+$ with $W^T(t) = \{w_{jk}(t)\}_{k,j=1}^n$ the transposed matrix, with $\sigma^{Max}(t)$ the largest singular value of $W(t)$ and with $|W(t)| = \sigma^{Max}$ the spectral norm [32]. In addition, $\|W(t)\| = \sup_{\xi\in[0,t]} |W(\xi)|, t \in \bar{\mathbb{R}}_+$ and for simplicity we will use the notation $D_{0+}^{\alpha} = {}_C D_{0+}^{\alpha}$ for the left side Caputo fractional derivative with lower terminal zero.

Below we will study the inhomogeneous linear delayed system of incommensurate type and distributed delay in the following general form

$$D^{\alpha}_{0+}X(t) = \int_{-h}^{0} [\mathrm{d}_\theta U(t,\theta)]X(t+\theta) + F(t),\ t \in \mathbb{R}_+ \tag{1}$$

or described in rows

$$D^{\alpha_k}_{0+}x_k(t) = \sum_{j=1}^{n} \int_{-h}^{0} x_j(t+\theta)d_\theta u_{kj}(t,\theta)) + f_k(t), t \in \mathbb{R}_+, k \in \langle n \rangle$$

where $X(t) = (x_1(t), \ldots, x_n(t))^T, D^{\alpha}_{0+} = \mathrm{diag}(D^{\alpha_1}_{0+}, \ldots, D^{\alpha_n}_{0+}), h \in \mathbb{R}_+$ is an arbitrary fixed number, $\alpha = (\alpha_1, \ldots, \alpha_n), \alpha_k \in (0,1), U : \bar{\mathbb{R}}_+ \times \mathbb{R} \to \mathbb{R}^{n\times n}, U(t,\theta) = \{u_{kj}(t,\theta)\}^n_{k,j=1}, F(t) = (f_1(t), \ldots, f_n(t))^T : \bar{R}_+ \to \mathbb{R}^n, \alpha_M = \max_{k\in\langle n \rangle} \alpha_k$ and $\alpha_m = \min_{k\in\langle n \rangle} \alpha_k$.

**Definition 1.** *With $\tilde{\mathbf{C}}$ we denote the Banach space of all bounded vector functions $\Phi(t) \in L^{loc}_1([-h,0],\mathbb{R}^n)$, with finite many jumps and norm $\|\Phi\| = \sup_{t\in[-h,0]} |\Phi(t)| = \max_{k\in\langle n \rangle}( \sup_{t\in[-h,0]} |\phi_k(t)|) < \infty$ and the subspace of all continuous functions by $\mathbf{C} = C([-h,0],\mathbb{R}^n)$, i.e., $\mathbf{C} \subset \tilde{\mathbf{C}}$. Below we assume for convenience, that every $\Phi \in \tilde{\mathbf{C}}$ is prolonged as $\Phi(t) = \mathbf{0}$ for $t \in (-\infty,-h)$ and by $S^\Phi$ we will denote the set of the jump points of $\Phi$.*

For the system, (1) introduces the following initial conditions:

$$X(t) = \Phi(t)\ \ (x_k(t) = \phi_k(t), k \in \langle n \rangle),\ \ t \in (-\infty,0], \Phi \in \tilde{\mathbf{C}}. \tag{2}$$

We say that for the kernel $U : \bar{\mathbb{R}}_+ \times \mathbb{R} \to \mathbb{R}^{n\times n}$ the conditions **(S)** hold for some $h \in \mathbb{R}_+$ if the following conditions are fulfilled:

**(S1)** The functions $(t,\theta) \to U(t,\theta) = \{u_{kj}(t,\theta)\}^n_{k,j=1}$ are measurable in $(t,\theta) \in \bar{\mathbb{R}}_+ \times \mathbb{R}$ and normalized so that for $t \in \bar{\mathbb{R}}_+, U(t,\theta) = 0$ when $\theta \in \bar{\mathbb{R}}_+$ and $U(t,\theta) = U(t,-h)$ for all $\theta \in (-\infty,-h]$. For all $t \in \bar{\mathbb{R}}_+$ the matrix valued function $\bar{U}(t,0) = Var_{\theta\in[-h,0]}U(t,\theta) = \{Var_{\theta\in[-h,0]}u_{k,j}(t,\theta)\}^n_{k,j=1}, \bar{U}(t,0) \in L^{loc}_1(\mathbb{R}_+,\mathbb{R}^{n\times n})$ is locally bounded and $\max_{k,j\in\langle n \rangle} Var_{\theta\in[-h,0]}u_{k,j}(t,\theta) < \infty$.

**(S2)** The Lebesgue decomposition of the kernel $U(t,\theta)$ for $t \in \bar{\mathbb{R}}_+$ and $\theta \in [-h,0]$ has the form:

$$U(t,\theta) = U_J(t,\theta) + U_{AC}(t,\theta) + U_S(t,\theta)$$

where $U_J(t,\theta) = \sum_{i=0}^{m} A^i(t)H(\theta + \sigma_i(t)),\ m \in \mathbb{N},\ A^i(t) = \{a^i_{kj}(t)\}^n_{k,j=1} \in L^{loc}_1(\mathbb{R}_+,\mathbb{R}^{n\times n})$ are locally bounded on $\mathbb{R}_+$, $H(t)$ is the Heaviside function, the delays $\sigma_i(t) \in C(\bar{\mathbb{R}}_+,\bar{\mathbb{R}}_+)$ are bounded with $\sigma_i = \sup_{t\in\bar{\mathbb{R}}_+} \sigma_i(t), \max_{i\in\langle m \rangle} \sigma_i = h, i \in \langle m \rangle, \sigma_0(t) \equiv 0, U_{AC} = \{ \int_{-h}^{\theta} b^j_k(t,s)\mathrm{d}s\}^n_{k,j=1} \in L^{loc}_1(\bar{\mathbb{R}}_+ \times \mathbb{R},\mathbb{R}^{n\times n})$ are locally bounded on $\bar{\mathbb{R}}_+$ and $U_S(t,\theta) \in C(\bar{\mathbb{R}}_+ \times \mathbb{R},\mathbb{R}^{n\times n})$.

**(S3)** For every $t^* \in \mathbb{R}_+$ the following relation hold: $\lim_{t\to t_*} \int_{-h}^{0} |U(t,\theta) - U(t_*,\theta)|\mathrm{d}\theta = 0$.

**(S4)** The set $S_U = \{t \in \bar{\mathbb{R}}_+ \mid t - \sigma_i(t) \in S^\Phi, i \in \langle m \rangle\}$ do not have limit points.

**Remark 1.** *At first glance, it seems that condition (S4) imposes certain restrictions on the initial function (more preciously on its jump set $S^\Phi$, which is a finite set). But the leading role in this interaction belongs to the delays, i.e., the validity of (S4) depends only from the properties of the delays. For example, in the cases of constant delays or when the delays are strictly increasing, then (S4) is ultimately fulfilled.*

Let us consider the following auxiliary system in matrix form

$$X(t) = \Phi(0) + I_{-1}(\Gamma(\alpha))[\int_0^t I_{\alpha-1}(t-\eta)\int_{-h}^0 [\mathrm{d}_\theta U(\eta,\theta)]X(\eta+\theta)\mathrm{d}\eta + \int_0^t I_{\alpha-1}(t-\eta)F(\eta)\mathrm{d}\eta] \tag{3}$$

where $I_{-1}(\Gamma(\alpha)) = \mathrm{diag}(\Gamma^{-1}(\alpha_1),\ldots,\Gamma^{-1}(\alpha_n))$, or for $k \in \langle n \rangle$ in row form

$$x_k(t) = \phi_k(0) + \frac{1}{\Gamma(\alpha_k)}[\int_0^t (t-\eta)^{\alpha_k-1}(\sum_{j=1}^n \int_{-h}^0 x_j(\eta+\theta)\mathrm{d}_\theta u_{kj}(\eta,\theta))\mathrm{d}\eta + \int_0^t (t-\eta)^{\alpha_k-1} f_k(\eta)\mathrm{d}\eta]$$

with the initial condition (2).

In our exposition below we will use the abbreviation IP for Initial Problem.

**Definition 2.** *The vector function $X(t) = (x_1(t),\ldots,x_n(t))^T$ is a solution of the IP (1), (2) or IP (3), (2) in $\bar{\mathbb{R}}_+$, if $X \in C(\bar{\mathbb{R}}_+, \mathbb{R}^n)$ satisfies the system (1) respectively (3) for all $t \in \mathbb{R}_+$ and the initial condition (2) for each $t \in [-h, 0]$.*

In virtue of Lemma 3.3 in [33] every solution $X(t)$ of IP (1), (2) is a solution of IP (3), (2) and vice versa. Moreover, the IP (3), (2) possess a unique solution $X \in C(\bar{\mathbb{R}}_+, \mathbb{R}^n)$ according Corollary 1 in [34] and hence IP (1), (2) too.

For the corresponding homogeneous system of the system (1) (i.e., $F(t) \equiv \mathbf{0}$ for $t \in \mathbb{R}_+$):

$$D^\alpha_{0+}X(t) = \int_{-h}^0 [\mathrm{d}_\theta U(t,\theta)]X(t+\theta), t \in \mathbb{R}_+ \tag{4}$$

and for arbitrary fixed $s \in [-h, \infty)$ introduce the matrix system

$$D^\alpha_{0+}W(t,s) = \int_{-h}^0 [\mathrm{d}_\theta U(t,\theta)]W(t+\theta,s), t \in \mathbb{R}_+ \cap [s,\infty). \tag{5}$$

as well as the special kind initial matrix valued functions $\Phi_1, \Phi_2 : \mathbb{R}^2 \to \mathbb{R}^{n\times n}$

$$\begin{aligned}\Phi_1(t,s) &= \begin{cases} I, & t = s, \\ \Theta, & t < s \end{cases}, s \in \bar{\mathbb{R}}_+, \\ \Phi_2(t,s) &= \begin{cases} I, & -h \le s \le t \le 0, \\ \Theta, & t < s \text{ or } s < -h \end{cases}, s \in [-h, 0]\end{aligned} \tag{6}$$

and consider the matrix integral equations

$$C(t,s) = \Phi_1(t,s) + I_{-1}(\Gamma(\alpha)) \int_s^t I_{\alpha-1}(t-\eta) \int_{-\sigma}^0 [\mathrm{d}U(\eta,\theta)]C(\eta+\theta,s)\mathrm{d}\eta, s \in \bar{\mathbb{R}}_+, t \in (s,\infty) \tag{7}$$

$$T_{-h}(t,s) = \Phi_2(0,s) + I_{-1}(\Gamma(\alpha)) \int_0^t I_{\alpha-1}(t-\eta) \int_{-\sigma}^0 [\mathrm{d}U(\eta,\theta)]T_{-h}(\eta+\theta,s)\mathrm{d}\eta, s \in [-h,0], t \in \mathbb{R}_+ \tag{8}$$

For arbitrary fixed $s \in \bar{\mathbb{R}}_+$, the solution $C(t,s)$ of (7) for $t \in (s,\infty)$ with initial condition $C(t,s) = \Phi_1(t,s), t \in (-\infty, s]$ is called fundamental matrix of the system (4).

By $T_{-h}(t,s)$ for arbitrary fixed $s \in (-\infty, 0]$ we denote the solution of (8) for $t \in \mathbb{R}_+$ with initial condition $T_{-h}(t,s) = \Phi_2(t,s), t \in (-\infty, 0]$ and we note that $C(t,0) = T_0(t,0)$.

The existence and uniqueness of the fundamental matrix $C(t,s)$ of the system (4) and the matrix $T_{-h}(t,s)$ as well as their properties are proved in [31]. Please note that these matrices are absolutely continuous concerning $t$ and continuous in $s$ on every compact subinterval in $\bar{\mathbb{R}}_+$ if $s \neq t$ and for $s = t$ possess first kind jumps [31].

Everywhere below we will use the notations:

$$\|\bar{U}(t,0)\| = \sup_{\xi\in[0,t]} |\bar{U}(\xi,0)| = \sup_{\xi\in[0,t]} |Var_{\theta\in[-h,0]}U(\xi,\theta)|,$$

$$\bar{C}(t,s) = Var_{\eta\in[0,s]}C(t,\eta) = \{Var_{\eta\in[0,s]}c_{kj}(t,\eta)\}_{k,j=1}^{n},$$

$$\|\bar{C}(t,s)\| = \sup_{\xi\in[0,t]} |\bar{C}(\xi,s)| = \sup_{\xi\in[0,t]} |Var_{\eta\in[0,s]}C(\xi,\eta)|,$$

$$\bar{T}_{-h}(t,s) = Var_{\eta\in[-h,s]}T_{-h}(t,\eta) = \{Var_{\eta\in[-h,s]}\vartheta_{kj}(t,\eta)\}_{k,j=1}^{n},$$

$$\|\bar{T}_{-h}(t,s)\| = \sup_{\xi\in[0,t]} |\bar{T}_{-h}(\xi,s)| = \sup_{\xi\in[0,t]} |Var_{\eta\in[-h,s]}\bar{T}_{-h}(\xi,\eta)|.$$

We recall some needed properties of the gamma function $\Gamma(z), z \in \mathbb{R}_+$.

It is well known that $\Gamma(z)$ has a local minimum at $z_{min} \approx 1.46163$, where it attains the value $\Gamma(z_{min}) \approx 0.885603$. Since $\Gamma(z)$ for $z \in (0, z_{min})$ is strictly decreasing, then for arbitrary $\alpha_k \in (0,1)$ we have that

$$\max_{k\in\langle n\rangle} \frac{1}{\Gamma(\alpha_k)} < \max_{k\in\langle n\rangle} \frac{1}{\Gamma(1+\alpha_k)} \le \frac{1}{\Gamma(z_{min})} \le 1.1279$$

For the function $I_{\alpha-1}(t-\eta) = (\mathrm{diag}((t-\eta)^{\alpha_1-1}, \ldots, (t-\eta)^{\alpha_n-1})$ we will use below the notations $\alpha_* = \alpha_m$ when $t-\eta \le 1$ and $\alpha_* = \alpha_M$ when $t-\eta \ge 1$. Then we have that for $t \in \bar{\mathbb{R}}_+, \eta \in [0,t)$, the following relations hold

$$|I_{\alpha-1}(t-\eta)| = (t-\eta)^{\alpha_*-1}; \ |I_{-1}(\Gamma(\alpha))| = \frac{1}{\Gamma(\alpha_M)} = \Gamma^{-1}(\alpha_M) = C_0 \tag{9}$$

where $\Gamma^{-1}(\alpha_M)$ and $(t-\eta)^{\alpha_*-1}$ are the largest singular values for the diagonal matrices $I_{-1}(\Gamma(\alpha))$ and $I_{\alpha-1}(t-\eta)$ respectively.

**Theorem 1.** *[35] Let the following conditions hold:*

1. *The functions $a(t), u(t) \in L^1_{loc}([0,T), \bar{\mathbb{R}}_+)$ for some $T \in \mathbb{R}_+$ and $\alpha > 0$.*
2. *The function $g(t) \in C([0,T), [0,M])$ for some $M \in \mathbb{R}_+$ and is nondecreasing.*
3. *For every $t \in [0,T)$ the following inequality holds:*

$$u(t) \le a(t) + g(t) \int_0^t (t-\eta)^{\alpha-1} u(\eta) d\eta.$$

*Then the following inequality holds for $t \in [0,T)$:*

$$u(t) \le a(t) + \int_0^t [\sum_{q=1}^{\infty} \frac{(g(\eta)(\Gamma(\alpha))^q}{\Gamma(\alpha q)} (t-\eta)^{\alpha q-1}] a(\eta) d\eta.$$

**Corollary 1.** *[35] Let the conditions of Theorem 1 hold and let the function $a(t)$ be nondecreasing on $[0,T)$.*

*Then for $t \in [0,T)$ the inequality $u(t) \le a(t)E_\alpha[g(t)\Gamma(\alpha)t^\alpha]$ holds, where $E_\alpha$ denotes the one parameter Mittag-Leffler function.*

**Definition 3.** *[27] The fractional system given by (1) satisfying the initial state (2) is finite-time stable with respect to $\{0, J_T, \delta, \varepsilon, h\}$ with $t \in J_T$ and $\delta \le \varepsilon$ if and only if the inequality $\|\Phi\| < \delta$ implies that $\|X(t)\| < \varepsilon$ for each $t \in J_T$, where $X(t)$ is the unique solution of IP (1), (2).*

## 3. A Priory Estimates of the Solutions of IP (1), (2)—Gronwall's Inequality Approach

In this section, we obtain some a priori estimates of the solutions of IP (1), (2) and IP (4), (2) in different cases, depending from the properties of the initial function $\Phi$ and the function $F$. The different a priori estimates of the solutions in this section are obtained using approaches based on Gronwall's inequality.

**Theorem 2.** *Let $T \in \mathbb{R}_+$ be an arbitrary fixed number and the following conditions are fulfilled:*
*1. Conditions (S) hold.*
*2. The function $F(t) \in L_1^{loc}(\mathbb{R}_+, \mathbb{R}^n)$ is locally bounded.*
*Then for every initial function $\Phi \in \tilde{C}$ the corresponding unique solution $X(t)$ of IP (1), (2) for every $t \in J_T$ satisfies the estimation*

$$\max(\|X(t)\|, \|\Phi\|) \le (\|\Phi\| + \alpha_*^{-1} C_0 \|F(t)\| t^{\alpha_*}) E_\alpha(\|\bar{U}(t,0)\| C_0 \Gamma(\alpha_*) t^{\alpha_*}). \tag{10}$$

**Proof.** Let $\Phi \in \tilde{C}$ be an arbitrary initial function and $X(t)$ be the corresponding unique solution of the IP (1), (2). Then if $\max(\|X(T)\|, \|\Phi\|) = \|\Phi\|$ the estimation (10) obviously holds.

Let assume that $\max(\|X(T)\|, \|\Phi\|) > \|\Phi\|$. From (3) for every $t \in J_T$ it follows that

$$X(t) = \Phi(0) + I_{-1}(\Gamma(\alpha))[\int_0^t I_{\alpha-1}(t-\eta)F(\eta)\mathrm{d}\eta + \int_0^t I_{\alpha-1}(t-\eta) \int_{-h}^0 [\mathrm{d}_\theta U(\eta,\theta)] X(\eta+\theta)\mathrm{d}\eta]. \tag{11}$$

Using (9) it is simple to check that

$$\begin{aligned} |I_{-1}(\Gamma(\alpha))[\int_0^t I_{\alpha-1}(t-\eta)F(\eta)\mathrm{d}\eta| &\le \frac{1}{\Gamma(\alpha_M)} \int_0^t (t-\eta)^{\alpha_*-1} |F(\eta)| \mathrm{d}\eta \\ &\le C_0 \|F(t)\| \int_0^t (t-\eta)^{\alpha_*-1} \mathrm{d}\eta = C_0 \alpha_*^{-1} \|F(t)\| t^{\alpha_*}. \end{aligned} \tag{12}$$

Since for each $\eta \in \bar{\mathbb{R}}_+$ with $\eta + \theta \le 0$ for some $\theta \in [-h, 0]$ we have that $|X(\eta + \theta)| \le \|\Phi\|$ and for each $\eta \in \bar{\mathbb{R}}_+$ with $\eta + \theta \in [0, \eta]$ for some $\theta \in [-h, 0]$ the estimation $|X(\eta + \theta)| \le \|X(\eta)\|$ holds, then for $t \in J_T$ we obtain

$$|\int_{-h}^0 [\mathrm{d}_\theta U(\eta,\theta)] X(\eta+\theta)| \le \|\bar{U}(t,0)\| \max(\|X(\eta)\|, \|\Phi\|). \tag{13}$$

Then from (9), (11)–(13) for $t \in J_T$ we obtain

$$\begin{aligned} \max(\|X(t)\|, \|\Phi\|) &\le \|\Phi\| + C_0 \int_0^t (t-\eta)^{\alpha_*-1} \|F(t)\| \mathrm{d}\eta \\ &+ \frac{1}{\Gamma(\alpha_M)} \int_0^t (t-\eta)^{\alpha_*-1} | \int_{-h}^0 [\mathrm{d}_\theta U(\eta,\theta)] X(\eta+\theta) | \mathrm{d}\eta \\ &\le \|\Phi\| + C_0 \alpha_*^{-1} t^{\alpha_*} \|F(t)\| \\ &+ C_0 \|\bar{U}(t,0)\| \int_0^t (t-\eta)^{\alpha_*-1} \max(\|X(\eta)\|)|, \|\Phi\|) \mathrm{d}\eta \end{aligned} \tag{14}$$

and denoting $u(t) = \max(\|X(t)\|, \|\Phi\|)$, from (14) it follows that

$$u(t) \leq (\|\Phi\| + C_0\alpha_*^{-1}t^{\alpha_*}\|F(t)\|) + C_0\|\bar{U}(t,0)\| \sup_{\xi\in[0,t]} \int_0^{\xi} (\xi-\eta)^{\alpha_*-1}u(\eta)\mathrm{d}\eta \tag{15}$$

Since $u(t)$ is positive and non-decreasing then for each $t \in J_T$ we have

$$\begin{aligned} \sup_{\xi\in[0,t]} \int_0^{\xi} (\xi-\eta)^{\alpha_*-1}u(\eta)\mathrm{d}\eta &= \sup_{\xi\in[0,t]} \int_0^{\xi} s^{\alpha_*-1}u(\xi-s)\mathrm{d}s \\ &\leq \int_0^{t} s^{\alpha_*-1}u(t-s)\mathrm{d}s = \int_0^{t} (t-\eta)^{\alpha_*-1}u(\eta)\mathrm{d}s \end{aligned} \tag{16}$$

and hence from (15) and (16) it follows for each $t \in J_T$ the estimation

$$u(t) \leq (\|\Phi\| + C_0\alpha_*^{-1}t^{\alpha_*}\|F(t)\|) + C_0\|\bar{U}(t,0)\| \int_0^{t} (t-\eta)^{\alpha_*-1}u(\eta)\mathrm{d}s \tag{17}$$

Then applying Corollary 1 to (17) we obtain (10). □

**Corollary 2.** *Let $T \in \mathbb{R}_+$ be an arbitrary fixed number and the following conditions are fulfilled:*

1. *The conditions (S) hold.*
2. $\|F(T)\| = 0$.

*Then for every initial function $\Phi \in \tilde{C}$ with $\|\Phi\| > 0$ the corresponding unique solution $X(t)$ of IP (1), (2) for every $t \in J_T$ satisfies the estimation*

$$\max(\|X(t)\|, \|\Phi\|) \leq \|\Phi\| E_\alpha(\|\bar{U}(t,0)\|C_0\Gamma(\alpha_*)t^{\alpha_*}). \tag{18}$$

**Proof.** The estimation (18) follows immediately from (10) using that $\|F(t)\| = 0$ for each $t \in [0,T]$. □

**Corollary 3.** *Let $T \in \mathbb{R}_+$ be an arbitrary fixed number and the following conditions are fulfilled:*

1. *The conditions (S) hold.*
2. *The function $F(t) \in L_1^{loc}(\mathbb{R}_+, \mathbb{R}^n)$ is locally bounded and $\|\Phi\| = 0$.*

*Then the corresponding unique solution $X(t)$ of IP (1), (2) satisfies the estimation*

$$\|X(t)\| \leq \alpha_*^{-1}C_0 t^{\alpha_*}\|F(t)\| E_\alpha(\|\bar{U}(t,0)\|C_0\Gamma(\alpha_*)t^{\alpha_*}). \tag{19}$$

**Proof.** The estimation (19) follows immediately from (10) using that $\|\Phi\| = 0$. □

The next theorem is devoted to obtaining another form of the estimation (10) based on the assumption that $\|\Phi\| > 0$. The approach used is the same as in Theorem 2 but the assumption that $\|\Phi\| > 0$ allows one technical stunt to be realized.

**Theorem 3.** *Let $T \in \mathbb{R}_+$ be an arbitrary fixed number and the following conditions are fulfilled:*

1. *The condition of Theorem 2 hold and $||F(T)|| > 0$.*
2. *The initial function $\Phi \in \tilde{C}$ satisfies the condition $\|\Phi\| > 0$.*

*Then the corresponding unique solution $X(t)$ of IP (1), (2) for every $t \in J_T$ satisfies the estimation*

$$\max(\|X(t)\|, \|\Phi\|) \leq \|\Phi\| E_\alpha((C_\Phi + \|\bar{U}(t,0)\|)C_0\Gamma(\alpha_*)t^{\alpha_*}), \tag{20}$$

*where $C_\Phi = \|\Phi\|^{-1}\|F(T)\|$.*

**Proof.** Let $X(t)$ be the corresponding unique solution of the IP (1), (2). Condition 2 implies that $||\Phi|| > 0$ and then since $\sup_{s\in[-h,t]} |X(s)|$ is not decreasing and $X(t) = \Phi(t)$ for $t \in [-h, 0]$, then we have that $\sup_{t\in[-h,0]} |X(t)| = ||\Phi||$. Let assume that $||\Phi|| > |X(0)|$ and let $\bar{t} \in [0, T]$ be arbitrary with $||\Phi|| \geq |X(\bar{t})|$. Then for $C_\Phi = ||\Phi||^{-1}||F(T)||$ we have

$$C_\Phi \max(|X(\bar{t})|, ||\Phi||) = C_\Phi||\Phi|| = ||\Phi||\frac{||F(T)||}{||\Phi||} = ||F(T)|| \geq ||F(\bar{t})|| \geq |F(\bar{t})|.$$

For arbitrary $\bar{t} \in [0, T]$ with $||\Phi|| \leq |X(\bar{t})|$ we obtain that the inequality

$$C_\Phi \max(|X(\bar{t})|, ||\Phi||) = C_\Phi|X(\bar{t})| \geq ||\Phi||\frac{||F(T)||}{||\Phi||} = ||F(T)|| \geq ||F(\bar{t})|| \geq |F(\bar{t})|$$

holds and hence for each $t \in J_T$ the inequality $||F(t)|| \leq C_\Phi \max(|X(t)|, ||\Phi||)$ holds.

Then for each $t \in J_T$ from (11) as in the proof of Theorem 2 we obtain that (14) holds.

From (14) and taking into account the inequality $||F(t)|| \leq C_\Phi \max(|X(t)|, ||\Phi||)$ it follows that

$$\begin{aligned}\max(|X(t)|, ||\Phi||) &\leq ||\Phi|| + C_0C_\Phi \int_0^t (t-\eta)^{\alpha_*-1} \max(|X(\eta)|, ||\Phi||)d\eta \\ &\quad + C_0||\bar{U}(t,0)|| \int_0^t (t-\eta)^{\alpha_*-1} \max(|X(\eta)|, ||\Phi||)d\eta \\ &\leq ||\Phi|| + C_0(C_\Phi + ||\bar{U}(t,0)||) \int_0^t (t-\eta)^{\alpha_*-1} \max(|X(\eta)|, ||\Phi||)d\eta\end{aligned} \tag{21}$$

and hence from (21) as in the proof of Theorem 2 we obtain

$$u(t) \leq ||\Phi||C_0(C_\Phi + ||\bar{U}(t,0)||) \int_0^t (t-\eta)^{\alpha_*-1}u(\eta)d\eta. \tag{22}$$

Then applying Corollary 1 to (22) we obtain (20). □

**Remark 2.** *At first glance, it looks like the estimate (20) is better at least as it has a more appropriate form for the applications in compare with (10). However, the most important question is which estimate is more accurate since in general the approach used in both proofs is the same. It is simple to establish that if $||\Phi|| = 0$ then the estimate (19) can be used and in the case when $||\Phi|| > 0$ the estimate (10) can be rewritten in the form*

$$max(||X(t)||, ||\Phi||) \leq ||\Phi||(1 + \alpha_*^{-1}C_0C_\Phi t^{\alpha_*})E_\alpha(||\bar{U}(t,0)||C_0\Gamma(\alpha_*)t^{\alpha_*}). \tag{23}$$

*These simple considerations limit the impact to linear (no more than power-law) growth in the right side of the estimation (23) and allow avoiding the high nonlinear impact of $C_\Phi = ||\Phi||^{-1}||F(T)||$ as argument in the Mittag-Leffler function $E_\alpha(\cdot)$ in (20).*

## 4. A Priory Estimates of the Solutions Obtained via Their Integral Representations

The next different a priori estimations are obtained using the other most popular approach, which is essentially based on the different kinds integral representations of the solutions of the considered systems obtained in [31,33] and applying the superposition principle.

**Theorem 4.** *Let $T \in \mathbb{R}_+$ be an arbitrary fixed number and following conditions are fulfilled:*

*1. The conditions of Theorem 2 hold.*

*2. The initial function $\Phi(t) \equiv \mathbf{0}$ for $t \in [-h, 0]$ (i.e., $\|\Phi\| = 0$).*

*Then the corresponding unique solution $X^F(t)$ of the IP (1), (2) for every $t \in J_T$ satisfies the estimation*

$$\|X^F(t)\| \le \alpha_*^{-1} t^{\alpha_*} C_0 \|F(t)\| (1 + \| \bar{C}(t,t) \|). \tag{24}$$

**Proof.** Let $\Phi \in \tilde{C}$ and $\Phi(t) \equiv \mathbf{0}$ for $t \in [-h, 0]$. Then according Theorem 4.3 in [33] the unique solution $X^F(t)$ of the IP (1), (2) for every $t \in \mathbb{R}_+$ has the following representation:

$$X^F(t) = \int_0^t C(t,s)_{RL} D_{a+}^{1-\alpha} F(s) \mathrm{d}s, \tag{25}$$

where $C(t,s)$ is the fundamental matrix of the system (5). Then from (25) after simple calculations and integrating by parts we obtain for $t \in \mathbb{R}_+$

$$\begin{aligned} X^F(t) &= \int_0^t C(t,s)_{RL} D_{0+}^{1-\alpha} F(s) \mathrm{d}s = I_{-1}(\Gamma(\alpha)) \int_0^t C(t,s) (\frac{\mathrm{d}}{\mathrm{d}s} \int_0^s I_{\alpha-1}(s-\eta) F(\eta) \mathrm{d}\eta) \mathrm{d}s \\ &= I_{-1}(\Gamma(\alpha)) \int_0^t C(t,s) \mathrm{d}_s (\int_0^s I_{\alpha-1}(s-\eta) F(\eta) \mathrm{d}\eta) \\ &= I_{-1}(\Gamma(\alpha)) \int_0^t I_{\alpha-1}(t-\eta) F(\eta) \mathrm{d}\eta) - I_{-1}(\Gamma(\alpha)) \int_0^t (\int_0^s I_{\alpha-1}(s-\eta) F(\eta) \mathrm{d}\eta) \mathrm{d}_s (C(t,s)) \end{aligned} \tag{26}$$

Then for the first addend in the right side of (26) using (12) we obtain that

$$|I_{-1}(\Gamma(\alpha)) \int_0^t I_{\alpha-1}(t-\eta) F(\eta) \mathrm{d}\eta)| \le C_0 \int_0^t |I_{\alpha-1}(t-\eta)| \|F(\eta)\| \mathrm{d}\eta = C_0 \int_0^t (t-\eta)^{\alpha_*-1} \|F(\eta)\| \mathrm{d}\eta$$

and hence in virtue of (16) we obtain

$$\left\| I_{-1}(\Gamma(\alpha)) \int_0^t I_{\alpha-1}(t-\eta) F(\eta) \mathrm{d}\eta) \right\| \le C_0 \int_0^t (t-\eta)^{\alpha_*-1} \|F(\eta)\| \mathrm{d}\eta \le \alpha_*^{-1} C_0 t^{\alpha_*} \|F(t)\|. \tag{27}$$

For the second addend in the right side of (26) we obtain the estimation

$$\begin{aligned} &\sup_{s\in[0,t]} |I_{-1}(\Gamma(\alpha)) \int_0^t (\int_0^s I_{\alpha-1}(s-\eta) F(\eta) \mathrm{d}\eta) \mathrm{d}_s (C(t,s))| \\ &\le C_0 \|\bar{C}(t,t)\| \sup_{s\in[0,t]} | \int_0^s I_{\alpha-1}(s-\eta) F(\eta) \mathrm{d}\eta| \le C_0 \|\bar{C}(t,t)\| \sup_{s\in[0,t]} \int_0^s |I_{\alpha-1}(s-\eta)| \|F(\eta)\| \mathrm{d}\eta \\ &= C_0 \|F(t)\| \|\bar{C}(t,t)\| \sup_{s\in[0,t]} \int_0^s (t-\eta)^{\alpha_*-1} \mathrm{d}\eta = \alpha_*^{-1} C_0 t^{\alpha_*} \|F(t)\| \|\bar{C}(t,t)\|. \end{aligned} \tag{28}$$

Then the statement of the theorem follows from (27) and (28). □

**Theorem 5.** *Let $T \in \mathbb{R}_+$ be an arbitrary fixed number and the following conditions are fulfilled:*

*1. The conditions (S) hold.*

*2. $\|F(T)\| = 0$.*

*3. The initial function $\Phi \in BV([-h, 0], \mathbb{R}^n) \cap \tilde{C}$ and its Lebesgue decomposition does not include a singular term.*

*Then the corresponding unique solution $X_\Phi(t)$ of the IP (1), (2) for every $t \in J_T$ satisfies the estimation*

$$\|X_\Phi(t)\| \leq |Var_{\eta\in[-h,0]}\Phi(\eta)| \sup_{s\in[-h,0]} \|T_{-h}(t,s)\| + |\Phi(-h)| \|T_{-h}(t-h)\|. \tag{29}$$

**Proof.** According Theorem 9 in [31] the unique solution $X_\Phi(t)$ of the IP (1), (2) for every $t \in \mathbb{R}_+$ has the following representation:

$$X_\Phi(t) = \int_{-h}^{0} T_{-h}(t,s)\mathrm{d}\Phi(s) + T_{-h}(t,-h)\Phi(-h). \tag{30}$$

From (30) we obtain

$$\begin{aligned} \|X_\Phi(t)\| &\leq \int_{-h}^{0} \|T_{-h}(t,s)\|\mathrm{d}\|Var_{\eta\in[-h,s]}\Phi(\eta)\| + |\Phi(-h)| \|T_{-h}(t,-h)\| \\ &\leq |Var_{\eta\in[-h,0]}\Phi(\eta)| \sup_{s\in[-h,0]} \|T_{-h}(t,s)\| + |\Phi(-h)| \|T_{-h}(t-h)\| \end{aligned} \tag{31}$$

and from (31) it follows (29), which complete the proof. □

**Corollary 4.** *Let $T \in \mathbb{R}_+$ be an arbitrary fixed number and the following conditions are fulfilled:*
1. *The conditions (S) hold.*
2. *The initial functions $\Phi(t) \equiv \Phi_0 \neq \mathbf{0}, \Phi_0 \in \mathbb{R}^n$ for $t \in [-h,0]$.*

*Then the corresponding unique solution $X_\Phi(t)$ of the IP (1), (2) for every $t \in J_T$ satisfies the estimation*

$$\|X_\Phi(t)\| \leq |\Phi(-h)| \|T_{-h}(t,-h)\| = |\Phi_0| \|T_{-h}(t,-h)\| \tag{32}$$

**Proof.** According Theorem 9 in [31] the unique solution $X(t)$ of the IP (1), (2) for every $t \in \mathbb{R}_+$ has the representation (30) and hence we obtain that $X_\Phi(t) = T_{-h}(t,-h)\Phi(-h)$ which completes the proof. □

**Corollary 5.** *Let $T \in \mathbb{R}_+$ be an arbitrary fixed number and the following conditions are fulfilled:*
1. *The conditions (S) hold.*
2. *The function $F(t) \in L_1^{loc}(\mathbb{R}_+, \mathbb{R}^n)$ and is locally bounded.*
3. *The initial function $\Phi \in BV([-h,0], \mathbb{R}^n) \cap \tilde{C}$ and its Lebesgue decomposition does not include a singular term.*

*Then the corresponding unique solution $X_\Phi^F(t)$ of the IP (1), (2) for every $t \in J_T$ satisfies the estimation*

$$\begin{aligned} \|X_\Phi^F(t)\| &\leq |Var_{\eta\in[-h,0]}\Phi(\eta)| \sup_{s\in[-h,0]} \|T_{-h}(t,s)\| + |\Phi(-h)| \|T_{-h}(t-h)\| \\ &+ \alpha_*^{-1} t^{\alpha_*} C_0 \|F(t)\| (1 + \|\bar{C}(t,t)\|) \end{aligned} \tag{33}$$

**Proof.** Using the superposition principle, i.e., $X_\Phi^F(t) = X_\Phi(t) + X^F(t)$ we obtain that the estimation (33) follows immediately from Theorems 4 and 5. □

**Remark 3.** *It is clear that if $\|\Phi\| \|F(T)\| > 0$, then (33) can be rewritten in the form*

$$\begin{aligned} \|X_\Phi^F(t)\| &\leq \max(\|\Phi\|, |Var_{\eta\in[-h,0]}\Phi(\eta)|)[\sup_{s\in[-h,0]} \|T_{-h}(t,s)\| + \|T_{-h}(t-h)\| \\ &+ \alpha_*^{-1} t^{\alpha_*} C_0 C_\Phi (1 + \|\bar{C}(t,t)\|)] \end{aligned} \tag{34}$$

The next theorem establishes explicit bounds for the matrix functions involved in (33) and (34), which allows obtaining a new form of these estimations more convenient for practical computer calculations.

**Theorem 6.** *Let $T \in \mathbb{R}_+$ be an arbitrary fixed number and the following conditions are fulfilled:*

*1. The conditions (S) hold.*

*2. The function $F(t) \in L_1^{loc}(\mathbb{R}_+, \mathbb{R}^n)$ and is locally bounded and $\|\Phi\|\|F(T)\| > 0$.*

*3. The initial function $\Phi \in BV([-h,0], \mathbb{R}^n) \cap \tilde{C}$ and its Lebesgue decomposition does not include a singular term.*

*Then the corresponding unique solution $X_\Phi^F(t)$ of the IP (1), (2) for every $t \in J_T$ satisfies the estimation*

$$\begin{aligned}\|X_\Phi^F(t)\| \le (|Var_{\eta\in[-h,0]}\Phi(\eta)| + |\Phi(-h)|)E_\alpha(\|\bar{U}(t,0)\|C_0\Gamma(\alpha_*)t^{\alpha_*}) \\ + \alpha_*^{-1}t^{\alpha_*}C_0\|F(t)\|(1 + 2E_\alpha(\|\bar{U}(t,0)\|C_0\Gamma(\alpha_*)t^{\alpha_*}))\end{aligned} \tag{35}$$

**Proof.** From (7) it follows that $\|\Phi_1(t,s)\| = 1, t \in (-\infty, s]$ and $\|\Phi_2(t,s)\| = 1, s \in [-h,0], t \in [s,0]$.

Let $s \in \bar{\mathbb{R}}_+$ be an arbitrary fixed number and $C(t,s)$ is the solution for $t \in (s,\infty)$ of the (7) with initial condition $C(t,s) = \Phi_1(t,s), t \in (-\infty, s]$. Then from (7), (8) it follows that

$$C(t,s) = I + I_{-1}(\Gamma(\alpha))\int_s^t I_{\alpha-1}(t-\eta)\int_{-h}^0 [d_\theta U(\eta,\theta)]C(\eta+\theta,s)d\eta \tag{36}$$

and respectively for $s \in [-h,0], t \in \mathbb{R}_+$ we have that

$$T_{-h}(t,s) = I + I_{-1}(\Gamma(\alpha))\int_s^t I_{\alpha-1}(t-\eta)\int_{-h}^0 [d_\theta U(\eta,\theta)]T_{-h}(\eta+\theta,s)d\eta \tag{37}$$

where $T_{-h}(t,s) = \Phi_2(t,s), t \in (-\infty, 0]$.

For arbitrary fixed $s \in \bar{\mathbb{R}}_+$, since $\|C(t,s)\|$ is nonnegative and nondecreasing in $t$ from the first system (36) and (16) we obtain that

$$\begin{aligned}\|C(t,s)\| &= \sup_{\xi\in[0,t]}|C(\xi,s) \le 1 + C_0\sup_{\xi\in[0,t]}\int_s^\xi |I_{\alpha-1}(\xi-\eta)|\left|\int_{-h}^0 [d_\theta U(\eta,\theta)]C(\eta+\theta,s)\right|d\eta \\ &\le 1 + C_0\|\bar{U}(t,0)\|\sup_{\xi\in[0,t]}\int_0^\xi (\xi-\eta)^{\alpha_*-1}\sup_{\eta+\theta\in[-h,\xi]}|C(\eta+\theta,s)|d\eta \\ &\le 1 + C_0\|\bar{U}(t,0)\|\sup_{\xi\in[0,t]}\int_0^\xi (\xi-\eta)^{\alpha_*-1}\|C(\eta,s)\|d\eta \\ &\le 1 + C_0\|\bar{U}(t,0)\|\int_0^t (t-\eta)^{\alpha_*-1}\|C(\eta,s)\|d\eta\end{aligned} \tag{38}$$

and then in virtue of Corollary 1 we have that

$$\|C(t,s)\| \le E_\alpha(\|\bar{U}(t,0)\|C_0\Gamma(\alpha_*)t^{\alpha_*}) \le E_\alpha(\|\bar{U}(T,0)\|C_0\Gamma(\alpha_*)T^{\alpha_*}), s \in \bar{\mathbb{R}}_+ \tag{39}$$

Analogical way when $T_{-h}(t,s)$ is a solution of the (8) with initial condition $T_{-h}(t,s) = \Phi_2(t,s), t \in (-\infty, 0]$ and since $\|T_{-h}(t,s)\|$ is nonnegative and nondecreasing in $t$ from (16) and (37) we obtain

$$\begin{aligned}
\|T_{-h}(t,s)\| &\leq 1 + C_0 \sup_{\xi\in[0,t]} \int_s^{\xi} |I_{\alpha-1}(\xi-\eta)| \left| \int_{-h}^{0} [d_\theta U(\eta,\theta)] T_{-h}(\eta+\theta,s) \right| d\eta \\
&\leq 1 + C_0 \|\bar{U}(t,0)\| \sup_{\xi\in[0,t]} \int_0^{t} (\xi-\eta)^{\alpha_*-1} \sup_{\theta\in[-h,0]} |T_{-h}(\eta+\theta,s)| d\eta \\
&\leq 1 + C_0 \|\bar{U}(t,0)\| \sup_{\xi\in[0,t]} \int_0^{\xi} (\xi-\eta)^{\alpha_*-1} \|T_{-h}(\eta,s)\| d\eta \\
&\leq 1 + C_0 \|\bar{U}(t,0)\| \int_0^{t} (t-\eta)^{\alpha_*-1} \|T_{-h}(\eta,s)\| d\eta
\end{aligned}$$

and hence in virtue of Corollary 1 we have

$$|T_{-h}(t,s)\| \leq E_\alpha(\|\bar{U}(t,0)\| C_0 \Gamma(\alpha_*) t^{\alpha_*}) \leq E_\alpha(\|\bar{U}(T,0)\| C_0 \Gamma(\alpha_*) T^{\alpha_*}), s \in [-h,0]. \quad (40)$$

Since for fixed $t$ the matrix function $\|\bar{C}(t,s)\|$ is nondecreasing for $s \in [0,T]$ , then taking into account (39) and (40) we have that

$$\|\bar{C}(T,T)\| = \|C(T,T) - C(T,0)\| \leq \|C(T,T)\| + \|C(T,0)\| \leq 2E_\alpha(\|\bar{U}(T,0)\| C_0 \Gamma(\alpha_*) T^{\alpha_*}). \quad (41)$$

Then from (40) and (41) we obtain that for every $t \in J_T$ the estimation (35) holds. □

**Remark 4.** *Please note that if $\|\Phi\|\|F(T)\| > 0$, then (35) can be rewritten in the form*

$$\begin{aligned}
\|X_\Phi^F(t)\| \leq \max(\|\Phi\|, |Var_{\eta\in[-h,0]}\Phi(\eta)|) \\
[2E_\alpha(\|\bar{U}(t,0)\| C_0 \Gamma(\alpha_*) t^{\alpha_*}) + \alpha_*^{-1} t^{\alpha_*} C_0 C_\Phi (1 + 2E_\alpha(\|\bar{U}(t,0)\| C_0 \Gamma(\alpha_*) t^{\alpha_*})]
\end{aligned} \quad (42)$$

**5. Finite-Time Stability Results**

In this section, we study the finite-time stability (FTS) properties of the system (1), with the initial condition (2) as an application of the different a priori estimations obtained in Sections 4 and 5. In addition, we will study these properties for different types initial functions. A special attention obtains the case when $\|\Phi\| = 0$ too.

First, we start with the homogeneous case, i.e., the IP (4), (2).

**Theorem 7.** *Let $T \in \mathbb{R}_+$ be an arbitrary fixed number and the following conditions are fulfilled:*
1. *The conditions (S) hold and $F(t) \equiv \mathbf{0}$ for $t \in J_T$.*
2. *There exist numbers $\varepsilon \geq \delta > 0$ such that the following inequality holds*

$$\delta E_\alpha(\|\bar{U}(T,0)\| C_0 \Gamma(\alpha_*) T^{\alpha_*}) \leq \varepsilon \quad (43)$$

*Then for every initial function $\Phi \in \tilde{C}$ with $\|\Phi\| < \delta$ the corresponding unique solution $X(t)$ of the IP (1), (2) (in this case this is IP (4), (2)) is finite-time stable with respect to $\{0, J_T, \delta, \varepsilon, h\}$.*

**Proof.** Let $\Phi \in \tilde{C}$ with $\|\Phi\| < \delta$ be an arbitrary initial function. Then if $\max(\|X(T)\|, \|\Phi\|) = \|\Phi\|$ then the statement of the theorem holds. The nontrivial case obviously is when $\max(\|X(T)\|, \|\Phi\|) > \|\Phi\|$. In this case from condition 1 it follows that Corollary 2 holds and from (18) for $t \in J_T$ we obtain that

$$\|X(t)\| \leq \|\Phi\| E_\alpha(\|\bar{U}(t,0)\| C_0 \Gamma(\alpha_*) t^{\alpha_*}) \quad (44)$$

and hence from (43) and (44) it follows that

$$\|X(t)\| < \|\Phi\| E_\alpha(\|\bar{U}(t,0)\| C_0 \Gamma(\alpha_*) t^{\alpha_*}) \leq \delta E_\alpha(\|\bar{U}(T,0)\| C_0 \Gamma(\alpha_*) T^{\alpha_*}) \leq \varepsilon$$

which completes the proof. □

The next theorem considers a special nonhomogeneous case of the system (1) when $\|\Phi\| = 0$.

**Theorem 8.** *Let the following conditions be fulfilled:*

1. *The conditions of Theorem 2 hold and* $\|\Phi\| = 0$.
2. *There exist numbers* $\varepsilon \geq \delta > 0$ *such that if* $\|F(T)\| < \delta$ *then the following inequality holds*

$$\delta \alpha_*^{-1} C_0 T^{\alpha_*} E_\alpha(\|\bar{U}(t,0)\| C_0 \Gamma(\alpha_*) T^{\alpha_*}) \leq \varepsilon \tag{45}$$

*Then the corresponding unique solution* $X(t)$ *of the IP (1), (2) is finite-time stable with respect to* $\{0, J_T, \delta, \varepsilon, h\}$.

**Proof.** Let us consider the case when $\max(\|X(T)\|, \|\Phi\|) > \|\Phi\|$. Since Corollary 3 holds, from (19) and (45) for $t \in J_T$ it follows that

$$\begin{aligned} \|X(t)\| &\leq \alpha_*^{-1} C_0 t^{\alpha_*} \|F(t)\| E_\alpha(\|\bar{U}(t,0)\| C_0 \Gamma(\alpha_*) t^{\alpha_*}) \\ &\leq \delta \alpha_*^{-1} C_0 T^{\alpha_*} E_\alpha(\|\bar{U}(t,0)\| C_0 \Gamma(\alpha_*) T^{\alpha_*}) \leq \varepsilon \end{aligned} \tag{46}$$

Thus, from (46) it follows that the corresponding unique solution $X(t)$ of the IP (1), (2) is finite-time stable with respect to $\{0, J_T, \delta, \varepsilon, h\}$ for every locally bounded $F(t) \in L_1^{loc}(\mathbb{R}_+, \mathbb{R}^n)$. □

**Theorem 9.** *Let the following conditions be fulfilled:*

1. *The conditions of Theorem 2 hold and* $\|\Phi\| > 0$.
2. *There exist numbers* $\varepsilon \geq \delta > 0$ *such that if* $\|\Phi\| < \delta$ *then the following inequality holds*

$$\delta(1 + \alpha_*^{-1} C_0 C_\Phi T^{\alpha_*}) E_\alpha(\|\bar{U}(T,0)\| C_0 \Gamma(\alpha_*) T^{\alpha_*}) \leq \varepsilon \tag{47}$$

*Then for every initial function* $\Phi \in \tilde{C}$ *with* $\|\Phi\| \in (0, \delta)$ *the corresponding unique solution* $X(t)$ *of the IP (1), (2) is finite-time stable with respect to* $\{0, J_T, \delta, \varepsilon, h\}$.

**Proof.** Let $\Phi \in \tilde{C}$ with $\|\Phi\| \in (0, \delta)$ be an arbitrary initial function and assume that $\max(\|X(T)\|, \|\Phi\|) > \|\Phi\|$. Then since Theorem 2 holds, from (23) and (47) for $t \in J_T$ it follows that

$$\begin{aligned} \|X(t)\| &\leq \|\Phi\|(1 + \alpha_*^{-1} C_0 C_\Phi t^{\alpha_*}) E_\alpha(\|\bar{U}(t,0)\| C_0 \Gamma(\alpha_*) t^{\alpha_*}) \\ &\leq \delta(1 + \alpha_*^{-1} C_0 C_\Phi t^{\alpha_*}) E_\alpha(\|\bar{U}(T,0)\| C_0 \Gamma(\alpha_*) T^{\alpha_*}) \leq \varepsilon \end{aligned} \tag{48}$$

Thus, from (48) it follows that for every initial function $\Phi \in \tilde{C}$ with $\|\Phi\| \in (0, \delta)$ the corresponding unique solution $X(t)$ of the IP (1), (2) is finite-time stable with respect to $\{0, J_T, \delta, \varepsilon, h\}$. □

Below we present FTS results based on estimations obtained via different kind integral representations of the solutions and superposition principle.

**Theorem 10.** *Let the following conditions be fulfilled:*

1. *The conditions of Theorem 4 hold.*
2. *There exist numbers* $\varepsilon \geq \delta > 0$ *such that if* $\|F(T)\| < \delta$ *then the following inequality holds*

$$\delta \alpha_*^{-1} C_0 T^{\alpha_*} (1 + \|\bar{C}(T,T)\|) \leq \varepsilon \tag{49}$$

*Then for the initial function $\Phi \in \tilde{C}$ with $||\Phi|| = 0$ and locally bounded function $F(t) \in L_1^{loc}(\mathbb{R}_+, \mathbb{R}^n)$ with $||F(T)|| < \delta$ the corresponding unique solution $X(t)$ of the IP (1), (2) is finite-time stable with respect to $\{0, J_T, \delta, \varepsilon, h\}$.*

**Proof.** Theorem 4 implies that for each $t \in J_T$ the inequality (24) holds and then from (24) and (49) for every $t \in J_T$ it follows that

$$||X(t)|| \leq \alpha_*^{-1} C_0 t^{\alpha_*} ||F(t)||(1 + ||\bar{C}(t,t)||) < \delta\alpha_*^{-1} C_0 t^{\alpha_*}(1 + ||\bar{C}(t,t)||) \leq \delta\alpha_*^{-1} C_0 T^{\alpha_*}(1 + ||\bar{C}(T,T)||) \leq \varepsilon$$

which completes the proof. □

**Theorem 11.** *Let the following conditions be fulfilled:*

*1. The conditions of Theorem 5 hold.*

*2. There exist numbers $\varepsilon \geq \delta > 0$ such that if $\max(|\Phi(-h)|, |Var_{\eta \in [-h,0]} \Phi(\eta)|) < \delta$ then the following inequality holds*

$$\delta(\sup_{s \in [-h,0]} ||T_{-h}(T,s)|| + ||T_{-h}(T,-h)||) \leq \varepsilon \tag{50}$$

*Then the corresponding unique solution $X(t)$ of the IP (1), (2) is finite-time stable with respect to $\{0, J_T, \delta, \varepsilon, h\}$.*

**Proof.** Theorem 5 implies that for each $t \in J_T$ the inequality (29) holds and then from (29) and (50) same way as above for every $t \in J_T$ we obtain that

$$\begin{aligned} ||X(t)|| &\leq |Var_{\eta \in [-h,0]} \Phi(\eta)| \sup_{s \in [-h,0]} ||T_{-h}(t,s)|| + ||\Phi(-h)|| ||T_{-h}(t,-h)|| \\ &\leq \delta(\sup_{s \in [-h,0]} ||T_{-h}(T,s)|| + ||T_{-h}(T,-h)||) \leq \varepsilon \end{aligned}$$

and hence the corresponding unique solution $X(t)$ of the IP (1), (2) is finite-time stable with respect to $\{0, J_T, \delta, \varepsilon, h\}$. □

**Corollary 6.** *Let the following conditions be fulfilled:*

*1. The conditions of Corollary 4, hold.*

*2. There exist numbers $\varepsilon \geq \delta > 0$ such that if $|\Phi(-h)| < \delta$ then the following inequality holds*

$$\delta||T_{-h}(T,-h)|| \leq \varepsilon \tag{51}$$

*Then the corresponding unique solution $X(t)$ of the IP (1), (2) is finite-time stable with respect to $\{0, J_T, \delta, \varepsilon, h\}$.*

**Proof.** Since $||\Phi|| = |\Phi_0| = |\Phi(-h)| < \delta$ then using (32) and (51)we obtain

$$||X(t)|| \leq |\Phi(-h)| ||T_{-h}(t,-h)|| = |\Phi_0| ||T_{-h}(t,-h)|| \leq \delta||T_{-h}(t,-h)|| \leq \varepsilon$$

and then the result follows from Theorem 11. □

**Remark 5.** *The FTS results obtained in Theorem 11 and Corollary 6 are new even in the cases considered in [25] when the initial function $\Phi \in C^1([-h,0], \mathbb{R}^n)$. Our results are more accurate not only in the case when the initial function $\Phi \in BV([-h,0], \mathbb{R}^n)$ has finite set of jump points $S_\Phi \neq \varnothing$, (i.e., $\Phi$ is not continuous), but also when $\Phi$ is continuous.*

*We illustrate this fact with two simple examples:*

*Let $\Phi(-h) = (0.75, 0)^T, \Phi(t) = (1,0)^T, t \in (-h, 0]$. Then $|\Phi(-h)| = 0.75, ||\Phi|| = 1, |Var_{\eta \in [-h,0]} \Phi(\eta)| = 0.25$ and $\max(|Var_{\eta \in [-h,0]} \Phi(\eta)|, |\Phi(-h)|) = |\Phi(-h)| = 0.75 < ||\Phi|| = 1$.*

*Let* $h = 1$ *and* $\Phi(t) = (0.4t + 1, 0)^T, t \in (-1, 0], \Phi(-1) = (0.6, 0)^T, |Var_{\eta\in[-1,0]}\Phi(\eta)| = 0.6, ||\Phi|| = 1$ *and hence* $\max(|Var_{\eta\in[-1,0]}\Phi(\eta)|, |\Phi(-1)|) = 0.6 < ||\Phi|| = 1$.

*These examples show, that we can establish FTS in some cases, where the conditions presented in [25] are not directly applicable.*

**Remark 6.** *The FTS result for the general case* $||\Phi||\,||F(T)|| > 0$ *needs some preliminary comments.*

*It is clear that the estimations (32) and (33) will be essentially used, but to obtain a practical applicable estimation we need to solve (clarify) two problems:*

**(a)** *First, we need to clarify which impact is leading for the process, the impact hereditary of the process expressed by* $||\Phi||$*, the impact of the outer perturbations expressed by* $||F(T)||$*, or the complex of both factors expressed by the ratio* $C_\Phi = ||\Phi||^{-1}||F(T)||$.

**(b)** *As second, an explicit estimation is needed in the general case for the fundamental matrix* $C(t,s)$ *as well as the matrix* $T_{-h}(t,s)$ *too.*

*Concerning point* **(a)***, it is clear that a reasonable response can be given only on the basis of real empirical data from the process which is described by the mathematical model. From a mathematical point of view, as was mentioned above by the construction of the proofs, we must limit the impact of* $||\Phi||$ *and* $||F(T)||$ *to linear or no more than power-law growth as in the right side of the estimation (23) and avoid the high nonlinear impact of* $C_\Phi = ||\Phi||^{-1}||F(T)||$ *if it is involved as an argument in the Mittag-Leffler function* $E_\alpha(\cdot)$ *in (20).*

*About* **(b)** *it is possible to obtain the needed estimations in the general case, for example we can use the estimations obtained in the previous sections.*

**Theorem 12.** *Let* $T \in \mathbb{R}_+$ *be an arbitrary fixed number and the following conditions are fulfilled:*

1. *The conditions (S) hold.*
2. *The function* $F(t) \in L_1^{loc}(\mathbb{R}_+, \mathbb{R}^n)$ *and is locally bounded.*
3. *The initial function* $\Phi \in BV([-h,0], \mathbb{R}^n) \cap \tilde{C}$ *and its Lebesgue decomposition does not include a singular term.*
4. $||\Phi||\,||F(T)|| > 0$ *and there exist numbers* $\varepsilon \geq \delta > 0$ *such that if* $\max(|\Phi(-h)|, |Var_{\eta\in[-h,0]}\Phi(\eta)|) < \delta$ *then the following inequality holds*

$$\delta[\sup_{s\in[-h,0]} ||T_{-h}(T,s)|| + ||T_{-h}(T,-h)|| + \alpha_*^{-1}T^{\alpha_*}C_0C_\Phi(1 + ||\bar{C}(T,T)||)] \leq \varepsilon \tag{52}$$

*Then the corresponding unique solution* $X(t)$ *of the IP (1), (2) for every* $t \in J_T$ *is finite-time stable with respect to* $\{0, J_T, \delta, \varepsilon, h\}$.

**Proof.** Condition 4 of the theorem implies that the estimate (34) holds. Then from (34) and (52) for every $t \in J_T$ it follows

$$\begin{aligned}
||X(t)|| &\leq |Var_{\eta\in[-h,0]}\Phi(\eta)| \sup_{s\in[-h,0]} ||T_{-h}(t,s)|| + |\Phi(-h)|\,||T_{-h}(t,-h)|| \\
&+ \alpha_*^{-1}t^{\alpha_*}C_0||F(t)||(1 + ||\bar{C}(t,t)||) \\
&\leq \delta[\sup_{s\in[-h,0]} ||T_{-h}(t,s)|| + ||T_{-h}(t,-h)|| + \alpha_*^{-1}t^{\alpha_*}C_0C_\Phi(1 + ||\bar{C}(t,t)||)] \\
&\leq \delta[\sup_{s\in[-h,0]} ||T_{-h}(T,s)|| + ||T_{-h}(T,-h)|| + \alpha_*^{-1}t^{\alpha_*}C_0C_\Phi(1 + ||\bar{C}(T,T)||)] \leq \varepsilon
\end{aligned}$$

which completes the proof. □

**Corollary 7.** *Let* $T \in \mathbb{R}_+$ *be an arbitrary fixed number and the following conditions are fulfilled:*

1. *The conditions (S) hold.*
2. *The function* $F(t) \in L_1^{loc}(\mathbb{R}_+, \mathbb{R}^n)$ *and is locally bounded.*
3. *The initial function* $\Phi \in BV([-h,0], \mathbb{R}^n) \cap \tilde{C}$ *and its Lebesgue decomposition does not include a singular term.*

*4.* $\|\Phi\|\|F(T)\| > 0$ *and there exist numbers* $\varepsilon \geq \delta > 0$ *such that if* $\max(|\Phi(-h)|, |Var_{\eta\in[-h,0]}\Phi(\eta)|) < \delta$ *then the following inequality holds*

$$\delta[2E_\alpha(\|\bar{U}(T,0)\|C_0\Gamma(\alpha_*)T^{\alpha_*}) + \alpha_*^{-1}T^{\alpha_*}C_0C_\Phi(1+2E_\alpha(\|\bar{U}(T,0)\|C_0\Gamma(\alpha_*)T^{\alpha_*})] \leq \varepsilon \quad (53)$$

*Then the corresponding unique solution* $X(t)$ *of the IP* (1), (2) *for every* $t \in J_T$ *is finite-time stable with respect to* $\{0, J_T, \delta, \varepsilon, h\}$.

**Proof.** The statement follows from Theorem 12 and Theorem 6. □

## 6. Examples and Comments

**Remark 7.** *From a practical point of view, it is important to establish a sharp upper bound of the constant* $\alpha_*^{-1}C_0$ *appearing in all estimates except* (29) *and answer the question does the constant* $\alpha_*^{-1}C_0$ *attain its upper bound.*

*Let us consider the case when* $\alpha_* = \alpha_M$. *Then we have that* $\alpha_*^{-1}C_0 = \alpha_M^{-1}C_0 = \Gamma^{-1}(1+\alpha_M) \leq \Gamma^{-1}(z_{min})$. *Thus if* $\alpha_M = z_{min} - 1$ *then* $\alpha_*^{-1}C_0$ *attains its upper bound, namely* $\alpha_*^{-1}C_0 = \Gamma^{-1}(z_{min}) \approx 1.1279$. *Please note that in the partial case when all orders of the differentiation coincide (i.e.,* $\alpha_1 = \cdots = \alpha_n = \alpha$*) then all estimates can be essentially simplified. For example in this case we have that* $\alpha_*^{-1}C_0 = \Gamma^{-1}(1+\alpha) \leq \Gamma^{-1}(z_{min})$ *and* $C_0\Gamma\alpha_* = 1$.

**Remark 8.** *First, it must be noted that in the commented works are used different norms. In the works [24,25] the so-called 1-norm is used (i.e., for* $W = \{w_{ij}\}_{i,j\in\langle n\rangle} \in \mathbb{R}^{n\times n}$ *the matrix norm* $|W| = \max_{j\in\langle n\rangle}\sum_{i=1}^{n}|w_{ij}|$*) while in [26,27] is used the spectral norm as well as in our work. A direct comparison shows that the condition* (43) *in our work based on the estimate* (18) *is more accurate in compare with the condition (9) in Theorem 4.1 [24] proved via the integral representation approach and condition (16) in Theorem 3.2 in [27] proved by Gronwall's approach, even in the partial cases considered in these works.*

*Please note that for the partial case when* $\Phi$ *is a constant both conditions* (43) *and (9) in [24] coincide. In this case the same results can be established by using* (50) *obtained via the integral representation* (30). *In the homogeneous case* ($\gamma = 0$) *of the considered in [26] partial cases of the system* (4) *(variable matrices and one variable delay), our condition* (43) *coincides with condition (5) of Theorem 1 in [26] proved by Gronwall's approach.*

Below on the base of the considered in the work [24] example we will establish that generally speaking the results obtained via the integral representation approach can be more accurate in comparison with these obtained via the Gronwall's approach but the results depend essentially from the norm choice and from the constructions of their proofs.

**Example 1.** *[24] Consider*

$$\begin{cases} D_{0+}^{\alpha}X(t) = AX(t-\sigma), & t > 0 \\ X(t) = \Phi(t), & t \in [-\sigma, 0] \end{cases} \quad (54)$$

*where* $A = \begin{pmatrix} 0.2 & 0 \\ 0 & 0.8 \end{pmatrix}$, $\alpha = 0.2, \sigma = 0.2, T = 0.8, \Phi(t) = (0.1, 0.2)^T$.

*The system* (54) *is a partial case of* (4) *in the case when:* $n = 2, \alpha_1 = \alpha_2 = \alpha = 0.2, U_{AC}(t,\theta) = U_S(t,\theta) \equiv \Theta, U_J(t,\theta) = A^1H(\theta+\sigma), A^1 = A, A^0 = \Theta, \sigma = h = 0.2, \|\bar{U}(T,0)\| = \|A\|_1 = \|A\|_2 = 0.8$ $\|\Phi\|_2 = |\Phi(-0.2)| = 0.2236$.

*Using system Wolfram Mathematica, we obtain* $|\Phi(-0.2)|E_{0.2}(0.8 * 0.8^{0.2}) = 0.2236 * 1.25913 = 0.9292$ *and hence* (54) *is finite-time stable with respect to* $\{0, J_T, \delta, \varepsilon, \sigma\}$ *for* $\varepsilon \geq 0.9292$.

*The compared results are given in Table 1 below:*

**Table 1.** Compared Results.

| Theorem/Work | $\|\|\Phi\|\|$ | $\sigma = h$ | $\delta$ | $\|\|X(t)\|\|$ | *FTS* |
|---|---|---|---|---|---|
| Th. 4.1 in [24] | 0.3 | 0.2 | 0.31 | 1.2882 | Yes |
| Th. 4.2 in [24] | 0.3 | 0.2 | 0.31 | 2.0586 | Yes |
| Theorem 7 | 0.2236 | 0.2 | 0.2237 | 0.9292 | Yes |
| Corollary 6 | 0.2236 | 0.2 | 0.2237 | 0.9292 | Yes |
| Th. 1 ($\gamma = 0$) [26] | 0.2236 | 0.2 | 0.2237 | 0.9292 | Yes |

**Remark 9.** *Please note that the results essentially depend from the used norm and we can show that the spectral norm bring some advantages.*

*For example for the initial function* $\Phi(t) = \begin{pmatrix} 0.222 \\ 0.2 \end{pmatrix}$, $||\Phi||_1 = 0.422$, $||\Phi||_2 = 0.299$ *and for* $\varepsilon = 1.2882$ *concerning the spectral norm* (54) *is FTS, which cannot be established using the 1-norm.*

*The same remark is also true concerning the matrix* $A = \begin{pmatrix} 0.2 & 0 \\ 0 & 0.8 \end{pmatrix}$. *Since A is a diagonal matrix then* $||A||_1 = ||A||_2 = 0.8$ *but if for example we have* $\bar{A} = \begin{pmatrix} 0.2 & 0.3 \\ 0 & 0.8 \end{pmatrix}$ *then* $||A||_1 = 1.1$, *but* $||A||_2 = 0.85742$ *and then if we use some of the proved estimations, without direct calculation which for example we present, then the differences between the estimations will increase.*

*One direct calculation via the integral representation established in [24] for sharp upper bounds for the 1-norm and the spectral norm of the state vector for* $T = 0.8$ *give us* $||X(0.8||_1 = 0.95702$ *and* $||X(0.8||_2 = 0.84059$. *Namely the solution of* (54) *according Theorem 3.2 in [24] has the following representation* $X(t) = \mathbf{E}_{\sigma}^{Bt^{\alpha}}\Phi(-\sigma)$, *where* $\Phi$ *is a constant vector and* $\mathbf{E}_{\sigma}^{Bt^{\alpha}} = I + \sum_{k=1}^{\infty} A^k \frac{(t-(k-1)\sigma)^{k\alpha}}{\Gamma(\alpha k+1)} H(k\sigma - t), t \in \bar{\mathbb{R}}_+, \mathbf{E}_{\theta}^{Bt_{\theta}^{\alpha}} = \Theta$ *for* $t < -\sigma$ *and* $\mathbf{E}_{\sigma}^{Bt^{\alpha}} = I$ *for* $-\sigma \leq t \leq 0$ *is the introduced in the same work delayed matrix with Mittag-Leffler functions. For the values in the example above we have that*

$$X(t) = \mathbf{E}_{0.2}^{At^{0.2}}\Phi(-0.2) = \begin{pmatrix} E_{0.2}^{0.2t^{0.2}} & 0 \\ 0 & E_{0.2}^{0.8t^{0.2}} \end{pmatrix} \begin{pmatrix} 0.1 \\ 0.2 \end{pmatrix}$$

*where the matrix entries are standard scalar Mittag-Leffler functions.*

*Calculating by system Wolfram Mathematica we obtain*

$$X(0.8) = \begin{pmatrix} 1.25913 & 0 \\ 0 & 4.15554 \end{pmatrix} \begin{pmatrix} 0.1 \\ 0.2 \end{pmatrix} = \begin{pmatrix} 0.125913 \\ 0.8311 \end{pmatrix}$$

*and hence* $||X(0.8)||_1 = 0.95702$ *and* $||X(0.8)||_2 = 0.84059$.

*Finally, we note that the integral representation of the solution of* (54) *proved in Theorem 3.2 in [24] for the case when* $\Phi \in C^1([-\tau, 0], \mathbb{R}^n$ *is partial case from the integral representation (4.7) in [31] proved for* $\Phi \in BV([-\tau, 0], \mathbb{R}^n)$. *For the system* (54) *the both presentations coincide when* $\Phi \in AC([-\tau, 0], \mathbb{R}^n)$.

Analogically as in the homogeneous case consider one partial case of the IP (1), (2) as follows:

**Example 2.** *Consider*

$$\begin{cases} D_{0+}^{\alpha} X(t) = A_0(t)X(t) + A_1(t)X(t - \sigma(t)) + f(t, X(t)), & t > 0 \\ X(t) = \Phi(t), & t \in [-\sigma, 0] \end{cases} \tag{55}$$

*The system* (55) *is considered in [25] in the case when* $\boldsymbol{f} \in C(\bar{\mathbb{R}}_+ \times \mathbb{R}^n, \mathbb{R}^n)$, $A_0(t) \equiv \Theta$, $A_1(t) \equiv B \in \mathbb{R}^{n \times n}$, $\sigma(t) \equiv \sigma$ *for* $t \in \bar{\mathbb{R}}_+$. *In the same work an example is given to clear the applicability of the theoretical results by using the following data:* $\alpha_1 = \alpha_2 = \alpha = 0.6, \sigma = 0.2, T = 0.6, \Phi(t) = (t, 2t)^T, \omega(t) = \psi(t) = 2t^2$, $A^0 = \Theta, A_1 = \begin{pmatrix} 0.3 & 0 \\ 0 & 0.5 \end{pmatrix}$ *and* $\|f(t, Y)\|_1 \leq \omega(t)$ *for all* $t \in [0, T]$ *and* $Y \in \mathbb{R}^n$.

*Let define* $\|F(t)\|_1 = \sup_{Y \in \sim n} \|f(t, Y)\|_1 \leq 2t^2$. *We will use the estimation (47) and then apply Theorem 9. In our notations we have:* $\|\bar{U}(T, 0)\| = 0.5, \|F(T)\|_2 \leq \|F(T)\|_1 = \sup_{Y \in \mathbb{R}^n} \|f(t, Y)\|_1 \leq \|\omega(T)\| = 2T^2 = 0.72, \|\Phi\|_2 = 0.4473, C_\Phi = \frac{\|F(T)\|_1}{\|\Phi\|_2} = 1.61, C_0 = \frac{1}{\Gamma(0.6)} = 1.11917, T^{0.6} = 0.6^{0.6} = 0.736022$ *and* $E_{0.6}(0.5 * 0.6^{0.6}) = 1.57201$. *Then if* $\delta = \|\Phi\|_2 = 0.4473$ *we obtain that* $\|X(T)\|_2 = \|X(0.6)\|_2 = 1.64291$. *Using the same* $\delta = 0.61$ *as in [25] we obtain that* $\|X(T)\|_2 = \|X(0.6)\|_2 = 1.89127$. *Then applying Theorem 9 we obtain that (55) is finite-time stable with respect to* $\{0, J_T, \delta, \varepsilon, \sigma\}$ *when* $\varepsilon \geq 1.89127$.

*Please note that our result is better than the best result given in Table 1 in [25] and hence our estimation (47) is more accurate than the estimations (12) and (13) used for the best results in Table 1.*

**Example 3.** *Consider*

$$\begin{cases} D^{\alpha}_{0+}X(t) = A_0(t)X(t) + A_1(t)X(t - \sigma(t)) + Dw(t) + f(t, X(t), X(t - \sigma(t), w(t))), & t > 0 \\ X(t) = \Phi(t), & t \in [-\sigma, 0] \end{cases} \quad (56)$$

*The IP (56) is considered in [26] for* $A_0 = \begin{pmatrix} 0 & 1 \\ -2 & 0 \end{pmatrix}, A_1 = \begin{pmatrix} 0 & 0 \\ 3 & 4 \end{pmatrix}, D = \begin{pmatrix} 1 \\ 0 \end{pmatrix}, w(t) \in C(\bar{\mathbb{R}}_+, \mathbb{R}^n)$ *with* $\|w(t)\|_2 = 0.1, \alpha = 0.5, T = 5, \delta = 0.1$ *and* $\sigma(t) = 0.1\sin^2 t$ . *For simplicity we will assume that* $f(t, X(t), X(t - \sigma(t), w(t))) \equiv 0, t \in \bar{\mathbb{R}}_+$. *Then via (47) we obtain that* $\|X(5)\|_2 = 1.95384E + 106$ *and then (55) is finite-time stable with respect to* $\{0, J_T, \delta, \varepsilon, \sigma\}$ *when* $\varepsilon \geq 1.95384E + 106$, *which result coincides with the result calculated by us for this case via condition (5) in [27].*

## 7. Conclusions

As was mentioned above, in this work we set out some considerations illustrating our point of view concerning the different sources of the impacts of the finite-time stability. It is easy to see that they appear not only as an influence on the finite-time stability connecting with the impact of the aftereffect (the delay effect) described in the mathematical model through the initial function and the fractional derivatives, but it seems to be reasonable to include into account the impact of external influences too. From a physical point of view, we can interpret as an influence of external forces the existence in the model different kind of functions $F(t, X(t), X_t(\theta))$, etc..., mathematically understood as nonlinear perturbations. Namely, if we apply the formal definition to the nonhomogeneous system (1), when $F(t) \not\equiv \mathbf{0}$ for $t \in J_T$ and $\|\Phi\| = 0$ we obtain a case when the inequality $\|\Phi\| < \delta$ is fulfilled for all $\delta \in \mathbb{R}_+$ but this fact is not useful to establish the possible existing finite-time stability.

Our attempt to clarify which impact is leading for the process, the impact hereditary of the process expressed by $\|\Phi\|$, the impact of the outer perturbations expressed by $\|F(T)\|$, or the complex of both factors expressed by the ratio $C_\Phi = \|\Phi\|^{-1}\|F(T)\|$ imposes a more detailed study not only of the homogeneous case when$\|F(T)\| = 0$, but also the important case when $\|\Phi\| = 0$ . This reason focuses our attention on the case of the nonhomogeneous system with $\|\Phi\| = 0$ and it was very strange for us that we could not find some extra consideration of this case. Please note that conditions of the type "there exists $M \in \mathbb{R}_+$ , such that $\|\Phi\|^{-1}\|F(T)\| \leq M$ " are often used without to clime that $\|\Phi\| \neq 0$.

The result from this study is in general a pure mathematical answer, that is the mean by the construction of the proofs, we must limit the impact of $\|\Phi\|$ and $\|F(T)\|$ to linear or no more than power-law growth as in the right side of the estimation (23) and avoid the high nonlinear impact of $C_\Phi = \|\Phi\|^{-1}\|F(T)\|$ if it is involved as an argument in the Mittag-Leffler function as in estimation (20).

Our comparison between the two most used approaches leads to the following conclusions: The most accurate estimation can be obtained by direct numerical calculation from the integral representation of the solutions, but before them, it is needed to simplify symbolically these presentations, which essentially increase the accuracy of the results (see Example 54).

Since the estimation via Mittag-Leffler functions of the fundamental matrices involved in the integral representation are not accurate enough, then generally speaking we cannot unequivocally point to one of the compared methods as better. It seems from the examples that this maybe, in general, be not possible, because it depends essentially also from the possibility to have explicit presentation of the fundamental matrices.

**Author Contributions:** Conceptualization, H.K., M.V., E.M. and A.Z. Writing—Review and Editing, H.K., M.V., E.M. and A.Z. All authors contributions in the article are equal. All authors have read and agreed to the published version of the manuscript.

**Funding:** This research was partially supported by project FP21-FMI-002 of the Scientific Fund of the University of Plovdiv Paisii Hilendarski, Bulgaria. The third AUTHOR (E.M.) is supported by the Bulgarian Ministry of Education and Science under the National Research Program "Young scientists and postdoctoral students", Stage III-2021/2022.

**Institutional Review Board Statement:** Not applicable.

**Informed Consent Statement:** Not applicable.

**Data Availability Statement:** Not applicable.

**Conflicts of Interest:** The authors declare no conflict of interest.

## References

1. Kilbas, A.A.; Srivastava, H.M.; Trujillo, J.J. *Theory and Applications of Fractional Differential Equations;* Elsevier Science B.V: Amsterdam, The Netherlands, 2006.
2. Podlubny, I. *Fractional Differential Equation;* Academic Press: San Diego, CA, USA, 1999.
3. Jiao, Z.; Chen, Y.Q.; Podlubny, I. *Distributed-Order Dynamic Systems: Stability, Simulation, Applications and Perspectives;* Springer: Berlin, Germany, 2012.
4. Diethelm, K. *The Analysis of Fractional Differential Equations, an Application-Oriented Exposition Using Differential Operators of Caputo Type;* Lecture Notes in Mathematics; Springer: Berlin, Germany, 2010; Volume 2004.
5. Stamova, I.; Stamov, G. *Functional and Impulsive Differential Equations of Fractional Order;* Qualitative Analysis and Applications; CRC Press: Boca Raton, FL, USA, 2017.
6. Jiang, S.; Zhang, J.; Zhang, Q.; Zhang, Z. Fast evaluation of the Caputo fractional derivative and its applications to fractional diffusion equations. *Commun. Comput. Phys.* **2017**, *21*, 650–678. [CrossRef]
7. Gu, X.-M.; Wu, S.-L. A parallel-in-time iterative algorithm for Volterra partial integro-differential problems with weakly singular kernel. *J. Comput. Phys.* **2020**, *471*, 109576. [CrossRef]
8. Li, C.P.; Zhang, F.R. A survey on the stability of fractional differential equations. *Eur. Phys. J. Spec. Top.* **2011**, *193*, 27–47. [CrossRef]
9. Krol, K. Asymptotic properties of fractional delay differential equations. *Appl. Math. Comput.* **2011**, *218*, 1515–1532. [CrossRef]
10. Zhang, F.R.; Li, C.P. Stability Analysis of Fractional Differential Systems with Order Lying in (1, 2). *Adv. Differ. Equ.* **2011**, 1–17. [CrossRef]
11. Veselinova, M.; Kiskinov, H.; Zahariev, A. Stability analysis of linear fractional differential system with distributed delays. *AIP Conf. Proc.* **2015**, *1690*, 040013-1–040013-8.
12. Veselinova, M.; Kiskinov, H.; Zahariev, A. Explicit conditions for stability of neutral linear fractional system with distributed delays. *AIP Conf. Proc.* **2016**, *1789*, 040005-1–040005-13.
13. Cermak, J.; Hornicek, J.; Kisela, T. Stability regions for fractional differential systems with a time delay. *Commun. Nonlinear Sci. Numer. Simul.* **2015**, *31*, 108–123. [CrossRef]
14. Cong, N.D.; Doan, T.S.; Siegmund, S.; Tuan, H.T. Linearized asymptotic stability for fractional differential equations. *Electron. J. Qual. Theory Diff. Equ.* **2016**, *39*, 1–13. [CrossRef]
15. Boyadzhiev, D.; Kiskinov, H.; Veselinova, M.; Zahariev, A. Stability analysis of linear distributed order fractional systems with distributed delays. *Fract. Calc. Appl. Anal.* **2017**, *20*, 914–935. [CrossRef]
16. Liu, S.; Zhou, X.; Li, X.; Jiang, W. Asymptotical stability of Riemann–Liouville fractional singular systems with multiple time-varying delays. *Appl. Math. Lett.* **2017**, *65*, 32–39. [CrossRef]

17. Zahariev, A.; Kiskinov, H. Asymptotic stability of the solutions of neutral linear fractional system with nonlinear perturbation. *Mathematics* **2020**, *8*, 390. [CrossRef]
18. Kaslik, E.; Sivasundaram, S. An analytical and numerical methods for the stability analysis of linear fractional delay differential equations. *J. Comput. Appl. Math.* **2012**, *236*, 4027–4041. [CrossRef]
19. Kamenkov, G. On stability of motion over a finite interval of time. *J. Appl. Math. Mech. (PMM)* **1953**, *17*, 529–540. (In Russian)
20. Dorato, P. *An Overview of Finite-Time Stability*; Current Trends in Nonlinear Systems and Control; Birkhaeuser: Boston, MA, USA, 2006; pp. 185–194.
21. Lazarevic, M.P.; Spasic, A.M. Finite-time stability analysis of fractional order time-delay systems: Gronwall's approach. *Math. Comput. Model.* **2009**, *49*, 475–481. [CrossRef]
22. Zhang, X. Some results of linear fractional order time-delay system. *Appl. Math. Comput.* **2008**, *197*, 407–411. [CrossRef]
23. Ma, Y.; Wu, B.; Wang, Y. Finite-time stability and finite-time boundedness of fractional order linear systems. *Neurocomputing* **2016**, *173*, 2076–2082. [CrossRef]
24. Li, M.; Wang, J. Finite time stability of fractional delay differential equations. *Appl. Math. Lett.* **2017**, *64*, 170–176. [CrossRef]
25. Li, M.; Wang, J. Exploring delayed Mittag-Leffler type matrix functions to study finite time stability of fractional delay differential equations. *Appl. Math. Comput.* **2018**, *324*, 254–265. [CrossRef]
26. Phat, N.; Thanhb, N. New criteria for finite-time stability of nonlinear fractional-order delay systems: A Gronwall inequality approach. *Appl. Math. Lett.* **2018**, *83*, 169–175. [CrossRef]
27. Zhang, F.; Qian, D.; Li, C. Finite-time stability analysis of fractional differential systems with variable coefficients. *Chaos* **2019**, *29*, 013110. [CrossRef] [PubMed]
28. Du, F.; Jia, B. Finite-time stability of a class of nonlinear fractional delay difference systems. *Appl. Math. Lett.* **2019**, *98*, 233–239. [CrossRef]
29. Du, F.; Lu, J.G. New criterion for finite-time stability of fractional delay systems. *Appl. Math. Lett.* **2020**, *104*, 106248. [CrossRef]
30. Du, F.; Jia, B. Finite-time stability of nonlinear fractional order systems with a constant delay. *J. Nonlinear Model. Anal.* **2020**, *2*, 1–13.
31. Kiskinov, H.; Madamlieva, E.; Veselinova, M.; Zahariev, A. Existence of Absolutely Continuous Fundamental Matrix of Linear Fractional System with Distributed Delays. *Mathematics* **2021**, *9*, 150. [CrossRef]
32. Horn, R.A.; Johnson, C.R. *Matrix Analysis*, 2nd ed.; Cambridge University Press: Cambridge, UK, 2013.
33. Boyadzhiev, D.; Kiskinov, H.; Zahariev, A. Integral representation of solutions of fractional system with distributed delays. *Integral Transf. Special Funct.* **2018**, *29*, 725–744. [CrossRef]
34. Zahariev, A.; Kiskinov, H.; Angelova, E. Linear fractional system of incommensurate type with distributed delay and bounded Lebesgue measurable initial conditions. *Dyn. Syst. Appl.* **2019**, *28*, 491–506.
35. Ye, H.; Gao, J.; Ding, Y. A generalized Gronwall inequality and its application to a fractional differential equation. *J. Math. Anal. Appl.* **2007**, *328*, 1075–1081. [CrossRef]

*axioms*

MDPI

*Article*

# Non-Instantaneous Impulsive Boundary Value Problems Containing Caputo Fractional Derivative of a Function with Respect to Another Function and Riemann–Stieltjes Fractional Integral Boundary Conditions

**Suphawat Asawasamrit [1], Yasintorn Thadang [1], Sotiris K. Ntouyas [2,3] and Jessada Tariboon [1,*]**

1 Intelligent and Nonlinear Dynamic Innovations Research Center, Department of Mathematics, Faculty of Applied Science, King Mongkut's University of Technology North Bangkok, Bangkok 10800, Thailand; suphawat.a@sci.kmutnb.ac.th (S.A.); yasintorn009@hotmail.com (Y.T.)
2 Department of Mathematics, University of Ioannina, 451 10 Ioannina, Greece; sntouyas@uoi.gr
3 Nonlinear Analysis and Applied Mathematics (NAAM)-Research Group, Department of Mathematics, Faculty of Science, King Abdulaziz University, P.O. Box 80203, Jeddah 21589, Saudi Arabia
* Correspondence: jessada.t@sci.kmutnb.ac.th

**Abstract:** In the present article we study existence and uniqueness results for a new class of boundary value problems consisting by non-instantaneous impulses and Caputo fractional derivative of a function with respect to another function, supplemented with Riemann–Stieltjes fractional integral boundary conditions. The existence of a unique solution is obtained via Banach's contraction mapping principle, while an existence result is established by using Leray–Schauder nonlinear alternative. Examples illustrating the main results are also constructed.

**Keywords:** impulsive differential equations; fractional impulsive differential equations; instantaneous impulses; non-instantaneous impulses

**Citation:** Asawasamrit, S.; Thadang, Y.; Ntouyas, S.K.; Tariboon, J. Non-Instantaneous Impulsive Boundary Value Problems Containing Caputo Fractional Derivative of a Function with Respect to Another Function and Riemann–Stieltjes Fractional Integral Boundary Conditions. *Axioms* **2021**, *10*, 130. https://doi.org/10.3390/axioms10030130

Academic Editor: Jorge E. Macías Díaz

Received: 5 June 2021
Accepted: 22 June 2021
Published: 23 June 2021



## 1. Introduction and Preliminaries

Fractional calculus is a generalization of classical differentiation and integration to an arbitrary real order. Fractional differential equations has gained much attention in literature because of its applications for description of hereditary properties in many fields, such as physics, mechanics, engineering, game theory, stability and optimal control. With the help of fractional calculus, the natural phenomena and mathematical models can be described more accurately. Many researchers have shown their interests in fractional differential equations, and the theory and applications of the fractional differential equations have been greatly developed. For the basic theory of fractional calculus and fractional differential equations we refer to the monographs [1–8] and references therein.

The theory of impulsive differential equations arise naturally in biology, physics, engineering, and medical fields where at certain moments they change their state rapidly. There are two type of impulses. One is called instantaneous impulses in which the duration of these changes is relatively short, and the other is called non-instantaneous impulses in which an impulsive action, starting abruptly at some points and continue to be active on a finite time interval. Some examples of such processes can be found in physics, biology, population dynamics, ecology, pharmacokinetics, and others. For results with instantaneous impulses see, e.g., the monographs [9–14], the papers [15–19], and the references cited therein. Non-instantaneous impulsive differential equation was introduced by Hernández and O'Regan in [20] pointed out that the instantaneous impulses cannot characterize some processes such as evolution processes in pharmacotherapy. Some practical problems involving non-instantaneous impulses within the area of psychology have been reviewed in [21]. For some recent works, on non-instantaneous impulsive fractional differential equations we refer the reader to [22–25] and references therein.

The scope of this investigation is to establish existence results of the new class of boundary value problems consisting by non-instantaneous impulses and Caputo fractional derivative of a function with respect to another function, supplemented with Riemann–Stieltjes fractional integral boundary conditions of the form

$$\begin{cases} {}_{s_i}D_{g_i}^{\alpha_i}x(t) = f(t,x(t)), & t \in [s_i,t_{i+1}), \quad i = 0,1,2,\dots,m, \\ x(t) = \varphi_i(t) + \psi_i(t)x(t_i^-), & t \in [t_i,s_i), \quad i = 1,2,3,\dots,m, \\ \beta_1 x(0) + \beta_2 x(T) = \sum\limits_{k=0}^{m} \mu_k \int_{s_k}^{t_{k+1}} \left({}_{s_k}I_{g_k}^{\gamma_k}x\right)(u)\, dH_k(u). \end{cases} \tag{1}$$

Here ${}_{s_i}D_{g_i}^{\alpha_i}$ is the Caputo fractional derivative of order $\alpha_i \in (0,1)$, with respect to a function $g_i$ starting at the point $s_i$, over the interval $[s_i,t_{i+1})$, ${}_{s_i}I_{g_i}^{\gamma_i}$ is the Riemann–Liouville fractional integral with respect to the function $g_i$ on $[s_i,t_{i+1})$ of order $\gamma_i > 0$, $\mu_i \in \mathbb{R}$, the bounded variation function $H_i$ of the Riemann–Stieltjes on $[s_i,t_{i+1})$ and a function $f : \bigcup[s_i,t_{i+1}) \to \mathbb{R}$, for $i = 0,1,2,\dots,m$. (For details on Riemann–Stieltjes integral we refer to [26]). In impulsive interval $[t_i,s_i)$, $\varphi_i, \psi_i, i = 1,2,3,\dots,m$, are given functions. The points

$$0 = s_0 < t_1 < s_1 < t_2 < s_2 < \cdots < t_m < s_m < t_{m+1} = T,$$

are fixed in $[0,T]$ and $\beta_1, \beta_2$ are known constants. Note that in problem (1), we have $x(s_i^+) = x(s_i^-)$ and if $\psi_i(t) \neq 1$, $\varphi_i(t) \neq 0$ at $t_i$ for all $i = 1,2,3,\dots,m$, then $x(t_i^+) \neq x(t_i^-)$.

For $\gamma > 0$, the Riemann–Liouville fractional integral of an integrable function $h : [a,b] \to \mathbb{R}$ with respect to another function $g \in C^1([a,b],\mathbb{R})$ such that $g'(t) > 0$, for all $t \in [a,b]$ is defined by [2,27,28]

$${}_aI_g^{\gamma}h(t) = \frac{1}{\Gamma(\gamma)} \int_a^t \frac{g'(s)h(s)}{[g(t)-g(s)]^{1-\gamma}} ds, \tag{2}$$

where $\Gamma$ is the gamma function. The Riemann–Liouville type of fractional derivative of a function $h$, with respect to another function $g$ on $[a,b]$ is defined as

$${}_a^{\star}D_g^{\alpha}h(t) = D_g^n\, {}_aI_g^{n-\alpha}h(t) = \frac{1}{\Gamma(n-\alpha)} D_g^n \int_a^t \frac{g'(s)h(s)}{[g(t)-g(s)]^{1+\alpha-n}} ds, \tag{3}$$

while the Caputo type is defined by

$${}_aD_g^{\alpha}h(t) = {}_aI_g^{n-\alpha} D_g^n h(t) = \frac{1}{\Gamma(n-\alpha)} \int_a^t \frac{g'(s)D_g^n h(s)}{[g(t)-g(s)]^{1+\alpha-n}} ds, \tag{4}$$

where $D_g^n = \underbrace{D_g \cdots D_g}_{n-times}$, $n-1 < \alpha < n$, $n$ is a positive integer and $D_g$ is defined by

$$D_g = \frac{1}{g'(t)} \frac{d}{dt}. \tag{5}$$

There are relations of fractional integral and derivatives of the Riemann–Liouville and Caputo types which will be used in our investigation, see [2], as

$${}_aI_g^{\gamma}\left({}_a^{\star}D_g^{\gamma}h\right)(t) = h(t) - \sum_{j=1}^{n} \frac{(g(t)-g(a))^{\gamma-j}}{\Gamma(\gamma-j+1)} D_g^{n-j}\left({}_aI_g^{n-\gamma}h\right)(a), \tag{6}$$

and

$${}_aI_g^{\gamma}\left({}_aD_g^{\gamma}h\right)(t) = h(t) - \sum_{j=0}^{n-1} \frac{(g(t)-g(a))^{j}}{j!} D_g^{j}h(a). \tag{7}$$

In addition, for $\gamma, \delta > 0$, the relation

$$ {}_aI_g^{\gamma}(g(t) - g(a))^{\delta} = \frac{\Gamma(\delta+1)}{\Gamma(\gamma+\delta+1)}(g(t) - g(a))^{\gamma+\delta}, \tag{8} $$

is applied in the main results ([2]). For some recent results we refer the interesting reader to the papers [29–31].

Note that (2) is reduced to the Riemann–Liouville and Hadamard fractional integrals when $g(t) = t$ and $g(t) = \log t$, respectively, where $\log(\cdot) = \log_e(\cdot)$. The Hadamard and Hadamard–Caputo types fractional derivatives can be obtained by substituting $g(t) = \log t$ in (3) and (4), respectively. Also the Riemann–Liouville and Caputo fractional derivatives are presented by replacing $g(t) = t$ in (3) and (4), respectively. Therefore, the problem (1) generates many types and also mixed types of impulsive fractional differential equations with boundary conditions. There are some papers that have studied either Hadamard or Caputo fractional derivatives containing in noninstantaneous impulsive equations, see [32–34].

The significance of this studying is to mixed different calculus within the system of non-instantaneous impulsive differential equations. For example if putting $m = 1$, $t_1 = 1$, $s_1 = 2$, $t_2 = 3$, $\alpha_0 = \alpha_1 = 1/2$, $g_0(t) = t$ and $g_1(t) = \log_e t$ in the first two equations of (1), then we obtain

$$ \begin{cases} \left(\dfrac{d}{dt}\right)^{\frac{1}{2}} x = f(t, x(t)), & t \in [0,1), \\ x(t) = \varphi(t) + \psi(t)x(1^-), & t \in [1,2), \\ \left(t\dfrac{d}{dt}\right)^{\frac{1}{2}} x = f(t, x(t)), & t \in [2,3), \end{cases} $$

which is a special case of mixed Riemann–Liouville and Hadamard fractional impulsive system. In addition, if $H_k(t) = g_k(t)$, for all $t \in [s_i, t_{i+1})$, $k = 0,1,2,\ldots,m$, then the nonlocal condition in (1), is reduced to

$$ \beta_1 x(0) + \beta_2 x(T) = \sum_{k=0}^{m} \mu_k \left( {}_{s_k}I_{g_k}^{\gamma_k+1} x \right)(t_{k+1}). $$

If $\varphi_i(t) = 0$, $\psi_i(t) = 1$ and $s_i \to t_i$, $i = 1,2,3,\ldots,m$, then (1) is reduced to a non impulsive fractional boundary value problem.

In fact, to the best of the authors knowledge, this is the first paper investigating Riemann–Stieltjes integration acting on fractional integral boundary conditions. Existence and uniqueness results are established for the the non-instantaneous impulsive Riemann–Stieltjes fractional integral boundary value problem (1) by using classical fixed point theorems. We make use of Banach's contraction mapping principle to obtain the uniqueness result, while the Leray–Schauder nonlinear alternative is applied to obtain the existence result. The main results are presented in Section 3. In Section 2 we prove an auxiliary result concerning a linear variant of the problem (1) which is of great importance in the proof of main results. Illustrative examples are also presented.

## 2. An Auxiliary Result

Let us set some constants which will be used in our proofs.

$$ \Lambda_k = \frac{1}{\Gamma(\gamma_k+1)} \int_{s_k}^{t_{k+1}} (g_k(u) - g_k(s_k))^{\gamma_k} dH_k(u), \quad k = 1,2,3,\ldots,m, \tag{9} $$

$$ \Lambda^*(i) = \sum_{j=1}^{i} \left( \prod_{j}^{i-1} \psi_{j+1}(s_{j+1}) \right) \varphi_j(s_j), \qquad i = 1,2,3,\ldots,m, \tag{10} $$

$$ \Omega = \beta_1 + \beta_2 \left( \prod_{j=1}^{m} \psi_j(s_j) \right) - \sum_{k=0}^{m} \mu_k \left( \prod_{j=1}^{k} \psi_j(s_j) \right) \Lambda_k. \tag{11} $$

**Lemma 1.** *Let $\Omega \neq 0$ and $h \in C([0,T],\mathbb{R})$. Then the integral equation equivalent to problem (1) can be written as*

$$\begin{aligned} x(t) &= \frac{1}{\Omega}\left(\prod_{j=1}^{i}\psi_j(s_j)\right)\left\{\sum_{k=0}^{m}\mu_k\Lambda^*(k)\Lambda_k - \beta_2\Lambda^*(m)\right. \\ &+ \sum_{k=0}^{m}\mu_k\sum_{j=1}^{k}\left[\left(\prod_{j}^{k}\psi_j(s_j)\right)_{s_{j-1}}I_{g_{j-1}}^{\alpha_{j-1}}f_x(t_j^-)\right]\Lambda_k \\ &+ \sum_{k=0}^{m}\mu_k\int_{s_k}^{t_{k+1}}{}_{s_k}I_{g_k}^{\alpha_k+\gamma_k}f_x(u)\,dH_k(u) \\ &\left.-\beta_2\sum_{j=1}^{m+1}\left[\left(\prod_{j}^{m}\psi_j(s_j)\right)_{s_{j-1}}I_{g_{j-1}}^{\alpha_{j-1}}f_x(t_j^-)\right]\right\} \\ &+\Lambda^*(i) + \sum_{j=1}^{i}\left[\left(\prod_{j}^{i}\psi_j(s_j)\right)_{s_{j-1}}I_{g_{j-1}}^{\alpha_{j-1}}f_x(t_j^-)\right] + {}_{s_i}I_{g_i}^{\alpha_i}f_x(t), \end{aligned} \tag{12}$$

*for $t \in [s_i, t_{i+1})$, $i = 0,1,2,\ldots,m$, and*

$$\begin{aligned} x(t) &= \varphi_i(t) + \psi_i(t)\left[\frac{1}{\Omega}\left(\prod_{j=1}^{i-1}\psi_j(s_j)\right)\left\{\sum_{k=0}^{m}\mu_k\Lambda^*(i)\Lambda_k\right.\right. \\ &+ \sum_{k=0}^{m}\mu_k\sum_{j=1}^{k}\left[\left(\prod_{j}^{k}\psi_j(s_j)\right)_{s_{j-1}}I_{g_{j-1}}^{\alpha_{j-1}}f_x(t_j^-)\right]\Lambda_k \\ &+ \sum_{k=0}^{m}\mu_k\int_{s_k}^{t_{k+1}}{}_{s_k}I_{g_k}^{\alpha_k+\gamma_k}f_x(u)\,dH_k(u) - \beta_2\Lambda^*(m) \\ &\left.-\beta_2\sum_{j=1}^{m+1}\left[\left(\prod_{j}^{m}\psi_j(s_j)\right)_{s_{j-1}}I_{g_{j-1}}^{\alpha_{j-1}}f_x(t_j^-)\right]\right\} \\ &\left.+\Lambda^*(i-1) + \sum_{j=1}^{i}\left(\prod_{j}^{i-1}\psi_j(s_j)\right)_{s_{j-1}}I_{g_{j-1}}^{\alpha_{j-1}}f_x(t_j^-)\right], \end{aligned} \tag{13}$$

*for $t \in [t_i, s_i)$, $i = 1,2,3,\ldots,m$, where $f_x(t) = f(t,x(t))$.*

**Proof.** For $t \in (s_0, t_1]$, taking the fractional integral with respect to a function $g_0(t)$ of order $\alpha_0 > 0$, from $s_0$ to $t$ in the first equation of (1) and setting $x(0) = A$, we have

$$x(t) = A + {}_{s_0}I_{g_0}^{\alpha_0}f_x(t). \tag{14}$$

In particular, we get for $t = t_1^-$, that $x(t_1^-) = A + {}_{s_0}I_{g_0}^{\alpha_0}f_x(t_1^-)$.

In the second interval $[t_1, s_1)$, we have from the second equation of (1) as

$$\begin{aligned} x(t) &= \varphi_1(t) + \psi_1(t)x(t_1^-) \\ &= \varphi_1(t) + A\psi_1(t) + \psi_1(t)_{s_0}I_{g_0}^{\alpha_0}f_x(t_1^-), \end{aligned} \tag{15}$$

and also $x(s_1) = \varphi_1(s_1) + A\psi_1(s_1) + \psi_1(s_1)_{s_0}I_{g_0}^{\alpha_0}f_x(t_1^-)$.

In the third interval $[s_1, t_2)$, again taking the Riemann–Liouville fractional integral with respect to a function $g_1(t)$ of order $\alpha_1$, we obtain

$$\begin{aligned} x(t) &= x(s_1) + {}_{s_1}I_{g_1}^{\alpha_1}f_x(t) \\ &= \varphi_1(s_1) + A\psi_1(s_1) + \psi_1(s_1)_{s_0}I_{g_0}^{\alpha_0}f_x(t_1^-) + {}_{s_1}I_{g_1}^{\alpha_1}f_x(t), \end{aligned}$$

which has particular case as $x(t_2^-) = \varphi_1(s_1) + A\psi_1(s_1) + \psi_1(s_1)_{s_0}I_{g_0}^{\alpha_0}f_x(t_1^-) + {}_{s_1}I_{g_1}^{\alpha_1}f_x(t_2^-)$.

In the fourth interval $[t_2, s_2)$, it follows that

$$x(t) = \varphi_2(t) + \psi_2(t)\left[\varphi_1(s_1) + A\psi_1(s_1) + \psi_1(s_1)_{s_0}I_{g_0}^{\alpha_0} f_x(t_1^-) + {}_{s_1}I_{g_1}^{\alpha_1} f_x(t_2^-)\right].$$

By the previous procedure we can find that

$$x(t) = \begin{cases} A\left(\prod_{j=1}^{i}\psi_j(s_j)\right) + \sum_{j=1}^{i}\left(\prod_{j}^{i-1}\psi_{j+1}(s_{j+1})\right)\varphi_j(s_j) \\ + \sum_{j=1}^{i}\left[\left(\prod_{j}^{i}\psi_j(s_j)\right)_{s_{j-1}}I_{g_{j-1}}^{\alpha_{j-1}} f_x(t_j^-)\right] + {}_{s_i}I_{g_i}^{\alpha_i} f_x(t), \\ \qquad t \in [s_i, t_{i+1}),\ i = 0, 1, 2, \ldots, m, \\ \varphi_i(t) + \psi_i(t)\left[A\prod_{j=1}^{i-1}\psi_j(s_j) + \sum_{j=1}^{i-1}\left(\prod_{j}^{i-2}\psi_{j+1}(s_{j+1})\right)\varphi_j(s_j)\right. \\ \left. + \sum_{j=1}^{i}\left(\prod_{j}^{i-1}\psi_j(s_j)\right)_{s_{j-1}}I_{g_{j-1}}^{\alpha_{j-1}} f_x(t_j^-)\right], \quad t \in [t_i, s_i),\ i = 1, 2, 3, \ldots, m. \end{cases} \tag{16}$$

By using the mathematical induction, we will claim that the formula (16) holds. Putting $i = 0$ and $i = 1$ in the first and second parts of (16), respectively, we have results in (14) and (15). Assume that the first part of (16) is true for $i = k$, that is, for $t \in [s_k, t_{k+1})$,

$$\begin{aligned} x(t) &= A\left(\prod_{j=1}^{k}\psi_j(s_j)\right) + \sum_{j=1}^{k}\left(\prod_{j}^{k-1}\psi_{j+1}(s_{j+1})\right)\varphi_j(s_j) \\ &\quad + \sum_{j=1}^{k}\left[\left(\prod_{j}^{k}\psi_j(s_j)\right)_{s_{j-1}}I_{g_{j-1}}^{\alpha_{j-1}} f_x(t_j^-)\right] + {}_{s_k}I_{g_k}^{\alpha_k} f_x(t). \end{aligned}$$

Then for $t \in [t_{k+1}, s_{k+1})$, we have

$$\begin{aligned} x(t) &= \varphi_{k+1}(t) + \psi_{k+1}(t)x(t_{k+1}^-) \\ &= \varphi_{k+1}(t) + \psi_{k+1}(t)\left\{A\left(\prod_{j=1}^{k}\psi_j(s_j)\right) + \sum_{j=1}^{k}\left(\prod_{j}^{k-1}\psi_{j+1}(s_{j+1})\right)\varphi_j(s_j),\right. \\ &\quad \left. + \sum_{j=1}^{k}\left[\left(\prod_{j}^{k}\psi_j(s_j)\right)_{s_{j-1}}I_{g_{j-1}}^{\alpha_{j-1}} f_x(t_j^-)\right] + {}_{s_k}I_{g_k}^{\alpha_k} f_x(t_{k+1})\right\} \\ &= \varphi_{k+1}(t) + \psi_{k+1}(t)\left\{A\left(\prod_{j=1}^{k}\psi_j(s_j)\right) + \sum_{j=1}^{k}\left(\prod_{j}^{k-1}\psi_{j+1}(s_{j+1})\right)\varphi_j(s_j),\right. \\ &\quad \left. + \sum_{j=1}^{k+1}\left[\left(\prod_{j}^{k}\psi_j(s_j)\right)_{s_{j-1}}I_{g_{j-1}}^{\alpha_{j-1}} f_x(t_j^-)\right]\right\}, \end{aligned}$$

which implies that the second part of (16) holds. Similarly suppose that the second part of (16) is satisfied for $i = k$. Then for $t \in [s_k, t_{k+1})$, we obtain

$$\begin{aligned} x(t) &= x(s_k) + {}_{s_k}I_{g_k}^{\alpha_k} f_x(t) \\ &= \varphi_k(s_k) + \psi_k(s_k)\left[A\prod_{j=1}^{k-1}\psi_j(s_j) + \sum_{j=1}^{k-1}\left(\prod_{j}^{k-2}\psi_{j+1}(s_{j+1})\right)\varphi_j(s_j)\right. \\ &\quad \left. + \sum_{j=1}^{k}\left(\prod_{j}^{k-1}\psi_j(s_j)\right)_{s_{j-1}}I_{g_{j-1}}^{\alpha_{j-1}} f_x(t_j^-)\right] + {}_{s_k}I_{g_k}^{\alpha_k} f_x(t) \end{aligned}$$

$$
\begin{aligned}
&= A\left(\prod_{j=1}^{k}\psi_j(s_j)\right)+\sum_{j=1}^{k}\left(\prod_{j}^{k-1}\psi_{j+1}(s_{j+1})\right)\varphi_j(s_j)\\
&\quad+\sum_{j=1}^{k}\left[\left(\prod_{j}^{k}\psi_j(s_j)\right)_{s_{j-1}}I_{g_{j-1}}^{\alpha_{j-1}}f_x(t_j^-)\right]+{}_{s_k}I_{g_k}^{\alpha_k}f_x(t).
\end{aligned}
$$

Thus the first part of (16) is fulfilled. Therefore, the relation (16) holds for all $t\in[0,T]$. Now, we put $t=T$ in (16), we have

$$
\begin{aligned}
x(T) &= A\left(\prod_{j=1}^{m}\psi_j(s_j)\right)+\sum_{j=1}^{m}\left(\prod_{j}^{m-1}\psi_{j+1}(s_{j+1})\right)\varphi_j(s_j)\\
&\quad+\sum_{j=1}^{m}\left[\left(\prod_{j}^{m}\psi_j(s_j)\right)_{s_{j-1}}I_{g_{j-1}}^{\alpha_{j-1}}f_x(t_j^-)\right]+{}_{s_m}I_{g_m}^{\alpha_m}f_x(T)\\
&= A\left(\prod_{j=1}^{m}\psi_j(s_j)\right)+\Lambda^*(m)+\sum_{j=1}^{m+1}\left[\left(\prod_{j}^{m}\psi_j(s_j)\right)_{s_{j-1}}I_{g_{j-1}}^{\alpha_{j-1}}f_x(t_j^-)\right]. \quad (17)
\end{aligned}
$$

By taking the Riemann–Liouville fractional integral of order $\gamma_k>0$ to (16), with respect to a function $g_k(t)$ on $[s_k,t_{k+1})$ for $k=0,1,2,\ldots,m$, we obtain

$$
\begin{aligned}
{}_{s_k}I_{g_k}^{\gamma_k}x(t) &= A\frac{\big(g_k(t)-g_k(s_k)\big)^{\gamma_k}}{\Gamma(\gamma_k+1)}\left(\prod_{j=1}^{k}\psi_j(s_j)\right)\\
&\quad+\left[\sum_{j=1}^{k}\left(\prod_{j}^{k-1}\psi_{j+1}(s_{j+1})\right)\varphi_j(s_j)\right]\times\frac{\big(g_k(t)-g_k(s_k)\big)^{\gamma_k}}{\Gamma(\gamma_k+1)}\\
&\quad+\sum_{j=1}^{k}\left[\left(\prod_{j}^{k}\psi_j(s_j)\right)_{s_{j-1}}I_{g_{j-1}}^{\alpha_{j-1}}f_x(t_j^-)\right]\frac{\big(g_k(t)-g_k(s_k)\big)^{\gamma_k}}{\Gamma(\gamma_k+1)}+{}_{s_k}I_{g_k}^{\alpha_k+\gamma_k}f_x(t),
\end{aligned}
$$

which yields

$$
\begin{aligned}
&\sum_{k=0}^{m}\mu_k\int_{s_k}^{t_{k+1}}\left({}_{s_k}I_{g_k}^{\gamma_k}x\right)(u)\,dH_k(u)\\
&= A\sum_{k=0}^{m}\mu_k\left(\prod_{j=1}^{k}\psi_j(s_j)\right)\Lambda_k+\sum_{k=0}^{m}\mu_k\Lambda^*(k)\Lambda_k\\
&\quad+\sum_{k=0}^{m}\mu_k\sum_{j=1}^{k}\left[\left(\prod_{j}^{k}\psi_j(s_j)\right)_{s_{j-1}}I_{g_{j-1}}^{\alpha_{j-1}}f_x(t_j^-)\right]\Lambda_k\\
&\quad+\sum_{k=0}^{m}\mu_k\int_{s_k}^{t_{k+1}}{}_{s_k}I_{g_k}^{\alpha_k+\gamma_k}f_x(u)\,dH_k(u). \quad (18)
\end{aligned}
$$

The condition in (1) with (17) and (18) implies

$$
\begin{aligned}
A &= \frac{1}{\Omega}\Bigg\{\sum_{k=0}^{m}\mu_k\Lambda^*(k)\Lambda_k+\sum_{k=0}^{m}\mu_k\sum_{j=1}^{k}\left[\left(\prod_{j}^{k}\psi_j(s_j)\right)_{s_{j-1}}I_{g_{j-1}}^{\alpha_{j-1}}f_x(t_j^-)\right]\Lambda_k\\
&\quad+\sum_{k=0}^{m}\mu_k\int_{s_k}^{t_{k+1}}{}_{s_k}I_{g_k}^{\alpha_k+\gamma_k}f_x(u)\,dH_k(u)-\beta_2\Lambda^*(m)\\
&\quad-\beta_2\sum_{j=1}^{m+1}\left[\left(\prod_{j}^{m}\psi_j(s_j)\right)_{s_{j-1}}I_{g_{j-1}}^{\alpha_{j-1}}f_x(t_j^-)\right]\Bigg\}. \quad (19)
\end{aligned}
$$

By substituting the constant $A$, (19), into (16), the obtained integral Equations (12) and (13) are presented.

Conversely, by taking the operator ${}_{s_i}D^{\alpha_i}_{g_i}$ over $[s_i, t_{i+1})$ to (12), we get ${}_{s_i}D^{\alpha_i}_{g_i}x(t) = f(t, x(t))$. Putting $t = t_i$ and replacing $i$ by $i-1$ in (12), then (13) implies $x(t) = \varphi_i(t) + \psi_i(t)x(t_i^-)$, $t \in [t_i, s_i)$. By direct computation as substituting $t = 0$, $t = T$ and applying the Riemann–Stieltjes fractional integral of order $\gamma_k$ with respect to $g_k$ to the unknown function $x(t)$ in (12) over $[s_k, t_{k+1})$, then the condition in (1) is satisfied. Therefore the proof is completed. □

## 3. Existence and Uniqueness Results

Before going to prove our main results, we have to define the space of functions and the operator which are involved to problem (1). Let $J = [0, T]$ be an interval and let $PC(J,\mathbb{R})$ and $PC^1(J,\mathbb{R})$ be the spaces of piecewise continuous function defined by $PC(J,\mathbb{R}) = \{x : J \to \mathbb{R} |\ x(t)$ is continuous everywhere except for some $t_i$ at which $x(t_i^+)$ and $x(t_i^-)$ exist for $i = 1, 2, 3, \ldots, m\}$ and $PC^1(J,\mathbb{R}) = \{x \in PC(J,\mathbb{R}) |\ x'(t)$ is continuous everywhere except for some $t_i$ at which $x'(t_i^+)$ and $x'(t_i^-)$ exist for $i = 1, 2, 3, \ldots, m\}$. Let $E = PC(J,\mathbb{R}) \cap PC^1(J,\mathbb{R})$. Then $E$ is the Banach space with norm $\|x\| = \sup\{|x(t)|, t \in J\}$. Now, we define the operator on $E$ by

$$\mathcal{Q}x(t) = \begin{cases} \dfrac{1}{\Omega}\left(\displaystyle\prod_{j=1}^{i}\psi_j(s_j)\right)\left\{\displaystyle\sum_{k=0}^{m}\mu_k\Lambda^*(k)\Lambda_k - \beta_2\Lambda^*(m)\right. \\ \quad + \displaystyle\sum_{k=0}^{m}\mu_k\sum_{j=1}^{k}\left[\left(\prod_{j}^{k}\psi_j(s_j)\right){}_{s_{j-1}}I^{\alpha_{j-1}}_{g_{j-1}}f_x(t_j^-)\right]\Lambda_k \\ \quad + \displaystyle\sum_{k=0}^{m}\mu_k\int_{s_k}^{t_{k+1}}{}_{s_k}I^{\alpha_k+\gamma_k}_{g_k}f_x(u)\,dH_k(u) \\ \quad \left. -\beta_2\displaystyle\sum_{j=1}^{m+1}\left[\left(\prod_{j}^{m}\psi_j(s_j)\right){}_{s_{j-1}}I^{\alpha_{j-1}}_{g_{j-1}}f_x(t_j^-)\right]\right\} \\ \quad +\Lambda^*(i) + \displaystyle\sum_{j=1}^{i}\left[\left(\prod_{j}^{i}\psi_j(s_j)\right){}_{s_{j-1}}I^{\alpha_{j-1}}_{g_{j-1}}f_x(t_j^-)\right] + {}_{s_i}I^{\alpha_i}_{g_i}f_x(t), \\ \qquad\qquad t \in [s_i, t_{i+1}),\ i = 0, 1, 2, \ldots, m, \\ \varphi_i(t) + \psi_i(t)\left[\dfrac{1}{\Omega}\left(\displaystyle\prod_{j=1}^{i-1}\psi_j(s_j)\right)\left\{\displaystyle\sum_{k=0}^{m}\mu_k\Lambda^*(i)\Lambda_k\right.\right. \\ \quad + \displaystyle\sum_{k=0}^{m}\mu_k\sum_{j=1}^{k}\left[\left(\prod_{j}^{k}\psi_j(s_j)\right){}_{s_{j-1}}I^{\alpha_{j-1}}_{g_{j-1}}f_x(t_j^-)\right]\Lambda_k \\ \quad + \displaystyle\sum_{k=0}^{m}\mu_k\int_{s_k}^{t_{k+1}}{}_{s_k}I^{\alpha_k+\gamma_k}_{g_k}f_x(u)\,dH_k(u) - \beta_2\Lambda^*(m) \\ \quad \left. -\beta_2\displaystyle\sum_{j=1}^{m+1}\left[\left(\prod_{j}^{m}\psi_j(s_j)\right){}_{s_{j-1}}I^{\alpha_{j-1}}_{g_{j-1}}f_x(t_j^-)\right]\right\} \\ \quad \left. +\Lambda^*(i-1) + \displaystyle\sum_{j=1}^{i}\left(\prod_{j}^{i-1}\psi_j(s_j)\right){}_{s_{j-1}}I^{\alpha_{j-1}}_{g_{j-1}}f_x(t_j^-)\right], \\ \qquad\qquad t \in [t_i, s_i),\ i = 1, 2, 3, \ldots, m. \end{cases}$$

Next, by applying the Banach's contraction mapping principle, and Leray–Schauder's nonlinear alternative, we derive the existence and uniqueness of solutions to problem (1). Some constants are set as follows:

$$\Phi_1 = \frac{1}{|\Omega|}\left(\prod_{j=1}^{m}|\psi_j(s_j)|\right), \quad \Phi_2 = \sum_{k=0}^{m}|\mu_k||\Lambda^*(k)||\Lambda_k|,$$

$$
\begin{aligned}
\Phi_3 &= \sum_{k=0}^{m} |\mu_k| \sum_{j=1}^{k} \left[ \left( \prod_{j}^{k} |\psi_j(s_j)| \right) \left( \frac{(g_{j-1}(t_j) - g_{j-1}(s_{j-1}))^{\alpha_{j-1}}}{\Gamma(\alpha_{j-1}+1)} \right) \right] |\Lambda_k|, \\
\Phi_4 &= \sum_{k=0}^{m} \frac{|\mu_k|}{\Gamma(\alpha_k+\gamma_k+1)} \int_{s_k}^{t_{k+1}} (g_k(u) - g_k(s_k))^{\alpha_k+\gamma_k} \, dH_k(u), \\
\Phi_5 &= \sum_{j=1}^{m+1} \left[ \left( \prod_{j}^{m} |\psi_j(s_j)| \right) \left( \frac{(g_{j-1}(t_j) - g_{j-1}(s_{j-1}))^{\alpha_{j-1}}}{\Gamma(\alpha_{j-1}+1)} \right) \right], \\
\Phi_6 &= \Phi_1(\Phi_3 + \Phi_4) + \Phi_5(|\beta_2|\Phi_1 + 1).
\end{aligned} \tag{20}
$$

**Theorem 1.** *Suppose that the nonlinear function $f\colon J \times \mathbb{R} \to \mathbb{R}$ satisfies the condition:*
*$(H_1)$ There exists a constant $L > 0$ such that for all $t \in J$ and $x, y \in \mathbb{R}$,*

$$|f(t,x) - f(t,y)| \le L|x - y|.$$

*If $L\Phi_6 < 1$, where $\Phi_6$ is defined by (20), then the non-instantaneous impulsive Riemann–Stieltjes fractional integral boundary value problem (1) has a unique solution on $J$.*

**Proof.** Let $B_r$ be the subset of $E$ defined by $B_r = \{x \in E : \|x\| \le r\}$, where a fixed constant $r$ satisfies

$$r \ge \frac{\Phi_1\Phi_2 + |\Lambda^*(m)|(|\beta_2|\Phi_1 + 1) + M\Phi_6}{1 - L\Phi_6}. \tag{21}$$

Now we will prove that $\mathcal{Q}B_r \subset B_r$. Setting $M = \sup\{|f(t,0)|, t \in J|\}$, we have, from triangle inequality and $(H_1)$, that $|f(t,x)| \le |f(t,x) - f(t,0)| + |f(t,0)| \le Lr + M$. Then we obtain

$$
\begin{aligned}
|\mathcal{Q}x(t)| \le\ & \frac{1}{|\Omega|} \left( \prod_{j=1}^{i} |\psi_j(s_j)| \right) \Bigg\{ \sum_{k=0}^{m} |\mu_k||\Lambda^*(k)||\Lambda_k| + |\beta_2||\Lambda^*(m)| \\
& + \sum_{k=0}^{m} |\mu_k| \sum_{j=1}^{k} \left[ \left( \prod_{j}^{k} |\psi_j(s_j)| \right) {}_{s_{j-1}}I_{g_{j-1}}^{\alpha_{j-1}} |f_x|(t_j^-) \right] |\Lambda_k| \\
& + \sum_{k=0}^{m} |\mu_k| \int_{s_k}^{t_{k+1}} {}_{s_k}I_{g_k}^{\alpha_k+\gamma_k} |f_x|(u) \, dH_k(u) \\
& + |\beta_2| \sum_{j=1}^{m+1} \left[ \left( \prod_{j}^{m} |\psi_j(s_j)| \right) {}_{s_{j-1}}I_{g_{j-1}}^{\alpha_{j-1}} |f_x|(t_j^-) \right] \Bigg\} \\
& + |\Lambda^*(i)| + \sum_{j=1}^{i} \left[ \left( \prod_{j}^{i} |\psi_j(s_j)| \right) {}_{s_{j-1}}I_{g_{j-1}}^{\alpha_{j-1}} |f_x|(t_j^-) \right] + {}_{s_i}I_{g_i}^{\alpha_i} |f_x|(t)
\end{aligned}
$$

for $t \in [s_i, t_{i+1})$, $i = 0, 1, 2, \ldots, m$, and

$$
\begin{aligned}
|\mathcal{Q}x(t)| \le\ & |\varphi_i(t)| + |\psi_i(t)| \Bigg[ \frac{1}{|\Omega|} \left( \prod_{j=1}^{i-1} |\psi_j(s_j)| \right) \Bigg\{ \sum_{k=0}^{m} |\mu_k||\Lambda^*(i)||\Lambda_k| \\
& + \sum_{k=0}^{m} |\mu_k| \sum_{j=1}^{k} \left[ \left( \prod_{j}^{k} |\psi_j(s_j)| \right) {}_{s_{j-1}}I_{g_{j-1}}^{\alpha_{j-1}} |f_x|(t_j^-) \right] \Lambda_k \\
& + \sum_{k=0}^{m} |\mu_k| \int_{s_k}^{t_{k+1}} {}_{s_k}I_{g_k}^{\alpha_k+\gamma_k} |f_x|(u) \, dH_k(u) + |\beta_2||\Lambda^*(m)| \\
& + |\beta_2| \sum_{j=1}^{m+1} \left[ \left( \prod_{j}^{m} |\psi_j(s_j)| \right) {}_{s_{j-1}}I_{g_{j-1}}^{\alpha_{j-1}} |f_x|(t_j^-) \right] \Bigg\}
\end{aligned}
$$

$$+|\Lambda^*(i-1)|+\sum_{j=1}^{i}\left(\prod_{j}^{i-1}|\psi_j(s_j)|\right){}_{s_{j-1}}I_{g_{j-1}}^{\alpha_{j-1}}|f_x|(t_j^-)\Bigg],$$

for $t\in[t_i,s_i)$, $i=1,2,3,\ldots,m$. Then we have

$$\begin{aligned}
\sup_{t\in J}|\mathcal{Q}x(t)| &\le \frac{1}{|\Omega|}\left(\prod_{j=1}^{m}|\psi_j(s_j)|\right)\Bigg\{\sum_{k=0}^{m}|\mu_k||\Lambda^*(k)||\Lambda_k|+|\beta_2||\Lambda^*(m)| \\
&\quad +(Lr+M)\sum_{k=0}^{m}|\mu_k|\sum_{j=1}^{k}\left[\left(\prod_{j}^{k}|\psi_j(s_j)|\right){}_{s_{j-1}}I_{g_{j-1}}^{\alpha_{j-1}}(1)(t_j^-)\right]|\Lambda_k| \\
&\quad +(Lr+M)\sum_{k=0}^{m}|\mu_k|\int_{s_k}^{t_{k+1}}{}_{s_k}I_{g_k}^{\alpha_k+\gamma_k}(1)(u)\,dH_k(u) \\
&\quad +(Lr+M)|\beta_2|\sum_{j=1}^{m+1}\left[\left(\prod_{j}^{m}|\psi_j(s_j)|\right){}_{s_{j-1}}I_{g_{j-1}}^{\alpha_{j-1}}(1)(t_j^-)\right]\Bigg\} \\
&\quad +|\Lambda^*(m)|+(Lr+M)\sum_{j=1}^{m}\left[\left(\prod_{j}^{m}|\psi_j(s_j)|\right){}_{s_{j-1}}I_{g_{j-1}}^{\alpha_{j-1}}(1)(t_j^-)\right] \\
&\quad +(Lr+M){}_{s_m}I_{g_m}^{\alpha_m}(1)(T) \\
&= \Phi_1\Phi_2+|\Lambda^*(m)|(|\beta_2|\Phi_1+1)+rL\{\Phi_1(\Phi_3+\Phi_4)+\Phi_5(|\beta_2|\Phi_1+1)\} \\
&\quad +M\{\Phi_1(\Phi_3+\Phi_4)+\Phi_5(|\beta_2|\Phi_1+1)\} \\
&= \Phi_1\Phi_2+|\Lambda^*(m)|(|\beta_2|\Phi_1+1)+rL\Phi_6+M\Phi_6,
\end{aligned}$$

since

$$\begin{aligned}
{}_{s_{j-1}}I_{g_{j-1}}^{\alpha_{j-1}}(1)(t_j^-) &= \frac{(g_{j-1}(t_j)-g_{j-1}(s_{j-1}))^{\alpha_{j-1}}}{\Gamma(\alpha_{j-1}+1)}, \\
\int_{s_k}^{t_{k+1}}{}_{s_k}I_{g_k}^{\alpha_k+\gamma_k}(1)(u)\,dH_k(u) &= \int_{s_k}^{t_{k+1}}\frac{(g_k(u)-g_k(s_k))^{\alpha_k+\gamma_k}}{\Gamma(\alpha_k+\gamma_k+1)}\,dH_k(u).
\end{aligned}$$

Thus $\|\mathcal{Q}x\|\le r$, where $r$ satisfies (21). Therefore, we conclude that $\mathcal{Q}B_r\subset B_r$.

Next we will prove that the operator $\mathcal{Q}$ is a contraction. For any $x,y\in B_r$ we have

$$\begin{aligned}
&|\mathcal{Q}x(t)-\mathcal{Q}y(t)| \\
&\le \frac{1}{|\Omega|}\left(\prod_{j=1}^{i}|\psi_j(s_j)|\right)\Bigg\{\sum_{k=0}^{m}|\mu_k|\sum_{j=1}^{k}\left[\left(\prod_{j}^{k}|\psi_j(s_j)|\right){}_{s_{j-1}}I_{g_{j-1}}^{\alpha_{j-1}}|f_x-f_y|(t_j^-)\right]|\Lambda_k| \\
&\quad +\sum_{k=0}^{m}|\mu_k|\int_{s_k}^{t_{k+1}}{}_{s_k}I_{g_k}^{\alpha_k+\gamma_k}|f_x-f_y|(u)\,dH_k(u) \\
&\quad +|\beta_2|\sum_{j=1}^{m+1}\left[\left(\prod_{j}^{m}|\psi_j(s_j)|\right){}_{s_{j-1}}I_{g_{j-1}}^{\alpha_{j-1}}|f_x-f_y|(t_j^-)\right]\Bigg\} \\
&\quad +\sum_{j=1}^{i}\left[\left(\prod_{j}^{i}|\psi_j(s_j)|\right){}_{s_{j-1}}I_{g_{j-1}}^{\alpha_{j-1}}|f_x-f_y|(t_j^-)\right]+{}_{s_i}I_{g_i}^{\alpha_i}|f_x-f_y|(t)
\end{aligned}$$

for $t\in[s_i,t_{i+1})$, $i=0,1,2,\ldots,m$, and

$$\begin{aligned}
&|\mathcal{Q}x(t)-\mathcal{Q}y(t)| \\
&\le |\varphi_i(t)|+|\psi_i(t)|\Bigg[\frac{1}{|\Omega|}\left(\prod_{j=1}^{i-1}|\psi_j(s_j)|\right)\Bigg\{\sum_{k=0}^{m}|\mu_k|\sum_{j=1}^{k}\Bigg[\left(\prod_{j}^{k}|\psi_j(s_j)|\right)
\end{aligned}$$

$$
\times {}_{s_{j-1}}I_{g_{j-1}}^{\alpha_{j-1}}|f_x - f_y|(t_j^-)\Bigg]\Lambda_k + \sum_{k=0}^{m}|\mu_k|\int_{s_k}^{t_{k+1}} {}_{s_k}I_{g_k}^{\alpha_k+\gamma_k}|f_x - f_y|(u)\,dH_k(u)
$$

$$
+ |\beta_2|\sum_{j=1}^{m+1}\left[\left(\prod_{j}^{m}|\psi_j(s_j)|\right){}_{s_{j-1}}I_{g_{j-1}}^{\alpha_{j-1}}|f_x - f_y|(t_j^-)\right]\Bigg\}
$$

$$
+ \sum_{j=1}^{i}\left(\prod_{j}^{i-1}|\psi_j(s_j)|\right){}_{s_{j-1}}I_{g_{j-1}}^{\alpha_{j-1}}|f_x - f_y|(t_j^-)\Bigg]
$$

for $t \in [t_i, s_i)$, $i = 1, 2, 3, \ldots, m$. Consequently

$$
\begin{aligned}
&|\mathcal{Q}x(t) - \mathcal{Q}y(t)| \\
\leq\ & \frac{1}{|\Omega|}\left(\prod_{j=1}^{m}|\psi_j(s_j)|\right)\Bigg\{L\|x-y\|\sum_{k=0}^{m}|\mu_k|\sum_{j=1}^{k}\left[\left(\prod_{j}^{k}|\psi_j(s_j)|\right){}_{s_{j-1}}I_{g_{j-1}}^{\alpha_{j-1}}(1)(t_j^-)\right]|\Lambda_k| \\
&+ L\|x-y\|\sum_{k=0}^{m}|\mu_k|\int_{s_k}^{t_{k+1}} {}_{s_k}I_{g_k}^{\alpha_k+\gamma_k}(1)(u)\,dH_k(u) \\
&+ L\|x-y\||\beta_2|\sum_{j=1}^{m+1}\left[\left(\prod_{j}^{m}|\psi_j(s_j)|\right){}_{s_{j-1}}I_{g_{j-1}}^{\alpha_{j-1}}(1)(t_j^-)\right]\Bigg\} \\
&+ L\|x-y\|\sum_{j=1}^{m+1}\left[\left(\prod_{j}^{m}|\psi_j(s_j)|\right){}_{s_{j-1}}I_{g_{j-1}}^{\alpha_{j-1}}(1)(t_j^-)\right] \\
=\ & L\Phi_6\|x-y\|,
\end{aligned}
$$

which yields $\|\mathcal{Q}x - \mathcal{Q}y\| \leq L\Phi_6\|x-y\|$. As $L\Phi_6 < 1$, $\mathcal{Q}$ is a contraction. Therefore, we deduce by Banach's contraction mapping principle, that $\mathcal{Q}$ has a fixed point which is the solution of the boundary value problem (1). The proof is completed. □

**Remark 1.** *If $\beta_1 \neq 0$, $\beta_2 = 0$, then the problem (1) is reduced to the initial and integral values problem. The constants $\Omega^*$, $\Phi_6^*$ and $\Phi_1^*$, given by*

$$
\Omega^* = \beta_1 - \sum_{k=0}^{m}\mu_k\left(\prod_{j=1}^{k}\psi_j(s_j)\right)\Lambda_k,\quad \Phi_6^* = \Phi_1^*(\Phi_3 + \Phi_4) + \Phi_5,\quad \Phi_1^* = \frac{1}{|\Omega^*|}\left(\prod_{j=1}^{m}|\psi_j(s_j)|\right),
$$

*with conditions $(H_1)$ and $L\Phi_6^* < 1$ are used to obtain the existence of a unique solution of such a problem on $J$.*

The following theorem of Leray–Schauder's nonlinear alternative will be applied to the next result.

**Theorem 2** ([35]). *Given E is a Banach space, and B is a closed, convex subset of E. In addition let G be an open subset of B such that $0 \in G$. Suppose that $\mathcal{Q} : \overline{G} \to B$ is a continuous, compact (that is, $\mathcal{Q}(\overline{G})$ is a relatively compact subset of B) map. Then either*

*(i) $\mathcal{Q}$ has a fixed point in $\overline{G}$,*

*(ii) there is a $x \in \partial G$ (the boundary of G in B) and $\lambda \in (0,1)$ with $x = \lambda\mathcal{Q}(x)$.*

**Theorem 3.** *Suppose that $f : J \times \mathbb{R}$ is a continuous function. In addition we assume that:*

*$(H_2)$ There exist a continuous nondecreasing function $\Psi : [0,\infty) \to (0,\infty)$ and continuous function $w : J \to \mathbb{R}^+$, such that*

$$
|f(t,x)| \leq w(t)\Psi(|x|),
$$

*for each $(t,x) \in J \times \mathbb{R}$;*

$(H_3)$ *There exists a constant $N > 0$ such that*

$$\frac{N}{\Phi_1\Phi_2 + |\Lambda^*(m)|(|\beta_2|\Phi_1 + 1) + \|w\|\Psi(N)\Phi_6} > 1.$$

*Then the non-instantaneous impulsive Riemann–Stieltjes fractional integral boundary value problem (1) has at least one solution on $J$.*

**Proof.** Let $\rho$ be a radius of a ball $B_\rho = \{x \in E : \|x\| \le \rho\}$. It is obvious that $B_\rho$ is a closed, convex subset of $E$. Now, we will show that the operator $\mathcal{Q}$ is fulfilled all conditions of Theorem 2. Firstly the continuity of operator $\mathcal{Q}$ is proved by defining a sequence $\{x_n\}$ which is converse to $x$. Then

$$\begin{aligned}
&|\mathcal{Q}x_n(t) - \mathcal{Q}x(t)| \\
\le\ & \frac{1}{|\Omega|}\left(\prod_{j=1}^{i}|\psi_j(s_j)|\right)\left\{\sum_{k=0}^{m}|\mu_k|\sum_{j=1}^{k}\left[\left(\prod_{j}^{k}|\psi_j(s_j)|\right){}_{s_{j-1}}I_{g_{j-1}}^{\alpha_{j-1}}|f_{x_n} - f_y|(t_j^-)\right]|\Lambda_k|\right. \\
&+ \sum_{k=0}^{m}|\mu_k|\int_{s_k}^{t_{k+1}} {}_{s_k}I_{g_k}^{\alpha_k+\gamma_k}|f_{x_n} - f_x|(u)\,dH_k(u) \\
&\left.+ |\beta_2|\sum_{j=1}^{m+1}\left[\left(\prod_{j}^{m}|\psi_j(s_j)|\right){}_{s_{j-1}}I_{g_{j-1}}^{\alpha_{j-1}}|f_{x_n} - f_x|(t_j^-)\right]\right\} \\
&+ \sum_{j=1}^{i}\left[\left(\prod_{j}^{i}|\psi_j(s_j)|\right){}_{s_{j-1}}I_{g_{j-1}}^{\alpha_{j-1}}|f_x - f_y|(t_j^-)\right] + {}_{s_i}I_{g_i}^{\alpha_i}|f_{x_n} - f_x|(t) \\
\to\ & 0, \qquad \text{as} \quad n \to \infty,
\end{aligned}$$

for $t \in [s_i, t_{i+1})$, $i = 0, 1, 2, \ldots, m$, and

$$\begin{aligned}
&|\mathcal{Q}x_n(t) - \mathcal{Q}x(t)| \\
\le\ & |\varphi_i(t)| + |\psi_i(t)|\left[\frac{1}{|\Omega|}\left(\prod_{j=1}^{i-1}|\psi_j(s_j)|\right)\left\{\sum_{k=0}^{m}|\mu_k|\sum_{j=1}^{k}\left[\left(\prod_{j}^{k}|\psi_j(s_j)|\right)\right.\right.\right. \\
&\left.\times {}_{s_{j-1}}I_{g_{j-1}}^{\alpha_{j-1}}|f_{x_n} - f_x|(t_j^-)\right]\Lambda_k + \sum_{k=0}^{m}|\mu_k|\int_{s_k}^{t_{k+1}} {}_{s_k}I_{g_k}^{\alpha_k+\gamma_k}|f_{x_n} - f_x|(u)\,dH_k(u) \\
&\left.+ |\beta_2|\sum_{j=1}^{m+1}\left[\left(\prod_{j}^{m}|\psi_j(s_j)|\right){}_{s_{j-1}}I_{g_{j-1}}^{\alpha_{j-1}}|f_{x_n} - f_x|(t_j^-)\right]\right\} \\
&\left.+ \sum_{j=1}^{i}\left(\prod_{j}^{i-1}|\psi_j(s_j)|\right){}_{s_{j-1}}I_{g_{j-1}}^{\alpha_{j-1}}|f_{x_n} - f_x|(t_j^-)\right] \to 0, \qquad \text{as} \quad n \to \infty,
\end{aligned}$$

for $t \in [t_i, s_i)$, $i = 1, 2, 3, \ldots, m$. Then $\mathcal{Q}$ is continuous.

Next the compactness of the operator $Q$ will be proved. Assume that $x \in B_\rho$, then we have

$$\begin{aligned}
|\mathcal{Q}x(t)| \le\ & \frac{1}{|\Omega|}\left(\prod_{j=1}^{m}|\psi_j(s_j)|\right)\left\{\sum_{k=0}^{m}|\mu_k||\Lambda^*(k)||\Lambda_k| + |\beta_2||\Lambda^*(m)|\right. \\
&+ \|w\|\Psi(\rho)\sum_{k=0}^{m}|\mu_k|\sum_{j=1}^{k}\left[\left(\prod_{j}^{k}|\psi_j(s_j)|\right){}_{s_{j-1}}I_{g_{j-1}}^{\alpha_{j-1}}(1)(t_j^-)\right]|\Lambda_k| \\
&+ \|w\|\Psi(\rho)\sum_{k=0}^{m}|\mu_k|\int_{s_k}^{t_{k+1}} {}_{s_k}I_{g_k}^{\alpha_k+\gamma_k}(1)(u)\,dH_k(u)
\end{aligned}$$

$$
\begin{aligned}
& + \|w\|\Psi(\rho)|\beta_2| \sum_{j=1}^{m+1}\left[\left(\prod_{j}^{m}|\psi_j(s_j)|\right)_{s_{j-1}}I_{g_{j-1}}^{\alpha_{j-1}}(1)(t_j^-)\right]\Bigg\} \\
& + |\Lambda^*(m)| + \|w\|\Psi(\rho)\sum_{j=1}^{m}\left[\left(\prod_{j}^{m}|\psi_j(s_j)|\right)_{s_{j-1}}I_{g_{j-1}}^{\alpha_{j-1}}(1)(t_j^-)\right] \\
& + \|w\|\Psi(\rho)_{s_m}I_{g_m}^{\alpha_m}(1)(T) \\
= \;& \Phi_1\Phi_2 + |\Lambda^*(m)|(|\beta_2|\Phi_1 + 1) + \|w\|\Psi(\rho)\Phi_6 \\
:= \;& \Phi_7, \qquad (22)
\end{aligned}
$$

which yields $\|\mathcal{Q}x\| \leq \Phi_7$ and then $\mathcal{Q}B_\rho$ is a uniformly bounded set. To prove equicontinuity of $\mathcal{Q}B_\rho$, we let the points $\theta_1, \theta_2 \in [0,T]$ such that $\theta_1 < \theta_2$. Then for any $x \in B_\rho$, it follows that

$$
\begin{aligned}
& |\mathcal{Q}x(\theta_2) - \mathcal{Q}x(\theta_1)| \\
= \;& \left|{}_{s_i}I_{g_i}^{\alpha_i}f_x(\theta_2) - {}_{s_i}I_{g_i}^{\alpha_i}f_x(\theta_1)\right| \\
\leq \;& \|w\|\Psi(\rho)\left|{}_{s_i}I_{g_i}^{\alpha_i}(1)(\theta_2) - {}_{s_i}I_{g_i}^{\alpha_i}(1)(\theta_1)\right| \\
= \;& \frac{\|w\|\Psi(\rho)}{\Gamma(\alpha_i+1)}\left\{2(g(\theta_2)-g(\theta_1))^{\alpha_i} + \left|g((\theta_2)-g(s_i))^{\alpha_i} - (g(\theta_1)-g(s_i))^{\alpha_i}\right|\right\} \to 0,
\end{aligned}
$$

as $\theta_1 \to \theta_2$ for $t \in [s_i, t_{i+1})$, $i = 0,1,2,\ldots,m$, and

$$
\begin{aligned}
|\mathcal{Q}x(\theta_2) - \mathcal{Q}x(\theta_1)| \;&=\; |\varphi_i(\theta_2) - \varphi_i(\theta_1)| + |\psi_i(\theta_2) - \psi_i(\theta_1)| \times \text{const.} \\
&\to\; 0, \qquad \text{as} \quad \theta_1 \to \theta_2,
\end{aligned}
$$

for $t \in [t_i, s_i)$, $i = 1,2,3,\ldots,m$. The above two inequalities are convergent to zero independently of $x$. Then $\mathcal{Q}B_\rho$ is equicontinuous set. Therefore, we deduce that $\mathcal{Q}B_\rho$ is relatively compact which implies by the Arzelá–Ascoli theorem, that the operator $\mathcal{Q}$ is completely continuous.

In the last step, we will illustrate that the condition $(ii)$ of Theorem 2 dose not hold. Let $x$ be a solution of problem (1). Now, we consider the operator equation $x = \lambda\mathcal{Q}x$ for any fixed constant $\lambda \in (0,1)$. Consequently, from above computation getting (22), we obtain

$$
\frac{\|x\|}{\Phi_1\Phi_2 + |\Lambda^*(m)|(|\beta_2|\Phi_1 + 1) + \|w\|\Psi(\|x\|)\Phi_6} \leq 1.
$$

The hypothesis $(H_3)$ implies that there exists a positive constants $N$ such that $\|x\| \neq N$. Define the open subset of $B_\rho$ by $G = \{x \in B_\rho : \|x\| < N\}$. It is easy to see that $\mathcal{Q} : \overline{G} \to E$ is continuous and completely continuous. Thus, there is no $x \in \partial G$ such that $x = \lambda\mathcal{Q}x$ for some $\lambda \in (0,1)$. Hence the condition $(ii)$ of Theorem 2 is not true. Therefore, by the conclusion from Theorem 2 $(i)$, the operator $\mathcal{Q}$ has a fixed point $x \in \overline{G}$ which is a solution of the problem (1) on $J$. This is the end of the proof. □

A special case can be obtain by setting $p(t) \equiv 1$ and $\Psi(x) = \kappa_1 x + \kappa_2$, $\kappa_1 \geq 0$, $\kappa_2 > 0$ in Theorem 3.

**Corollary 1.** *If*

$$
|f(t,x)| \leq \kappa_1 x + \kappa_2,
$$

*and if $\kappa_1\Phi_6 < 1$, then the non-instantaneous impulsive Riemann–Stieltjes fractional integral boundary value problem (1) has at least one solution on $J$.*

**Remark 2.** *In the same way of Remark 1, if $\beta_1 \neq 0$, $\beta_2 = 0$, and conditions $(H_2)$-$(H_3)$ are fulfilled with*

$$
\frac{N}{\Phi_1^*\Phi_2 + |\Lambda^*(m)| + \|w\|\Psi(N)\Phi_6^*} > 1,
$$

*then the initial and integral values problem has at least one solution on $J$.*

**Example 1.** *Consider the non-instantaneous impulsive Riemann–Stieltjes fractional integral boundary value problem*

$$\begin{cases} {}_{2i}D^{\frac{4i+5}{4i+6}}_{\frac{e^t}{(e^t+4+i-t)}} x(t) = f(t,x(t)), \quad t \in [2i,2i+1), \quad i=0,1,2,3, \\ x(t) = \dfrac{1}{2}\log_e(i+t) + \left(\dfrac{1}{i+\tan^{-1}(t)}\right)x(t_i^-), \quad t \in [2i-1,2i), \quad i=1,2,3, \\ \dfrac{3}{11}x(0) + \dfrac{4}{13}x(7) = \dfrac{5}{17}\displaystyle\int_0^1 \left({}_0I^{\frac{1}{4}}_{(\frac{e^u}{(e^u+4-u)}} x\right)(u)\, d(u^2+u) \\ \qquad + \dfrac{6}{19}\displaystyle\int_2^3 \left({}_2I^{\frac{1}{2}}_{\frac{e^u}{(e^u+5-u)}} x\right)(u)\, d(u^2+2u) \\ \qquad + \dfrac{7}{23}\displaystyle\int_4^5 \left({}_4I^{\frac{3}{4}}_{\frac{e^u}{(e^u+6-u)}} x\right)(u)\, d(u^2+3u) \\ \qquad + \dfrac{8}{29}\displaystyle\int_6^7 \left({}_6I^{\frac{3}{2}}_{\frac{e^u}{(e^u+7-u)}} x\right)(u)\, d(u^2+4u). \end{cases} \tag{23}$$

Here $\alpha_i = (4i+5)/(4i+6)$, $g_i(t) = e^t/(e^t+4+i-t)$, for $t \in [2i,2i+1)$, $i=0,1,2,3$, $\varphi_i(t) = (1/2)\log_e(i+t)$, $\psi_i(t) = 1/(i+\tan^{-1}t)$, $t \in [2i-1,2i)$, $i=1,2,3$, $\beta_1 = 3/11$, $\beta_2 = 4/13$. Since $[2i,2i+1) \cup [2j-1,2j) \cup \{7\} = [0,7]$, for $i=0,1,2,3$, $j=1,2,3$, we put $T=7$. Setting $\mu_0 = 5/17$, $\mu_1 = 6/19$, $\mu_2 = 7/23$, $\mu_3 = 8/29$, $H_i(t) = t^2+it$, $i=1,2,3,4$, $\gamma_0 = 1/4$, $\gamma_1 = 1/2$, $\gamma_2 = 3/4$, $\gamma_3 = 3/2$. Remark that $g_i'(t) > 0$ for all $t \in [0,7]$, $i=0,1,2,3$. Then from all information, we can compute that $|\Omega| \approx 0.5181070744$, $\Phi_1 \approx 0.06251397190$, $\Phi_2 \approx 0.8574153788$, $\Phi_3 \approx 0.1639270834$, $\Phi_4 \approx 0.1706687388$, $\Phi_5 \approx 0.1889629435$, $\Phi_6 \approx 0.2135145724$ and $\Lambda^*(3) \approx 1.376938726$.

(i) Consider a nonlinear function $f: [0,7] \times \mathbb{R} \to \mathbb{R}$ by

$$f(t,x) = \frac{4}{3}e^{-t}\left(\frac{2x^2+3|x|}{1+|x|}\right) + \frac{1}{2}t + 1. \tag{24}$$

It is easy to check that the function $f(t,x)$ satisfies the Lipchitz condition with $L=4$, as $|f(t,x) - f(t,y)| \le 4|x-y|$, for all $t \in [0,7]$ and $x,y \in \mathbb{R}$. Since $L\Phi_6 \approx 0.8540582896 < 1$, by applying the result in Theorem 1, we have that the problem (23), with $f$ given by (24), has a unique solution on $[0,7]$.

(ii) Let now a nonlinear function $f$ defined by

$$f(t,x) = \frac{1}{t+2}\left(\frac{x^{16}}{1+x^{14}} + \frac{2}{3}\sin^2 x + \frac{1}{3}e^{-x^2}\right). \tag{25}$$

Note that

$$|f(t,x)| \le \frac{1}{t+2}\left(x^2+1\right),$$

which satisfies $(H_2)$ with $p(t) = 1/(t+2)$ and $\Psi(x) = x^2+1$. Accordingly, $\|p\| = 1/2$ and there exists a constant $N \in (1.984010360, 7.383031794)$ satisfying the condition $(H_3)$ of Theorem 3. Therefore, by applying Theorem 3, we deduce that the problem (23), with $f$ given by (25), has at least one solution on $[0,7]$.

(iii) If the term $x^{16}$ is replaced by $|x|^{15}$ in (25) then

$$f(t,x) = \frac{1}{t+2}\left(\frac{|x|^{15}}{1+x^{14}} + \frac{2}{3}\sin^2 x + \frac{1}{3}e^{-x^2}\right). \tag{26}$$

Hence we get $|f(t,x)| \le (1/2)|x| + (1/2)$. Putting $\kappa_1 = 1/2$ and $\kappa_2 = 1/2$, it follows that $\kappa_1\Phi_6 \approx 0.1067572862 < 1$, which implies, by Corollary 1, that the problem (23) with (26) has at least one solution on $[0,7]$.

## 4. Conclusions

We have presented the sufficient criteria for the existence and uniqueness of solutions for a non-instantaneous impulsive Riemann–Stieltjes fractional integral boundary value problem. The given boundary value problem is converted into an equivalent fixed point operator equation, which is solved by applying the standard fixed point theorems. We make use of Banach's contraction mapping principle to obtain the uniqueness result, while the Leray–Schauder nonlinear alternative is applied to obtain the existence result. We have demonstrated the application of the obtained results by constructing examples.

Our problem generates many types and also mixed types of impulsive fractional boundary value problems. For example, our results are reduced to Riemann–Liouville and Hadamard impulsive fractional boundary value problems when $g(t) = t$ and $g(t) = \log t$, respectively. Our results are new in the given configuration and contributes to the theory of fractional boundary value problems.

**Author Contributions:** conceptualization, S.K.N. and J.T.; methodology, S.A., Y.T., S.K.N. and J.T.; formal analysis, S.A., Y.T., S.K.N. and J.T.; funding acquisition, J.T. All authors have read and agreed to the published version of the manuscript.

**Funding:** This research was funded by King Mongkut's University of Technology North Bangkok. Contract no. KMUTNB-61-KNOW-015.

**Institutional Review Board Statement:** Not applicable.

**Informed Consent Statement:** Not applicable.

**Data Availability Statement:** Not applicable.

**Conflicts of Interest:** The authors declare no conflict of interest.

## References

1. Diethelm, K. *The Analysis of Fractional Differential Equations: An Application-Oriented Exposition Using Differential Operators of Caputo Type*; Springer: New York, NY, USA, 2010.
2. Kilbas, A.A.; Srivastava, H.M.; Trujillo, J.J. *Theory and Applications of the Fractional Differential Equations*; Elseiver: Amsterdam, The Netherlands, 2006.
3. Lakshmikantham, V.; Leela, S.; Devi, J.V. *Theory of Fractional Dynamic Systems*; Cambridge Scientific Publishers: Cambridge, UK, 2009.
4. Miller, K.S.; Ross, B. *An Introduction to the Fractional Calculus and Differential Equations*; John Wiley: New York, NY, USA, 1993.
5. Podlubny, I. *Fractional Differential Equations: An Introduction to Fractional Derivatives, Fractional Differential Equations, to Methods of Their Solution and Some of Their Applications*; Academic Press: New York, NY, USA, 1998.
6. Ahmad, B.; Alsaedi, A.; Ntouyas, S.K.; Tariboon, J. *Hadamard-Type Fractional Differential Equations, Inclusions and Inequalities*; Springer International Publishing: Cham, Switzerland, 2017.
7. Samko, S.G.; Kilbas, A.A.; Marichev, O.I. *Fractional Integrals and Derivatives Theory and Applications*; Gordon and Breach: New York, NY, USA, 1993.
8. Zhou, Y.; Wang, J.R.; Zhang, L. *Basic Theory of Fractional Differential Equations*; World Scientific: Singapore, 2014.
9. Samoilenko, A.M.; Perestyuk, N.A. *Impulsive Differential Equations*; World Scientific Publishing: Singapore, 1995.
10. Lakshmikantham, V.; Bainov, D.D.; Simeonov, P.S. *Theory of Impulsive Differential Equations*; World Scientific: Singapore, 1989.
11. Benchohra, M.; Henderson, J.; Ntouyas, S.K. *Impulsive Differential Equations and Inclusions*; Hindawi Publishing Corporation: New York, NY, USA, 2006.
12. Kostic, M. *Abstract Voltera Integro-Differential Equations*; ORC Press: Boca Raton, FL, USA, 2015.
13. Song, X.; Gno, H.; Shi, X. *Theory and Applications of Impulsive Differential Equations*; Science Press: Beijing, China, 2011.
14. Stamov, G.T. *Almost Periodic Solutions of Impulsive Differential Equations*; Springer: Berlin, Germany, 2012.
15. Yukunthorn, W.; Ntouyas, S.K.; Tariboon, J. Impulsive multiorders Riemann-Liouville fractional differential equations. *Discret. Dyn. Nat. Soc.* **2015**, *2015*, 603893. [CrossRef]
16. Thaiprayoon, C.; Tariboon, J.; Ntouyas, S.K. Impulsive fractional boundary-value problems with fractional integral jump conditions. *Boun. Value Probl.* **2014**, *2014*, 16. [CrossRef]
17. Yukunthorn, W.; Ahmad, B.; Ntouyas, S.K.; Tariboon, J. On Caputo- Hadamard type fractional impulsive hybrid systems with nonlinear fractional integral conditions. *Nonlinear Anal. Hybrid Syst.* **2016**, *19*, 77–92. [CrossRef]
18. Heidarkhani, S.; Caristi, G.; Salari, A. Nontrivial solutions for impulsive elastic beam equations of Kirchhoff-type. *J. Nonlinear Funct. Anal.* **2020**, *2020*, 4.

19. Kamenski, M.; Petrosyan, G.; Wen, C.F. An existence result for a periodic boundary value problem of fractional semilinear differential equations in Banach spaces. *J. Nonlinear Var. Anal.* **2021**, *5*, 155–177.
20. Hernández, E.; O'Regan, D. On a new class of abstract impulsive differential equation. *Proc. Am. Math. Soc.* **2013**, *141*, 1641–1649. [CrossRef]
21. Terzieva, R. Some phenomena for non-instantaneous impulsive differential equations. *Int. J. Pure Appl. Math.* **2018**, *119*, 483–490.
22. Li, P.L.; Xu, C.J. Mild solution of fractional order differential equations with not instantaneous impulses. *Open Math.* **2015**, *23*, 436–443. [CrossRef]
23. Wang, J.; Li, Z. Periodic BVP for integer/fractional order nonlinear differential equations with non-instantaneous impulses. *J. Appl. Math. Comput.* **2014**, *46*, 321–334. [CrossRef]
24. Agarwal, R.; Hristova, S.; O'Regan, D. non-instantaneous impulses in Caputo fractional differential equations and practical stability via Lyapunov functions. *J. Frankl. Inst.* **2017**, *354*, 3097–3119. [CrossRef]
25. Agarwal, R.; O'Regan, D.; Hristova, S. Monotone iterative technique for the initial value problem for differential equations with non-instantaneous impulses. *Appl. Math. Comput.* **2017**, *298*, 45–56. [CrossRef]
26. Rudin, W. *Principles of Mathematical Analysis*; McGraw-Hill: New York, NY, USA, 1964.
27. Almeida, R. A Caputo fractional derivative of a function with respect to another function. *Commun. Nonlinear Sci. Numer. Simulat.* **2017**, *44*, 460–481. [CrossRef]
28. Almeida, R.; Malinowska, A.; Monteiro, T. Fractional differential equations with a Caputo derivative with respect to a kernel function and their applications. *Math. Methods Appl. Sci.* **2018**, *41*, 336–352. [CrossRef]
29. Ameen, R.; Jarad, F.; Abdeljawad, T. Ulam stability for delay fractional differential equations with a generalized Caputo derivative. *Filomat* **2018**, *32*, 5265–5274. [CrossRef]
30. Samet, B.; Aydi, H. Lyapunov-type inequalities for an anti-periodic fractional boundary value problem involving $\psi$-Caputo fractional derivative. *J. Inequal. Appl.* **2018**, *2018*, 286. [CrossRef] [PubMed]
31. Katugampola, U. A new approach to generalized fractional derivatives. *Bull. Math. Anal. Appl.* **2014**, *6*, 1–15.
32. Zhang, X.; Liu, Z.; Peng, H.; Zhang, X.; Yang, S. The general solution of differential equations with Caputo-Hadamard fractional derivatives and nininstantaneous impulses. *Adv. Math. Phy.* ***2017***, 2017, *3094173*.
33. Agarwal, R.; Hristova, S.; O'Regan, D. Lipschitz stability for non- instantaneous impulsive Caputo fractional differential equations with state dependent delays. *Axioms* **2019**, *8*, 4, doi:10.3390/axioms8010004. [CrossRef]
34. Hristova, S.; Ivanova, K. Caputo fractional differential equations with non-instantaneous random Erlang distributed impulses. *Fractal Fract.* **2019**, *3*, 28. [CrossRef]
35. Granas, A.; Dugundji, J. *Fixed Point Theory*; Springer: New York, NY, USA, 2003.

axioms

MDPI

Article

# A Novel Numerical Method for Solving Fractional Diffusion-Wave and Nonlinear Fredholm and Volterra Integral Equations with Zero Absolute Error

**Mutaz Mohammad [1,*], Alexandre Trounev [2] and Mohammed Alshbool [1,3,*]**

1 Department of Mathematics & Statistics, Zayed University, Abu Dhabi 144543, United Arab Emirates
2 Department of Computer Technology and Systems, Kuban State Agrarian University, 350044 Krasnodar, Russia; trounev.a@edu.kubsau.ru
3 Department of Applied Mathematics, Abu Dhabi University, Abu Dhabi P.O. Box 59911, United Arab Emirates
* Correspondence: Mutaz.Mohammad@zu.ac.ae (M.M.); alshbool.mohammed@gmail.com (M.A.)

**Abstract:** In this work, a new numerical method for the fractional diffusion-wave equation and nonlinear Fredholm and Volterra integro-differential equations is proposed. The method is based on Euler wavelet approximation and matrix inversion of an $M \times M$ collocation points. The proposed equations are presented based on Caputo fractional derivative where we reduce the resulting system to a system of algebraic equations by implementing the Gaussian quadrature discretization. The reduced system is generated via the truncated Euler wavelet expansion. Several examples with known exact solutions have been solved with zero absolute error. This method is also applied to the Fredholm and Volterra nonlinear integral equations and achieves the desired absolute error of $0. \times 10^{-31}$ for all tested examples. The new numerical scheme is exceptional in terms of its novelty, efficiency and accuracy in the field of numerical approximation.

**Keywords:** time-fractional diffusion-wave equations; Euler wavelets; integral equations; numerical approximation

**MSC:** 26A33, 35R11, 45B05

**Citation:** Mohammad, M.; Trounev, A.; Alshbool, M. A Novel Numerical Method for Solving Fractional Diffusion-Wave and Nonlinear Fredholm and Volterra Integral Equations with Zero Absolute Error. *Axioms* **2021**, *10*, 165. https://doi.org/10.3390/axioms10030165

Academic Editor: Jorge E. Macías Díaz

Received: 19 April 2021
Accepted: 8 June 2021
Published: 28 July 2021



## 1. Introduction

Fractional calculus is very useful and widely used in many applications in science, numerical computations and engineering, where the mathematical modeling of several real world problems is presented in terms of fractional differential equations, see, e.g., [1–8]. For example, the authors in [8] approximated the Caputo fractional derivative by quadratic segmentary interpolation. That raised a new approach of approximating fractional derivatives and provides some insights for a new applications where the numerical resolution of ordinary fractional differential equations is achieved.

The definition of such fractional order involves an integration represented as a non-local operator. This important feature allows to capture the previous history (memory) when calculating, for example, the time-fractional diffusion wave derivative value of a given function within certain period of time. This could not be achieved based on the classical (integer) derivative order.

The fractional diffusion-wave equation and some types of integral equations, as a mathematical models, are widely used in many physical phenomena, where the exact solution usually is difficult to obtain. Note that the authors of [9] introduced a mathematical model that intermediates between the wave, heat, and transport equations, both time and spatial variations of the corresponding dynamical law are expressed in fractional form (Caputo derivative for the time-variable and Riesz pseudo-differential operator for the spatial one), so that pure wavelike propagation is connected with pure diffusion and transport processes in unified form.

Several authors have reported the higher precision numerical solution with absolute error of $10^{-16}$–$10^{-20}$ for nonlinear Volterra integral equation as in [10] and for fractional diffusion wave equation in [11]. They used the popular collocation method based on some wavelet systems to solve the nontrivial mathematical problems.

Since the number of collocation points is limited by 16 for 1–dimensional or $4 \times 4$ for 2–dimensional problems, we have noticed kind of a numerical phenomenon for each case and specifically for the absolute error. In this paper, we propose a novel numerical method to solve the fractional diffusion-wave equations and nonlinear Fredholm and Volterra integro-differential problems with zero absolute error. We also discuss the proposed method in [10] and proposed a new one to solve the nonlinear Volterra integral equation with absolute error of $0 \times 10^{-31}$. As it has been shown, in every case, there is a numerical phenomenon of error cancellation.

## 2. Fractional Diffusion-Wave Equation

We consider the following fractional diffusion-wave equation involved by the Caputo fractional derivative of order $\alpha > 0$:

$$\mathcal{D}_c^{\alpha} u + \mu u_t - u_{xx} = Q(x,t), \quad 0 \le x,t \le 1, \tag{1}$$

where $u = u(x,t)$, $\mu$ is a damping parameter, and the Caputo fractional derivative for this work is defined as

$$\mathcal{D}_c^{\alpha} u = \frac{1}{\Gamma(2-\alpha)} \int_0^t \frac{u_{\tau\tau}(x,\tau)}{(t-\tau)^{2-\alpha}} d\tau, \quad 1 < \alpha \le 2. \tag{2}$$

The initial and boundary conditions for Equation (1) is given as follows

$$u(x,0) = f_0(x), \quad u_t(x,0) = f_1(x), \quad u(0,t) = g_0(t), \quad u(1,t) = g_1(t), \tag{3}$$

where $\alpha, f_0, f_1, g_0, g_1, Q$ are known functions.

We simulate the problem defined in Equations (1)–(3) based on these given functions. We propose a new numerical method based on Euler wavelets with different sets of collocation points. Surprisingly, the numerical scheme used in this paper achieved zero absolute error. The absolute error of the numerical algorithm is defined on the grid only, which is why we were able to estimate zero absolute error. All examples in the manuscript are not trivial, which is why we believe that this method can be interesting to the international community.

## 3. The New Numerical Scheme

Wavelets are basis set, very well localized functions, and known as a useful tool for solving various types of differential and integral equations. In particular, orthogonal wavelets are used extensively to approximate different types of fractional differential equations in the literature. To solve the proposed problem in Equations (1)–(3), we use wavelets based on Euler polynomials. We define the Euler polynomials $E_1(x), E_2(x)$ and the needed functions for our novel numerical algorithm as follows:

$$
\begin{aligned}
E_1(x) &= -\frac{1}{2} + x, \ E_2(x) = -x + x^2, && (4)\\
I_1^1 &= \int_0^x E_1(t)dt = -\frac{x}{2} + \frac{x^2}{2}, && (5)\\
I_2^1 &= \int_0^x E_2(t)dt = -\frac{x^2}{2} + \frac{x^3}{3}, && (6)\\
I_1^2 &= \int_0^x I_1^1(t)dt = -\frac{x^2}{4} + \frac{x^3}{6}, && (7)\\
I_2^2 &= \int_0^x I_2^1(t)dt = -\frac{x^3}{6} + \frac{x^4}{12}, && (8)\\
I_1^\alpha &= \int_0^x \frac{E_1(\xi)}{(x-\xi)^{2-\alpha}}d\xi = \frac{x^{2-\alpha}(-3+\alpha+2x)}{2(-2+\alpha)(-3+\alpha)} && (9)\\
I_2^\alpha &= \int_0^x \frac{E_2(\xi)}{(x-\xi)^{2-\alpha}}d\xi = -\frac{x^{3-\alpha}(-4+\alpha+2x)}{-6+11(\alpha-1)-6(\alpha-1)^2+(\alpha-1)^3}. && (10)
\end{aligned}
$$

Define $\Psi$ to be the set of all functions given in Equations (4)–(10). For any function $f \in \Psi$, we define the function $\psi(x)$ as follows

$$
\begin{aligned}
\psi(x) &= f(x), \ on \ [0,1],\\
&= 0, \ otherwise.
\end{aligned}
$$

Now, assume that

$$\psi_1 = E_1, \psi_2 = E_2, \psi_{1,1} = I_1^1, \psi_{2,1} = I_2^1, \psi_{1,2} = I_1^2, \psi_{2,2} = I_2^2, \psi_{1,\alpha} = I_1^\alpha, \psi_{2,\alpha} = I_2^\alpha,$$

we define the following set of functions (wavelets) depending on $j,k \in \mathbb{Z}$ as

$$
\begin{aligned}
\psi_1(j,k,x) &= \psi_1(2^jx-k),\\
\psi_2(j,k,x) &= \psi_2(2^jx-k,),\\
\psi(j,k,x) &= (\psi_1(j,k,x)+\psi_2(j,k,x)),\\
\psi^{1,1}(j,k,x) &= \psi_{1,1}(2^jx-k),\\
\psi^{1,2}(j,k,x) &= \psi_{1,2}(2^jx-k),\\
\psi^{2,1}(j,k,x) &= \psi_{2,1}(2^jx-k),\\
\psi^{2,2}(j,k,x) &= \psi_{2,2}(2^jx-k),\\
\psi^{1}(j,k,x) &= (\psi^{1,1}(j,k,x)+\psi^{2,1}(j,k,x))/j,\\
\psi^{2}(j,k,x) &= (\psi^{2,1}(j,k,x)+\psi^{2,2}(j,k,x))/j^2,\\
\psi^{1,\alpha}(j,k,x) &= \psi_{1,\alpha}(2^jx-k),\\
\psi^{2,\alpha}(j,k,x) &= \psi_{2,\alpha}(2^jx-k),\\
\psi^{\alpha}(j,k,x) &= (\psi^{1,\alpha}(j,k,x)+\psi^{2,\alpha}(j,k,x))/j^{\alpha-2}.
\end{aligned}
$$

Recall that, see, e.g., [12], a function $f \in L_2(\mathbb{R})$ can be expanded using the following series,

$$f(x) = \sum_{\ell=1}^{2} \sum_{j,k\in\mathbb{Z}}^{\infty} d^\ell(j,k)\psi^\ell(j,k,x), \tag{11}$$

where,

$$d^\ell(j,k) = \left\langle f, \psi^\ell(j,k,x) \right\rangle = \int_{\mathbb{R}} f(x)\psi^\ell(j,k,x)w(x)dx,$$

for which $\langle \cdot, \cdot \rangle$ denotes the usual inner product over the space $L_2(\mathbb{R})$ and $w$ is a proper weight function. One may truncate Equation (11) by $f_{n,M}$ as

$$f_{n,M} = \sum_{\ell=1}^{2} \sum_{j=0}^{n} \sum_{k=0}^{M-1} d^\ell(j,k)\psi^\ell(j,k,x). \tag{12}$$

In order to solve the proposed problem, we construct a vector $\Psi_f$ of length $M = 2^{n+1}, n \in \mathbb{N}$, such that

$$\Psi_f = (\psi_f, \sigma^\rho(1,0,x), \ldots, \sigma^\rho(2^j,k,x), \ldots, \sigma^\rho(2^n, 2^{n-1}, x)), j = 0,1,2,\ldots,n; k = 0,1,2,\ldots,2^{j-1}, \tag{13}$$

where,

$$\begin{cases} \psi_f = 1, \sigma^\rho = \psi & if\ f = E_1, E_2,\ \rho = 1, \\ \psi_f = x, \sigma^\rho = \psi^1 & if\ f = I_1^1, I_2^1,\ \rho = j, \\ \psi_f = x^2/2, \sigma^\rho = \psi^2 & if\ f = I_1^2, I_2^2,\ \rho = j^2, \\ \psi_f = I_1^\alpha(x), \sigma^\rho = \psi^\alpha & if\ f = I_1^\alpha, I_2^\alpha,\ \rho = j^{\alpha-2}. \end{cases}$$

For example, for $n = 2, \alpha = 3/2$, we have the following:

- When $\psi_f = 1, \rho = 1$, we have

$$\Psi_f = \begin{cases} (1,0,0,0,0,0,0,0) & x \geq 1\ or\ x < 0 \\ \left(1, x^2 - \frac{1}{2}, 0, (2x-1)^2 - \frac{1}{2}, 0,0,0, (4x-3)^2 - \frac{1}{2}\right) & \frac{3}{4} \leq x < 1 \\ \left(1, x^2 - \frac{1}{2}, 0, (2x-1)^2 - \frac{1}{2}, 0,0, (4x-2)^2 - \frac{1}{2}, 0\right) & \frac{1}{2} \leq x < \frac{3}{4} \\ \left(1, x^2 - \frac{1}{2}, 4x^2 - \frac{1}{2}, 0,0, (4x-1)^2 - \frac{1}{2}, 0,0\right) & \frac{1}{4} \leq x < \frac{1}{2} \\ \left(1, x^2 - \frac{1}{2}, 4x^2 - \frac{1}{2}, 0, 16x^2 - \frac{1}{2}, 0,0,0\right) & \text{True} \end{cases}$$

- When $\psi_f = x, \rho = j$, we have

$$\Psi_f = \begin{cases} (x,0,0,0,0,0,0,0) & x \geq 1\ or\ x < 0 \\ \left(x, \frac{1}{6}x(2x^2-3), 0, \frac{1}{12}(16x^3 - 24x^2 + 6x + 1), 0,0,0, \frac{1}{12}(4x-3)^3 + \frac{1}{8}(3-4x)\right) & \frac{3}{4} \leq x < 1 \\ \left(x, \frac{1}{6}x(2x^2-3), 0, \frac{1}{12}(16x^3 - 24x^2 + 6x + 1), 0,0, \frac{1}{12}(64x^3 - 96x^2 + 42x - 5), 0\right) & \frac{1}{2} \leq x < \frac{3}{4} \\ \left(x, \frac{1}{6}x(2x^2-3), \frac{1}{6}x(8x^2-3), 0,0, \frac{16x^3}{3} - 4x^2 + \frac{x}{2} + \frac{1}{24}, 0,0\right) & \frac{1}{4} \leq x < \frac{1}{2} \\ \left(x, \frac{1}{6}x(2x^2-3), \frac{1}{6}x(8x^2-3), 0, \frac{1}{6}x(32x^2-3), 0,0,0\right) & \text{True} \end{cases}$$

- When $\psi_f = x^2/2, \rho = j^2$, we have

$$\Psi_f = \begin{cases} \left(\frac{x^2}{2}, 0,0,0,0,0,0,0\right) & x \geq 1\ or\ x < 0 \\ \left(\frac{x^2}{2}, \frac{1}{12}x^2(x^2-3), 0, \frac{1}{24}(1-2x)^2(2x^2-2x-1), 0,0,0, \frac{1}{96}(3-4x)^2(8x^2-12x+3)\right) & \frac{3}{4} \leq x < 1 \\ \left(\frac{x^2}{2}, \frac{1}{12}x^2(x^2-3), 0, \frac{1}{24}(1-2x)^2(2x^2-2x-1), 0,0, \frac{1}{48}(1-2x)^2(16x^2-16x+1), 0\right) & \frac{1}{2} \leq x < \frac{3}{4} \\ \left(\frac{x^2}{2}, \frac{1}{12}x^2(x^2-3), \frac{1}{12}x^2(4x^2-3), 0,0, \frac{1}{96}(1-4x)^2(8x^2-4x-1), 0,0\right) & \frac{1}{4} \leq x < \frac{1}{2} \\ \left(\frac{x^2}{2}, \frac{1}{12}x^2(x^2-3), \frac{1}{12}x^2(4x^2-3), 0, \frac{4x^4}{3} - \frac{x^2}{4}, 0,0,0\right) & \text{True} \end{cases}$$

- When $\psi_f = I_1^\alpha, \rho = j^{\alpha-2}$, we have

$$\Psi_f = \begin{cases} (2\sqrt{x}, 0,0,0,0,0,0,0) & x \geq 1\ or\ x < 0 \\ \left(2\sqrt{x}, x^2 - \frac{1}{2}, 0, \frac{8x^2-8x+1}{\sqrt{2}}, 0,0,0, 32x^2 - 48x + 17\right) & \frac{3}{4} \leq x < 1 \\ \left(2\sqrt{x}, x^2 - \frac{1}{2}, 0, \frac{8x^2-8x+1}{\sqrt{2}}, 0,0, 32x^2 - 32x + 7, 0\right) & \frac{1}{2} \leq x < \frac{3}{4} \\ \left(2\sqrt{x}, x^2 - \frac{1}{2}, \frac{8x^2-1}{\sqrt{2}}, 0,0, 32x^2 - 16x + 1, 0,0\right) & \frac{1}{4} \leq x < \frac{1}{2} \\ \left(2\sqrt{x}, x^2 - \frac{1}{2}, \frac{8x^2-1}{\sqrt{2}}, 0, 32x^2 - 1, 0,0,0\right) & \text{True} \end{cases}$$

Now, define the solution of the proposed system given in Equations (1)–(3) in the form of a matrix system by the following equation,

$$u_{xxtt} \approx \Psi_E^T(x) \cdot U \cdot \Psi_E(t), \tag{14}$$

where $U$ is a matrix of order $M \times M$ that should be determined using some collocation points, $\Psi_E^T$ is the transpose of the vector $\Psi_E$ and $E$ denotes the set of both functions $E_1$ and $E_1$ that are defined earlier.

Integrating Equation (14) step by step two times with respect to $t$ yields:

$$\begin{aligned} u_{xxt}(x,t) &\approx \Psi_E^T(x) \cdot U \cdot \Psi_{I^1}(t) + F_1''(x), \\ u_{xx}(x,t) &\approx \Psi_E^T(x) \cdot U \cdot \Psi_{I^2}(t) + tF_1''(x) + F_2''(x), \end{aligned}$$

Now, integrating Equation (14) step by step two times for $x$, reveals the following:

$$\begin{aligned} u_x(x,t) &\approx \Psi_{I^1}^T(x) \cdot U \cdot \Psi_{I^2}(t) + t(F_1'(x) - F_1'(0)) + F_2'(x) - F_2'(0) + F_3(t), \\ u(x,t) &\approx \Psi_{I^2}^T(x) \cdot U \cdot \Psi_{I^2}(t) + t(F_1(x) - F_1(0) - xF_1'(0)) + F_2(x) - F_2(0) - xF_2'(0) + xF_3(t) + F_4(t), \end{aligned}$$

where

$$I^1 = \{I_1^1, I_2^1\}, I^2 = \{I_1^2, I_2^2\},$$

and $F_1(x), F_2(x), F_3(t), F_4(t)$ are arbitrary functions that can be determined using the initial and boundary conditions given in Equation (3).

Hence, we have

$$\begin{aligned} u(x,t) &\approx \Psi_{I^2}^T(x) \cdot U \cdot \Psi_{I^2}(t) + t(f_1(x) - (xF_3'(0) + F_4'(0))) + f_0(x) - xF_3(0) - F_4(0) + xF_3(t) + g_0(t), \\ u_t(x,t) &\approx \Psi_{I^2}^T(x) \cdot U \cdot \Psi_{I^1}(t) + f_1(x) - xF_3'(0) - F_4'(0) + xF_3'(t) + g_0'(t), \\ u_{xx}(x,t) &\approx \Psi_E^T(x) \cdot U \cdot \Psi_{I^2}(t) + tf_1''(x) + f_0''(x), \\ u_{tt}(x,t) &\approx \Psi_{I^2}^T(x) \cdot U \cdot \Psi_E(t) + xF_3''(t) + g_0''(t), \\ \mathcal{D}_c^\alpha u(x,t) &\approx \frac{1}{\Gamma(2-\alpha)}\left(-x\Psi_{I^2}^T(x) \cdot U \cdot \Psi_{I^\alpha}(t) + \Psi_{I^2}^T(x) \cdot U \cdot \Psi_{I^\alpha}(t) + F_5(t) + xF_6(t)\right), \end{aligned}$$

where

$$I^\alpha = \{I_1^\alpha, I_2^\alpha\}.$$

Here, we define the functions $F_i$ as follows

$$\begin{aligned} F_4(t) &= g_0(t), \\ F_3(t) &= g_1(t) - g_0(t) - \Psi_{I^2}^T(t) \cdot U \cdot \Psi_{I^2}(t) + tc_1 + c_2, \\ F_5(t) &= \int_0^t \frac{g_0''(\tau)}{(t-\tau)^{2-\alpha}} d\tau, \\ F_6(t) &= \int_0^t \frac{g_1''(\tau) - g_0''(\tau)}{(t-\tau)^{2-\alpha}} d\tau, \\ c_0 &= g_1(0) - 2g_0(0) + f_0(1), \\ c_1 &= -f_1(1) + c_0/2 + g_0(0), \\ c_2 &= -f_0(1) + c_0/2 + g_0(0). \end{aligned}$$

Now, we have all functions needed for the numerical simulation. Let us define $M = 2^{1+n}, n = 1, 2, ..$ as a collocation points and

$$\Delta x = 1/M, s_0 = 0, s_i = s_{i-1} + \Delta x, i = 1, 2, .., M; x_i = t_i = \frac{1}{2}(s_{i-1} + s_i), i = 1, 2, ..., M.$$

Then, we substitute the above equations into the propose system and calculate Equation (1) for each pair of the collocation points as follows

$$\mathcal{D}_c^{\alpha}u(x_i,t_j)+\mu u_t(x_i,t_j)-u_{xx}(x_i,t_j)=Q(x_i,t_j),\quad i,j=1,2,\dots,M. \tag{15}$$

Therefore,

$$\frac{1}{\Gamma(2-\alpha)}\left(-x_i\Psi_{I^2}^T(x_i)\cdot U\cdot\Psi_{I^{\alpha}}(t_j)+\Psi_{I^2}^T(x_i)\cdot U\cdot\Psi_{I^{\alpha}}(t_j)+F_5(t_j)+x_iF_6(t_j)\right)+ \tag{16}$$

$$\mu\left(\Psi_{I^2}^T(x_i)\cdot U\cdot\Psi_{I^1}(t_j)+f_1(x_i)-x_iF_3'(0)-F_4'(0)+x_iF_3'(t_j)+g_0'(t_i)\right)- \tag{17}$$

$$\left(\Psi_E^T(x)\cdot U\cdot\Psi_{I^2}(t)+tf_1''(x)+f_0''(x)\right)=Q(x_i,t_j) \tag{18}$$

Note that Equations (16)–(18) generates an $M\times M$ system of algebraic equations in order to produce our matrix $U$.

## 4. Numerical Performance

In this section, we present some examples of the problem proposed in Equations (1)–(3). The numerical solution demonstrated here achieved a zero absolute error and that was independent from the number of collocation points, damping parameter $\mu$ and fractional value $\alpha$. We noticed that there is a numerical phenomenon behind the error cancellation in this method.

The generated system of algebraic equations given in Equation (15) is not so simple and it is also a matrix; however, for all examples that we consider, the numerical solution is not different from the exact solution in all collocation points and that makes this technique a special and powerful tool capable of achieving such an excellent order of accuracy.

**Example 1.** *Consider the equation*

$$\mathcal{D}_c^{\alpha}u(x,t)+\mu u_t(x,t)-u_{xx}(x,t)=Q(x,t), \tag{19}$$

*where,*

$$Q(x,t)=\frac{1}{\Gamma(2-\alpha)}\int_0^t\frac{u_{\tau\tau}(x,\tau)}{(t-\tau)^{2-\alpha}}d\tau, 1<\alpha\le 2,$$

*with the following initial and boundary condition given as*

$$u(x,0)=x, u_t(x,0)=0, u(0,t)=(2-\alpha)t^2, u(1,t)=1+(2-\alpha)t^2. \tag{20}$$

*The exact solution for this formulation is*

$$u_e(x,t)=x+(2-\alpha)t^2.$$

*Applying our algorithm, Figure 1 presents the exact solution (left) and exact solution with numerical solution (middle and right) computed at $M=8,\mu=1,\alpha=3/2$. The maximum absolute error for the numerical solution is calculated by Mathematica as zero and so it is less than the minimal machine number $2.22507\times10^{-308}$, which means*

$$max|u(x_i,t_j)-u_e(x_i,t_j)|<2.22507\times10^{-308}, i,j=1,2,\dots,M.$$

*Figure 2 shows the visual representation of the values of elements in the matrix generated during solving the related system of algebraic equations for this example.*

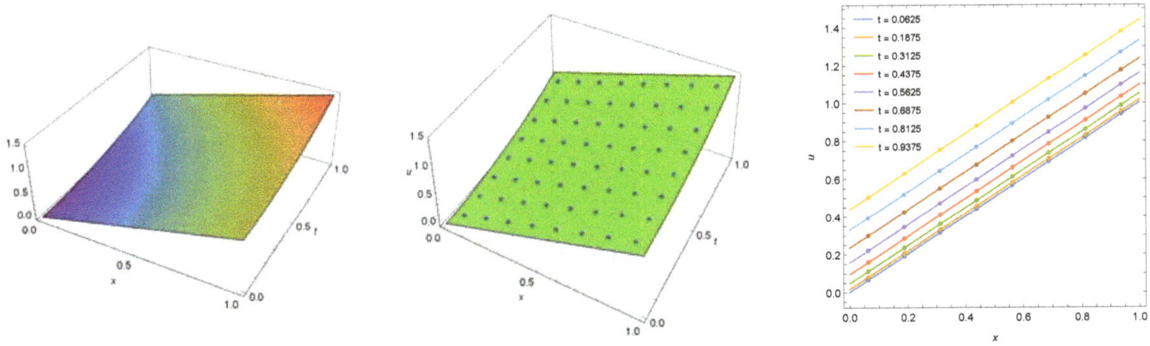


**Figure 1.** The exact solution (**left**) and numerical solution (points) with exact solution (**middle** and **right**) computed for Example 1 when $M = 8, \mu = 1, \alpha = 3/2$.

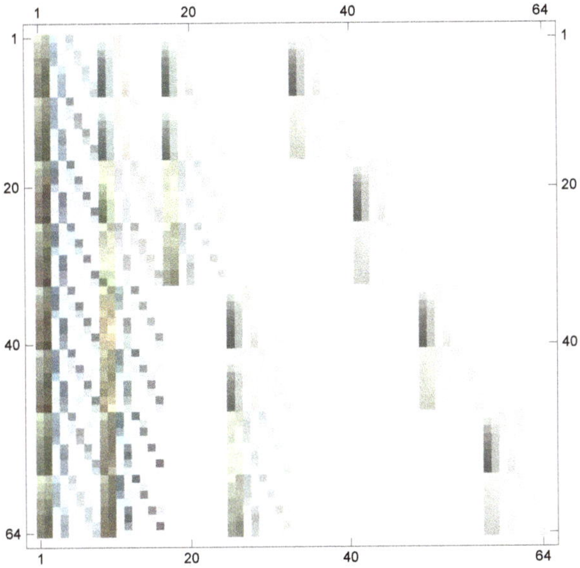


**Figure 2.** The visual representation of the matrix coefficient computed for Example 1 when $M = 8$, $\mu = 1, \alpha = 3/2$.

**Example 2.** *Consider the equation*

$$\mathcal{D}_c^{\alpha} u(x,t) + \mu u_t(x,t) - u_{xx}(x,t) = 0. \tag{21}$$

*with the following initial and boundary condition given as*

$$u(x,0) = \frac{x^2}{2}, u_t(x,0) = \frac{1}{\mu}, u(0,t) = \frac{t}{\mu}, u(1,t) = \frac{1}{2} + \frac{t}{\mu}. \tag{22}$$

*The exact solution for this formulation is*

$$u_e(x,t) = \frac{x^2}{2} + \frac{t}{\mu}.$$

*In Figure 3, we show the exact solution (left) and exact solution with numerical solution (middle and right) computed at $M = 16, \mu = 1, \alpha = 19/10$. Again, the maximum absolute error* *for the numerical solution is recognized by Mathematica as zero. Thus, it is less than the minimal machine number* $2.22507 \times 10^{-308}$.

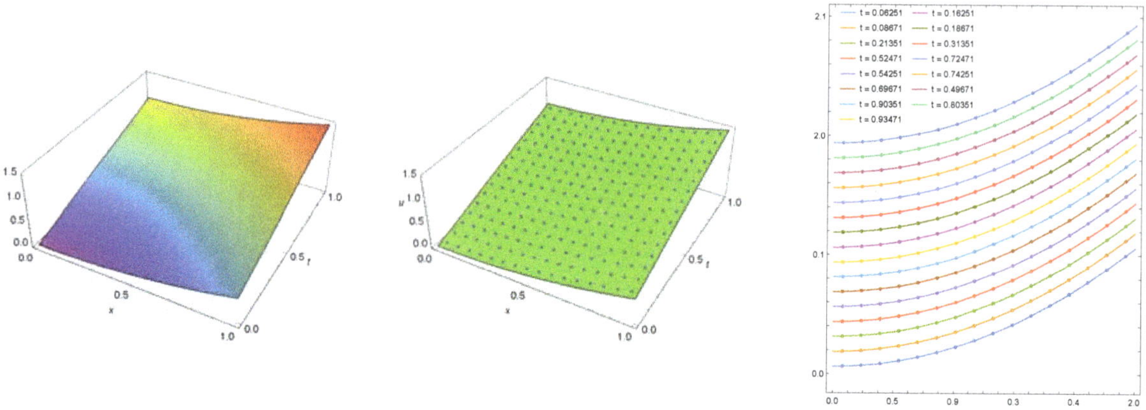


**Figure 3.** The numerical solution (points) with exact solution computed for Example 2 when $M = 16$, $\mu = 1, \alpha = 19/10$.

Figure 4 shows the visual representation of the values of elements in the matrix generated during solving the related system of algebraic equations.

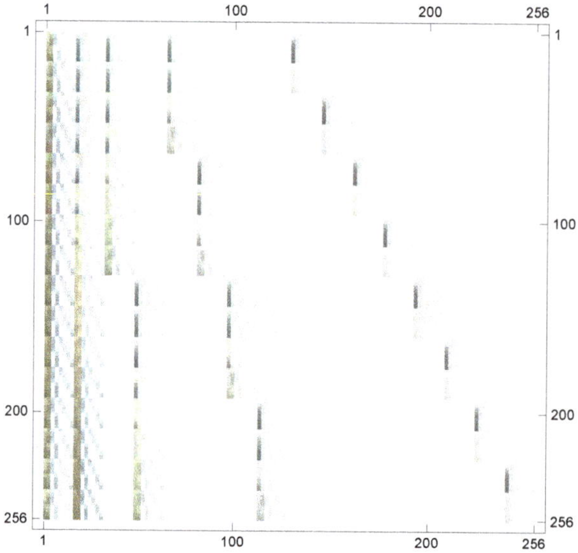

**Figure 4.** The visual representation of the matrix coefficient computed for Example 2 when $M = 16$, $\mu = 1, \alpha = 19/10$.

**Example 3.** *The numerical phenomenon of the error cancellation also occurs for the wave equation. In this case, we have* $\alpha = 2$, *and so Equation (1) turns to the common form of the wave equation given by*

$$u_{tt}(x,t) + \mu u_t(x,t) - u_{xx}(x,t) = Q(x,t), \tag{23}$$

*where,*

$$Q(x,t) = \mu.$$

*The initial and boundary conditions are given as*

$$u(x,0) = x, u_t(x,0) = 1, u(0,t) = t, u(1,t) = 1 + t. \quad (24)$$

*The exact solution of this problem is $u_e(x,t) = x + t$. In Figure 5, we present the exact solution (left) and exact solution with numerical solution (middle and right) computed at $M = 8, \mu = 1, \alpha = 2$. The maximum absolute error for the numerical solution is zero for this case as well.*

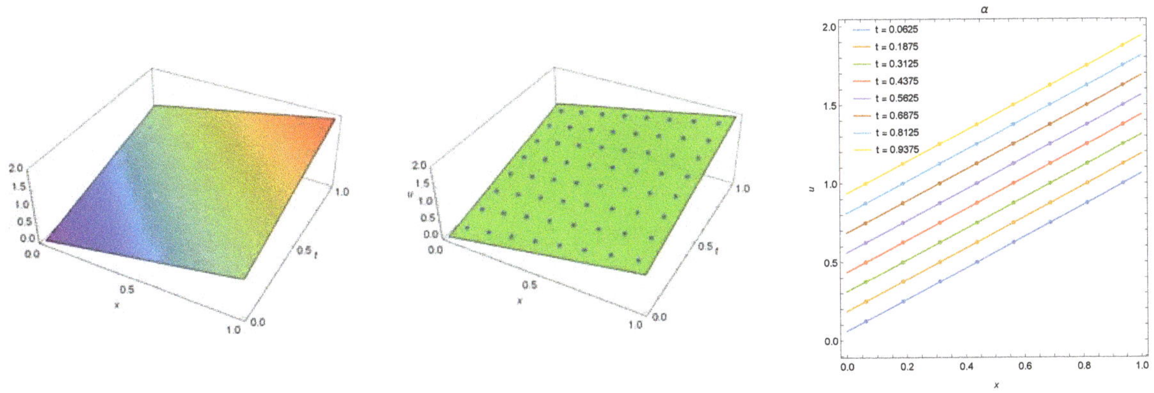


**Figure 5.** The exact solution (**left**) and numerical solution (points) with exact solution (**middle** and **right**) computed for Example 3 with $M = 8, \mu = 1, \alpha = 2$.

**Example 4.** *The numerical phenomenon of the error cancellation also occurs for the wave equation. In this case, we choose $\alpha = 3/2$, and so Equation (1) turns to the common form of the wave equation given by*

$$\mathcal{D}_C^{\alpha} u(x,t) + \mu u_t(x,t) - u_{xx}(x,t) = Q(x,t), \quad (25)$$

*where,*

$$Q(x,t) = \mu x.$$

*The initial and boundary conditions are given as*

$$u(x,0) = 0, u_t(x,0) = x, u(0,t) = 0, u(1,t) = t. \quad (26)$$

*The exact solution of this problem is $u_e(x,t) = xt$. In Figure 6, we present the exact solution (left) and exact solution with numerical solution (middle and right) computed at $M = 8, \mu = 1, \alpha = 2$. The maximal absolute error for the numerical solution is zero. This result does not depend on the number of collocation points, nor the fractional parameters $\alpha$ and $\mu$.*

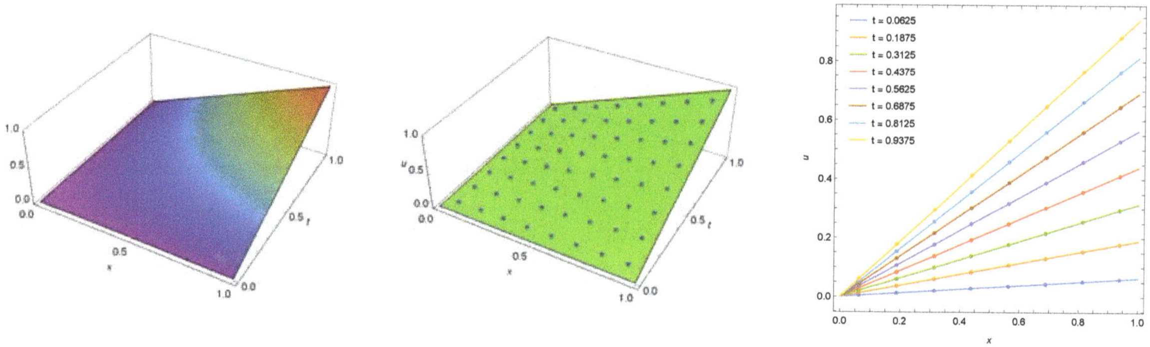


**Figure 6.** The exact solution (**left**) and numerical solution (points) with exact solution (**middle** and **right**) computed for Example 4 with $M = 8, \mu = 1, \alpha = 3/2$.

**Example 5.** *Let us consider another example by involving the fractional parameter* $\alpha$ *in the function* $Q$ *as follows*

$$\mathcal{D}_c^{\alpha} u(x,t) + \mu u_t(x,t) - u_{xx}(x,t) = \frac{2x(1-x)t^{2-\alpha}}{(2-\alpha)\Gamma(2-\alpha)} + 2tx(1-x) + 2t^2. \quad (27)$$

*The initial and boundary conditions are given as*

$$u(x,0) = 0, u_t(x,0) = 0, u(0,t) = 0, u(1,t) = 0. \quad (28)$$

*This example has been considered and discussed for* $\mu = 1$ *by many authors, see, e.g., [11,13,14]. The exact solution for this case has the following form* $u_e = t^2x(1-x)$*. Using our technique, we are able to solve it with a proper setting of precision of the numerical technique. For instance, in Figure 7, we provide the exact solution and numerical solution (points) computed with machine precision of* $1.11022 \times 10^{-16}$ *( shown in Figure 8, left). Increasing precision up to* $10^{-30}$*, we get the numerical solution with zero absolute error (as it shown in Figure 8, right).*

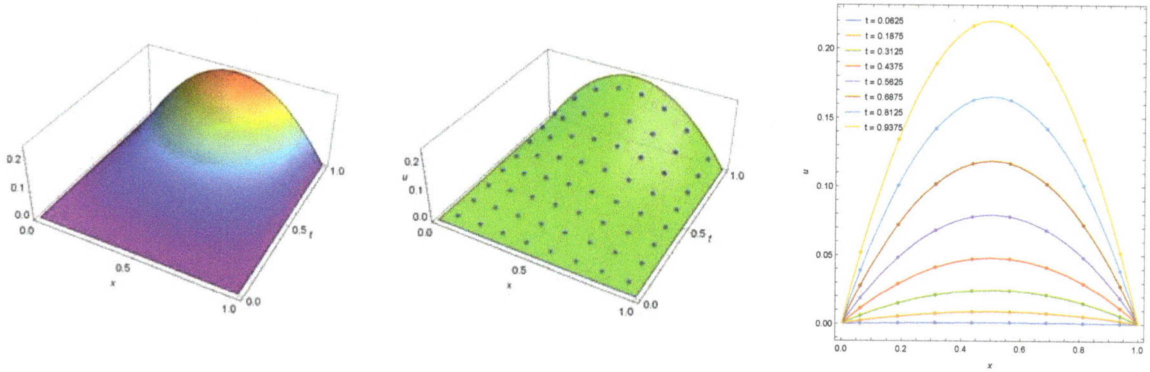


**Figure 7.** The exact solution (**left**) and numerical solution (points) with exact solution (**middle** and **right**) computed for Example 7 for $M = 8, \mu = 1, \alpha = 3/2$.

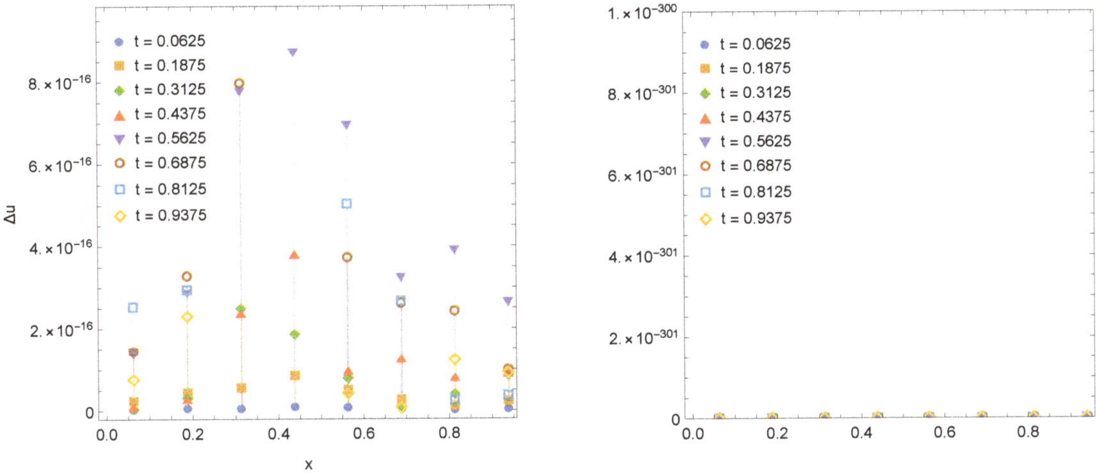


**Figure 8.** The absolute error computed for Example 5 given that $M = 8, \mu = 1, \alpha = 3/2$ with machine precision (**left** sub-figure) and with double precision (**right** sub-figure).

## 5. Numerical Technique for Nonlinear Fredholm and Volterra Integral Equation

Let us now consider the following form of Volterra integral equation of the second kind

$$u(x) = g(x) + \int_0^x K(x,t,u(t))dt, 0 \le x \le 1, \tag{29}$$

where $g$ and $K$ (the kernel) are known functions. It is well known that Equation (29) has a unique solution under following conditions [15]:

(1) $g(x)$ is continues and bounded on $0 \le x \le 1$;
(2) The kernel $K(x,t,u)$ is bounded and uniformly continuous in both $x$ and $t$, for all finite $u$ where $0 \le t \le x \le 1$;
(3) The kernel $K(x,t,u)$ satisfies the uniform Lipschitz condition

$$|K(x,t,u_1) - K(x,t,u_2)| \le L|u_1 - u_2|, \tag{30}$$

for all finite $u_{1,2}$ and $0 \le t \le x \le 1$.

To solve Equation (29), we use Euler wavelets in the form of vector $\Psi_E$ that we defined earlier. Then, we proposed that the numerical solution has the following setting:

$$u(x) = A \cdot \Psi_E(x), \tag{31}$$

where the vector $A = (a_1, a_2, \ldots, a_M)$ can be computed using the collocation technique such that

$$M = 2^{1+n}, n = 1, 2, \ldots,$$

and $\Psi_E(x)$ is defined considering $\rho(j) = 2$.

To do this, we first transform the integral in Equation (29) by substituting

$$t = \frac{x}{2}(s+1), -1 \le s \le 1.$$

Then, this integral turns to the fixed limit integral, and so it can be approximated by a finite sum using the Gauss quadrature rule as follows:

$$\int_0^x K(x,t,u(t))dt = \frac{x}{2}\int_{-1}^{1} K(x, x(s+1)/2, u(x(s+1)/2))ds \tag{32}$$

$$= \frac{x}{2}\sum_{i=1}^{2M} w_i K(x, x(s_i+1)/2, u(x(s_i+1)/2)) + \Delta, \tag{33}$$

where $w_i$ are weights, $s_i$ are points of the Gauss quadrature rule defined on $(-1,1)$, and $\Delta$ is the error of approximation. Substituted Equations (31) and (32) in Equation (29) and using the assumed collocation points, we get a system of algebraic equations:

$$A \cdot \Psi_E(x_j) = g(x_j) + \frac{x_j}{2}\sum_{i=1}^{2M} w_i K(x_j, x_j(s_i+1)/2, A \cdot \Psi_E(x_j(s_i+1)/2)), \tag{34}$$

for $j = 1, 2, ..., M$ and $\Delta = 0$.

The system of nonlinear algebraic equations given in Equation (34) can be solved by using several method. In this work, we use Newton's iterative technique.

## 6. Numerical Examples

The parameters of the Gauss quadrature rule are not exact; however, it can be calculated with high precision of $10^{-60}$, it is possible to solve the system in Equation (34) with absolute error of $0. \times 10^{-31}$. We can consider this solution as a numerical solution with zero absolute error without future estimation. For the examples in this section, the numerical solution has absolute error as of $0. \times 10^{-31}$. Furthermore, we consider some intermediate results computed with machine precision as of $1.11022 \times 10^{-16}$.

**Example 6.** *This example has been discussed by many authors, see for example [16–18]:*

$$u(x) = \frac{x^2}{2}(1 + \cos x^2) + \int_0^x tx^2 \sin(u(t))dt \tag{35}$$

*The exact solution of this equation is given by $u = x^2$. Using an iterative multistep kernel method [16] it is possible to get the numerical solution of Equation (35) with absolute error of $7.8974 \times 10^{-10}$, and using the method proposed in [17], the best result has absolute error of $10^{-6}$. Using our method, we get numerical solution with maximum absolute error of $2.77556 \times 10^{-17}$ computed with the machine precision (Figure 9, left and middle) and of $0 \times 10^{-31}$ computed with double precision and with precision of $10^{-60}$ for the Gauss quadrature rule parameters $w_i, s_i$ (Figure 9, right). Note that, we have used $\rho(j) = 2$ for this case.*

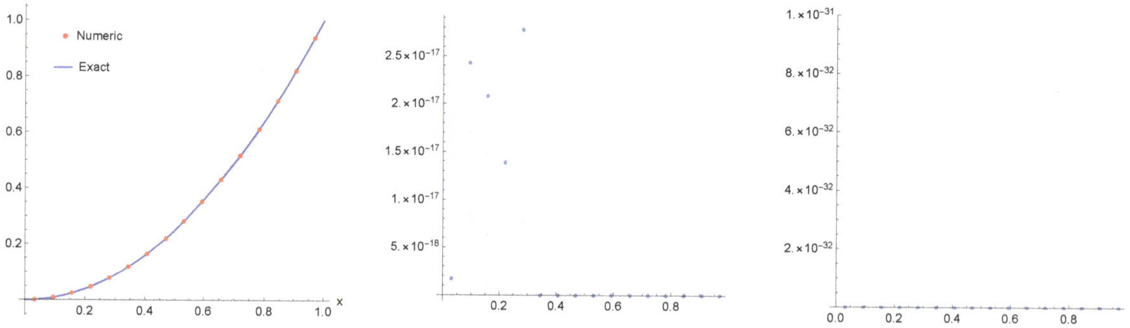


**Figure 9.** The numerical solution (points) with exact solution (**left**) and the absolute error computed for Example 6 with machine precision (**middle**), and with double precision (**right**).

**Example 7.** *Now, we consider the following nonlinear Fredholm integral Equation [19,20]:*

$$u(x) = -x^2 - \frac{x}{3}(2\sqrt{2}-1) + 2 + \int_0^1 xt\sqrt{u(t)}dt \tag{36}$$

*The exact solution for this problem is* $u(x) = 2 - x^2$. *This problem can be solved by the Haar wavelets method as in [19,20] with absolute error of* $3.1 \times 10^{-5}$, $4.2 \times 10^{-6}$, *respectively, where they used 128 collocation points to get into these bounds. With our method, with only 16 collocation points, we have achieved a numerical solution with absolute error of* $6.64685 \times 10^{-20}$ *computed using the machine precision, and as of* $0 \times 10^{-31}$ *computed using a double precision as shown in Figure 10.*

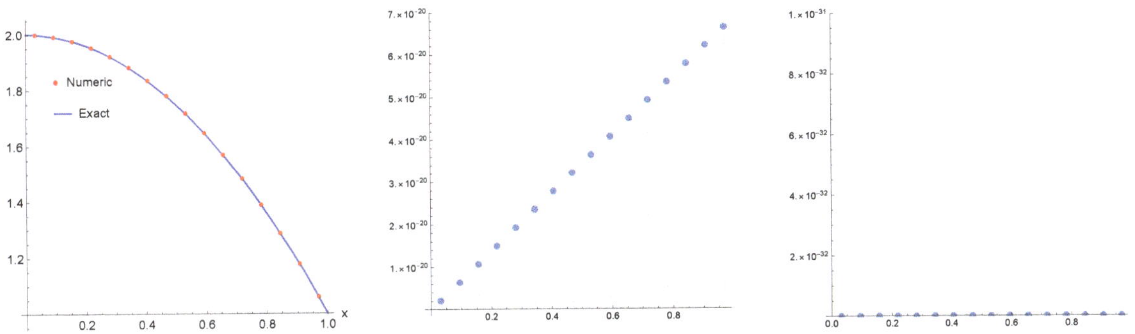


**Figure 10.** The numerical solution (points) with exact solution (**left**) and the absolute error computed for Example 7 with machine precision (**middle**), and with double precision (**right**).

**Example 8.** *We consider now the following nonlinear Volterra integral equation based on two parameters such that*

$$u(x) = x^2 - \frac{x^{5+\beta+\gamma}}{5+\gamma} + \int_0^x x^\beta t^\gamma u^2(t)dt. \tag{37}$$

*The exact solution of this equation is* $u = x^2$. *Numerical experiments with different* $\beta, \gamma$ *shown that for any integer* $\beta, \gamma = 0, 1, 2, \ldots, 27$ *the numerical solution has zero absolute error for all collocation points and for* $n = 3$. *For integer* $\gamma = 0, 1, 2, \ldots, 27$ *and for some* $1 \leq \beta \leq 27$ *including* $\pi$ *and e the numerical solution has zero absolute error. For non integer* $\beta, \gamma > 1$ *there is absolute error that varies from zero up to* $10^{-15}$. *However, we cannot check every* $\beta, \gamma$ *due to numerical limitations. The graphs of the exact, numerical and error results are depicted in Figure 11.*

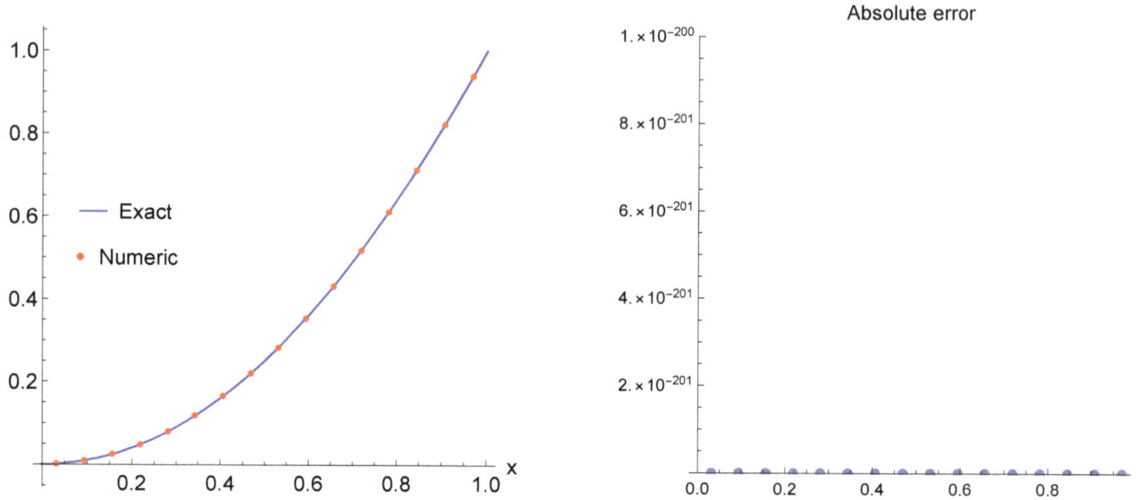


**Figure 11.** The numerical solution (points) with exact solution (**left**) and the absolute error computed for Example 8 (**right**).

**Example 9.** *Finally, we consider the generalized form of Equation (35) based on two parameters as*

$$u(x) = x^2 - \frac{{}_1F_2(\frac{3+\gamma}{4}; \frac{3}{2}, \frac{7+\gamma}{4}; -\frac{x^4}{4})}{3+\gamma} x^{3+\beta+\gamma} + \int_0^x x^{\beta} t^{\gamma} \sin(u(t))dt, \tag{38}$$

*where ${}_1F_2(a;b;z)$ is the generalized hyper-geometric function. The exact solution of this formulation is $u = x^2$. Note that, Equation (35) is a special case of Equation (38) when $\beta = 2, \gamma = 1$. The numerical experiments for any integer $\beta, \gamma = 0, 1, 2, \ldots, 80$ demonstrate a numerical solution with zero absolute error up to $\beta = 30, \gamma = 30$, and then maximum absolute error increases from $9 \times 10^{-50}$ for $\beta = 31, \gamma = 31$ to $1.01 \times 10^{-28}$ for $\beta = 80, \gamma = 80$. For any integer $\gamma = 0, 1, 2, \ldots, 30$ and real $0 \le \beta \le 30$, the numerical solution has zero absolute error for all tested points including $\pi$ and $e$. We present the exact, numerical and error results in Figure 12.*

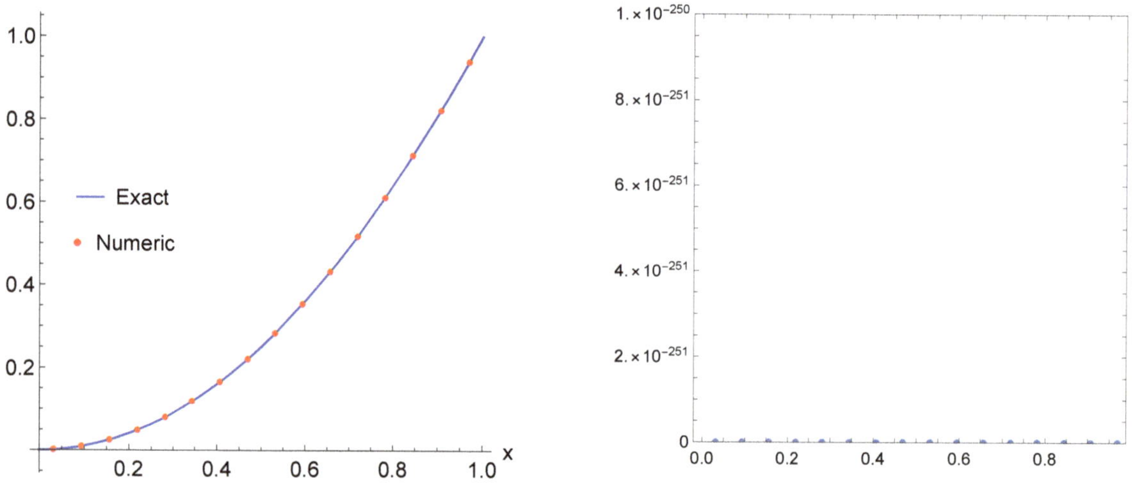


**Figure 12.** The numerical solution (points) with exact solution (**left**) and the absolute error computed for Example 9 (**right**).

## 7. Conclusions

In this work, a novel numerical method based on a proper wavelet systems generated via Euler functions is proposed. The collocation algorithm based on Euler wavelets has been applied to the time-fractional diffusion wave and nonlinear Fredholm and Volterra integral equations. We used some truncated representations based on Euler wavelets to convert the proposed equations to a system of algebraic equations based on specific discretization. The reduced system was converted to a matrix form and simulated using Mathematica software.

We numerically solved a series of examples related to the proposed equations, where the numerical results achieved an exceptional absolute error among other numerical schemes in the literature. We provided some graphical illustrations to show the efficiency of the method.

**Author Contributions:** Conceptualization, M.M. and A.T.; formal analysis, M.M.; investigation, M.M.; resources, M.M. and A.T.; data curation, A.T.; writing—original draft preparation, A.T.; writing—review and editing, M.M. and M.A.; visualization, M.M. and A.T.; supervision, M.M.; project administration, M.M.; funding acquisition, M.A. All authors have read and agreed to the published version of the manuscript.

**Funding:** This research was funded by Abu Dhabi University research fund Grant number/center 19300514.

**Institutional Review Board Statement:** Not applicable.

**Informed Consent Statement:** Not applicable.

**Data Availability Statement:** Not applicable.

**Acknowledgments:** We would like to thank the anonymous reviewers for their valuable comments and suggestions.

**Conflicts of Interest:** The authors declare no conflict of interest.

## References

1. Ghanbari, B.; Atangana, A. A new application of fractional Atangana–Baleanu derivatives: Designing ABC-fractional masks in image processing. *Phys. A Stat. Mech. Appl.* **2020**, *542*, 123516. [CrossRef]
2. Mohammad, M.; Trounev, A.; Cattani, C. An efficient method based on framelets for solving fractional Volterra integral equations. *Entropy* **2020**, *22*, 824. [CrossRef] [PubMed]
3. Mohammad, M.; Trounev, A. On the dynamical modeling of COVID-19 involving Atangana-Baleanu fractional derivative and based on Daubechies framelet simulations. *Chaos Solitons Fractals* **2020**, *140*, 110171. [CrossRef] [PubMed]
4. Mohammad, M.; Trounev, A. Fractional nonlinear Volterra–Fredholm integral equations involving Atangana–Baleanu fractional derivative: Framelet applications. *Adv. Differ. Equ.* **2020**, *618*, 1–15. [CrossRef]
5. Mohammad, M.; Trounev, A.; Cattani, C. The dynamics of COVID-19 in the UAE based on fractional derivative modeling using Riesz wavelets simulation. *Adv. Differ. Equ.* **2021**, *2021*, 1–14. [CrossRef] [PubMed]
6. Alshbool, H.M.; Isik, O.; Hashim, I. Fractional Bernstein series solution of fractional diffusion equations with error estimate. *Axioms* **2021**, *10*, 6. [CrossRef]
7. Mohammad, M. Biorthogonal-Wavelet-Based Method for Numerical Solution of Volterra Integral Equations. *Entropy* **2019**, *2019*, 21. [CrossRef]
8. Ferrari, A.; Gadella, M.; Lara, L.P.; Santillan, E. Approximate solutions of one dimensional systems with fractional calculus. *Int. J. Mod. Phys. C* **2020**, *31*, 2050092. [CrossRef]
9. Fernando, O.R.; Oscar, R.O. Transition from the Wave Equation to Either the Heat or the Transport Equations through Fractional Differential Expressions. *Symmetry* **2018**, *10*, 524. [CrossRef]
10. Rajagopal, N.; Balaji, S.; Seethalakshmi, R.; Balaji, V.S. A new numerical method for fractional order volterra integro-differential equations. *Ain Shams Eng. J.* **2020**, *11*, 171–177. [CrossRef]
11. Zhou, F.; Xu, X. Numerical solution of time-fractional diffusion-wave equations via chebyshev wavelets collocation method. *Adv. Math. Phys.* **2017**, *2017*, 1–17. [CrossRef]
12. Mohammad, M.; Lin, E.B. Gibbs phenomenon in tight framelet expansions. *Commun. Nonlinear Sci. Numer. Simul.* **2018**, *55*, 84–92. [CrossRef]
13. Heydari, M.H.; Hooshmandasl, M.R.; Maalek Ghaini, F.M.; Cattani, C. Wavelets method for the time fractional diffusion-wave equation. *Phys. Lett. A* **2015**, *379*, 71–76.

14. Chen, J.; Liu, F.; Anh, V.; Shen, S.; Liu, Q.; Liao, C. The analytical solution and numerical solution of the fractional diffusion-wave equation with damping. *Appl. Math. Comput.* **2012**, *219*, 1737–1748. [CrossRef]
15. Tricomi, F.G. Integral equations. In *Pure and Applied Mathematics*; Dover Publications: New York, NY, USA, 1957; Volume 5, p. 238.
16. Heydari, M.; Shivanian, E.; Azarnavid, B.; Abbasbandy, S. An iterative multistep kernel based method for nonlinear volterra integral and integro-differential equations of fractional order. *J. Comput. Appl. Math.* **2019**, *361*, 97–112. [CrossRef]
17. Babolian, E.; Javadi, S.; Moradi, E. Error analysis of re- producing kernel hilbert space method for solving functional integral equations. *J. Comput. Appl. Math.* **2016**, *300*, 300–311. [CrossRef]
18. Ketabchi, R.; Mokhtari, R.; Babolian, E. Some error estimates for solving volterra integral equations by using the reproducing kernel method. *J. Comput. Appl. Math.* **2015**, *273*, 245–250. [CrossRef]
19. Aziz, I. New algorithms for the numerical solution of nonlinear fredholm and volterra integral equations using haar wavelets. *J. Comput. Appl. Math.* **2013**, *239*, 333–345. [CrossRef]
20. Lepik, Ü.; Tamme, E. Solution of nonlinear fredholm integral equations via the haar wavelet method. *Proc. Est. Acad. Sci. Phys. Math.* **2007**, *56*, 17–27.

*axioms* MDPI

*Article*

# Sequential Riemann–Liouville and Hadamard–Caputo Fractional Differential Systems with Nonlocal Coupled Fractional Integral Boundary Conditions

**Chanakarn Kiataramkul [1,†], Weera Yukunthorn [2,†], Sotiris K. Ntouyas [3,4,†] and Jessada Tariboon [1,*]**

1 Intelligent and Nonlinear Dynamic Innovations Research Center, Department of Mathematics, Faculty of Applied Science, King Mongkut's University of Technology North Bangkok, Bangkok 10800, Thailand; chanakarn.k@sci.kmutnb.ac.th
2 Faculty of Science and Technology, Kanchanaburi Rajabhat University, Kanchanaburi 71000, Thailand; w.yukunthorn@kru.ac.th
3 Department of Mathematics, University of Ioannina, 451 10 Ioannina, Greece; sntouyas@uoi.gr
4 Nonlinear Analysis and Applied Mathematics (NAAM)-Research Group, Department of Mathematics, Faculty of Science, King Abdulaziz University, P.O. Box 80203, Jeddah 21589, Saudi Arabia
* Correspondence: jessada.t@sci.kmutnb.ac.th
† These authors contributed equally to this work.

**Abstract:** In this paper, we initiate the study of existence of solutions for a fractional differential system which contains mixed Riemann–Liouville and Hadamard–Caputo fractional derivatives, complemented with nonlocal coupled fractional integral boundary conditions. We derive necessary conditions for the existence and uniqueness of solutions of the considered system, by using standard fixed point theorems, such as Banach contraction mapping principle and Leray–Schauder alternative. Numerical examples illustrating the obtained results are also presented.

**Keywords:** coupled systems; Riemann–Liouville fractional derivative; Hadamard–Caputo fractional derivative; nonlocal boundary conditions; existence; fixed point

**Citation:** Kiataramkul, C.; Yukunthorn, W.; Ntouyas, S.K.; Tariboon, J. Sequential Riemann–Liouville and Hadamard–Caputo Fractional Differential Systems with Nonlocal Coupled Fractional Integral Boundary Conditions. *Axioms* **2021**, *10*, 174. https://doi.org/10.3390/axioms10030174

Academic Editor: Jorge E. Macías Díaz

Received: 30 June 2021
Accepted: 30 July 2021
Published: 31 July 2021



## 1. Introduction

Fractional differential equations have played a very important role in almost all branches of applied sciences because they are considered a valuable tool to model many real world problems. For details and applications, we refer the reader to monographs [1–11]. The study of coupled systems of fractional differential equations is important as such systems appear in various problems in applied sciences, see [12–16].

On the other hand, multi-term fractional differential equations also gained considerable importance in view of their occurrence in the mathematical models of certain real world problems, such as behavior of real materials [17], continuum and statistical mechanics [18], an inextensible pendulum with fractional damping terms [19], etc.

Fractional differential equations have several kinds of fractional derivatives, such as Riemann–Liouville fractional derivative, Caputo fractional derivative, Hadamard fractional derivative, and so on. In the literature, there are many papers studying existence and uniqueness results for boundary value problems and coupled systems of fractional differential equations and used mixed types of fractional derivatives, see [20–29]. In [23], the following boundary value problem is considered:

$$\begin{cases} {}^{RL}D^q[{}^CD^r x(t) - g(t,x(t))] = f(t,x(t)), \ \ 0 < t < T, \\ x(\eta) = \phi(x), \ \ I^p x(T) = h(x), \end{cases} \tag{1}$$

where ${}^{RL}D^{q}$, ${}^{C}D^{r}$ are Riemann–Liouville and Caputo fractional derivatives of orders $q, r \in (0,1)$, respectively, $I^{p}$ is the Riemann–Liouville fractional integral of order $p > 0$, $f, g : J \times \mathbb{R} \to \mathbb{R}$ are given continuous functions and $\phi, h : C(J, \mathbb{R}) \to \mathbb{R}$ are two given functionals.

In [24], the authors initiated the study of a coupled system of sequential mixed Caputo and Hadamard fractional differential equations supplemented with coupled separated boundary conditions. To be more precisely, in [24], existence and uniqueness results are established for the following couple system:

$$\begin{cases} {}^{C}D^{p_1}\,{}^{H}D^{q_1}x(t) = f(t, x(t), y(t)), & t \in [a,b], \\ {}^{H}D^{q_2}\,{}^{C}D^{p_2}y(t) = g(t, x(t), y(t)), & t \in [a,b], \\ \alpha_1 x(a) + \alpha_2\,{}^{C}D^{p_2}y(a) = 0, & \beta_1 x(b) + \beta_2\,{}^{C}D^{p_2}y(b) = 0, \\ \alpha_3 y(a) + \alpha_4\,{}^{H}D^{q_1}x(a) = 0, & \beta_3 y(b) + \beta_4\,{}^{H}D^{q_1}x(b) = 0, \end{cases} \tag{2}$$

where ${}^{C}D^{p_i}$ and ${}^{H}D^{q_i}$ are notations of the Caputo and Hadamard fractional derivatives of orders $p_i$ and $q_i$, respectively, $0 < p_i, q_i \leq 1$, $i = 1,2$, $f, g : [a,b] \times \mathbb{R} \times \mathbb{R} \to \mathbb{R}$ are nonlinear continuous functions, $a > 0$, $\alpha_i \in \mathbb{R} \setminus \{0\}$, $\beta_i \in \mathbb{R}$, $i = 1, \ldots, 4$.

In [25], the existence and uniqueness of solutions for neutral fractional order coupled systems containing mixed Caputo and Riemann–Liouville sequential fractional derivatives were studied, complemented with nonlocal multi-point and Riemann–Stieltjes integral multi-strip conditions of the form:

$$\begin{cases} {}^{c}D^{q}({}^{RL}D^{p}x(t) + f(t, x(t)) = g(t, x(t), y(t)), \ t \in (0,1), \\ {}^{c}D^{q_1}({}^{RL}D^{p_1}y(t) + f_1(t, y(t)) = g_1(t, x(t), y(t)), \ t \in (0,1), \\ x(0) = 0, \quad bx(1) = a\displaystyle\int_0^1 y(s)dH(s) + \sum_{i=1}^{n} \alpha_i \int_{\xi_i}^{\eta_i} y(s)ds, \\ y(0) = 0, \quad b_1 y(1) = a_1 \displaystyle\int_0^1 x(s)dH(s) + \sum_{j=1}^{m} \beta_j \int_{\theta_j}^{\zeta_j} x(s)ds, \end{cases} \tag{3}$$

where ${}^{RL}D^{p}, {}^{RL}D^{p_1}$, and ${}^{c}D^{q}, {}^{c}D^{q_1}$ denote the Riemann–Liouville and Caputo fractional derivatives of order $p, p_1$ and $q, q_1$, respectively, $0 < p, p_1, q, q_1 \leq 1$, with $1 < p + q \leq 2, 1 < p_1 + q_1 \leq 2$, $f, f_1$ and $g, g_1$ are given continuous functions, $0 < \xi_i < \eta_i < 1$, $0 < \theta_j < \zeta_j < 1$, $\alpha_i, \beta_j \in \mathbb{R}, i = 1, 2, \ldots, n$, $j = 1, 2, \ldots, m, a, a_1, b, b_1 \in \mathbb{R}$, and $H(\cdot)$ is a function of bounded variation.

To the best of the authors' knowledge, there are some papers dealing with sequential mixed type fractional derivatives, but we not find in the literature papers dealing with coupled systems with sequential Riemann–Liouville and Hadamard–Caputo fractional differential equations. Motivated by this fact, and to fill this gap, in the present paper, we investigate the existence and uniqueness of solutions for the following coupled system of sequential Riemann–Liouville and Hadamard–Caputo fractional differential equations supplemented with nonlocal coupled fractional integral boundary conditions

$$\begin{cases} {}^{RL}D^{p_1}\left({}^{HC}D^{q_1}x\right)(t) = f(t, x(t), y(t)), & t \in [0,T], \\ {}^{RL}D^{p_2}\left({}^{HC}D^{q_2}y\right)(t) = g(t, x(t), y(t)), & t \in [0,T], \\ {}^{HC}D^{q_1}x(0) = 0, \quad x(T) = \displaystyle\sum_{i=1}^{m} \alpha_i\,{}^{RL}I^{\beta_i}y(\xi_i), \\ {}^{HC}D^{q_2}y(0) = 0, \quad y(T) = \displaystyle\sum_{j=1}^{k} \lambda_j\,{}^{RL}I^{\delta_j}x(\eta_j), \end{cases} \tag{4}$$

where ${}^{RL}D^{p_r}$ and ${}^{HC}D^{q_r}$ are the Riemann–Liouville and Hadamard–Caputo fractional derivatives of orders $p_r$ and $q_r$, respectively, $0 < p_r, q_r < 1$, $r = 1, 2$, the nonlinear continuous functions $f, g : [0, T] \times \mathbb{R}^2 \to \mathbb{R}$, ${}^{RL}I^{\phi}$ is the Riemann–Liouville fractional integral of orders $\phi > 0$, $\phi \in \{\beta_i, \delta_j\}$ and given constants $\alpha_i, \lambda_j \in \mathbb{R}$, $\xi_i, \eta_j \in (0, T)$, $i = 1, \ldots, m$, $j = 1, \ldots, k$.

Let us compare the coupled system (4) with the coupled system (2) studied in [24].

(i) In (2), we studied a coupled system consisting by mixed Caputo and Hadamard fractional derivatives, while, in (4), we consider mixed Riemann–Liouville and Hadamard–Caputo fractional derivatives.

(ii) In (2), the coupled system was subjected to coupled separated boundary conditions, while, in (4), the coupled system is subjected to nonlocal coupled fractional integral boundary conditions.

(iii) In both problems (4) and (2), the same method is used to establish the existence and uniqueness results, and based on standard fixed point theorems, but their presentation in the framework of mixed coupled Caputo and Hadamard and Riemann–Liouville and Hadamard–Caputo fractional derivatives is new.

We also notice that the conditions ${}^{HC}D^{q_1}x(0) = 0$ and ${}^{HC}D^{q_2}y(0) = 0$ are necessary for the well-posedness of the problem.

By using standard tools from fixed point theory in the present study, we establish existence and uniqueness results for the coupled system (4). The Banach contraction mapping principle is used to obtain the existence and uniqueness result, while an existence result is derived via the Leray–Schauder alternative.

The rest of the paper is organized as follows. In Section 2, some basic definitions and lemmas from fractional calculus are recalled. In addition, an auxiliary lemma, concerning a linear variant of (4), which plays a key role in obtaining the main results, is proved. The main results are presented in Section 3, which also include examples illustrating the basic results. We emphasize that our results are new and significantly enhance the existing literature on the topic, and, as far as we know, they are the first results concerning a coupled system with sequential mixed Riemann–Liouville and Hadamard–Caputo fractional derivatives.

## 2. Preliminaries

In this section, we introduce some notations and definitions of fractional calculus [2,30] and present preliminary results needed in our proofs later.

**Definition 1.** *The Riemann–Liouville fractional derivative of order $p > 0$ of a continuous function $f : (0, \infty) \to \mathbb{R}$ is defined by*

$$ {}^{RL}D^{p} f(t) = \frac{1}{\Gamma(n-p)} \left(\frac{d}{dt}\right)^{n} \int_0^t (t-s)^{n-p-1} f(s) ds, \quad n-1 < p < n, $$

*where $n = [p] + 1$, $[p]$ denotes the integer part of a real number $p$ and $\Gamma$ is the Gamma function defined by $\Gamma(p) = \int_0^{\infty} e^{-s} s^{p-1} ds$.*

**Definition 2.** *The Riemann–Liouville fractional integral of order $p$ of a function $f : (0, \infty) \to \mathbb{R}$, is defined as*

$$ {}^{RL}I^{p} f(t) = \frac{1}{\Gamma(q)} \int_0^t (t-s)^{p-1} f(s) ds, \quad p > 0, $$

*provided the right side is pointwise defined on $\mathbb{R}_+$.*

**Definition 3.** *For an at least n-times differentiable function $g : (0,\infty) \to \mathbb{R}$, the Hadamard–Caputo derivative of fractional order $q > 0$ is defined as*

$$^{HC}D^q g(t) = \frac{1}{\Gamma(n-q)} \int_0^t \left(\log\frac{t}{s}\right)^{n-q-1} \delta^n g(s)\frac{ds}{s}, \quad n-1 < q < n, \quad n = [q]+1,$$

*where $\delta = t\frac{d}{dt}$ and $\log(\cdot) = \log_e(\cdot)$.*

**Definition 4.** *The Hadamard fractional integral of order $q > 0$ is defined as*

$$^{H}I^q g(t) = \frac{1}{\Gamma(\alpha)} \int_0^t \left(\log\frac{t}{s}\right)^{q-1} g(s)\frac{ds}{s},$$

*provided the integral exists.*

**Lemma 1** (see [2]). *Let $p > 0$. Then, for $y \in C(0,T) \cap L(0,T)$, it holds that*

$$^{RL}I^p\left(^{RL}D^p y\right)(t) = y(t) + c_1 t^{p-1} + c_2 t^{p-2} + \cdots + c_n t^{p-n},$$

*where $c_i \in \mathbb{R}$, $i = 1,2,\ldots,n$ and $n-1 < p < n$.*

**Lemma 2** ([30]). *Let $u \in AC^n_\delta[0,T]$ or $C^n_\delta[0,T]$ and $q \in \mathbb{C}$, where $X^n_\delta[0,T] = \{g : [0,T] \to \mathbb{C} : \delta^{n-1}g(t) \in X[0,T]\}$. Then, we have*

$$^{H}I^q(^{HC}D^q)u(t) = u(t) + c_0 + c_1\log t + c_2(\log t)^2 + \cdots + c_{n-1}(\log t)^{n-1},$$

*where $c_i \in \mathbb{R}$, $i = 0,1,2,\ldots,n-1$ $(n = [q]+1)$.*

**Lemma 3** ([2], p. 113). *Let $q > 0$ and $\beta > 0$ be given constants. Then, the following formula*

$$^{H}I^q t^\beta = \beta^{-q} t^\beta,$$

*holds.*

Next, the integral equations are obtained by transformation of a linear variant of problem (4). For convenience in computation, we set some constants

$$\Omega_1 = \sum_{i=1}^{m} \frac{\alpha_i \xi_i^{\beta_i}}{\Gamma(\beta_i+1)}, \quad \Omega_2 = \sum_{j=1}^{k} \frac{\lambda_j \eta_j^{\delta_j}}{\Gamma(\delta_j+1)}$$

and $\Lambda = \Omega_1\Omega_2 - 1 \neq 0$.

**Lemma 4.** *Let $f^*, g^* \in C([a,b],\mathbb{R})$ be two given functions. Then, the linear system equivalent to problem (4) of sequential Riemann–Liouville and Hadamard–Caputo fractional differential equations*

$$\begin{cases} ^{RL}D^{p_1}\left(^{HC}D^{q_1}x\right)(t) = f^*(t), & t \in [0,T], \\ ^{RL}D^{p_2}\left(^{HC}D^{q_2}y\right)(t) = g^*(t), & t \in [0,T], \\ ^{HC}D^{q_1}x(0) = 0, & x(T) = \sum_{i=1}^{m} \alpha_i {}^{RL}I^{\beta_i}y(\xi_i), \\ ^{HC}D^{q_2}y(0) = 0, & y(T) = \sum_{j=1}^{k} \lambda_j {}^{RL}I^{\delta_j}x(\eta_j), \end{cases} \tag{5}$$

*can be written into integral equations as*

$$
\begin{aligned}
x(t) \quad &= \quad -\frac{1}{\Lambda}\sum_{i=1}^{m}\alpha_i\,{}^{RL}I^{\beta_i}\Big({}^{H}I^{q_2}\Big({}^{RL}I^{p_2}g^*\Big)\Big)(\xi_i)+\frac{1}{\Lambda}{}^{H}I^{q_1}\Big({}^{RL}I^{p_1}f^*\Big)(T)\\
&\quad +\frac{\Omega_1}{\Lambda}{}^{H}I^{q_2}\Big({}^{RL}I^{p_2}g^*\Big)(T)-\frac{\Omega_1}{\Lambda}\sum_{j=1}^{k}\lambda_j\,{}^{RL}I^{\delta_j}\Big({}^{H}I^{q_1}\Big({}^{RL}I^{p_1}f^*\Big)\Big)(\eta_j)\\
&\quad +{}^{H}I^{q_1}\Big({}^{RL}I^{p_1}f^*\Big)(t), \qquad (6)
\end{aligned}
$$

*and*

$$
\begin{aligned}
y(t) \quad &= \quad -\frac{\Omega_2}{\Lambda}\sum_{i=1}^{m}\alpha_i\,{}^{RL}I^{\beta_i}\Big({}^{H}I^{q_2}\Big({}^{RL}I^{p_2}g^*\Big)\Big)(\xi_i)+\frac{\Omega_2}{\Lambda}{}^{H}I^{q_1}\Big({}^{RL}I^{p_1}f^*\Big)(T)\\
&\quad +\frac{1}{\Lambda}{}^{H}I^{q_2}\Big({}^{RL}I^{p_2}g^*\Big)(T)-\frac{1}{\Lambda}\sum_{j=1}^{k}\lambda_j\,{}^{RL}I^{\delta_j}\Big({}^{H}I^{q_1}\Big({}^{RL}I^{p_1}f^*\Big)\Big)(\eta_j)\\
&\quad +{}^{H}I^{q_2}\Big({}^{RL}I^{p_2}g^*\Big)(t). \qquad (7)
\end{aligned}
$$

**Proof.** For $t \in [0, T]$ and by taking the Riemann–Liouville fractional integral of order $p_1$ to the first equation of (5), we obtain

$$ {}^{HC}D^{q_1}x(t) = c_1 t^{p_1-1} + {}^{RL}I^{p_1}f^*(t), \quad c_1 \in \mathbb{R}. \qquad (8)$$

Similarly, for the second equation of (5), we have

$$ {}^{HC}D^{q_2}y(t) = d_1 t^{p_2-1} + {}^{RL}I^{p_2}g^*(t), \quad d_1 \in \mathbb{R}. \qquad (9)$$

Since $0 < p_r < 1, r = 1, 2$, the conditions ${}^{HC}D^{q_1}x(0) = 0$ and ${}^{HC}D^{q_2}y(0) = 0$ imply $c_1 = 0$ and $d_1 = 0$, respectively. Applying the Hadamard fractional integral of orders $q_1$ and $q_2$ to (8) and (9), respectively, and substituting the values of $c_1, d_1$, we get

$$ x(t) = c_0 + {}^{H}I^{q_1}\Big({}^{RL}I^{p_1}f^*\Big)(t), \qquad (10)$$

and

$$ y(t) = d_0 + {}^{H}I^{q_2}\Big({}^{RL}I^{p_2}g^*\Big)(t). \qquad (11)$$

Now, we consider the terms

$$ \sum_{i=1}^{m}\alpha_i\,{}^{RL}I^{\beta_i}y(\xi_i) = d_0\sum_{i=1}^{m}\frac{\alpha_i\xi_i^{\beta_i}}{\Gamma(\beta_i+1)}+\sum_{i=1}^{m}\alpha_i\,{}^{RL}I^{\beta_i}\Big({}^{H}I^{q_2}\Big({}^{RL}I^{p_2}g^*\Big)\Big)(\xi_i) \qquad (12)$$

and

$$ \sum_{j=1}^{k}\lambda_j\,{}^{RL}I^{\delta_j}x(\eta_j) = c_0\sum_{j=1}^{k}\frac{\lambda_j\eta_j^{\delta_j}}{\Gamma(\delta_j+1)}+\sum_{j=1}^{k}\lambda_j\,{}^{RL}I^{\delta_j}\Big({}^{H}I^{q_1}\Big({}^{RL}I^{p_1}f^*\Big)\Big)(\eta_j). \qquad (13)$$

Consequently, by (10)–(13) and boundary fractional integral conditions in (5), it follows that

$$
\begin{aligned}
c_0 \quad &= \quad -\frac{1}{\Lambda}\sum_{i=1}^{m}\alpha_i\,{}^{RL}I^{\beta_i}\Big({}^{H}I^{q_2}\Big({}^{RL}I^{p_2}g^*\Big)\Big)(\xi_i)+\frac{1}{\Lambda}{}^{H}I^{q_1}\Big({}^{RL}I^{p_1}f^*\Big)(T)\\
&\quad +\frac{\Omega_1}{\Lambda}{}^{H}I^{q_2}\Big({}^{RL}I^{p_2}g^*\Big)(T)-\frac{\Omega_1}{\Lambda}\sum_{j=1}^{k}\lambda_j\,{}^{RL}I^{\delta_j}\Big({}^{H}I^{q_1}\Big({}^{RL}I^{p_1}f^*\Big)\Big)(\eta_j),
\end{aligned}
$$

and

$$
\begin{aligned}
d_0 &= -\frac{\Omega_2}{\Lambda}\sum_{i=1}^{m}\alpha_i\,{}^{RL}I^{\beta_i}\left({}^{H}I^{q_2}\left({}^{RL}I^{p_2}g^*\right)\right)(\xi_i) + \frac{\Omega_2}{\Lambda}{}^{H}I^{q_1}\left({}^{RL}I^{p_1}f^*\right)(T) \\
&\quad + \frac{1}{\Lambda}{}^{H}I^{q_2}\left({}^{RL}I^{p_2}g^*\right)(T) - \frac{1}{\Lambda}\sum_{j=1}^{k}\lambda_j\,{}^{RL}I^{\delta_j}\left({}^{H}I^{q_1}\left({}^{RL}I^{p_1}f^*\right)\right)(\eta_j),
\end{aligned}
$$

Substituting the values of $c_0$ and $d_0$ in (10) and (11), we obtain integral equations in (6) and (7), respectively, as desired.

The converse follows by direct computation. This completes the proof. □

Next, we establish formulas for multiple fractional integrals of Riemann–Liouville and Hadamard types.

**Lemma 5.** *Let $a, b, c > 0$ be constants. Then, we have*

*(i)*

$$
{}^{H}I^{b}\left({}^{RL}I^{a}(1)\right)(t) = \frac{a^{-b}t^{a}}{\Gamma(a+1)}.
$$

*(ii)*

$$
{}^{RL}I^{c}\left({}^{H}I^{b}\left({}^{RL}I^{a}(1)\right)\right)(t) = \frac{a^{-b}}{\Gamma(a+c+1)}t^{a+c}.
$$

**Proof.** Since ${}^{RL}I^{a}(1) = \dfrac{t^{a}}{\Gamma(a+1)}$, we have

$$
{}^{H}I^{b}\left({}^{RL}I^{a}(1)\right)(t) = \frac{1}{\Gamma(a+1)}{}^{H}I^{b}t^{a} = \frac{a^{-b}t^{a}}{\Gamma(a+1)}, \tag{14}
$$

by using Lemma 3, and (i) is proved. To prove (ii), taking the Riemann–Liouville fractional integral of order $c > 0$ in (14), we have

$$
{}^{RL}I^{c}\left({}^{H}I^{b}\left({}^{RL}I^{a}(1)\right)\right)(t) = \frac{a^{-b}}{\Gamma(a+1)}{}^{RL}I^{c}t^{a} = \frac{a^{-b}}{\Gamma(a+c+1)}t^{a+c},
$$

from ${}^{RL}I^{c}t^{a} = \dfrac{\Gamma(a+1)}{\Gamma(a+c+1)}t^{a+c}$. The proof is completed. □

**Corollary 1.** *Let constants $p_r, q_r$, $r = 1, 2$, $\beta_i, \xi_i, \delta_j, \eta_j$ be defined in problem (4). Then, from Lemma 5, we have*

$$
\begin{aligned}
{}^{H}I^{q_1}\left({}^{RL}I^{p_1}1\right)(T) &= \frac{p_1^{-q_1}T^{p_1}}{\Gamma(p_1+1)}, \\
{}^{H}I^{q_2}\left({}^{RL}I^{p_2}1\right)(T) &= \frac{p_2^{-q_2}T^{p_2}}{\Gamma(p_2+1)}, \\
{}^{RL}I^{\beta_i}\left({}^{H}I^{q_2}\left({}^{RL}I^{p_2}1\right)\right)(\xi_i) &= \frac{p_2^{-q_2}}{\Gamma(p_2+\beta_i+1)}\xi_i^{p_2+\beta_i}, \\
{}^{RL}I^{\delta_j}\left({}^{H}I^{q_1}\left({}^{RL}I^{p_1}1\right)\right)(\eta_j) &= \frac{p_1^{-q_1}}{\Gamma(p_1+\delta_j+1)}\eta_j^{p_1+\delta_j},
\end{aligned}
$$

*which will be used in the next section.*

## 3. Main Results

Let $\mathcal{C} = C([0,T],\mathbb{R})$ be the Banach space of all continuous functions from $[0,T]$ to $\mathbb{R}$. Let $X = \{x(t) : x(t) \in C^2([0,T],\mathbb{R})\}$ be the space endowed with the norm $\|x\| =$

$\sup\{|x(t)|, t \in [0,T]\}$. Obviously, $(X, \|\cdot\|)$ is a Banach space. Next, we set $Y = \{y(t) : y(t) \in C^2([0,T],\mathbb{R})\}$ with the norm $\|y\| = \sup\{|y(t)|, t \in [0,T]\}$. The product space $(X \times Y, \|(x,y)\|)$ is Banach space with the norm $\|(x,y)\| = \|x\| + \|y\|$.

In the following, for brevity, we use the subscript notation

$$h_{x,y}(t) = h(t, x(t), y(t)), \ \ h \in \{f, g\}, \tag{15}$$

in fractional integral as

$${}^{RL}I^{p}h_{x,y}(\phi) = \frac{1}{\Gamma(p)}\int_a^{\phi}(\phi - s)^{p-1}h(s, x(s), y(s))\,ds, \tag{16}$$

where $\phi \in \{t, T, \xi_i, \eta_j\}$. In addition, we use it in multiple fractional integrations.

In view of Lemma 4, we define the operator $\mathcal{P} : X \times Y \to X \times Y$ by

$$\mathcal{P}(x,y)(t) = \begin{pmatrix} \mathcal{P}_1(x,y)(t) \\ \mathcal{P}_2(x,y)(t) \end{pmatrix},$$

where

$$\begin{aligned}
\mathcal{P}_1(x,y)(t) \ =\ & -\frac{1}{\Lambda}\sum_{i=1}^{m}\alpha_i\, {}^{RL}I^{\beta_i}\left({}^{H}I^{q_2}\left({}^{RL}I^{p_2}g_{x,y}\right)\right)(\xi_i) + \frac{1}{\Lambda}{}^{H}I^{q_1}\left({}^{RL}I^{p_1}f_{x,y}\right)(T) \\
& + \frac{\Omega_1}{\Lambda}{}^{H}I^{q_2}\left({}^{RL}I^{p_2}g_{x,y}\right)(T) - \frac{\Omega_1}{\Lambda}\sum_{j=1}^{k}\lambda_j\, {}^{RL}I^{\delta_j}\left({}^{H}I^{q_1}\left({}^{RL}I^{p_1}f_{x,y}\right)\right)(\eta_j) \\
& + {}^{H}I^{q_1}\left({}^{RL}I^{p_1}f_{x,y}\right)(t)
\end{aligned}$$

and

$$\begin{aligned}
\mathcal{P}_2(x,y)(t) \ =\ & -\frac{\Omega_2}{\Lambda}\sum_{i=1}^{m}\alpha_i\, {}^{RL}I^{\beta_i}\left({}^{H}I^{q_2}\left({}^{RL}I^{p_2}g_{x,y}\right)\right)(\xi_i) + \frac{\Omega_2}{\Lambda}{}^{H}I^{q_1}\left({}^{RL}I^{p_1}f_{x,y}\right)(T) \\
& + \frac{1}{\Lambda}{}^{H}I^{q_2}\left({}^{RL}I^{p_2}g_{x,y}\right)(T) - \frac{1}{\Lambda}\sum_{j=1}^{k}\lambda_j\, {}^{RL}I^{\delta_j}\left({}^{H}I^{q_1}\left({}^{RL}I^{p_1}f_{x,y}\right)\right)(\eta_j) \\
& + {}^{H}I^{q_2}\left({}^{RL}I^{p_2}g_{x,y}\right)(t).
\end{aligned}$$

For computational convenience, we set

$$\begin{aligned}
M_1 &= \left(\frac{1+|\Lambda|}{|\Lambda|}\right)\left(\frac{p_1^{-q_1}T^{p_1}}{\Gamma(p_1+1)}\right) + \frac{|\Omega_1|}{|\Lambda|}\left(p_1^{-q_1}\sum_{j=1}^{k}\frac{|\lambda_j|\eta_j^{p_1+\delta_j}}{\Gamma(p_1+\delta_j+1)}\right), \\
M_2 &= \frac{|\Omega_1|}{|\Lambda|}\left(\frac{p_2^{-q_2}T^{p_2}}{\Gamma(p_2+1)}\right) + \frac{1}{|\Lambda|}\left(p_2^{-q_2}\sum_{i=1}^{m}\frac{|\alpha_i|\xi_i^{p_2+\beta_i}}{\Gamma(p_2+\beta_i+1)}\right), \\
M_3 &= \frac{|\Omega_2|}{|\Lambda|}\left(\frac{p_1^{-q_1}T^{p_1}}{\Gamma(p_1+1)}\right) + \frac{1}{|\Lambda|}\left(p_1^{-q_1}\sum_{j=1}^{k}\frac{|\lambda_j|\eta_j^{p_1+\delta_j}}{\Gamma(p_1+\delta_j+1)}\right), \\
M_4 &= \left(\frac{1+|\Lambda|}{|\Lambda|}\right)\left(\frac{p_2^{-q_2}T^{p_2}}{\Gamma(p_2+1)}\right) + \frac{|\Omega_2|}{|\Lambda|}\left(p_2^{-q_2}\sum_{i=1}^{m}\frac{|\alpha_i|\xi_i^{p_2+\beta_i}}{\Gamma(p_2+\beta_i+1)}\right).
\end{aligned}$$

In the first result, Banach's contraction mapping principle is used to prove existence and uniqueness of solutions of system (4).

**Theorem 1.** *Suppose that $f, g : [0,T] \times \mathbb{R}^2 \to \mathbb{R}$ are continuous functions. In addition, we assume that $f, g$ satisfies the Lipchitz condition:*
*$(H_1)$ there exist constants $m_i, n_i$, $i = 1,2$*

$$|f(t,u_1,v_1) - f(t,u_2,v_2)| \le m_1|u_1 - u_2| + m_2|v_1 - v_2|$$

*and*

$$|g(t,u_1,v_1) - g(t,u_2,v_2)| \leq n_1|u_1 - u_2| + n_2|v_1 - v_2|,$$

*for all* $t \in [0,T]$ *and* $u_i, v_i \in \mathbb{R}$, $i = 1,2$. *Then, the system (4) has a unique solution on* $[0,T]$, *if*

$$(M_1 + M_3)(m_1 + m_2) + (M_2 + M_4)(n_1 + n_2) < 1. \tag{17}$$

**Proof.** Let us define $\sup_{t\in[0,T]} f(t,0,0) = N_1 < \infty$ and $\sup_{t\in[0,T]} g(t,0,0) = N_2 < \infty$. Choose a constant $r > 0$ satisfying

$$r > \frac{(M_1 + M_3)N_1 + (M_2 + M_4)N_2}{1 - [(M_1 + M_3)(m_1 + m_2) + (M_2 + M_4)(n_1 + n_2)]}.$$

At first, we shall show that the set $\mathcal{P}B_r \subset B_r$, where a ball $B_r = \{(x,y) \in X \times Y : \|(x,y)\| \leq r\}$. For $(x,y) \in B_r$, and using

$$|f_{x,y}| \leq |f_{x,y} - f_{0,0}| + |f_{0,0}| \leq m_1\|x\| + m_2\|y\| + N_1,$$

and

$$|g_{x,y}| \leq |g_{x,y} - g_{0,0}| + |g_{0,0}| \leq n_1\|x\| + n_2\|y\| + N_2,$$

we get relations

$$\begin{aligned}
&|\mathcal{P}_1(x,y)(t)| \\
\leq\ & \frac{1}{|\Lambda|}\sum_{i=1}^{m}|\alpha_i|\,{}^{RL}I^{\beta_i}\left({}^{H}I^{q_2}\left({}^{RL}I^{p_2}|g_{x,y}|\right)\right)(\xi_i) + \frac{1}{|\Lambda|}{}^{H}I^{q_1}\left({}^{RL}I^{p_1}|f_{x,y}|\right)(T) \\
&+ \frac{|\Omega_1|}{|\Lambda|}{}^{H}I^{q_2}\left({}^{RL}I^{p_2}|g_{x,y}|\right)(T) + \frac{|\Omega_1|}{|\Lambda|}\sum_{j=1}^{k}|\lambda_j|\,{}^{RL}I^{\delta_j}\left({}^{H}I^{q_1}\left({}^{RL}I^{p_1}|f_{x,y}|\right)\right)(\eta_j) \\
&+ {}^{H}I^{q_1}\left({}^{RL}I^{p_1}|f_{x,y}|\right)(T) \\
\leq\ & \frac{1}{|\Lambda|}\sum_{i=1}^{m}|\alpha_i|\,{}^{RL}I^{\beta_i}\left({}^{H}I^{q_2}\left({}^{RL}I^{p_2}1\right)\right)(\xi_i)(n_1\|x\| + n_2\|y\| + N_2) \\
&+ \frac{1}{|\Lambda|}{}^{H}I^{q_1}\left({}^{RL}I^{p_1}1\right)(T)(m_1\|x\| + m_2\|y\| + N_1) \\
&+ \frac{|\Omega_1|}{|\Lambda|}{}^{H}I^{q_2}\left({}^{RL}I^{p_2}1\right)(T)(n_1\|x\| + n_2\|y\| + N_2) \\
&+ \frac{|\Omega_1|}{|\Lambda|}\sum_{j=1}^{k}|\lambda_j|\,{}^{RL}I^{\delta_j}\left({}^{H}I^{q_1}\left({}^{RL}I^{p_1}1\right)\right)(\eta_j)(m_1\|x\| + m_2\|y\| + N_1) \\
&+ {}^{H}I^{q_1}\left({}^{RL}I^{p_1}1\right)(T)(m_1\|x\| + m_2\|y\| + N_1) \\
=\ & \frac{1}{|\Lambda|}\left(p_2^{-q_2}\sum_{i=1}^{m}\frac{|\alpha_i|\xi_i^{p_2+\beta_i}}{\Gamma(p_2+\beta_i+1)}\right)(n_1\|x\| + n_2\|y\| + N_2) \\
&+ \frac{1}{|\Lambda|}\left(\frac{p_1^{-q_1}T^{p_1}}{\Gamma(p_1+1)}\right)(m_1\|x\| + m_2\|y\| + N_1) \\
&+ \frac{|\Omega_1|}{|\Lambda|}\left(\frac{p_2^{-q_2}T^{p_2}}{\Gamma(p_2+1)}\right)(n_1\|x\| + n_2\|y\| + N_2) \\
&+ \frac{|\Omega_1|}{|\Lambda|}\left(p_1^{-q_1}\sum_{j=1}^{k}\frac{|\lambda_j|\eta_j^{p_1+\delta_j}}{\Gamma(p_1+\delta_j+1)}\right)(m_1\|x\| + m_2\|y\| + N_1) \\
&+ \left(\frac{p_1^{-q_1}T^{p_1}}{\Gamma(p_1+1)}\right)(m_1\|x\| + m_2\|y\| + N_1) \\
=\ & M_1(m_1\|x\| + m_2\|y\| + N_1) + M_2(n_1\|x\| + n_2\|y\| + N_2) \\
=\ & (M_1m_1 + M_2n_1)\|x\| + (M_1m_2 + M_2n_2)\|y\| + M_1N_1 + M_2N_2 \\
\leq\ & [M_1(m_1 + m_2) + M_2(n_1 + n_2)]r + M_1N_1 + M_2N_2.
\end{aligned}$$

Therefore, we deduce that

$$\|\mathcal{P}_1(x,y)\| \leq [M_1(m_1+m_2)+M_2(n_1+n_2)]r + M_1N_1 + M_2N_2.$$

In a similar way of computation, we get

$$\begin{aligned}
|\mathcal{P}_2(x,y)(t)| \leq\ & \frac{|\Omega_2|}{|\Lambda|}\sum_{i=1}^{m}|\alpha_i|\,{}^{RL}I^{\beta_i}\left({}^{H}I^{q_2}\left({}^{RL}I^{p_2}1\right)\right)(\xi_i)(n_1\|x\|+n_2\|y\|+N_2) \\
&+\frac{|\Omega_2|}{|\Lambda|}{}^{H}I^{q_1}\left({}^{RL}I^{p_1}1\right)(T)(m_1\|x\|+m_2\|y\|+N_1) \\
&+\frac{1}{|\Lambda|}{}^{H}I^{q_2}\left({}^{RL}I^{p_2}1\right)(T)(n_1\|x\|+n_2\|y\|+N_2) \\
&+\frac{1}{|\Lambda|}\sum_{j=1}^{k}|\lambda_j|\,{}^{RL}I^{\delta_j}\left({}^{H}I^{q_1}\left({}^{RL}I^{p_1}1\right)\right)(\eta_j)(m_1\|x\|+m_2\|y\|+N_1) \\
&+{}^{H}I^{q_2}\left({}^{RL}I^{p_2}1\right)(T)(n_1\|x\|+n_2\|y\|+N_2) \\
=\ & \frac{|\Omega_2|}{|\Lambda|}\left(p_2^{-q_2}\sum_{i=1}^{m}\frac{|\alpha_i|\xi_i^{p_2+\beta_i}}{\Gamma(p_2+\beta_i+1)}\right)(n_1\|x\|+n_2\|y\|+N_2) \\
&+\frac{|\Omega_2|}{|\Lambda|}\left(\frac{p_1^{-q_1}T^{p_1}}{\Gamma(p_1+1)}\right)(m_1\|x\|+m_2\|y\|+N_1) \\
&+\frac{1}{|\Lambda|}\left(\frac{p_2^{-q_2}T^{p_2}}{\Gamma(p_2+1)}\right)(n_1\|x\|+n_2\|y\|+N_2) \\
&+\frac{1}{|\Lambda|}\left(p_1^{-q_1}\sum_{j=1}^{k}\frac{|\lambda_j|\eta_j^{p_1+\delta_j}}{\Gamma(p_1+\delta_j+1)}\right)(m_1\|x\|+m_2\|y\|+N_1) \\
&+\left(\frac{p_2^{-q_2}T^{p_2}}{\Gamma(p_2+1)}\right)(n_1\|x\|+n_2\|y\|+N_2) \\
=\ & M_3(m_1\|x\|+m_2\|y\|+N_1)+M_4(n_1\|x\|+n_2\|y\|+N_2),
\end{aligned}$$

which yields

$$\|\mathcal{P}_2(x,y)\| \leq [M_3(m_1+m_2)+M_4(n_1+n_2)]r + M_3N_1 + M_4N_2.$$

Then, we conclude that

$$\begin{aligned}
\|\mathcal{P}(x,y)\| \leq\ & [M_1(m_1+m_2)+M_2(n_1+n_2)]r + M_1N_1 + M_2N_2 \\
&+[M_3(m_1+m_2)+M_4(n_1+n_2)]r + M_3N_1 + M_4N_2 \leq r,
\end{aligned}$$

which leads to $\mathcal{P}B_r \subset B_r$.

In the next step, we will show that the $\mathcal{P}$ is a contraction operator. For any $(x_1,y_1)$, $(x_2,y_2) \in X \times Y$, we have

$$
\begin{aligned}
& |\mathcal{P}_1(x_1,y_1)(t) - \mathcal{P}_1(x_2,y_2)(t)| \\
\leq\ & \frac{1}{|\Lambda|}\sum_{i=1}^{m}|\alpha_i|\, {}^{RL}I^{\beta_i}\left({}^{H}I^{q_2}\left({}^{RL}I^{p_2}|g_{x_1,y_1} - g_{x_2,y_2}|\right)\right)(\xi_i) \\
& + \frac{1}{|\Lambda|}{}^{H}I^{q_1}\left({}^{RL}I^{p_1}|f_{x_1,y_1} - f_{x_2,y_2}|\right)(T) + \frac{|\Omega_1|}{|\Lambda|}{}^{H}I^{q_2}\left({}^{RL}I^{p_2}|g_{x_1,y_1} - g_{x_2,y_2}|\right)(T) \\
& + \frac{|\Omega_1|}{|\Lambda|}\sum_{j=1}^{k}|\lambda_j|\, {}^{RL}I^{\delta_j}\left({}^{H}I^{q_1}\left({}^{RL}I^{p_1}|f_{x_1,y_1} - f_{x_2,y_2}|\right)\right)(\eta_j) \\
& + {}^{H}I^{q_1}\left({}^{RL}I^{p_1}|f_{x_1,y_1} - f_{x_2,y_2}|\right)(T) \\
\leq\ & \frac{1}{|\Lambda|}\sum_{i=1}^{m}|\alpha_i|\, {}^{RL}I^{\beta_i}\left({}^{H}I^{q_2}\left({}^{RL}I^{p_2}1\right)\right)(\xi_i)(n_1\|x_1 - x_2\| + n_2\|y_1 - y_2\|) \\
& + \frac{1}{|\Lambda|}{}^{H}I^{q_1}\left({}^{RL}I^{p_1}1\right)(T)(m_1\|x_1 - x_2\| + m_2\|y_1 - y_2\|) \\
& + \frac{|\Omega_1|}{|\Lambda|}{}^{H}I^{q_2}\left({}^{RL}I^{p_2}1\right)(T)(n_1\|x_1 - x_2\| + n_2\|y_1 - y_2\|) \\
& + \frac{|\Omega_1|}{|\Lambda|}\sum_{j=1}^{k}|\lambda_j|\, {}^{RL}I^{\delta_j}\left({}^{H}I^{q_1}\left({}^{RL}I^{p_1}1\right)\right)(\eta_j)(m_1\|x_1 - x_2\| + m_2\|y_1 - y_2\|) \\
& + {}^{H}I^{q_1}\left({}^{RL}I^{p_1}1\right)(T)(m_1\|x_1 - x_2\| + m_2\|y_1 - y_2\|) \\
=\ & M_1(m_1\|x_1 - x_2\| + m_2\|y_1 - y_2\|) + M_2(n_1\|x_1 - x_2\| + n_2\|y_1 - y_2\|) \\
=\ & (M_1m_1 + M_2n_1)\|x_1 - x_2\| + (M_1m_2 + M_2n_2)\|y_1 - y_2\|.
\end{aligned}
$$

Then, we get the result that

$$
\|\mathcal{P}_1(x_1,y_1) - \mathcal{P}_1(x_2,y_2)\| \leq M_1(m_1 + m_2) + M_2(n_1 + n_2)(\|x_1 - x_2\| + \|y_1 - y_2\|). \tag{18}
$$

In addition, we have

$$
\begin{aligned}
& |\mathcal{P}_2(x_1,y_1)(t) - \mathcal{P}_2(x_2,y_2)(t)| \\
\leq\ & \frac{|\Omega_2|}{|\Lambda|}\sum_{i=1}^{m}|\alpha_i|\, {}^{RL}I^{\beta_i}\left({}^{H}I^{q_2}\left({}^{RL}I^{p_2}1\right)\right)(n_1\|x_1 - x_2\| + n_2\|y_1 - y_2\|) \\
& + \frac{|\Omega_2|}{|\Lambda|}{}^{H}I^{q_1}\left({}^{RL}I^{p_1}1\right)(T)(m_1\|x_1 - x_2\| + m_2\|y_1 - y_2\|) \\
& + \frac{1}{|\Lambda|}{}^{H}I^{q_2}\left({}^{RL}I^{p_2}1\right)(T)(n_1\|x_1 - x_2\| + n_2\|y_1 - y_2\|) \\
& + \frac{1}{|\Lambda|}\sum_{j=1}^{k}|\lambda_j|\, {}^{RL}I^{\delta_j}\left({}^{H}I^{q_1}\left({}^{RL}I^{p_1}1\right)\right)(\eta_j)(m_1\|x_1 - x_2\| + m_2\|y_1 - y_2\|) \\
& + {}^{H}I^{q_2}\left({}^{RL}I^{p_2}1\right)(T)(n_1\|x_1 - x_2\| + n_2\|y_1 - y_2\|) \\
=\ & M_3(m_1\|x_1 - x_2\| + m_2\|y_1 - y_2\|) + M_4(n_1\|x_1 - x_2\| + n_2\|y_1 - y_2\|) \\
=\ & (M_3m_1 + M_4n_1)\|x_1 - x_2\| + (M_3m_2 + M_4n_2)\|y_1 - y_2\|,
\end{aligned}
$$

which yields

$$
\|\mathcal{P}_2(x_1,y_1) - \mathcal{P}_2(x_2,y_2)\| \leq M_3(m_1 + m_2) + M_4(n_1 + n_2)(\|x_1 - x_2\| + \|y_1 - y_2\|). \tag{19}
$$

The above results in (18) and (19) imply

$$
\begin{aligned}
\|\mathcal{P}(x_1,y_1) - \mathcal{P}(x_2,y_2)\| \leq\ & [(M_1 + M_3)(m_1 + m_2) + (M_2 + M_4)(n_1 + n_2)] \\
& \times(\|x_1 - x_2\| + \|y_1 - y_2\|).
\end{aligned}
$$

Since $(M_1 + M_3)(m_1 + m_2) + (M_2 + M_4)(n_1 + n_2) < 1$, then the operator $\mathcal{P}$ is a contraction. From the benefits of Banach's fixed point theorem, the operator $\mathcal{P}$ has a unique fixed point, which is the unique solution of (4) on $[0, T]$. The proof is completed. □

The Leray–Schauder alternative is applied to our second existence result.

**Lemma 6.** *(Leray–Schauder alternative) [31]. Let $Q : U \to U$ be a completely continuous operator. Let*

$$\mu(Q) = \{x \in U : x = \theta Q(x) \text{ for some } 0 < \theta < 1\}.$$

*Then, either the set $\mu(Q)$ is unbounded, or $Q$ has at least one fixed point.*

**Theorem 2.** *Suppose that there exist constants $a_r, b_r \geq 0$ for $r = 1, 2$ and $a_0, b_0 > 0$. In addition, for any $u, v \in \mathbb{R}$, we assume that*

$$\begin{aligned} |f(t,u,v)| &\leq a_0 + a_1|u| + a_2|v|, \\ |g(t,u,v)| &\leq b_0 + b_1|u| + b_2|v|. \end{aligned}$$

*If $(M_1 + M_3)a_1 + (M_2 + M_4)b_1 < 1$ and $(M_1 + M_3)a_2 + (M_2 + M_4)b_2 < 1$, then (4) has at least one solution on $[0, T]$.*

**Proof.** The first task of the proof is to show that the operator $\mathcal{P} : X \times Y \to X \times Y$ is completely continuous. The continuity of the functions $f, g$ on $[0, T] \times \mathbb{R} \times \mathbb{R}$ can be used to claim that the operator $\mathcal{P}$ is continuous. Now, we let $\Phi$ be the bounded subset of $X \times Y$. Then, there exist positive constants $G_1$ and $G_2$ such that

$$|f(t,x,y)| \leq G_1, \ |g(t,x,y)| \leq G_2, \ \forall (x,y) \in \Phi.$$

For any $(x, y) \in \Phi$, we have

$$\begin{aligned} |\mathcal{P}_1(x,y)(t)| \leq\ & \frac{1}{|\Lambda|}\sum_{i=1}^{m}|\alpha_i|\,{}^{RL}I^{\beta_i}\left({}^{H}I^{q_2}\left({}^{RL}I^{p_2}|g_{x,y}|\right)\right)(\xi_i) + \frac{1}{|\Lambda|}{}^{H}I^{q_1}\left({}^{RL}I^{p_1}|f_{x,y}|\right)(T) \\ & + \frac{|\Omega_1|}{|\Lambda|}{}^{H}I^{q_2}\left({}^{RL}I^{p_2}|g_{x,y}|\right)(T) + \frac{|\Omega_1|}{|\Lambda|}\sum_{j=1}^{k}|\lambda_j|\,{}^{RL}I^{\delta_j}\left({}^{H}I^{q_1}\left({}^{RL}I^{p_1}|f_{x,y}|\right)\right)(\eta_j) \\ & + {}^{H}I^{q_1}\left({}^{RL}I^{p_1}|f_{x,y}|\right)(T) \\ \leq\ & \frac{1}{|\Lambda|}\left(p_2^{-q_2}\sum_{i=1}^{m}\frac{|\alpha_i|\xi_i^{p_2+\beta_i}}{\Gamma(p_2+\beta_i+1)}\right)G_2 + \frac{1}{|\Lambda|}\left(\frac{p_1^{-q_1}T^{p_1}}{\Gamma(p_1+1)}\right)G_1 \\ & + \frac{|\Omega_1|}{|\Lambda|}\left(\frac{p_2^{-q_2}T^{p_2}}{\Gamma(p_2+1)}\right)G_2 + \frac{|\Omega_1|}{|\Lambda|}\left(p_1^{-q_1}\sum_{j=1}^{k}\frac{|\lambda_j|\eta_j^{p_1+\delta_j}}{\Gamma(p_1+\delta_j+1)}\right)G_1 \\ & + \left(\frac{p_1^{-q_1}T^{p_1}}{\Gamma(p_1+1)}\right)G_1, \end{aligned}$$

which leads to

$$\|\mathcal{P}_1(x,y)\| \leq G_1M_1 + G_2M_2.$$

Furthermore, we get

$$\begin{aligned}\|\mathcal{P}_2(x,y)\| &\leq \frac{|\Omega_2|}{|\Lambda|}\sum_{i=1}^{m}|\alpha_i|\,{}^{RL}I^{\beta_i}\left({}^{H}I^{q_2}\left({}^{RL}I^{p_2}1\right)\right)G_2+\frac{|\Omega_2|}{|\Lambda|}{}^{H}I^{q_1}\left({}^{RL}I^{p_1}1\right)(T)G_1\\&+\frac{1}{|\Lambda|}{}^{H}I^{q_2}\left({}^{RL}I^{p_2}1\right)(T)G_2+\frac{1}{|\Lambda|}\sum_{j=1}^{k}|\lambda_j|\,{}^{RL}I^{\delta_j}\left({}^{H}I^{q_1}\left({}^{RL}I^{p_1}1\right)\right)(\eta_j)G_1\\&+{}^{H}I^{q_2}\left({}^{RL}I^{p_2}1\right)(T)G_2\\&= G_1M_3+G_2M_4.\end{aligned}$$

Therefore, from above two results, we deduce that the set $\mathcal{P}\Phi$ is uniformly bounded. The next is to prove that the set $\mathcal{P}\Phi$ is equicontinuous. Choosing two points $\tau_1, \tau_2 \in [0,T]$ such that $\tau_1 < \tau_2$, we have, for any $(x,y) \in \Phi$, that

$$\begin{aligned}|\mathcal{P}_1(x,y)(\tau_2)-\mathcal{P}_1(x,y)(\tau_1)| &= \left|{}^{H}I^{q_1}\left({}^{RL}I^{p_1}f_{x,y}\right)(\tau_2)-{}^{H}I^{q_1}\left({}^{RL}I^{p_1}f_{x,y}\right)(\tau_1)\right|\\&\leq G_1\left|{}^{H}I^{q_1}\left({}^{RL}I^{p_1}1\right)(\tau_2)-{}^{H}I^{q_1}\left({}^{RL}I^{p_1}1\right)(\tau_1)\right|\\&= G_1\frac{p_1^{-q_1}}{\Gamma(p_1+1)}\left|\tau_2^{p_1}-\tau_1^{p_1}\right|,\end{aligned}$$

which implies

$$|\mathcal{P}_1(x,y)(\tau_2)-\mathcal{P}_1(x,y)(\tau_1)| \to 0, \quad \text{as } \tau_1 \to \tau_2.$$

In addition, we obtain

$$\begin{aligned}|\mathcal{P}_2(x,y)(\tau_2)-\mathcal{P}_2(x,y)(\tau_1)| &= \left|{}^{H}I^{q_2}\left({}^{RL}I^{p_2}g_{x,y}\right)(\tau_2)-{}^{H}I^{q_2}\left({}^{RL}I^{p_2}g_{x,y}\right)(\tau_1)\right|\\&\leq G_2\left|{}^{H}I^{q_2}\left({}^{RL}I^{p_2}1\right)(\tau_2)-{}^{H}I^{q_2}\left({}^{RL}I^{p_2}1\right)(\tau_1)\right|\\&= G_2\frac{p_2^{-q_2}}{\Gamma(p_2+1)}\left|\tau_2^{p_2}-\tau_1^{p_2}\right|.\end{aligned}$$

Then,

$$|\mathcal{P}_2(x,y)(\tau_2)-\mathcal{P}_2(x,y)(\tau_1)| \to 0, \quad \text{as } \tau_1 \to \tau_2.$$

Thus, the set $\mathcal{P}\Phi$ is equicontinuous. By taking into account the Arzelá-Ascoli theorem, the set $\mathcal{P}\Phi$ is relatively compact. Then, operator $\mathcal{P}$ is completely continuous.

Finally, we will claim that the set $\mu = \{(x,y) \in X \times Y : (x,y) = \theta\mathcal{P}(x,y), 0 \leq \theta \leq 1\}$ is bounded. For any $(x,y) \in \mu$, then $(x,y) = \theta\mathcal{P}(x,y)$. Hence, for $t \in [a,b]$, we have

$$x(t) = \theta\mathcal{P}_1(x,y)(t) \quad \text{and} \quad y(t) = \theta\mathcal{P}_2(x,y)(t).$$

Therefore, we obtain

$$\begin{aligned}\|x\| &\leq (a_0+a_1\|x\|+a_2\|y\|)M_1+(b_0+b_1\|x\|+b_2\|y\|)M_2,\\\|y\| &\leq (a_0+a_1\|x\|+a_2\|y\|)M_3+(b_0+b_1\|x\|+b_2\|y\|)M_4,\end{aligned}$$

which lead to

$$\begin{aligned}\|x\|+\|y\| &\leq (M_1+M_3)a_0+(M_2+M_4)b_0+[(M_1+M_3)a_1+(M_2+M_4)b_1]\|x\|\\&+[(M_1+M_3)a_2+(M_2+M_4)b_2]\|y\|.\end{aligned}$$

Thus, the following inequality holds:

$$\|(x,y)\| \leq \frac{(M_1+M_3)a_0+(M_2+M_4)b_0}{M^*}, \tag{20}$$

where $M^* = \min\{1-(M_1+M_3)a_1-(M_2+M_4)b_1, 1-(M_1+M_3)a_2-(M_2+M_4)b_2\}$. Hence, the set $\mu$ is a bounded set. Then, by using Lemma 6, the operator $\mathcal{P}$ has at least one fixed point. Therefore, we conclude that problem (4) has at least one solution on $[0,T]$. The proof is complete. □

If $a_r, b_r = 0$, $r = 1,2$, in Theorem 2, we have following corollary.

**Corollary 2.** *Assume that $|f(t,x,y)| \le a_0$ and $|g(t,x,y)| \le b_0$, where $a_0, b_0 > 0$, $\forall (t,x,y) \in [0,T] \times \mathbb{R}^2$. Then, problem (4) has at least one solution on $[0,T]$.*

Next, we present examples to illustrate our results.

**Example 1.** *Consider the following sequential Riemann–Liouville and Hadamard–Caputo fractional differential system with coupled fractional integral boundary conditions of the form*

$$\begin{cases} {}^{RL}D^{\frac{1}{5}}\left({}^{HC}D^{\frac{4}{5}}x\right)(t) = f(t,x(t),y(t)), & t \in [0,7/4], \\ {}^{RL}D^{\frac{2}{5}}\left({}^{HC}D^{\frac{3}{5}}y\right)(t) = g(t,x(t),y(t)), & t \in [0,7/4], \\ {}^{HC}D^{\frac{4}{5}}x(0) = 0, \quad x\left(\frac{7}{4}\right) = \frac{1}{3}{}^{RL}I^{\frac{3}{4}}y\left(\frac{1}{2}\right) + \frac{2}{7}{}^{RL}I^{\frac{5}{4}}y\left(\frac{5}{4}\right), \\ {}^{HC}D^{\frac{3}{5}}y(0) = 0, \ y\left(\frac{7}{4}\right) = \frac{3}{11}{}^{RL}I^{\frac{1}{2}}x\left(\frac{1}{4}\right) + \frac{4}{17}{}^{RL}I^{\frac{7}{8}}x\left(\frac{3}{4}\right) \\ \qquad\qquad + \frac{5}{19}{}^{RL}I^{\frac{11}{8}}x\left(\frac{3}{2}\right). \end{cases} \tag{21}$$

Here, $p_1 = 1/5$, $p_2 = 2/5$, $q_1 = 4/5$, $q_2 = 3/5$, $T = 7/4$, $m = 2$, $\alpha_1 = 1/3$, $\alpha_2 = 2/7$, $\beta_1 = 3/4$, $\beta_2 = 5/4$, $\xi_1 = 1/2$, $\xi_2 = 5/4$, $k = 3$, $\lambda_1 = 3/11$, $\lambda_2 = 4/17$, $\lambda_3 = 5/19$, $\delta_1 = 1/2$, $\delta_2 = 7/8$, $\delta_3 = 11/8$, $\eta_1 = 1/4$, $\eta_2 = 3/4$, $\eta_3 = 3/2$. Form all constants, we find that $\Omega_1 \approx 0.5489581728$, $\Omega_2 \approx 0.7217268652$, $|\Lambda| \approx 0.6038021388$, $M_1 \approx 13.82028787$, $M_2 \approx 3.420721316$, $M_3 \approx 9.093047627$, $M_4 \approx 7.354860071$.

Let the two nonlinear Lipschitzian functions $f, g : [0,7/4] \times \mathbb{R}^2 \longrightarrow \mathbb{R}$ be defined by

$$f(t,x,y) = \frac{1}{12(t+12)}\left(\frac{x^2+2|x|}{1+|x|}\right) + \frac{e^{-t}\sin y}{15(3t+5)} + \frac{1}{2}, \tag{22}$$

$$g(t,x,y) = \frac{\cos \pi t}{6(2t+9)}\tan^{-1}x + \frac{1}{36(4t+7)}\left(\frac{3y^2+4|y|}{1+|y|}\right) + \frac{3}{4}. \tag{23}$$

From (22)–(23), we see that

$$|f(t,x_1,y_1) - f(t,x_2,y_2)| \le \frac{1}{72}|x_1-x_2| + \frac{1}{75}|y_1-y_2|$$

and

$$|g(t,x_1,y_1) - g(t,x_2,y_2)| \le \frac{1}{54}|x_1-x_2| + \frac{1}{63}|y_1-y_2|,$$

for all $x_r, y_r \in \mathbb{R}$, $r = 1,2$, we obtain $(M_1+M_3)(1/72+1/75) + (M_2+M_4)(1/54+1/63) \approx 0.9943406888 < 1$. From the benefits of Theorem 1, the problem of a sequential Riemann–Liouville and Hadamard–Caputo fractional differential system with coupled fractional integral boundary conditions (21) with $f$ and $g$ given by (22)–(23), respectively, has a unique solution on $[0,7/4]$.

**Example 2.** *Consider the sequential Riemann–Liouville and Hadamard–Caputo fractional differential system with coupled fractional integral boundary conditions of the Example 1, where the nonlinear functions* $f, g : [0, 7/4] \times \mathbb{R}^2 \longrightarrow \mathbb{R}$ *are defined by*

$$f(t,x,y) = \frac{2e^{-t}}{13} + \frac{1}{2(5t+23)}\left(\frac{x^{16}}{1+|x|^{15}}\right) + \frac{\cos \pi t}{3(2t+15)} y \sin^2 x, \tag{24}$$

$$g(t,x,y) = \frac{4t}{3} + \frac{xe^{-y^2}}{2(4t+11)} + \frac{|y|^{19}\cos^4 x}{3(3t+8)(1+y^{18})}. \tag{25}$$

*It is easy to obtain that* $|f(t,x,y)| \leq (2/13) + (1/46)|x| + (1/45)|y|$ *and* $|g(t,x,y)| \leq (7/3) + (1/22)|x| + (1/24)|y|$. *By setting* $a_0 = 2/13$, $a_1 = 1/46$, $a_2 = 1/45$, $b_0 = 7/3$, $b_1 = 1/22$ *and* $b_2 = 1/24$, *we can find that* $(M_1 + M_3)a_1 + (M_2 + M_4)b_1 \approx 0.9879151432 < 1$ *and* $(M_1 + M_3)a_2 + (M_2 + M_4)b_2 \approx 0.9581677912 < 1$. *The conclusion of Theorem 2 can be implied that system (21) with f and g given by (24)–(25), respectively, has at least one solution on* $[0, 7/4]$.

**Example 3.** *Consider the sequential Riemann–Liouville and Hadamard–Caputo fractional differential system with coupled fractional integral boundary conditions of the Example 1, where the nonlinear functions* $f, g : [0, 7/4] \times \mathbb{R}^2 \longrightarrow \mathbb{R}$ *are given by*

$$f(t,x,y) = \frac{1}{2}(1+\cos^2 t) + \frac{|x|e^{-t}}{(1+|x|)} + \frac{2}{\pi}\tan^{-1} y, \tag{26}$$

$$g(t,x,y) = \frac{1}{4}(3+\sin^2 \pi t) + e^{-x^4} + \frac{3y^{22}}{1+y^{22}}. \tag{27}$$

*We can check that* $|f(t,x,y)| \leq 3$, $|g(t,x,y)| \leq 5$ *for all* $x, y \in \mathbb{R}$. *Using the Corollary 2, the problem (21) with f and g given by (26) and (27), respectively, has at least one solution on* $[0, 7/4]$.

## 4. Conclusions

In this paper, we studied a new system of sequential fractional differential equations which consists of mixed fractional derivatives of Riemann–Liouville and Hadamard–Caputo types, supplemented with nonlocal coupled fractional integral boundary conditions. To the best of our knowledge, this is the first system of this type that appeared in the literature. After proving a basic lemma, helping us to transform the considered system into a fixed point problem, we use the standard tools from functional analysis to establish existence and uniqueness results. We use a Banach contraction mapping principle to derive the uniqueness result and Leray–Schauder alternative to obtain an existence result. The obtained results are well illustrated by numerical examples. The obtained results enrich the existing literature on sequential systems of fractional differential equations. Other cases of fractional systems with other types of mixed fractional derivatives or other types of boundary conditions can be studied using the methodology of this paper.

**Author Contributions:** Conceptualization, C.K., W.Y., S.K.N., and J.T.; methodology, C.K., W.Y., S.K.N., and J.T.; formal analysis, C.K., W.Y., S.K.N., and J.T.; funding acquisition, J.T. All authors have read and agreed to the published version of the manuscript.

**Funding:** This research was funded by King Mongkut's University of Technology North Bangkok, Contract No. KMUTNB-61-KNOW-034.

**Conflicts of Interest:** The authors declare no conflict of interest.

## References

1. Diethelm, K. *The Analysis of Fractional Differential Equations*; Lecture Notes in Mathematics; Springer: New York, NY, USA, 2010.
2. Kilbas, A.A.; Srivastava, H.M.; Trujillo, J.J. *Theory and Applications of the Fractional Differential Equations*; North-Holland Mathematics Studies; Elsevier: Amsterdam, The Netherlands, 2006; Volume 204.
3. VLakshmikantham; Leela, S.; Devi, J.V. *Theory of Fractional Dynamic Systems*; Cambridge Scientific Publishers: Cottenham, UK, 2009.

4. Miller, K.S.; Ross, B. *An Introduction to the Fractional Calculus and Differential Equations*; John Wiley: NewYork, NY, USA, 1993.
5. Podlubny, I. *Fractional Differential Equations*; Academic Press: New York, NY, USA, 1999.
6. Samko, S.G.; Kilbas, A.A.; Marichev, O.I. *Fractional Integrals and Derivatives*; Gordon and Breach Science: Yverdon, Switzerland, 1993.
7. Ahmad, B.; Alsaedi, A.; Ntouyas, S.K.; Tariboon, J. *Hadamard-Type Fractional Differential Equations, Inclusions and Inequalities*; Springer: Cham, Switzerland, 2017.
8. Ahmad, B.; Ntouyas, S.K. *Nonlocal Nonlinear Fractional-Order Boundary Value Problems*; World Scientific: Singapore, 2021.
9. Zhou, Y. *Basic Theory of Fractional Differential Equations*; World Scientific: Singapore, 2014.
10. Tarasov, V.E. *Fractional Dynamics: Applications of Fractional Calculus to Dynamics of Particles, Fields, and Media*; Springer: Berlin/Heidelberg, Germany, 2011.
11. Uchaikin, V.; Sibatov, R. *Fractional Kinetics in Space: Anomalous Transport Models*; World Scientific: Singapore, 2018.
12. Ding, Y.; Wang, Z.; Ye, H. Optimal control of a fractional-order HIV-immune system with memory. *IEEE Trans. Control. Syst. Technol.* **2012**, *20*, 763–769. [CrossRef]
13. Faieghi, M.; Kuntanapreeda, S.; Delavari, H.; Baleanu, D. LMI-based stabilization of a class of fractional-order chaotic systems. *Nonlinear Dynam.* **2013**, *72*, 301–309. [CrossRef]
14. Zhang, F.; Li, G.C.C.; Kurths, J. Chaos synchronization in fractional differential systems. *Phys. Eng. Sci.* **2013**, *371*, 20120155. [CrossRef] [PubMed]
15. Javidi, M.; Ahmad, B. Dynamic analysis of time fractional order phytoplankton-toxic phytoplankton–zooplankton system. *Ecol. Model.* **2015**, *318*, 8–18. [CrossRef]
16. Carvalho, A.; Pinto, C.M.A. A delay fractional order model for the co-infection of malaria and HIV/AIDS. *Int. J. Dyn. Control* **2017**, *5*, 168–186. [CrossRef]
17. Torvik, P.J.; Bagley, R.L. On the appearance of the fractional derivative in the behavior of real materials. *J. Appl. Mech.* **1984**, *51*, 294–298. [CrossRef]
18. Mainardi, F. Some basic problems in continuum and statistical mechanics. In *Fractals and Fractional Calculus in Continuum Mechanics*; Carpinteri, A., Mainardi, F., Eds.; Springer: Berlin/Heidelberg, Germany, 1997; pp. 291–348.
19. Yin, C.; Liu, F.; Anh, V. Numerical simulation of the nonlinear fractional dynamical systems with fractional damping for the extensible and inextensible pendulum. *J. Algorithm Comput. Technol.* **2007**, *1*, 427–447. [CrossRef]
20. Ahmad, B.; Ntouyas, S.K. Existence and uniqueness of solutions for Caputo-Hadamard sequential fractional order neutral functional differential equations. *Electron. J. Differ. Equ.* **2017**, *36*, 1–11.
21. Promsakon, C.; Phuangthong, N.; Ntouyas, S.K.; Tariboon, J. Nonlinear sequential Riemann–Liouville and Caputo fractional differential equations with generalized fractional integral conditions. *Adv. Differ. Equ.* **2018**, *2018*, 385. [CrossRef]
22. Tariboon, J.; Cuntavepanit, A.; Ntouyas, S.K.; Nithiarayaphaks, W. Separated boundary value problems of sequential Caputo and Hadamard fractional differential equations. *J. Funct. Spaces* **2018**, *2018*, 6974046. [CrossRef]
23. Asawasamrit, S.; Phuangthong, N.; Ntouyas, S.K.; Tariboon, J. Nonlinear sequential Riemann–Liouville and Caputo fractional differential equations with nonlocal and integral boundary conditions. *Int. J. Anal. Appl.* **2019**, *17*, 47–63.
24. Asawasamrit, S.; Ntouyas, S.K.; Tariboon, J.; Nithiarayaphaks, W. Coupled systems of sequential Caputo and Hadamard fractional differential equations with coupled separated boundary conditions. *Symmetry* **2018**, *10*, 701. [CrossRef]
25. Ahmad, B.; Agarwal, R.P.; Alsaedi, A.; Ntouyas, S.K.; Alruwaily, Y. Fractional order coupled systems for mixed fractional derivatives with nonlocal multi-point and Riemann-Stieltjes integral-multi-strip conditions. *Dynam. Syst. Appl.* **2020**, *29*, 71–86.
26. Henderson, J.; Luca, R.; Tudorache, A. On a system of fractional differential equations with coupled integral boundary conditions. *Fract. Calc. Appl. Anal.* **2015**, *18*, 361–386. [CrossRef]
27. Wang, J.R.; Zhang, Y. Analysis of fractional order differential coupled systems. *Math. Methods Appl. Sci.* **2015**, *38*, 3322–3338. [CrossRef]
28. Ahmad, B.; Luca, R. Existence of solutions for a sequential fractional integro-differential system with coupled integral boundary conditions. *Chaos Solitons Fractals* **2017**, *104*, 378–388. [CrossRef]
29. Tariboon, J.; Ntouyas, S.K.; Ahmad, B.; Alsaedi, A. Existence results for sequential Riemann–Liouville and Caputo fractional differential inclusions with generalized fractional integral conditions. *Mathematics* **2020**, *8*, 1044 [CrossRef]
30. Jarad, F.; Abdeljawad, T.; Baleanu, D. Caputo-type modification of the Hadamard fractional derivatives. *Adv. Differ. Equ.* **2012**, *2012*, 142. [CrossRef]
31. Granas, A.; Dugundji, J. *Fixed Point Theory*; Springer: New York, NY, USA, 2003.

axioms
MDPI
Article

# Some New Fractional Estimates of Inequalities for LR-$p$-Convex Interval-Valued Functions by Means of Pseudo Order Relation

**Muhammad Bilal Khan [1], Pshtiwan Othman Mohammed [2,*], Muhammad Aslam Noor [1], Dumitru Baleanu [3,4,5,*] and Juan Luis García Guirao [6,7]**

1 Department of Mathematics, COMSATS University Islamabad, Islamabad 44000, Pakistan; bilal42742@gmail.com (M.B.K.); noomaslam@gamil.com (M.A.N.)
2 Department of Mathematics, College of Education, University of Sulaimani, Sulaimani 46001, Kurdistan Region, Iraq
3 Department of Mathematics, Faculty of Arts and Sciences, Cankaya University, 06530 Ankara, Turkey
4 Department of Medical Research, China Medical University Hospital, China Medical University, Taichung 40402, Taiwan
5 Institute of Space Sciences, P.O. Box MG-23, R 76900 Magurele-Bucharest, Romania
6 Departamento de Matemática Aplicada y Estadística, Campus de la Muralla, Universidad Politécnica de Cartagena, 30203 Cartagena, Murcia, Spain; Juan.Garcia@upct.es
7 Nonlinear Analysis and Applied Mathematics (NAAM)-Research Group, Department of Mathematics, Faculty of Science, King Abdulaziz University, P.O. Box 80203, Jeddah 21589, Saudi Arabia
* Correspondence: pshtiwansangawi@gmail.com (P.O.M.); dumitru@cankaya.edu.tr (D.B.)

**Abstract:** It is a familiar fact that interval analysis provides tools to deal with data uncertainty. In general, interval analysis is typically used to deal with the models whose data are composed of inaccuracies that may occur from certain kinds of measurements. In interval analysis, both the inclusion relation $(\subseteq)$ and pseudo order relation $(\leq_p)$ are two different concepts. In this article, by using pseudo order relation, we introduce the new class of nonconvex functions known as LR-$p$-convex interval-valued functions (LR-$p$-convex-IVFs). With the help of this relation, we establish a strong relationship between LR-$p$-convex-IVFs and Hermite-Hadamard type inequalities (*HH*-type inequalities) via Katugampola fractional integral operator. Moreover, we have shown that our results include a wide class of new and known inequalities for LR-$p$-convex-IVFs and their variant forms as special cases. Useful examples that demonstrate the applicability of the theory proposed in this study are given. The concepts and techniques of this paper may be a starting point for further research in this area.

**Keywords:** LR-$p$-convex interval-valued function; Katugampola fractional integral operator; Hermite-Hadamard type inequality; Hermite-Hadamard-Fejér inequality

**Citation:** Khan, M.B.; Mohammed, P.O.; Noor, M.A.; Baleanu, D.; Guirao, J.L.G. Some New Fractional Estimates of Inequalities for LR-$p$-Convex Interval-Valued Functions by Means of Pseudo Order Relation. *Axioms* **2021**, *10*, 175. https://doi.org/10.3390/axioms10030175

Academic Editors: Jorge E. Macías Díaz and Chris Goodrich

Received: 28 June 2021
Accepted: 23 July 2021
Published: 31 July 2021



## 1. Introduction

Hermite [1] and Hadamard [2] derived the familiar inequality known as Hermite-Hadamard inequality (*HH* inequality). This inequality establishes a strong relationship with a convex function such that:

Let $f : I \to \mathbb{R}$ be a convex function defined on an interval $I \subseteq \mathbb{R}$ and $u, v \in I$ such that $v > u$. Then

$$f\left(\frac{u+v}{2}\right) \leq \frac{1}{v-u}\int_u^v f(x)dx \leq \frac{f(u)+f(v)}{2} \tag{1}$$

If $f$ is a concave function, then both inequalities are reversed. We note that *HH*-inequality may be regarded as a refinement of the concept of convexity and it follows easily from Jensen's inequality. In the last few decades, *HH*-inequality has attracted many authors to devote themselves to this field. Therefore, many authors have proposed different varieties of convexities to introduce *HH*-type inequalities such as harmonic convexity [3], quasi convexity [4], Schur convexity [5,6], strong convexity [7,8], h-convexity [9], p-convexity [10], fuzzy convexity [11,12], fuzzy pre-invexity [13] and generalized convexity [14], *P*-convexity [15], etc. Fejér [16] considered the major generalization of *HH*-inequality which is known as *HH*-Fejér inequality. It can be expressed as follows:

Let $f : [u, v] \to \mathbb{R}$ be a convex function on an interval $[u, v]$ with $u \leq v$, and let $\mathcal{W} : [u, v] \subset \mathbb{R} \to \mathbb{R}$ with $\mathcal{W} \geq 0$ be an integrable and symmetric function with respect to $\frac{u+v}{2}$. Then, we have the following inequality:

$$f\left(\frac{u+v}{2}\right)\int_u^v \mathcal{W}(x)dx \leq \int_u^v f(x)\mathcal{W}(x)dx \leq \frac{f(u)+f(v)}{2}\int_u^v \mathcal{W}(x)dx \tag{2}$$

If $f$ is concave, then the double inequality (2) is reversed. If $\mathcal{W}(x) = 1$, then we obtain (1) from (2). With the assistance of inequality (2), several classical inequalities can be obtained through special convex functions. In addition, these inequalities have a very significant role for convex functions in both pure and applied mathematics. We urge the readers for a further analysis of the literature on the applications and properties of generalized convex functions and *HH*-integral inequalities, see [17–19] and the references therein.

On the other hand, it is a well-known fact that the interval-valued analysis was introduced as an attempt to overcome interval uncertainty, which occurs in the computer or mathematical models of some deterministic real-word phenomena. A classic example of an interval closure is Archimedes' technique, which is associated with the computation of the circumference of a circle. In 1966, Moore [20] gave the concept of interval analysis in his book and discussed its applications in computational Mathematics.

After that, several authors have developed a strong relationship between inequalities and IVFs by means of inclusion relation via different integral operators, as one can see by Costa [21], Costa and Roman-Flores [22], Roman-Flores et al. [23,24], and Chalco-Cano et al. [25,26], but also to more general set-valued maps by Nikodem et al. [27], and Matkowski and Nikodem [28]. In particular, Zhang et al. [29] derived the new version of Jensen's inequalities for set-valued and fuzzy set-valued functions by means of a pseudo order relation and proved that these Jensen's inequalities generalized a form of Costa Jensen's inequalities [21].

In the last two decades, in the development of pure and applied mathematics, fractional calculus has played a key role. Yet, it attains magnificent deliberation in the ongoing research work, which is due to its application in various directions such as image processing, signal processing, physics, biology, control theory, computer networking, and fluid dynamics [30–33].

As a further extension, several authors have introduced the refinements of classical inequalities through fractional integrals and discussed their applications, such as Budak et al. [34], who established a strong relationship between fractional interval *HH*-inequality and convex-IVF.

Through Katugampola fractional integral [35], Toplu et al. [36] established the following *HH*-inequality for p-convex functions:

Let $f$ be a real-valued Lebesgue integrable function and $p, \alpha > 0$. If $f \in SX([u, v], \mathbb{R}^+, p)$, then

$$f\left(\left[\frac{u^p+v^p}{2}\right]^{\frac{1}{p}}\right) \leq \frac{p^\alpha\Gamma(\alpha+1)}{2(v^p-u^p)^\alpha}\left[\mathcal{I}_{u^+}^{p,\alpha} f(v) + \mathcal{I}_{v^-}^{p,\alpha} f(u)\right] \leq \frac{f(u)+f(v)}{2}. \tag{3}$$

Due to the vast applications of convexity and fractional *HH*-inequality in mathematical analysis and optimization, many authors have discussed the applications, refinements, generalizations, and extensions, see [37–56] and the references therein.

Inspired by the ongoing research work, we generalize the class of p-convex function known as LR-$p$-convex-IVF, and establish the relationship between *HH*-type inequalities and LR-$p$-convex-IVF via Katugampola fractional integral.

## 2. Preliminaries

Let $\mathbb{R}$ be the set of real numbers and $\mathbb{R}_I$ be the collection of all closed and bounded intervals of $\mathbb{R}$ that is $\mathbb{R}_I = \left\{\left[\underline{\xi},\ \overline{\xi}\right] : \underline{\xi},\ \overline{\xi} \in \mathbb{R} \text{ and } \underline{\xi} \leq \overline{\xi}\right\}$. If $\underline{\xi} \geq 0$, then $\left[\underline{\xi},\ \overline{\xi}\right]$ is called positive interval. The set of all positive intervals is denoted by $\mathbb{R}_I^+$ and defined as

$$\mathbb{R}_I^+ = \left\{\left[\underline{\xi},\ \overline{\xi}\right] : \left[\underline{\xi},\ \overline{\xi}\right] \in \mathbb{R}_I \text{ and } \underline{\xi} \geq 0\right\}.$$

Let $\varrho \in \mathbb{R}$ and $\varrho\xi$ be defined as

$$\varrho\xi = \begin{cases} \left[\varrho\underline{\xi}, \varrho\overline{\xi}\right], & \varrho > 0, \\ \{0\}, & \varrho = 0, \\ \left[\varrho\overline{\xi}, \varrho\underline{\xi}\right], & \varrho < 0. \end{cases} \tag{4}$$

Then, the addition $\xi_1 + \xi_2$ and Minkowski difference $\xi_1 - \xi_2$ for $\xi_1, \xi_2 \in \mathbb{R}_I$ are defined by

$$\xi_1 + \xi_2 = \left[\underline{\xi}_1,\ \overline{\xi}_1\right] + \left[\underline{\xi}_2,\ \overline{\xi}_2\right] = \left[\underline{\xi}_1 + \underline{\xi}_2, \overline{\xi}_1 + \overline{\xi}_2\right] \tag{5}$$

and

$$\xi_1 - \xi_2 = \left[\underline{\xi}_1,\ \overline{\xi}_1\right] - \left[\underline{\xi}_2,\ \overline{\xi}_2\right] = \left[\underline{\xi}_1 - \overline{\xi}_2, \overline{\xi}_1 - \underline{\xi}_2\right] \tag{6}$$

respectively.

The inclusion relation "$\supseteq$" means that

$$\xi_2 \supseteq \xi_1 \Leftrightarrow \left[\underline{\xi}_2, \overline{\xi}_2\right] \supseteq \left[\underline{\xi}_1,\ \overline{\xi}_1\right] \Leftrightarrow \left[\underline{\xi}_1 \geq \underline{\xi}_2, \overline{\xi}_2 \geq \overline{\xi}_1\right] \tag{7}$$

**Remark 1.** ([29]). (i) *The relation "$\leq_p$" defined on $\mathbb{R}_I$ by*

$$\left[\underline{\xi},\ \overline{\xi}\right] \leq_p \left[\underline{\zeta},\ \overline{\zeta}\right] \text{ if and only if } \underline{\xi} \leq \underline{\zeta},\ \overline{\xi} \leq \overline{\zeta}, \tag{8}$$

*for all $\left[\underline{\xi},\ \overline{\xi}\right], \left[\underline{\zeta},\ \overline{\zeta}\right] \in \mathbb{R}_I$ is a pseudo order relation. In the interval analysis case, both the pseudo order relation ($\leq_p$) and partial order relation ($\leq$) behave alike, thus the relation $\left[\underline{\xi},\ \overline{\xi}\right] \leq_p \left[\underline{\zeta},\ \overline{\zeta}\right]$ is coincident to $\left[\underline{\xi},\ \overline{\xi}\right] \leq \left[\underline{\zeta},\ \overline{\zeta}\right]$ on $\mathbb{R}_I$, for more details see,* [21,29].

*(ii) It can be easily seen that "$\leq_p$" looks similar to "left and right" on the real line $\mathbb{R}$, so we call "$\leq_p$" is "left and right" (or "LR" order, in short).*

The concept of Riemann integral for IVF first introduced by Moore [20] is defined as follows:

**Theorem 1.** ([20]). *Let $f : [u, v] \subset \mathbb{R} \to \mathbb{R}_I$ is an IVF such that $f(x) = \left[\underline{f}(x),\ \overline{f}(x)\right]$. Then, $f$ is Riemann integrable over $[u, v]$ if and only if, $\underline{f}$ and $\overline{f}$ both are Riemann integrable over $[u, v]$ such that*

$$(IR)\int_u^v f(x)dx = \left[(R)\int_u^v \underline{f}(x)dx,\ (R)\int_u^v \overline{f}(x)dx\right] \tag{9}$$

Now, we discuss the concept of Katugampola fractional integral operator for IVF.

Let $q \geq 1$, $c \in \mathbb{R}$ and $x_c^q(u, v)$ be the set of all complex-valued Lebesgue integrable IVFs $f$ on $[u, v]$ for which the norm $\parallel f \parallel \mathcal{X}_c^q$ is defined by

$$\parallel f \parallel \mathcal{X}_c^q = \left(\int_u^v |\varrho^c f(x)|^q \frac{d\varrho}{\varrho}\right)^{\frac{1}{q}} < \infty$$

For $1 \leq q < \infty$ and

$$\parallel f \parallel \mathcal{X}_c^{\infty} = ess \sup_{u \leq \varrho \leq v} \varrho^c |f(\varrho)|$$

Katugampola [35] presented a new fractional integral to generalize the Riemann Liouville and Hadamard fractional integrals under certain conditions.

Let $p, \alpha > 0$ and $f \in \Im\mathcal{L}_{[u,v]}$ be the collection of all complex-valued Lebesgue integrable IVFs on $[u, v]$. Then, the interval left and right Katugampola fractional integrals of $f \in \Im\mathcal{L}_{[u,v]}$ with order are defined by

$$\mathcal{I}_{u^+}^{p,\alpha} f(x) = \frac{p^{1-\alpha}}{\Gamma(\alpha)} \int_u^x (x^p - \zeta^p)^{\alpha-1} \zeta^{p-1} f(\zeta) d(\zeta) \; (x > u), \tag{10}$$

and

$$\mathcal{I}_{v^-}^{p,\alpha} f(x) = \frac{p^{1-\alpha}}{\Gamma(\alpha)} \int_x^v (\zeta^p - x^p)^{\alpha-1} \zeta^{p-1} f(\zeta) d(\zeta) \; (x < v) \tag{11}$$

respectively, where $\Gamma(x) = \int\limits_0^\infty \zeta^{x-1} u^{-\zeta} d(\zeta)$ is the Euler gamma function.

The concept of $p$-convex functions were established by Zhang and Wang [10], and a number of properties of the functions were introduced.

**Definition 1.** ([54]). *Let $p \in \mathbb{R}$ with $p \neq 0$. Then, the interval $I$ is said to be $p$-convex if*

$$[\varrho x^p + (1-\varrho) y^p]^{\frac{1}{p}} \in I, \tag{12}$$

*for all $x,\ y \in I,\ \varrho \in [0,\ 1]$, where $p = 2n + 1$ and $n \in N$ or $p$ is an odd number.*

**Definition 2.** ([10]). *Let $p \in \mathbb{R}$ with $p \neq 0$ and $I = [u,\ v] \subseteq \mathbb{R}$. Then, the function $f : [u,\ v] \to \mathbb{R}^+$ is said to be $p$-convex function if*

$$f\left([\varrho x^p + (1-\varrho) y^p]^{\frac{1}{p}}\right) \leq \varrho f(x) + (1-\varrho) f(y), \tag{13}$$

*for all $x,\ y \in [u,\ v],\ \varrho \in [0,\ 1]$. If the inequality (13) is reversed, then $f$ is called $p$-concave function. The set of all $p$-convex (LR-$p$-concave, LR-$p$-affine) functions is denoted by*

$$SX([u,\ v],\ \mathbb{R}^+,\ p) \;\; (SV([u,\ v],\ \mathbb{R}^+,\ p),).$$

*Firstly, we introduce the new class of LR-$p$-convex-IVF.*

## 3. LR-$p$-Convex Interval-Valued Functions

Now, we introduce LR-$p$-convex interval-valued functions.

**Definition 3.** *The IVF $f : [u,\ v] \to \mathbb{R}_I^+$ is said to be LR-$p$-convex-IVF if for all $x,\ y \in [u,\ v]$ and $\varrho \in [0,\ 1]$ we have*

$$f\left([\varrho x^p + (1-\varrho) y^p]^{\frac{1}{p}}\right) \leq_p \varrho f(x) + (1-\varrho) f(y). \tag{14}$$

If inequality (14) is reversed, then $f$ is said to be LR-$p$-concave on $[u,\ v]$. The set of all LR-$p$-convex (LR-$p$-concave) IVFs is denoted by

$$LRSX([u,\ v],\ \mathbb{R}_I^+,\ p) \;\; (LRSV([u,\ v],\ \mathbb{R}_I^+,\ p),).$$

**Remark 2.** *If $p = 1$, then LR-$p$-convex-IVF reduces to LR-convex-IVF, see [24].*

If $p = -1$, then we obtain the class of harmonically convex functions, which is also a new one.

The next Theorem 2 establishes the relationship between Definition 3 and end point functions of IVFs.

**Theorem 2.** *Let $f : [u, v] \to \mathbb{R}_I^+$ be an IVF defined by $f(x) = \left[\underline{f}(x), \overline{f}(x)\right]$, for all $x \in [u, v]$. Then, $f \in LRSX([u, v], \mathbb{R}_I^+, p)$ if and only if, $\underline{f}, \overline{f} \in SX([u, v], \mathbb{R}^+, p)$.*

**Proof.** Assume that $\underline{f}, \overline{f} \in SX([u, v], \mathbb{R}^+, p)$. Then, for all $x, y \in [u, v]$, $\varrho \in [0, 1]$, we have

$$\underline{f}\left([\varrho x^p + (1-\varrho)y^p]^{\frac{1}{p}}\right) \le \varrho \underline{f}(x) + (1-\varrho)\underline{f}(y)$$

and

$$\overline{f}\left([\varrho x^p + (1-\varrho)y^p]^{\frac{1}{p}}\right) \le \varrho \overline{f}(x) + (1-\varrho)\overline{f}(y)$$

From Definition 3 and order relation $\le_p$, we have

$$\begin{aligned}
&\left[\underline{f}\left([\varrho x^p + (1-\varrho)y^p]^{\frac{1}{p}}\right), \overline{f}\left([\varrho x^p + (1-\varrho)y^p]^{\frac{1}{p}}\right)\right] \\
&\le_p \left[\varrho \underline{f}(x) + (1-\varrho)\underline{f}(y), \varrho \overline{f}(x) + (1-\varrho)\overline{f}(y)\right] \\
&= \varrho\left[\underline{f}(x), \overline{f}(x)\right] + (1-\varrho)\left[\underline{f}(y), \overline{f}(y)\right]
\end{aligned}$$

That is

$$f\left([\varrho x^p + (1-\varrho)y^p]^{\frac{1}{p}}\right) \le_p \varrho f(x) + (1-\varrho)f(y), \forall\, x, y \in [u, v],\ \varrho \in [0, 1].$$

Hence, $f \in LRSX([u, v], \mathbb{R}_I^+, p)$.

Conversely, let $f \in LRSX([u, v], \mathbb{R}_I^+, p)$. Then, for all $x, y \in [u, v]$ and $\varrho \in [0, 1]$, we have

$$f\left([\varrho x^p + (1-\varrho)y^p]^{\frac{1}{p}}\right) \le_p \varrho f(x) + (1-\varrho)f(y).$$

That is

$$\begin{aligned}
\left[\underline{f}\left([\varrho x^p + (1-\varrho)y^p]^{\frac{1}{p}}\right), \overline{f}\left([\varrho x^p + (1-\varrho)y^p]^{\frac{1}{p}}\right)\right] &\le_p \varrho\left[\underline{f}(x), \overline{f}(x)\right] + (1-\varrho)\left[\underline{f}(y), \overline{f}(y)\right] \\
&= \left[\varrho \underline{f}(x) + (1-\varrho)\underline{f}(y), \varrho \overline{f}(x) + (1-\varrho)\overline{f}(y)\right]
\end{aligned}$$

It follows that

$$\underline{f}\left([\varrho x^p + (1-\varrho)y^p]^{\frac{1}{p}}\right) \le \varrho \underline{f}(x) + (1-\varrho)\underline{f}(y),$$

and

$$\overline{f}\left([\varrho x^p + (1-\varrho)y^p]^{\frac{1}{p}}\right) \le \varrho \overline{f}(x) + (1-\varrho)\overline{f}(y),$$

Hence, the result follows. □

**Remark 3.** *If $\underline{f}(x) = \overline{f}(x)$, then p-convex-IVF reduces to the classical p-convex function, see [10].*

If $\underline{f}(x) = \overline{f}(x)$ with $\gamma = 1$ and $p = 1$, then $p$-convex-IVF reduces to the classical convex function.

**Example 1.** *Let $p$ be an odd number, $\alpha = \frac{1}{2}$, $x \in [2,3]$ and $f(x) = \left[-x^{\frac{p}{2}}, 2 - x^{\frac{p}{2}}\right]$. Then, we clearly see that both end point functions $\underline{f}(x) = -x^{\frac{p}{2}}$ and $\overline{f}(x) = 2 - x^{\frac{p}{2}}$ are p-convex functions. Hence, $f \in LRSX([u,\ v],\ \mathbb{R}_I^+,\ p)$.*

*Fractional Hermite-Hadamard Type Inequalities*

In this section, we will prove some new Hermite-Hadamard type inequalities for LR-$p$-convex-IVFs by means of the pseudo order relation via Katugampola fractional integral operator.

**Theorem 3.** *Let $p,\ \alpha > 0, u, v \in I$ such that $v > u$, $f \in \Im\mathcal{L}_{([u,v])}$. If $f \in LRSX([u,\ v],\ \mathbb{R}_I^+,\ p)$, then*

$$f\left(\left[\frac{u^p + v^p}{2}\right]^{\frac{1}{p}}\right) \leq_p \frac{p^\alpha \Gamma(\alpha+1)}{2(v^p - u^p)^\alpha}\left[\mathcal{I}_{u^+}^{p,\alpha} f(v) + \mathcal{I}_{v^-}^{p,\alpha} f(u)\right] \leq_p \frac{f(u) + f(v)}{2}. \tag{15}$$

*If $f \in LRSV([u,\ v],\ \mathbb{R}_I^+,\ p)([u,\ v],\ \mathbb{R}_I^+,\ p)$, then*

$$f\left(\left[\frac{u^p + v^p}{2}\right]^{\frac{1}{p}}\right) \geq_p \frac{p^\alpha \Gamma(\alpha+1)}{2(v^p - u^p)^\alpha}\left[\mathcal{I}_{u^+}^{p,\alpha} f(v) + \mathcal{I}_{v^-}^{p,\alpha} f(u)\right] \geq_p \frac{f(u) + f(v)}{2}. \tag{16}$$

**Proof.** Let $f \in LRSX([u,\ v],\ \mathbb{R}_I^+,\ p)$. Then, by hypothesis, we have

$$2f\left(\left[\frac{u^p + v^p}{2}\right]^{\frac{1}{p}}\right) \leq_p f\left([\varrho u^p + (1-\varrho)v^p]^{\frac{1}{p}}\right) + f\left([(1-\varrho)u^p + \varrho v^p]^{\frac{1}{p}}\right) \tag{17}$$

Multiplying both sides (17) by $\varrho^{\alpha-1}$ and integrating the obtained result with respect to $\varrho$ over $(0,1)$, we have

$$\begin{aligned} &2\int_0^1 \varrho^{\alpha-1} f\left(\left[\frac{u^p+v^p}{2}\right]^{\frac{1}{p}}\right) d\varrho \\ &\leq_p \int_0^1 \varrho^{\alpha-1}\left[f\left([\varrho u^p + (1-\varrho)v^p]^{\frac{1}{p}}\right) + f\left([(1-\varrho)u^p + \varrho v^p]^{\frac{1}{p}}\right)\right] d\varrho \end{aligned} \tag{18}$$

From (18), we get

$$\begin{aligned} 2\int_0^1 \varrho^{\alpha-1} f\left(\left[\tfrac{u^p+v^p}{2}\right]^{\frac{1}{p}}\right) d\varrho &= 2\left[\int_0^1 \varrho^{\alpha-1}\underline{f}\left(\left[\tfrac{u^p+v^p}{2}\right]^{\frac{1}{p}}\right) d\varrho, \int_0^1 \varrho^{\alpha-1}\overline{f}\left(\left[\tfrac{u^p+v^p}{2}\right]^{\frac{1}{p}}\right) d\varrho\right] \\ &= 2\left[\tfrac{1}{\alpha}\underline{f}\left(\left[\tfrac{u^p+v^p}{2}\right]^{\frac{1}{p}}\right), \tfrac{1}{\alpha}\overline{f}\left(\left[\tfrac{u^p+v^p}{2}\right]^{\frac{1}{p}}\right)\right] \\ &= 2\tfrac{1}{\alpha} f\left(\left[\tfrac{u^p+v^p}{2}\right]^{\frac{1}{p}}\right). \end{aligned} \tag{19}$$

and

$$\begin{aligned} &\int_0^1 \varrho^{\alpha-1}\left[f\left([\varrho u^p + (1-\varrho)v^p]^{\frac{1}{p}}\right) + f\left([(1-\varrho)u^p + \varrho v^p]^{\frac{1}{p}}\right)\right] d\varrho \\ &= \int_0^1 \varrho^{\alpha-1}\left[\underline{f}\left([\varrho u^p + (1-\varrho)v^p]^{\frac{1}{p}}\right), \underline{f}\left([\varrho u^p + (1-\varrho)v^p]^{\frac{1}{p}}\right)\right] d\varrho \\ &+ \int_0^1 \varrho^{\alpha-1}\left[\overline{f}\left([(1-\varrho)u^p + \varrho v^p]^{\frac{1}{p}}\right), \overline{f}\left([(1-\varrho)u^p + \varrho v^p]^{\frac{1}{p}}\right)\right] d\varrho \end{aligned}$$

Let $\varrho \in [0,1]$, $x^p = \varrho u^p + (1-\varrho)\nu^p$ and $y^p = (1-\varrho)u^p + \varrho\nu^p$. Then, we have

$$\begin{aligned}
&= \tfrac{p}{(\nu^p-u^p)^\alpha}\left[\int_u^\nu (\nu^p-y^p)^{\alpha-1}\tfrac{\underline{f}(y)}{y^{1-p}}dy, \int_u^\nu (\nu^p-y^p)^{\alpha-1}\tfrac{\overline{f}(y)}{y^{1-p}}dy\right]\\
&+\tfrac{p}{(\nu^p-u^p)^\alpha}\left[\int_u^\nu (x^p-u^p)^{\alpha-1}\tfrac{\underline{f}(x)}{x^{1-p}}dx, \int_u^\nu (x^p-u^p)^{\alpha-1}\tfrac{\overline{f}(x)}{x^{1-p}}dx\right],\\
&= \tfrac{p}{(\nu^p-u^p)^\alpha}\left[\int_u^\nu (\nu^p-u^p)^{\alpha-1}\tfrac{\underline{f}(y)}{y^{1-p}}dy, \int_u^\nu (x^p-u^p)^{\alpha-1}\tfrac{\overline{f}(x)}{x^{1-p}}dx\right],\\
&\leq_p \tfrac{p^\alpha\Gamma(\alpha)}{(\nu^p-u^p)^\alpha}\left[\mathcal{I}_{u^+}^{p,\alpha} f(\nu) + \mathcal{I}_{\nu^-}^{p,\alpha} f(u)\right].
\end{aligned} \tag{20}$$

Since $f \in LRSX([u,\ \nu],\ \mathbb{R}_I^+,\ p)$, we obtain

$$f\left([\varrho u^p + (1-\varrho)\nu^p]^{\frac{1}{p}}\right) \leq_p \varrho f(u) + (1-\varrho)f(\nu) \tag{21}$$

and

$$f\left([\varrho \nu^p + (1-\varrho)u^p]^{\frac{1}{p}}\right) \leq_p \varrho f(\nu) + (1-\varrho)f(u) \tag{22}$$

Adding (21) and (22), we get

$$f\left([\varrho u^p + (1-\varrho)\nu^p]^{\frac{1}{p}}\right) + f\left([\varrho \nu^p + (1-\varrho)u^p]^{\frac{1}{p}}\right) \leq_p f(u) + f(\nu) \tag{23}$$

Multiplying both sides (23) by $\varrho^{\alpha-1}$ and integrating both sides of the obtained result with respect to $\varrho$ over (0, 1), we get

$$\frac{p^\alpha\Gamma(\alpha)}{(\nu^p-u^p)^\alpha}\left[\mathcal{I}_{u^+}^{p,\alpha} f(\nu) + \mathcal{I}_{\nu^-}^{p,\alpha} f(u)\right] \leq_p \frac{f(u)+f(\nu)}{\alpha} \tag{24}$$

From (20) and (24), (19) becomes

$$f\left(\left[\frac{u^p+\nu^p}{2}\right]^{\frac{1}{p}}\right) \leq_p \frac{p^\alpha\Gamma(\alpha+1)}{2(\nu^p-u^p)^\alpha}\left[\mathcal{I}_{u^+}^{p,\alpha} f(\nu) + \mathcal{I}_{\nu^-}^{p,\alpha} f(u)\right] \leq_p \frac{f(u)+f(\nu)}{2},$$

and the theorem has been proved. □

**Remark 4.** *Let $p = 1$. Then, Theorem 3 reduces to the result for LR-convex-IVF, which is also a new one:*

$$f\left(\frac{u+\nu}{2}\right) \leq_p \frac{\Gamma(\alpha+1)}{2(\nu-u)^\alpha}\left[\mathcal{I}_{u^+}^{\alpha} f(\nu) + \mathcal{I}_{\nu^-}^{\alpha} f(u)\right] \leq_p \frac{f(u)+f(\nu)}{2}.$$

If $\alpha = 1$, then Theorem 3 reduces to the result for LR-$p$-convex-IVF, which is also a new one:

$$f\left(\left[\frac{u^p+\nu^p}{2}\right]^{\frac{1}{p}}\right) \leq_p \frac{p}{\nu^p-u^p}\ (IR)\int_u^\nu x^{p-1}f(x)dx \leq_p \frac{f(u)+f(\nu)}{2}$$

Let $p = \alpha = 1$. Then, Theorem 3 reduces to the result for LR-$p$-convex-IVF, which is also a new one:

$$f\left(\frac{u+\nu}{2}\right) \leq_p \frac{1}{\nu-u}\ (IR)\int_u^\nu f(x)dx \leq_p \frac{f(u)+f(\nu)}{2}$$

If $\underline{f} = \overline{f}$, then we get inequality (13) from Theorem 3.

If $p = 1$ and $\underline{f} = \overline{f}$, then from Theorem 3, we obtain fractional *HH*-inequality for convex function, see [41]:

$$f\left(\frac{u+v}{2}\right) \leq \frac{\Gamma(\alpha+1)}{2(v-u)^{\alpha}}\left[\mathcal{I}_{u^+}^{\alpha} f(v) + \mathcal{I}_{v^-}^{\alpha} f(u)\right] \leq \frac{f(u)+f(v)}{2}.$$

If $\alpha = 1$, and $\underline{f} = \overline{f}$, then Theorem 3 reduces to the result for LR-$p$-convex-IVF, see [10]:

$$f\left(\left[\frac{u^p+v^p}{2}\right]^{\frac{1}{p}}\right) \leq \frac{p}{v^p-u^p}\int_u^v x^{p-1} f(x)dx \leq \frac{f(u)+f(v)}{2}$$

If $\alpha = p = 1$ and $\underline{f} = \overline{f}$, then we obtain the classical inequality (1) from Theorem 3.

**Example 2.** Let $p$ be an odd number, $\alpha = \frac{1}{2}$, $x \in [2,3]$ and $f(x) = \left[2 - x^{\frac{p}{2}}, 2\left(2 - x^{\frac{p}{2}}\right)\right]$. Then, we clearly see that $f \in \Im\mathcal{L}_{([u,v])}$ and $f \in LRSX\left([u,\ v],\ \mathbb{R}_I^+,\ p\right)$. Since $\underline{f}(x) = 2 - x^{\frac{p}{2}}$ and $\overline{f}(x) = 2\left(2 - x^{\frac{p}{2}}\right)$. Now, we compute the following:

$$\underline{f}\left(\left[\frac{u^p+v^p}{2}\right]^{\frac{1}{p}}\right) = \underline{f}\left(\frac{5}{2}\right) = \frac{4-\sqrt{10}}{2}$$

$$\overline{f}\left(\left[\frac{u^p+v^p}{2}\right]^{\frac{1}{p}}\right) = \overline{f}\left(\frac{5}{2}\right) = 4-\sqrt{10},$$

$$\frac{\underline{f}(u)+\underline{f}(v)}{2} = 2 - \frac{\sqrt{2}-\sqrt{3}}{2},$$

$$\frac{\overline{f}(u)+\overline{f}(v)}{2} = 4-\sqrt{2}-\sqrt{3}.$$

*Note that*

$$\frac{p^{\alpha}\Gamma(\alpha+1)}{2(v^p-u^p)^{\alpha}}\left[\mathcal{I}_{u^+}^{p,\alpha}\underline{f}(v) + \mathcal{I}_{v^-}^{p,\alpha}\underline{f}(u)\right] = \frac{\Gamma\left(\frac{3}{2}\right)}{2}\frac{1}{\sqrt{\pi}}\int_2^3 (3^p - x^p)^{\frac{-1}{2}} x^{p-1}\left[2 - x^{\frac{p}{2}}, 2\left(2 - x^{\frac{p}{2}}\right)\right]dx$$
$$+\frac{\Gamma\left(\frac{3}{2}\right)}{2}\frac{1}{\sqrt{\pi}}\int_2^3 (x^p - 2^p)^{\frac{-1}{2}} x^{p-1}\left[2 - x^{\frac{p}{2}}, 2\left(2 - x^{\frac{p}{2}}\right)\right]dx$$
$$= \frac{1}{4}\left[\frac{7393}{5000} + \frac{9501}{5000}\right] = \frac{8447}{10{,}000}$$

*and*

$$\frac{p^{\alpha}\Gamma(\alpha)}{(v^p-u^p)^{\alpha}}\left[\mathcal{I}_{u^+}^{p,\alpha}\overline{f}(v) + \mathcal{I}_{v^-}^{p,\alpha}\overline{f}(u)\right] = \frac{\Gamma\left(\frac{3}{2}\right)}{2}\frac{1}{\sqrt{\pi}}\int_2^3 (3^p - x^p)^{\frac{-1}{2}} x^{p-1}\left(2 - x^{\frac{p}{2}}\right)dx$$
$$+\frac{\Gamma\left(\frac{3}{2}\right)}{2}\frac{1}{\sqrt{\pi}}\int_2^3 (x^p - 2^p)^{\frac{-1}{2}} x^{p-1}\left(2 - x^{\frac{p}{2}}\right)dx$$
$$= \frac{1}{4}\left[\frac{7393}{10{,}000} + \frac{9501}{10{,}000}\right] = \frac{8447}{20{,}000}.$$

*Therefore, we have*

$$\frac{4-\sqrt{10}}{2} \leq \frac{8447}{20{,}000} \leq 2 - \frac{\sqrt{2}+\sqrt{3}}{2}$$
$$4-\sqrt{10} \leq \frac{8447}{10{,}000} \leq 4-\sqrt{2}-\sqrt{3}$$

*and Theorem 3 is verified.*

The next Theorem 4 gives the *HH*-Fejér type inequality for LR-$p$-convex-IVFs.

**Theorem 4.** *Let $p, \alpha > 0$, $u, \nu \in I$ with $\nu > u$, $f \in \Im\mathcal{L}_{([u,\nu])}$ and $\mathcal{W}(x) = \mathcal{W}\left([u^p + \nu^p - x^p]^{\frac{1}{p}}\right) \geq 0$ for $x \in I$. If $f \in LRSX([u,\ \nu],\ \mathbb{R}_I^+,\ p)$, then we have the HH-Fejér type inequality as follows:*

$$\begin{aligned} & f\left(\left[\tfrac{u^p+\nu^p}{2}\right]^{\frac{1}{p}}\right)\left[\mathcal{I}_{u^+}^{p,\alpha}\, \mathcal{W}(\nu) + \mathcal{I}_{\nu^-}^{p,\alpha}\, \mathcal{W}(u)\right] \\ & \leq_p \left[\mathcal{I}_{u^+}^{p,\alpha}\, f\mathcal{W}(\nu) + \mathcal{I}_{\nu^-}^{p,\alpha}\, f\mathcal{W}(u)\right] \leq_p \tfrac{f(u)+f(\nu)}{2}\left[\mathcal{I}_{u^+}^{p,\alpha}\, \mathcal{W}(\nu) + \mathcal{I}_{\nu^-}^{p,\alpha}\, \mathcal{W}(u)\right]. \end{aligned} \tag{25}$$

*If $f \in LRSV([u,\ \nu],\ \mathbb{R}_I^+,\ p)$, then*

$$f\left(\left[\frac{u^p+\nu^p}{2}\right]^{\frac{1}{p}}\right)\left[\mathcal{I}_{u^+}^{p,\alpha}\, \mathcal{W}(\nu) + \mathcal{I}_{\nu^-}^{p,\alpha}\, \mathcal{W}(u)\right] \geq_p \left[\mathcal{I}_{u^+}^{p,\alpha}\, f\mathcal{W}(\nu) + \mathcal{I}_{\nu^-}^{p,\alpha}\, f\mathcal{W}(u)\right] \tag{26}$$

$$\geq_p \frac{f(u)+f(\nu)}{2}\left[\mathcal{I}_{u^+}^{p,\alpha}\, \mathcal{W}(\nu) + \mathcal{I}_{\nu^-}^{p,\alpha}\, \mathcal{W}(u)\right].$$

**Proof.** Since $f \in LRSX([u,\ \nu],\ \mathbb{R}_I^+,\ p)$, then for $\varrho \in [0,1]$, we have

$$f\left(\left[\frac{u^p+\nu^p}{2}\right]^{\frac{1}{p}}\right) \leq_p \frac{1}{2}\left(f\left([\varrho u^p + (1-\varrho)\nu^p]^{\frac{1}{p}}\right) + f\left([(1-\varrho)u^p + \varrho\nu^p]^{\frac{1}{p}}\right)\right). \tag{27}$$

Since $\mathcal{W}\left([\varrho u^p + (1-\varrho)\nu^p]^{\frac{1}{p}}\right) = \mathcal{W}\left([\varrho\nu^p + (1-\varrho)u^p]^{\frac{1}{p}}\right)$, then multiplying both sides of (27) by $\varrho^{\alpha-1}\mathcal{W}\left([(1-\varrho)u^p + \varrho\nu^p]^{\frac{1}{p}}\right)$, and integrating it with respect to $\varrho$ over $[0,\ 1]$, we have

$$\begin{aligned} & 2\int_0^1 \varrho^{\alpha-1} f\left(\left[\tfrac{u^p+\nu^p}{2}\right]^{\frac{1}{p}}\right)\mathcal{W}\left([(1-\varrho)u^p + \varrho\nu^p]^{\frac{1}{p}}\right)d\varrho \\ & \leq_p \int_0^1 \varrho^{\alpha-1} f\left([\varrho u^p + (1-\varrho)\nu^p]^{\frac{1}{p}}\right)\mathcal{W}\left([(1-\varrho)u^p + \varrho\nu^p]^{\frac{1}{p}}\right)d\varrho \\ & + \int_0^1 \varrho^{\alpha-1} f\left([(1-\varrho)u^p + \varrho\nu^p]^{\frac{1}{p}}\right)\mathcal{W}\left([(1-\varrho)u^p + \varrho\nu^p]^{\frac{1}{p}}\right)d\varrho \\ & = \int_0^1 \varrho^{\alpha-1}\left[\underline{f}\left([\varrho u^p + (1-\varrho)\nu^p]^{\frac{1}{p}}\right), \overline{f}\left([(1-\varrho)u^p + \varrho\nu^p]^{\frac{1}{p}}\right)\right] \times \mathcal{W}\left([(1-\varrho)u^p + \varrho\nu^p]^{\frac{1}{p}}\right)d\varrho + \\ & \int_0^1 \varrho^{\alpha-1}\left[\underline{f}\left([(1-\varrho)u^p + \varrho\nu^p]^{\frac{1}{p}}\right), \overline{f}\left([(1-\varrho)u^p + \varrho\nu^p]^{\frac{1}{p}}\right)\right] \times \mathcal{W}\left([(1-\varrho)u^p + \varrho\nu^p]^{\frac{1}{p}}\right)d\varrho. \end{aligned}$$

Let $x^p = \varrho v^p + (1-\varrho)u^p$. Then, we have

$$\frac{2p}{(v^p-u^p)^\alpha} f\left(\left[\frac{u^p+v^p}{2}\right]^{\frac{1}{p}}\right) \int_u^v (x^p-u^p)^{\alpha-1}\mathcal{W}(x)dx$$
$$\leq_p \frac{p}{(v^p-u^p)^\alpha}\int_u^v (x^p-u^p)^{\alpha-1}\left[\underline{f}\left([u^p-v^p-x^p]^{\frac{1}{p}}\right), \overline{f}\left([u^p+v^p-x^p]^{\frac{1}{p}}\right)\right]\mathcal{W}(x)x^{p-1}dx$$
$$+\int_u^v (x^p-u^p)^{\alpha-1}\left[\underline{f}(x), \overline{f}(x)\right]\mathcal{W}(x)x^{p-1}dx,$$
$$= \frac{p}{(v^p-u^p)^\alpha}\int_u^v (x^p-u^p)^{\alpha-1}\left[\underline{f}(x), \overline{f}(x)\right]\mathcal{W}\left([u^p-v^p-x^p]^{\frac{1}{p}}\right)x^{p-1}dx$$
$$+\int_u^v (x^p-u^p)^{\alpha-1}\left[\underline{f}(x), \overline{f}(x)\right]\mathcal{W}(x)x^{p-1}dx,$$
$$= \frac{p}{(v^p-u^p)^\alpha}\int_u^v (x^p-u^p)^{\alpha-1}\left[\underline{f}(x), \overline{f}(x)\right]\mathcal{W}(x)x^{p-1}dx$$
$$+\int_u^v (x^p-u^p)^{\alpha-1}\left[\underline{f}(x), \overline{f}(x)\right]\mathcal{W}(x)x^{p-1}dx,$$
$$= \frac{p}{(v^p-u^p)^\alpha}\left[\int_u^v (v^p-x^p)^{\alpha-1}f(x)\mathcal{W}(x)x^{p-1}dx + \int_u^v (x^p-u^p)^{\alpha-1}f(x)\mathcal{W}(x)x^{p-1}dx\right].$$

Therefore, we have

$$\frac{p^\alpha\Gamma(\alpha)}{(v^p-u^p)^\alpha} f\left(\left[\frac{u^p+v^p}{2}\right]^{\frac{1}{p}}\right)\left[\mathcal{I}_{u^+}^{p,\alpha}\,\mathcal{W}(v)+\mathcal{I}_{v^-}^{p,\alpha}\,\mathcal{W}(u)\right]$$
$$\leq_p \frac{p^\alpha\Gamma(\alpha)}{(v^p-u^p)^\alpha}\left[\mathcal{I}_{u^+}^{p,\alpha}\,f\mathcal{W}(v)+\mathcal{I}_{v^-}^{p,\alpha}\,f\mathcal{W}(u)\right]. \tag{28}$$

Now taking the multiplication of (23) by $\varrho^{\alpha-1}\mathcal{W}\left([\varrho v^p+(1-\varrho)u^p]^{\frac{1}{p}}\right)$, and integrating it with respect to $\varrho$ over $[0,\ 1]$, we get

$$\int_0^1 \varrho^{\alpha-1}\mathcal{W}\left([\varrho v^p+(1-\varrho)u^p]^{\frac{1}{p}}\right)f\left([\varrho u^p+(1-\varrho)v^p]^{\frac{1}{p}}\right)d\varrho$$
$$+\int_0^1 \varrho^{\alpha-1}\mathcal{W}\left([\varrho v^p+(1-\varrho)u^p]^{\frac{1}{p}}\right)f\left([\varrho v^p+(1-\varrho)u^p]^{\frac{1}{p}}\right)d\varrho$$
$$\leq_p [f(u)+f(v)]\int_0^1 \varrho^{\alpha-1}\mathcal{W}\left([\varrho v^p+(1-\varrho)u^p]^{\frac{1}{p}}\right)d\varrho.$$

Therefore, we have

$$\frac{p^\alpha\Gamma(\alpha)}{(v^p-u^p)^\alpha}\left[\mathcal{I}_{u^+}^{p,\alpha}\,f\mathcal{W}(v)\tilde{+}\mathcal{I}_{v^-}^{p,\alpha}\,f\mathcal{W}(u)\right] \leq_p \frac{p^\alpha\Gamma(\alpha)}{(v^p-u^p)^\alpha}.\frac{\mathcal{F}(u)\tilde{+}\mathcal{F}(v)}{2}\left[\mathcal{I}_{u^+}^{p,\alpha}\,\mathcal{W}(v)+\mathcal{I}_{v^-}^{p,\alpha}\,\mathcal{W}(u)\right]. \tag{29}$$

Combining (20) and (21), we get

$$f\left(\left[\frac{u^p+v^p}{2}\right]^{\frac{1}{p}}\right)\left[\mathcal{I}_{u^+}^{p,\alpha}\,\mathcal{W}(v)+\mathcal{I}_{v^-}^{p,\alpha}\,\mathcal{W}(u)\right]$$
$$\leq_p \left[\mathcal{I}_{u^+}^{p,\alpha}\,f\mathcal{W}(v)+\mathcal{I}_{v^-}^{p,\alpha}\,f\mathcal{W}(u)\right] \leq_p \frac{f(u)+f(v)}{2}\left[\mathcal{I}_{u^+}^{p,\alpha}\,\mathcal{W}(v)+\mathcal{I}_{v^-}^{p,\alpha}\,\mathcal{W}(u)\right]$$

and the theorem has been proved. □

**Remark 5.** *Let $p = 1$. Then, Theorem 4 reduces to the result for LR-convex-IVF, which is also a new one:*

$$f\left(\frac{u+v}{2}\right)\left[\mathcal{I}_{u^+}^{\alpha}\,\mathcal{W}(v)+\mathcal{I}_{v^-}^{\alpha}\,\mathcal{W}(u)\right] \leq_p \left[\mathcal{I}_{u^+}^{\alpha}\,f\mathcal{W}(v)+\mathcal{I}_{v^-}^{\alpha}\,f\mathcal{W}(u)\right] \leq_p \frac{f(u)+f(v)}{2}\left[\mathcal{I}_{u^+}^{\alpha}\,\mathcal{W}(v)+\mathcal{I}_{v^-}^{\alpha}\,\mathcal{W}(u)\right].$$

*Let $\alpha = 1$. Then, Theorem 4 reduces to the result for LR-p-convex-IVF, which is also a new one:*

$$f\left(\left[\frac{u^p+\nu^p}{2}\right]^{\frac{1}{p}}\right) \leq_p \frac{1}{\int_u^\nu x^{p-1}\mathcal{W}(x)dx}\int_u^\nu x^{p-1}f(x)\mathcal{W}(x)dx \leq_p \frac{f(u)+f(\nu)}{2}$$

*Let $p = \alpha = 1$. Then, Theorem 4 reduces to the result for LR-convex-IVF, which is also a new one:*

$$f\left(\frac{u+\nu}{2}\right) \leq_p \frac{1}{\int_u^\nu \mathcal{W}(x)dx}\int_u^\nu f(x)\mathcal{W}(x)dx \leq_p \frac{f(u)+f(\nu)}{2}$$

If $\underline{f} = \overline{f}$ and $\alpha = 1$, then from Theorem 4, we get Theorem 5 of [39].

If $\underline{f} = \overline{f}$ and $\alpha = 1$, then from Theorem 4, we obtain the classical *HH*-Fejér type inequality (2).

If $\underline{f} = \overline{f}$ and $\mathcal{W}(x) = p = \alpha = 1$, then from Theorem 4, we get the classical *HH*-inequality (1).

If $\mathcal{W}(x) = 1$, then from Theorem 4, we get Theorem 3.

**Theorem 5.** *Let $p, \alpha > 0, u, \nu \in I$ with $\nu > u$ and $f, g \in \Im\mathcal{L}_{([u,\nu])}$. If $f, g \in LRSX([u,\ \nu],\ \mathbb{R}_I^+,\ p)$, then we have*

$$\frac{p^\alpha\Gamma(\alpha)}{2(\nu^p-u^p)^\alpha}\left[\mathcal{I}_{u^+}^{p,\alpha} f(\nu)g(\nu) + \mathcal{I}_{\nu^-}^{p,\alpha} f(u)f(u)\right] \leq_p \left(\frac{1}{2} - \frac{\alpha}{(\alpha+1)(\alpha+2)}\right)M(u,\nu) + \left(\frac{\alpha}{(\alpha+1)(\alpha+2)}\right)N(u,\nu). \quad (30)$$

*If $f, g \in LRSV([u,\ \nu],\ \mathbb{R}_I^+,\ p)$, then*

$$\frac{p^\alpha\Gamma(\alpha)}{2(\nu^p-u^p)^\alpha}\left[\mathcal{I}_{u^+}^{p,\alpha} f(\nu)f(\nu) + \mathcal{I}_{\nu^-}^{p,\alpha} f(u)f(u)\right] \geq_p \left(\frac{1}{2} - \frac{\alpha}{(\alpha+1)(\alpha+2)}\right)M(u,\nu) + \left(\frac{\alpha}{(\alpha+1)(\alpha+2)}\right)N(u,\nu) \quad (31)$$

*where*

$$M(u,\nu) = [f(u)g(u) + f(\nu)g(\nu)]$$

*and*

$$N(u,\nu) = [f(u)g(\nu) + f(\nu)g(u)].$$

**Proof.** Since $f, g \in LRSX([u,\ \nu],\ \mathbb{R}_I^+,\ p)$, then for $\varrho \in [0,\ 1]$ we have

$$f\left([\varrho u^p + (1-\varrho)\nu^p]^{\frac{1}{p}}\right) \leq_p \varrho f(u) + (1-\varrho)f(\nu),$$

and

$$g\left([\varrho u^p + (1-\varrho)\nu^p]^{\frac{1}{p}}\right) \leq_p \varrho g(u) + (1-\varrho)g(\nu).$$

From the definition of $p$-convex-IVFs, it follows that $0 \leq_p f(x)$ and $0 \leq_p g(x)$, then we have

$$\begin{aligned}&f\left([\varrho u^p + (1-\varrho)\nu^p]^{\frac{1}{p}}\right)g\left([\varrho u^p + (1-\varrho)\nu^p]^{\frac{1}{p}}\right)\\ &\leq_p \varrho^2 f(u)g(u) + (1-\varrho)^2 f(\nu)g(\nu) + \varrho(1-\varrho)[f(\nu)g(u) + f(u)g(\nu)]\end{aligned} \quad (32)$$

Similarly, we have

$$\begin{aligned}&f\left([(1-\varrho)u^p + \varrho\nu^p]^{\frac{1}{p}}\right)g\left([(1-\varrho)u^p + \varrho\nu^p]^{\frac{1}{p}}\right)\\ &\leq_p (1-\varrho)^2 g(u)f(u) + \varrho^2 f(\nu)g(\nu) + \varrho(1-\varrho)[g(\nu)f(u) + g(u)f(\nu)]\end{aligned} \quad (33)$$

Adding (32) and (33), we get

$$\begin{aligned}&f\left([\varrho u^p+(1-\varrho)v^p]^{\frac{1}{p}}\right)g\left([\varrho u^p+(1-\varrho)v^p]^{\frac{1}{p}}\right)\\&+f\left([(1-\varrho)u^p+\varrho v^p]^{\frac{1}{p}}\right)g\left([(1-\varrho)u^p+\varrho v^p]^{\frac{1}{p}}\right)\\&\leq_p\left[\varrho^2+(1-\varrho)^2\right][f(u)g(u)+f(v)g(v)]+2\varrho(1-\varrho)[f(v)g(u)+f(u)g(v)]\end{aligned}\tag{34}$$

Multiplying both sides of (34) by $\varrho^{\alpha-1}$ and integrating the obtained result with respect to $\varrho$ over (0,1), we have

$$\begin{aligned}&\int_0^1\varrho^{\alpha-1}f\left([\varrho u^p+(1-\varrho)v^p]^{\frac{1}{p}}\right)g\left([\varrho u^p+(1-\varrho)v^p]^{\frac{1}{p}}\right)d\varrho\\&+\int_0^1\varrho^{\alpha-1}f\left([(1-\varrho)u^p+\varrho v^p]^{\frac{1}{p}}\right)g\left([(1-\varrho)u^p+\varrho v^p]^{\frac{1}{p}}\right)d\varrho\\&\leq_p M(u,v)\int_0^1\varrho^{\alpha-1}\left[\varrho^2+(1-\varrho)^2\right]+2N(u,v)\int_0^1\varrho^{\alpha-1}\varrho(1-\varrho)\,d\varrho.\end{aligned}\tag{35}$$

Form (35), we have

$$\begin{aligned}&\int_0^1\varrho^{\alpha-1}f\left([\varrho u^p+(1-\varrho)v^p]^{\frac{1}{p}}\right)g\left([\varrho u^p+(1-\varrho)v^p]^{\frac{1}{p}}\right)d\varrho\\&+\int_0^1\varrho^{\alpha-1}f\left([(1-\varrho)u^p+\varrho v^p]^{\frac{1}{p}}\right)g\left([(1-\varrho)u^p+\varrho v^p]^{\frac{1}{p}}\right)d\varrho\\&=\frac{p^\alpha\Gamma(\alpha)}{(v^p-u^p)^\alpha}\left[\mathcal{I}_{u^+}^{p,\alpha}f(v)g(v)+\mathcal{I}_{v^-}^{p,\alpha}f(u)g(u)\right].\end{aligned}\tag{36}$$

and

$$\begin{aligned}&M(u,v)\int_0^1\varrho^{\alpha-1}\left[\varrho^2+(1-\varrho)^2\right]+2N(u,v)\int_0^1\varrho^{\alpha-1}\varrho(1-\varrho)d\varrho\\&=\frac{2}{\alpha}\left(\frac{1}{2}-\frac{\alpha}{(\alpha+1)(\alpha+2)}\right)M(u,v)+\frac{2}{\alpha}\left(\frac{\alpha}{(\alpha+1)(\alpha+2)}\right)N(u,v).\end{aligned}\tag{37}$$

From (36) and (37), we have

$$\frac{p^\alpha\Gamma(\alpha)}{2(v^p-u^p)^\alpha}\left[\mathcal{I}_{u^+}^{p,\alpha}f(v)g(v)+\mathcal{I}_{v^-}^{p,\alpha}f(u)f(u)\right]\leq_p\left(\frac{1}{2}-\frac{\alpha}{(\alpha+1)(\alpha+2)}\right)M(u,v)+\left(\frac{\alpha}{(\alpha+1)(\alpha+2)}\right)N(u,v)$$

and the required result has been obtained. □

**Example 3.** *Let $p$ be an odd number, $[u,v]=[0,2]$, $\alpha=\frac{1}{2}$, $f(x)=\left[e^{x^p}-4,2x^p\right]$, and $g(x)=[x^p-3,2x^p]$. Then, $fg\in\Im\mathcal{L}_{([u,v])}$ and*

$$\begin{aligned}&\frac{p^\alpha\Gamma(1+\alpha)}{2(v^p-u^p)^\alpha}\left[\mathcal{I}_{u^+}^{p,\alpha}f(v)g(v)+\mathcal{I}_{v^-}^{p,\alpha}f(u)g(u)\right]\\&=\frac{\Gamma(\frac{3}{2})}{2\sqrt{2}}\frac{1}{\sqrt{\pi}}\int_0^2(2^p-x^p)^{\frac{-1}{2}}x^{p-1}\left[\left(4-e^{x^p}\right)(3-x^p),4x^{2p}\right]dx+\frac{\Gamma(\frac{3}{2})}{2\sqrt{2}}\frac{1}{\sqrt{\pi}}\int_0^2(x^p)^{\frac{-1}{2}}x^{p-1}\left[\left(4-e^{x^p}\right)(3-x^p),4x^{2p}\right]dx\\&\approx[2.6446,5.8664].\end{aligned}$$

*Note that*

$$M(u,v)=[f(u)g(u)+f(v)g(v)]=\left[13-e^2,16\right]$$

$$N(u,v)=[f(u)g(v)+f(v)g(u)]=\left[15-3e^2,0\right].$$

*Therefore, we have*

$$\left(\frac{1}{2}-\frac{\alpha}{(\alpha+1)(\alpha+2)}\right)M(u,\nu)+\left(\frac{\alpha}{(\alpha+1)(\alpha+2)}\right)N(u,\nu)=\frac{11}{15}\left[13-e^2,16\right]+\frac{2}{15}\left[15-3e^2,0\right]$$
$$\approx[3.1591,11.7333].$$

*It follows that*

$$[2.6446,5.8664]\leq_p[3.1591,11.7333],$$

*and Theorem 5 has been illustrated.*

**Theorem 6.** *Let $p,\alpha>0$, $u,\nu\in I$ with $\nu>u$ and $f,g\in\Im\mathcal{L}_{([u,\nu])}$. If $f,g\in LRSX([u,\ \nu],\ \mathbb{R}_I^+,\ p)$, then we have*

$$2f\left(\left[\frac{u^p+\nu^p}{2}\right]^{\frac{1}{p}}\right)g\left(\left[\frac{u^p+\nu^p}{2}\right]^{\frac{1}{p}}\right)\leq_p\frac{p^\alpha\Gamma(\alpha+1)}{2(\nu^p-u^p)^\alpha}\left[\mathcal{I}_{u^+}^{p,\alpha}f(\nu)g(\nu)+\mathcal{I}_{\nu^-}^{p,\alpha}f(u)g(u)\right]$$
$$+\left(\frac{1}{2}-\frac{\alpha}{(\alpha+1)(\alpha+2)}\right)N(u,\nu)+\left(\frac{\alpha}{(\alpha+1)(\alpha+2)}\right)M(u,\nu). \quad (38)$$

*If $f,g\in LRSV([u,\ \nu],\ \mathbb{R}_I^+,\ p)$, then*

$$f\left(\left[\frac{u^p+\nu^p}{2}\right]^{\frac{1}{p}}\right)g\left(\left[\frac{u^p+\nu^p}{2}\right]^{\frac{1}{p}}\right)\geq_p\frac{p^\alpha\Gamma(\alpha+1)}{4(\nu^p-u^p)^\alpha}\left[\mathcal{I}_{u^+}^{p,\alpha}f(\nu)g(\nu)+\mathcal{I}_{\nu^-}^{p,\alpha}f(u)g(u)\right]$$
$$+\frac{1}{2}\left(\frac{1}{2}-\frac{\alpha}{(\alpha+1)(\alpha+2)}\right)N(u,\nu)+\frac{1}{2}\left(\frac{\alpha}{(\alpha+1)(\alpha+2)}\right)M(u,\nu) \quad (39)$$

*where $M(u,\nu)$ and $N(u,\nu)$ are given in Theorem 5.*

**Proof.** Since $f,g\in LRSX([u,\ \nu],\ \mathbb{R}_I^+,\ p)$, then by hypothesis, for $\varrho\in[0,1]$ we have

$$\begin{aligned}
&f\left(\left[\frac{u^p+\nu^p}{2}\right]^{\frac{1}{p}}\right)g\left(\left[\frac{u^p+\nu^p}{2}\right]^{\frac{1}{p}}\right)\\
&=f\left[\frac{[(1-\varrho)u^p+\varrho\nu^p]^{\frac{1}{p}}}{2}+\frac{[\varrho u^p+(1-\varrho)\nu^p]^{\frac{1}{p}}}{2}\right]\times g\left[\frac{[(1-\varrho)u^p+\varrho\nu^p]^{\frac{1}{p}}}{2}+\frac{[\varrho u^p+(1-\varrho)\nu^p]^{\frac{1}{p}}}{2}\right]\\
&\leq_p\frac{1}{4}\left[f\left([\varrho u^p+(1-\varrho)\nu^p]^{\frac{1}{p}}\right)+f\left([(1-\varrho)u^p+\varrho\nu^p]^{\frac{1}{p}}\right)\right]\\
&\quad\times\left[g\left([\varrho u^p+(1-\varrho)\nu^p]^{\frac{1}{p}}\right)+g\left([(1-\varrho)u^p+\varrho\nu^p]^{\frac{1}{p}}\right)\right]\\
&=\frac{1}{4}\left[f\left([\varrho u^p+(1-\varrho)\nu^p]^{\frac{1}{p}}\right)g\left([\varrho u^p+(1-\varrho)\nu^p]^{\frac{1}{p}}\right)\right]\\
&\quad+\left[f\left([(1-\varrho)u^p+\varrho\nu^p]^{\frac{1}{p}}\right)g\left([(1-\varrho)u^p+\varrho\nu^p]^{\frac{1}{p}}\right)\right]\\
&\quad+\left[g\left([(1-\varrho)u^p+\varrho\nu^p]^{\frac{1}{p}}\right)f\left([\varrho u^p+(1-\varrho)\nu^p]^{\frac{1}{p}}\right)\right]\\
&\quad+\left[f\left([(1-\varrho)u^p+\varrho\nu^p]^{\frac{1}{p}}\right)g\left([\varrho u^p+(1-\varrho)\nu^p]^{\frac{1}{p}}\right)\right]\\
&\leq_p\frac{1}{4}\left[f\left([\varrho u^p+(1-\varrho)\nu^p]^{\frac{1}{p}}\right)+g\left([\varrho u^p+(1-\varrho)\nu^p]^{\frac{1}{p}}\right)\right.\\
&\quad\left.+f\left([(1-\varrho)u^p+\varrho\nu^p]^{\frac{1}{p}}\right)g\left([(1-\varrho)u^p+\varrho\nu^p]^{\frac{1}{p}}\right)\right]\\
&\quad+\frac{1}{4}(2\varrho^2-2\varrho+1)N(u,\nu)+\frac{1}{2}\varrho(1-\varrho)M(u,\nu).
\end{aligned} \quad (40)$$

Taking both multiplications of (40) with $\varrho^{\alpha-1}$ and integrating the result with respect to over (0,1), we have

$$\begin{aligned} &\int_0^1 \varrho^{\alpha-1} f\left(\left[\frac{u^p+v^p}{2}\right]^{\frac{1}{p}}\right) g\left(\left[\frac{u^p+v^p}{2}\right]^{\frac{1}{p}}\right) d\varrho \\ &\leq_p \frac{1}{4}\left[\int_0^1 \varrho^{\alpha-1} f\left([\varrho u^p+(1-\varrho)v^p]^{\frac{1}{p}}\right) g\left([\varrho u^p+(1-\varrho)v^p]^{\frac{1}{p}}\right) d\varrho \right. \\ &\left. + \int_0^1 \varrho^{\alpha-1} f\left([(1-\varrho)u^p+\varrho v^p]^{\frac{1}{p}}\right) g\left([(1-\varrho)u^p+\varrho v^p]^{\frac{1}{p}}\right) d\varrho \right] \\ &+ \frac{1}{4}\int_0^1 \varrho^{\alpha-1}(2\varrho^2-2\varrho+1) N(u,v) + \frac{1}{2}\int_0^1 \varrho^{\alpha-1}\varrho(1-\varrho) M(u,v) d\varrho. \end{aligned} \tag{41}$$

From (41), we get

$$\begin{aligned} &\int_0^1 \varrho^{\alpha-1} f\left(\left[\frac{u^p+v^p}{2}\right]^{\frac{1}{p}}\right) g\left(\left[\frac{u^p+v^p}{2}\right]^{\frac{1}{p}}\right) d\varrho \\ &= \left[\int_0^1 \varrho^{\alpha-1} \underline{f}\left(\left[\frac{u^p+v^p}{2}\right]^{\frac{1}{p}}\right) \underline{g}\left(\left[\frac{u^p+v^p}{2}\right]^{\frac{1}{p}}\right) d\varrho, \int_0^1 \varrho^{\alpha-1} \overline{f}\left(\left[\frac{u^p+v^p}{2}\right]^{\frac{1}{p}}\right) \overline{g}\left(\left[\frac{u^p+v^p}{2}\right]^{\frac{1}{p}}\right) d\varrho\right] \\ &= \left[\frac{1}{\alpha}\underline{f}\left(\left[\frac{u^p+v^p}{2}\right]^{\frac{1}{p}}\right) \underline{g}\left(\left[\frac{u^p+v^p}{2}\right]^{\frac{1}{p}}\right), \frac{1}{\alpha}\overline{f}\left(\left[\frac{u^p+v^p}{2}\right]^{\frac{1}{p}}\right) \overline{g}\left(\left[\frac{u^p+v^p}{2}\right]^{\frac{1}{p}}\right)\right] \\ &= \frac{1}{\alpha} f\left(\left[\frac{u^p+v^p}{2}\right]^{\frac{1}{p}}\right) g\left(\left[\frac{u^p+v^p}{2}\right]^{\frac{1}{p}}\right). \end{aligned} \tag{42}$$

On the other hand, from (42) and taking $\varrho x^p = \varrho u^p + (1-\varrho)v^p$ and $y^p = (1-\varrho)u^p + \varrho v^p$, we get

$$\begin{aligned} &\frac{1}{4}\left[\int_0^1 \varrho^{\alpha-1} f\left([\varrho u^p+(1-\varrho)v^p]^{\frac{1}{p}}\right) g\left([\varrho u^p+(1-\varrho)v^p]^{\frac{1}{p}}\right) d\varrho \right. \\ &\left. + \int_0^1 \varrho^{\alpha-1} f\left([(1-\varrho)u^p+\varrho v^p]^{\frac{1}{p}}\right) g\left([(1-\varrho)u^p+\varrho v^p]^{\frac{1}{p}}\right) d\varrho \right] \\ &+ \frac{1}{4}\int_0^1 \varrho^{\alpha-1}(2\varrho^2-2\varrho+1) N(u,v) d\varrho + \frac{1}{2}\int_0^1 \varrho^{\alpha-1}\varrho(1-\varrho) M(u,v) d\varrho \\ &= \frac{p}{4(v^p-u^p)^\alpha}\left[\begin{array}{c} \int_u^v (v^p-x^p)^{\alpha-1}\underline{f}(x)\underline{g}(x)x^{p-1}dx + \int_u^v (y^p-u^p)^{\alpha-1}\underline{f}(y)\underline{g}(y)y^{p-1}dy, \\ \int_0^1 (v^p-x^p)^{\alpha-1}\overline{f}(x)\overline{g}(x)x^{p-1}dx + \int_u^v (y^p-u^p)^{\alpha-1}\overline{f}(y)\overline{g}(y)y^{p-1}dy \end{array}\right] \\ &+ \frac{1}{2\alpha}\left(\frac{1}{2} - \frac{\alpha}{(\alpha+1)(\alpha+2)}\right) N(u,v) + \frac{1}{2\alpha}\left(\frac{\alpha}{(\alpha+1)(\alpha+2)}\right) M(u,v) \\ &= \frac{p^\alpha \Gamma(\alpha+1)}{4(v^p-u^p)^\alpha}\left[\mathcal{I}_{u^+}^{p,\alpha} f(v)g(v) + \mathcal{I}_{v^-}^{p,\alpha} f(u)g(u)\right] \\ &+ \frac{1}{2\alpha}\left(\frac{1}{2} - \frac{\alpha}{(\alpha+1)(\alpha+2)}\right) N(u,v) + \frac{1}{2\alpha}\left(\frac{\alpha}{(\alpha+1)(\alpha+2)}\right) M(u,v). \end{aligned} \tag{43}$$

From (42) and (43), (41) becomes

$$\begin{aligned} 2f\left(\left[\frac{u^p+v^p}{2}\right]^{\frac{1}{p}}\right) g\left(\left[\frac{u^p+v^p}{2}\right]^{\frac{1}{p}}\right) &\leq_p \frac{p^\alpha \Gamma(\alpha+1)}{2(v^p-u^p)^\alpha}\left[\mathcal{I}_{u^+}^{p,\alpha} f(v)g(v) + \mathcal{I}_{v^-}^{p,\alpha} f(u)g(u)\right] \\ &+ \left(\frac{1}{2} - \frac{\alpha}{(\alpha+1)(\alpha+2)}\right) N(u,v) + \left(\frac{\alpha}{(\alpha+1)(\alpha+2)}\right) M(u,v) \end{aligned}$$

Hence, Theorem 6 has been proved. □

**Example 4.** *Let $p$ be an odd number and $\alpha = 1$ for $\varrho \in [0,\ 1]$, and the LR-p-convex $f : [u,\ \vartheta] = [2,3] \to \mathbb{R}_I^+$ and LR-p-convex IVFs $g : [u,\ \vartheta] = [2,3] \to \mathbb{R}_I^+$ are respectively defined by $f(x) =$*

$\left[2 - x^{\frac{p}{2}}, 2\left(2 - x^{\frac{p}{2}}\right)\right]$ *and* $g(x) = [x^p, 2x^p]$. *Since* $f_*(x) = 2 - x^{\frac{p}{2}}$, $f^*(x) = 2\left(2 - x^{\frac{p}{2}}\right)$ *and* $g_*(x) = x^p$, $g^*(x) = 2x^p$, *then we compute the following*

$$2\, f_*\left(\left[\frac{u^p+\vartheta^p}{2}\right]^{\frac{1}{p}}\right) \times g_*\left(\left[\frac{u^p+\vartheta^p}{2}\right]^{\frac{1}{p}}\right) = \frac{20-5\sqrt{10}}{2}$$

$$2\, f^*\left(\left[\frac{u^p+\vartheta^p}{2}\right]^{\frac{1}{p}}\right) \times g^*\left(\left[\frac{u^p+\vartheta^p}{2}\right]^{\frac{1}{p}}\right) = 40 - 10\sqrt{10},$$

$$\frac{p^\alpha\Gamma(\alpha+1)}{2(\nu^p-u^p)^\alpha}\left[\mathcal{I}_{u^+}^{p,\alpha}\, f_*(\nu) \times g_*(\nu) + \mathcal{I}_{\nu^-}^{p,\alpha}\, f_*(u) \times g_*(u)\right] = 1$$

$$\frac{p^\alpha\Gamma(\alpha+1)}{2(\nu^p-u^p)^\alpha}\left[\mathcal{I}_{u^+}^{p,\alpha}\, f^*(\nu) \times g^*(\nu) + \mathcal{I}_{\nu^-}^{p,\alpha}\, f^*(u) \times g^*(u)\right] = 4,$$

$$\left(\frac{\alpha}{(\alpha+1)(\alpha+2)}\right)\mathcal{M}_*(u,\vartheta) = \frac{1}{6}\left(10 - 2\sqrt{2} - 3\sqrt{3}\right)$$

$$\left(\frac{\alpha}{(\alpha+1)(\alpha+2)}\right)\mathcal{M}^*(u,\vartheta) = \frac{4}{6}\left(10 - 2\sqrt{2} - 3\sqrt{3}\right),$$

$$\frac{1}{2} - \frac{\alpha}{(\alpha+1)(\alpha+2)}\mathcal{N}_*(u,\vartheta) = \frac{1}{3}\left(10 - 3\sqrt{2} - 2\sqrt{3}\right)$$

$$\frac{1}{2} - \frac{\alpha}{(\alpha+1)(\alpha+2)}\mathcal{N}^*(u,\vartheta) = \frac{4}{3}\left(10 - 3\sqrt{2} - 2\sqrt{3}\right),$$

*that means*

$$\frac{20-5\sqrt{10}}{2} \leq \left(1 + \frac{30-8\sqrt{2}-7\sqrt{3}}{6}\right),$$

$$40 - 10\sqrt{10} \leq \left(4 + \frac{60-16\sqrt{2}-14\sqrt{3}}{3}\right),$$

*hence, Theorem 6 has been illustrated.*

## 4. Conclusions

In this work, we introduced the new class of LR-$p$-convex interval-valued functions and established some new Hermite-Hadamard inequalities by means of the pseudo order relation via Katugampola fractional integral operator. Useful examples that verify the applicability of the theory developed in this study are presented. We intend to use various types of LR-convex interval-valued functions to construct interval inequalities of interval-valued functions. In the future, we will try to explore this concept for fuzzy-interval-valued functions by means of the fuzzy pseudo order relation.

**Author Contributions:** Conceptualization, M.B.K. and M.A.N.; validation, P.O.M., D.B. and J.L.G.G.; formal analysis, D.B. and J.L.G.G.; investigation, M.B.K., M.A.N. and D.B.; resources, M.B.K. and M.A.N.; writing—original draft, M.B.K. and M.A.N.; writing—review and editing, M.B.K., P.O.M. and D.B.; visualization, M.A.N., P.O.M. and D.B.; supervision, M.A.N. and P.O.M.; project administration, M.A.N. and J.L.G.G. All authors have read and agreed to the published version of the manuscript.

**Data Availability Statement:** No data were used to support this study.

**Acknowledgments:** The authors would like to thank the Rector, COMSATS University Islamabad, Islamabad, Pakistan, for providing excellent research and academic environments. This work has been partially supported by Ministerio de Ciencia, Innovaci ón y Universidades, grant number PGC2018-097198-B-I00 and by Fundaci ón Séneca of Región de Murcia, grant number 20783/PI/18.

**Conflicts of Interest:** The authors declare no conflict of interest.

## References

1. Hermite, C. Sur deux limites d'une intégrale définie. *Mathesis* **1883**, *3*, 82–97.
2. Hadamard, J. Étude sur les propriétés des fonctions entières et en particulier d'une fonction considérée par Riemann. *J. Mathématiques Pures Appliquées* **1893**, *7*, 171–215.
3. Awan, M.U.; Akhtar, N.; Iftikhar, S.; Noor, M.A.; Chu, Y.-M. New Hermite–Hadamard type inequalities for n-polynomial harmonically convex functions. *J. Inequal. Appl.* **2020**, *2020*, 125. [CrossRef]
4. Latif, M.A.; Rashid, S.; Dragomir, S.S.; Chu, Y.-M. Hermite–Hadamard type inequalities for co-ordinated convex and quasi-convex functions and their applications. *J. Inequal. Appl.* **2019**, *2019*, 317. [CrossRef]

5. Chu, Y.-M.; Wang, G.-D.; Zhang, X.-H. The Schur multiplicative and harmonic convexities of the complete symmetric function. *Math. Nachr.* **2011**, *284*, 653–663. [CrossRef]
6. Chu, Y.M.; Xia, W.-F.; Zhang, X.-H. The Schur concavity, Schur multiplicative and harmonic convexities of the second dual form of the Hamy symmetric function with applications. *J. Multivar. Anal.* **2012**, *105*, 412–442. [CrossRef]
7. Zaheer Ullah, S.; Adil Khan, M.; Khan, Z.A.; Chu, Y.-M. Integral majorization type inequalities for the functions in the sense of strong convexity. *J. Funct. Spaces* **2019**, *2019*, 9487823. [CrossRef]
8. Zaheer Ullah, S.; Adil Khan, M.; Chu, Y.-M. Majorization theorems for strongly convex functions. *J. Inequal. Appl.* **2019**, *2019*, 58. [CrossRef]
9. Varošanec, S. On h-convexity. *J. Math. Anal. Appl.* **2007**, *326*, 303–311. [CrossRef]
10. Zhang, K.-S.; Wan, J.-P. p-convex functions and their properties. *Pure Appl. Math.* **2007**, *23*, 130–133.
11. Chang, S.S.; Zhu, Y.G. On variational inequalities for fuzzy mappings. *Fuzzy Sets Syst.* **1989**, *32*, 359–367. [CrossRef]
12. Nanda, S.; Kar, K. Convex fuzzy mappings. *Fuzzy Sets Syst.* **1992**, *48*, 129–132. [CrossRef]
13. Noor, M.A. Fuzzy preinvex functions. *Fuzzy Sets Syst.* **1994**, *64*, 95–104. [CrossRef]
14. Zaheer Ullah, S.; Adil Khan, M.; Chu, Y.-M. A note on generalized convex functions. *J. Inequal. Appl.* **2019**, *2019*, 15. [CrossRef]
15. Liu, W. New integral inequalities involving beta function via P-convexity. *Miskolc. Math. Notes* **2014**, *15*, 585–591. [CrossRef]
16. Fej'er, L. Uberdie Fourierreihen II. *Math. Naturwise. Anz. Ungar. Akad. Wiss.* **1906**, *24*, 369–390.
17. Breckner, W.W. Stetigkeitsaussagen für eine Klasse verallgemeinerter konvexer funktionen in topologischen linearen Räumen. *Pupl. Inst. Math.* **1978**, *23*, 13–20.
18. Hudzik, H.; Maligranda, L. Some remarks on s-convex functions. *Aequat. Math.* **1994**, *48*, 100–111. [CrossRef]
19. Iscan, I. Hermite–Hadamard type inequalities for p-convex functions. *Int. J. Anal Appl.* **2016**, *11*, 137–145.
20. Moore, R.E. *Interval Analysis*; Prentice Hall: Englewood Cliffs, NJ, USA, 1966.
21. Costa, T.M. Jensen's inequality type integral for fuzzy-interval-valued functions. *Fuzzy Sets Syst.* **2017**, *327*, 31–47. [CrossRef]
22. Costa, T.M.; Roman-Flores, H. Some integral inequalities for fuzzy-interval-valued functions. *Inform. Sci.* **2017**, *420*, 110–125. [CrossRef]
23. Román-Flores, H.; Chalco-Cano, Y.; Lodwick, W.A. Some integral inequalities for interval-valued functions. *Comput. Appl. Math.* **2018**, *37*, 1306–1318. [CrossRef]
24. Roman-Flores, H.; Chalco-Cano, Y.; Silva, G.N. A note on Gronwall type inequality for interval-valued functions. In Proceedings of the IEEE IFSA World Congress and NAFIPS Annual Meeting, Edmonton, AB, Canada, 24–28 June 2013; Volume 35, pp. 1455–1458.
25. Chalco-Cano, Y.; Flores-Franulič, A.; Román-Flores, H. Ostrowski type inequalities for interval-valued functions using generalized Hukuhara derivative. *Comput. Appl. Math.* **2012**, *31*, 457–472.
26. Chalco-Cano, Y.; Lodwick, W.A.; Condori-Equice, W. Ostrowski type inequalities and applications in numerical integration for interval-valued functions. *Soft Comput.* **2015**, *19*, 3293–3300. [CrossRef]
27. Nikodem, K.; Snchez, J.L.; Snchez, L. Jensen and Hermite–Hadamard inequalities for strongly convex set-valued maps. *Math. Aterna* **2014**, *4*, 979–987.
28. Matkowski, J.; Nikodem, K. An integral Jensen inequality for convex multifunctions. *Results Math.* **1994**, *26*, 348–353. [CrossRef]
29. Zhang, D.; Guo, C.; Chen, D.; Wang, G. Jensen's inequalities for set-valued and fuzzy set-valued functions. *Fuzzy Sets Syst.* **2020**, *2020*, 1–27. [CrossRef]
30. Abdeljawad, T.; Baleanu, D. Monotonicity results for fractional difference operators with discrete exponential kernels. *Adv. Differ. Equ.* **2017**, *2017*, 78. [CrossRef]
31. Agarwal, R.; Purohit, S.D.; Kritika. A mathematical fractional model with nonsingular kernel for thrombin receptor activation in calcium signaling. *Math. Methods Appl. Sci.* **2019**, *42*, 7160–7171. [CrossRef]
32. Agarwal, R.; Yadav, M.P.; Baleanu, D.; Purohit, S.D. Existence and uniqueness of miscible flow equation through porous media with a non-singular fractional derivative. *AIMS Math.* **2019**, *5*, 1062–1073. [CrossRef]
33. Kumar, D.; Singh, J.; Purohit, S.D.; Swroop, R. A hybrid analytical algorithm for nonlinear fractional wave-like equations. *Math. Model. Nat. Phenom.* **2019**, *14*, 304. [CrossRef]
34. Budak, H.; Tunç, T.; Sarikaya, M.Z. Fractional Hermite–Hadamard type inequalities for interval-valued functions. *Proc. Am. Math. Soc.* **2019**, *148*, 705–718. [CrossRef]
35. Katugampola, U.N. A new approach to generalized fractional derivatives. *Bull. Math. Anal. Appl.* **2014**, *6*, 1–15.
36. Toplu, T.; Set, E.; İşcan, İ.; Maden, S. Hermite–Hadamard type inequalities for p-convex functions via Katugampola fractional integrals. *Facta Univ. Ser. Math. Inform.* **2019**, *34*, 149–164.
37. Adil Khan, M.; Begum, S.; Khurshid, Y.; Chu, Y.-M. Ostrowski type inequalities involving conformable fractional integrals. *J. Inequal. Appl.* **2018**, *2018*, 70. [CrossRef]
38. Fang, Z.B.; Shi, R. On the (p, h)-convex function and some integral inequalities. *J. Inequal. Appl.* **2014**, *2014*, 45. [CrossRef]
39. Kunt, M.; İşcan, İ. Hermite–Hadamard–Fejér type inequalities for p-convex functions. *Arab J. Math. Sci.* **2017**, *23*, 215–230. [CrossRef]
40. Liu, X.-L.; Ye, G.-J.; Zhao, D.-F.; Liu, W. Fractional Hermite–Hadamard type inequalities for interval-valued functions. *J. Inequal. Appl.* **2019**, *2019*, 26. [CrossRef]
41. Sarikaya, M.Z.; Set, E.; Yaldiz, H.; Başak, N. Hermite–Hadamard's inequalities for fractional integrals and related fractional inequalities. *Math. Comput. Model.* **2013**, *57*, 2403–2407. [CrossRef]

42. Zhao, T.-H.; Chu, Y.-M.; Wang, H. Logarithmically complete monotonicity properties relating to the gamma function. *Abstr. Appl. Anal.* **2011**, *2011*, 896483. [CrossRef]
43. Precup, R.E.; Teban, T.A.; Albu, A.; Borlea, A.B.; Zamfirache, I.A.; Petriu, E.M. Evolving fuzzy models for prosthetic hand myoelectric-based control. *IEEE Trans. Instrum. Meas.* **2020**, *69*, 4625–4636. [CrossRef]
44. Khan, M.B.; Noor, M.A.; Noor, K.I.; Chu, Y.-M. New Hermite-Hadamard Type Inequalities for (h1, h2)-Convex Fuzzy-Interval-Valued Functions. *Adv. Differ. Equ.* **2021**, *2021*, 6–20. [CrossRef]
45. Liu, P.; Khan, M.B.; Noor, M.A.; Noor, K.I. New Hermite–Hadamard and Jensen inequalities for log-s-convex fuzzy-interval-valued functions in the second sense. *Complex Intell. Syst.* **2021**, *2021*, 1–15.
46. Khan, M.B.; Noor, M.A.; Abdullah, L.; Chu, Y.M. Some New Classes of Preinvex Fuzzy-Interval-Valued Functions and Inequalities. *Int. J. Comput. Intell. Syst.* **2021**, *14*, 1403–1418. [CrossRef]
47. Khan, M.B.; Mohammed, P.O.; Noor, M.A.; Hamed, Y.S. New Hermite–Hadamard inequalities in fuzzy-interval fractional calculus and related inequalities. *Symmetry* **2021**, *13*, 673. [CrossRef]
48. Liu, P.; Khan, M.B.; Noor, M.A.; Noor, K.I. On Strongly Generalized Preinvex Fuzzy Mappings. *J. Math.* **2021**, *2021*, 6657602. [CrossRef]
49. Khan, M.B.; Noor, M.A.; Noor, K.I.; Ab Ghani, A.T.; Abdullah, L. Extended perturbed mixed variational-like inequalities for fuzzy mappings. *J. Math.* **2021**, *2021*, 6652930. [CrossRef]
50. Khan, M.B.; Noor, M.A.; Noor, K.I.; Almusawa, H.; Nisar, K.S. Exponentially Preinvex Fuzzy Mappings and Fuzzy Exponentially Mixed Variational-Like Inequalities. *Int. J. Anal. Appl.* **2021**, *19*, 518–541.
51. Khan, M.B.; Noor, M.A.; Al-Bayatti, H.M.; Noor, K.I. Some New Inequalities for LR-Log-h-Convex Interval-Valued Functions by Means of Pseudo Order Relation. *Appl. Math.* **2021**, *15*, 459–470.
52. Sana, G.; Khan, M.B.; Noor, M.A.; Mohammed, P.O.; Chu, Y.M. Harmonically Convex Fuzzy-Interval-Valued Functions and Fuzzy-Interval Riemann–Liouville Fractional Integral Inequalities. *Int. J. Comput. Intell. Syst.* **2021**, *14*, 1809–1822. [CrossRef]
53. Khan, M.B.; Noor, M.A.; Noor, K.I.; Chu, Y.M. Higher-Order Strongly Preinvex Fuzzy Mappings and Fuzzy Mixed Variational-Like Inequalities. *Int. J. Comput. Intell. Syst.* **2021**, *14*, 1856–1870. [CrossRef]
54. Khan, M.B.; Noor, M.A.; Noor, K.I. On Some Characterization of Preinvex Fuzzy Mappings. *Earth. J. Math. Sci.* **2021**, *5*, 17–42.
55. Khan, M.B.; Noor, M.A.; Noor, K.I. On Fuzzy Quasi-Invex Sets. *Int. J. Algeb. Stat.* **2021**, *9*, 11–26.
56. Mohammed, P.O. New generalized Riemann-Liouville fractional integral inequalities for convex functions. *J. Math. Inequal.* **2021**, *15*, 511–519. [CrossRef]

*axioms*

MDPI

*Article*

# The Approximate and Analytic Solutions of the Time-Fractional Intermediate Diffusion Wave Equation Associated with the Fokker–Planck Operator and Applications

**Entsar A. Abdel-Rehim**

Department of Mathematics, Faculty of Science, Suez Canal University, Eldaree Street, Ismailia 41522, Egypt; entsarabdelrehim@yahoo.com

**Abstract:** In this paper, the time-fractional wave equation associated with the space-fractional Fokker–Planck operator and with the time-fractional-damped term is studied. The concept of the Green function is implemented to drive the analytic solution of the three-term time-fractional equation. The explicit expressions for the Green function $G_3(t)$ of the three-term time-fractional wave equation with constant coefficients is also studied for two physical and biological models. The explicit analytic solutions, for the two studied models, are expressed in terms of the Weber, hypergeometric, exponential, and Mittag–Leffler functions. The relation to the diffusion equation is given. The asymptotic behaviors of the Mittag–Leffler function, the hypergeometric function $1F1$, and the exponential functions are compared numerically. The Grünwald–Letnikov scheme is used to derive the approximate difference schemes of the Caputo time-fractional operator and the Feller–Riesz space-fractional operator. The explicit difference scheme is numerically studied, and the simulations of the approximate solutions are plotted for different values of the fractional orders.

**Keywords:** space–fractional Fokker–Planck operator; time–fractional wave with the time–fractional damped term; Laplace transform; Mittag–Leffler function; Grünwald–Letnikov scheme; potential and current in an electric transmission line; random walk of a population

**MSC:** 26A33; 35L05; 35J05; 45K05; 60J60; 60G50; 60G51; 65N06; 80-99; 42A38; 33C20; 44A10

**Citation:** Abdel-Rehim, E.A. The Approximate and Analytic Solutions of the Time-Fractional Intermediate Diffusion Wave Equation Associated with the Fokker–Planck Operator and Applications. *Axioms* **2021**, *10*, 230. https://doi.org/10.3390/axioms10030230

Academic Editor: Jorge E. Macías Díaz

Received: 14 August 2021
Accepted: 13 September 2021
Published: 17 September 2021



## 1. Introduction and Important Definitions

The classical intermediate diffusion wave equation, the multiterm wave equation, can be written as:

$$\frac{\partial^2 u(x,t)}{\partial t^2} + k\,\frac{\partial u(x,t)}{\partial t} = L_{FP}\,(u(x,t))\ ,\ -\infty < x < \infty\,,\ t \geq 0\,, \tag{1}$$

where the right-hand side of this equation is the known Fokker–Planck operator; see [1]. The Fokker–Planck operator is always associated with the stochastic processes and is defined as:

$$L_{FP}\,(u(x,t)) = \frac{\partial^2\,(a(x)\,u(x,t))}{\partial x^2} - \frac{\partial}{\partial x}(b(x)\,u(x,t))\ , \tag{2}$$

where $-\infty < x < \infty$, $t \geq 0$. The Fokker–Planck operator $L_{FP}$ can be derived following the stochastic differential equations because it describes how a collection of initial data evolves in time. This wave equation is governed by the initial conditions:

$$u(x,0) = f(x_0),\ \ u_t(x,0) = 0\,, u_t(0,t) = 0\,, \tag{3}$$

and the boundary conditions:

$$u(-\infty,t) = u(\infty,t) = 0\ \ . \tag{4}$$

Equation (1) mathematically models sound propagation and many physical, chemical, biological, medical, and other real-life phenomena. The description of $u(x,t)$ depends on the nature of the model. Generally, $a(x)$ and $b(x)$ are predefined functions according to the model. $b(x)$ represents the drift (the external force) acting on the wave. The constant $k$ with $0 < k < 1$ is the friction coefficient of theresistance source. The telegraph equation or the cable equation is a special case of Equation (1); see for example [2–5].

Experimental evidence shows that over diagnostic ultrasound frequencies, the acoustic absorption in biological tissue and the wave propagation in many other natural phenomena exhibit a power law with a noninteger frequency, i.e., $t^{-\beta}$, with $1 < \beta < 2$; see [6–8]. Here, $\beta = 1$ represents the classical diffusion equation, $0 < \beta < 1$ represents the time-fractional diffusion equation, $1 < \beta < 2$ represents the intermediate diffusion wave equation, and $\beta = 2$ represents the classical wave equation. To mathematically model such real phenomena, the extension to the time-fractional derivatives is required.

Experimentally, many physical and chemical phenomena exhibit very sharp random walks (random jumps), and their continuous random walk is not a Brownian motion. Solutes that move through fractal media commonly exhibit large deviations from the stochastic processes of Brownian motion and do not require a finite velocity. The extension to Lévy-stable motion is a straightforward generalization due to the common properties of Lévy-stable motion and Brownian motion, but the Lévy flights differ from the regular Brownian motion due to the occurrence of extremely long jumps, whose length is distributed according to the Lévy long tail $\sim |x|^{-1-\gamma}$, $0 < \gamma < 2$. Therefore, in this paper, we are interested in studying the spacetime-fractional intermediate diffusion wave equation with the time-fractional-damped term, which reads:

$$\underset{t\ *}{D^{\beta}}\, u(x,t) + k \underset{t\ *}{D^{\alpha}}\, u(x,t) = L_{FP}^{\gamma}\left(u(x,t)\right), \tag{5}$$

where $0 < \beta < 2$, $0 < \alpha \leq 1$, and $0 < \gamma < 2$. The space-fractional Fokker–Planck operator is defined as:

$$L_{FP}^{\gamma} = \underset{0\ x}{D^{\gamma}} \left(a(x)\, u(x,t)\right) - \frac{\partial}{\partial x}\left(b(x)\, u(x,t)\right). \tag{6}$$

Here, $\underset{0\ x}{D^{\gamma}}$ is the Riesz–Feller potential operator [9]. This fractional operator allows us to simulate the discrete solution along all the $x$-dimension. The Fourier transformation of the Riesz–Feller operator is $-|\kappa|^{\gamma} \widehat{f}(\kappa)$ for a sufficiently well-behaved function $f(x)$. $\underset{t\ *}{D^{\beta}}$ is the Caputo time-fractional operator, $\underset{t\ *}{D^{\beta}}$, with $0 < \beta < 2$. The Caputo time-fractional operator (see [10]) is defined as:

$$\underset{*}{D^{\beta}} f(t) = \begin{cases} \frac{1}{\Gamma(m-\beta)} \{ \int\limits_0^t \frac{f^{(m)}(\tau)}{(t-\tau)^{\beta+1-m}} d\tau & \text{for } m-1 < \beta < m\,, \\ \frac{d^m}{dt^m} f(t) & \text{for } \beta = m\,, \end{cases} \tag{7}$$

where:

$$K_{\beta}(t-\tau) = \frac{(t-\tau)^{\beta+1-m}}{\Gamma(m-\beta)},$$

is its kernel and is called the memory function. This kernel reflects the memory effects on many physical, biological, and other processes. The Caputo fractional derivative $\underset{*}{D^{\beta}}$ is used as a time-fractional operator because of its image in the Laplace transform domain, which is:

$$\mathcal{L}\{\underset{*}{D^{\beta}} f(t); s\} = s^{\beta} \widetilde{f}(s) - s^{\beta-1} f(0) - \dot{f}(0) s^{\beta-2} - \cdots - f^{(m-1)}(0) s^{\beta-m}\,, \; s > 0\,.$$

As $\dot{(0)} = 0, \cdots, f^{(m-1)}(0) = 0$, then:

$$\mathcal{L}\{\underset{*}{D^{\beta}} f(t); s\} = s^{\beta} \widetilde{f}(s) - s^{\beta-1} f(0)\,, \; s > 0\,. \tag{8}$$

In other words, the Caputo time-fractional operator is dependent on the initial condition, and this is the main reason for using it as a time-fractional derivative operator.

Some attempts have been made to discuss such problems. Luchko [11] attempted to derive the fundamental solution of the multidimensional fractional wave equation in order to discuss its solution for some special cases in the form of convergent series. Gorenflo [12] discussed the stochastic processes related to the fractional wave equations and their distributed order. Anh and Leonenko [13] presented the Green functions and the spectral representations of the mean-squared solutions of the fractional diffusion–wave equations with random initial conditions. Chen et al. [14] discussed the analytical solution of the time-fractional telegraph equation with three kinds of nonhomogeneous boundary conditions, namely the Dirichlet, Neumann, and Robin boundary conditions. Wyss [15] used the Mellin transform theory to derive a closed-form solution of the fractional diffusion equation in terms of Fox's H-function. Abdel-Rehim et al. [16–18] studied the explicit approximate solutions of the multiterm time-fractional wave equation and its stationary solutions of different values of the fractional orders and their time evolutions. The Grünwald–Letnikov scheme and the common explicit finite difference rules were implemented to derive the approximate solutions that were proven to be convergent. Sarvestani et al. [19] drove a wavelet approach for the multiterm time-fractional diffusion–wave equation. Mainardi et al. investigated some numerical results to this equation in his book [20].

The aim of the paper is to derive the analytical solution of the classical (1) and the spacetime-fractional wave with time-fractional attenuation Equation (5). The analytic solutions are given by using the separation of variables and by implementing the concepts of the Green function of the three-term equations [9]. The resulting solutions are written in the form of some known special functions. The solutions are proven to be asymptotically convergent solutions. Two physical and biological applications to the time-fractional wave equation associated with the Fokker–Planck operator are also discussed. The stationary solutions are also given and compared. The approximate solutions of the two applications are obtained by implementing the common finite difference rule and the Grünwald–Letnikov scheme.

The organization of this paper is as follows: Section 1 is devoted to the Introduction. Section 2 introduces the two physical and biological applications. Section 3 derives the analytical solution of the classical models. Section 4 is devoted to the solution of the time-fractional models. Section 5 introduces the approximate solutions of the two studied models. Finally, Section 6 is devoted to simulating the approximate solutions and numerically discussing and comparing the asymptotic behaviors of the obtained special functions.

## 2. Applications

First, we begin by mathematically formulating the potential and current in an electric transmission line (the cable equation). Consider a transmission line being a coaxial cable containing the resistance $R$, inductance $L$, capacitance $C$, and leakage conductance $G$. Introduce the function $I(x,t)$ to represent the current and $V(x,t)$ for the potential. These variables satisfy the following coupled equations:

$$L\frac{\partial I}{\partial t} + R\,I = -\frac{\partial V}{\partial x}\,, \tag{9}$$

and:

$$C\frac{\partial V}{\partial t} + G\,V = -\frac{\partial I}{\partial x}\,. \tag{10}$$

Differentiate (9) with respect to $t$ and differentiate (10) with respect to $x$ in order to eliminate $I$ and $V$. After some minor algebra, one can prove that both $I$ and $V$ satisfy the same following equation:

$$\frac{\partial^2 I}{\partial t^2} + (p+q)\frac{\partial I}{\partial t} = c^2\,\frac{\partial^2 I}{\partial x^2} - pqI\,, \tag{11}$$

where $kc^2 = \frac{R}{C} + \frac{G}{C} = p + q$ and $bc^2 = pq$. Replacing $I(x,t)$ by $u(x,t)$, this equation is rewritten as:

$$\frac{\partial^2 u(x,t)}{\partial t^2} + kc^2 \frac{\partial u(x,t)}{\partial t} = c^2 \frac{\partial^2 u(x,t)}{\partial x^2} + bc^2 u(x,t) \; . \tag{12}$$

The function $V(x,t)$ satisfies the same Equations (11) and (12). This equation is called the telegraph equation (cable equation) and mathematically models the electrical signal traveling along the transmission cable in which the term $k\,\frac{\partial u(x,t)}{\partial t}$ is called the internal resistance of the wires comprising the transmission lines. For further applications in physics and to real phenomena, see [4,5,13]. For this model, the Fokker–Planck operator is $L_{FP} = c^2(D_{xx} + b)$.

*The Continuous-Time Random Walk of a Population*

This model describes a population of individuals moving either to the left or right along the $x$-axis. The probability density function of moving right and left is $w(x,t)$ and $v(x,t)$, respectively. The total population moving has density $u(x,t) = w(x,t) + v(x,t)$. At any time instant $\tau$, each instant $\tau$, any individual can move to the left with probability $\delta$ or to the right with probability $1 - k\tau$. At the next time step, one has:

$$\frac{\partial w(x,t)}{\partial t} = -\rho \frac{\partial w(x,t)}{\partial x} + k(v(x,t) - w(x,t)) \; , \tag{13}$$

and:

$$\frac{\partial v(x,t)}{\partial t} = \rho \frac{\partial v(x,t)}{\partial x} - k(v(x,t) - w(x,t)) \; . \tag{14}$$

Adding (13) and (14) and differentiating with respect to $t$, then subtracting (13) from (14) and differentiating with respect to $x$, we obtain:

$$\frac{\partial^2 (v+w)}{\partial t^2} = \rho \frac{\partial^2 (v-w)}{\partial x \partial t} \; , \tag{15}$$

and:

$$\frac{\partial^2 (v-w)}{\partial x \partial t} = \rho \frac{\partial^2 (v+w)}{\partial x^2} - 2k \frac{\partial (v-w)}{\partial x} \; . \tag{16}$$

Subtracting (16) from (15), we obtain:

$$\frac{\partial^2 u(x,t)}{\partial t^2} + 2k \frac{\partial u(x,t)}{\partial t} = \rho^2 \frac{\partial^2 u(x,t)}{\partial x^2} \; . \tag{17}$$

This means the Fokker–Planck operator in this case is $L_{FP} = \rho^2 D_{xx}$. Now, take the direction of the movement of the individuals into consideration. In other words, the individuals move to the right with probability $\lambda_1$ and move to left with probability $\lambda_2$. Make the suitable changes to the system of Equations (13) and (14) and follow the same mathematical manipulation to obtain:

$$\frac{\partial^2 u(x,t)}{\partial t^2} + (\lambda_1 + \lambda_2) \frac{\partial u(x,t)}{\partial t} = \rho^2 \frac{\partial^2 u(x,t)}{\partial x^2} + \rho(\lambda_1 - \lambda_2) \frac{\partial u(x,t)}{\partial x} \; . \tag{18}$$

Then, the Fokker–Planck operator is $L_{FP} = \rho^2 D_{xx} + \rho(\lambda_1 - \lambda_2) D_x$. If $\lambda_1 > \lambda_2$, the individual moves right, and if $\lambda_1 < \lambda_2$, the individual moves left. This is known as the simple random walk model. Now, suppose the individual is sitting at the position $x_j$ at the time instant $t_n$ and makes movements either to $x_j$, $x_j - 1$, or $x_j + 1$ with probabilities $\lambda_1, \lambda_2, \lambda_3$ at the next time instant $t_{n+1}$ with $\lambda_1 + \lambda_2 + \lambda_3 = 1$. Then, we obtain a similar wave equation, but with the Fokker–Planck operator defined as $L_{FP} u(x,t) = a D_{xx} u(x,t) + b D_x(x u(x,t))$. For more information about the random walk in biology, see [21].

The movement of the potential and electricity in the transmission line and the random movement of the population are stochastic processes. Therefore, mathematically modeling them in spacetime-fractional differential equations is a natural generalization to their classical partial differential equations. The numerical results show the effects of the fractional orders on the time evolution of approximate solutions.

### 3. The Analytical Solution of the Classical Models

To solve the above-defined partial differential equations, we use the separation of variables method:

$$u(x,t) = X(x)\,T(t) \ , \tag{19}$$

and the initial conditions (3) are rewritten as:

$$T(0) = 1\,,\ \dot{T}(0) = 0\,, X(0) = \delta(x)\,, \dot{X}(0) = 0\ , \tag{20}$$

while the boundary conditions (4) are rewritten as:

$$X(-\infty) = X(\infty) = 0\ . \tag{21}$$

Applying Equation (19) to Equation (12) (see [14]), we obtain two ordinary differential equations:

$$c^2 \frac{d^2}{X} dx^2 + mx + bc^2 = 0\ , \tag{22}$$

and:

$$\frac{d^2T}{dt^2} + k\frac{dT}{dt} + m\,T = 0\ , \tag{23}$$

where for the stability, the friction constant $k$ is chosen to satisfy $0 < k \leq 1$. Equation (23) models the harmonic oscillator in a resisting medium.

The solution of Equation (22) is:

$$X = c_1 + c_2 \cos\sqrt{\frac{m}{c^2}}x + c_3 \sin\sqrt{\frac{m}{c^2}}x\ ,$$

and by applying the initial conditions (20), we obtain:

$$X = -\frac{bc^2}{m} + \cos\sqrt{\frac{m}{c^2}}x \tag{24}$$

Applying the separation of variables on Equation (17), we obtain:

$$\frac{d^2X}{dx^2} = \frac{m}{\rho^2}X\ , \tag{25}$$

and the same Equation (23). By applying the initial conditions (20), Equation (25) has the solution $X(x) = \cos\sqrt{\frac{m}{\rho^2}}x$. Now, the analytic solution of Equation (18) is given by applying the separation, to obtain two ordinary differential equations:

$$\rho^2\frac{d^2X}{dx^2} + (\lambda_1 - \lambda_2)\rho\frac{dX}{dx} + mX = 0\ , \tag{26}$$

and the same Equation (23). Let $\frac{\lambda_1 - \lambda_2}{\rho} = B$, then by applying the initial conditions (20), Equation (26) has the solution $X(x) = e^{\frac{-B}{2}x}\cos\frac{\sqrt{B^2 - 4m\rho^2}}{2}x$. Now, we try to study the analytic solution of the general genetic random walk defined in Section 2, namely Equation (18). This classical partial differential equation is obtained from the general Fokker–Planck Equation (2) by choosing $a(x) = a$ and $b(x) = -bx$ to represent the diffusion constant and the attractive linear force, respectively. Equation (1) is rewritten as:

$$\frac{\partial^2 u(x,t)}{\partial t^2} + k\,\frac{\partial u(x,t)}{\partial t} = a\,\frac{\partial^2 u(x,t)}{\partial x^2} + b\,\frac{\partial}{\partial x}(x\,u(x,t))\,, \tag{27}$$

Substituting Equation (19) into Equation (27), we obtain the following two ordinary differential equations, defined as:

$$a\,\frac{d^2X}{dx^2} + bx\,\frac{dX}{dx} + (b+m)\,X(x) = 0\,, \tag{28}$$

The solution of Equation (28) is the Weber function $D_m(x)$ of order $m$ (see [22–25]),

$$X_m(x) = D_m\Big(\sqrt{\frac{b}{a}}x\Big)\,e^{-\frac{bx^2}{4a}}\,, \tag{29}$$

where the Weber function of variables $(n,y)$ is the solution of the ordinary differential equation $\frac{d^2Y}{dy^2} + y\,\frac{dY}{dy} + (1+n)\,Y(y) = 0$ and is defined as $D_n = (-1)^n\,e^{-y^2/4}\frac{d^n}{dy^n}\,e^{y^2/2}$; see [23]. The constant $A_m$ is calculated from:

$$A_m = \frac{1}{m!\sqrt{2\pi}}\int_{-\infty}^{\infty} u(x,0)D_m(x)\,e^{\frac{bx^2}{4a}}\,dx\,,$$

taking into consideration the boundary condition (4). Equation (23) is an ordinary differential equation with constant coefficients having the solution:

$$T(t) = e^{-\frac{kt}{2}}\Big[c_1\sin\Big(\sqrt{\frac{k^2-4m}{4}}\Big)t + c_2\cos\Big(\sqrt{\frac{k^2-4m}{4}}\Big)t\Big]$$

where $4m > k^2$ and the constants $c_1$ and $c_2$ are obtained from the initial conditions (20) as:

$$T(t) = e^{-\frac{kt}{2}}\cos\Big(\sqrt{\frac{k^2-4m}{4}}\Big)t\,. \tag{30}$$

The solution of Equation (27) is:

$$u(x,t) = e^{-\frac{kt}{2}}\sum_{m=0}^{\infty} A_m\,D_m\Big(\sqrt{\frac{b}{a}}x\Big)\,e^{-\frac{bx^2}{4a}}\,\cos\Big(\sqrt{\frac{k^2-4m}{4}}\Big)t\,, \tag{31}$$

where $A_m$ is a constant to be defined by using the initial conditions (3) as:

$$A_m = \frac{1}{m!\sqrt{2\pi}}\int_{-\infty}^{\infty} f(x_0)D_m(x)e^{\frac{bx^2}{4a}}\,dx\,. \tag{32}$$

Equation (23) could be solved by the three-term Green function method defined by Podlubny [9]. First, apply the Laplace transformation to both sides of Equation (23) to obtain:

$$(s^2 + sk + m)\,\tilde{T}(s) = 1 + k\,. \tag{33}$$

Let $1 + k = V_0 > 1$ represent the initial velocity of the wave propagation. Then, rewrite (33) as:

$$\tilde{T}(s) = \frac{s^{-2}}{1+\frac{k}{s}}\,\frac{V_0}{1-\frac{-ms^{-2}}{(1+k/s)}}\,. \tag{34}$$

Rewrite it again as an infinite series form (see [9]):

$$\tilde{T}(s) = V_0\sum_{n=0}^{\infty}(-1)^n\,m^n\,\frac{s^{(-2n-2)}}{(1+\frac{k}{s})^{n+1}}\,, \tag{35}$$

and we need to use the Laplace inverse of two convoluted functions $f(t)$ and $g(t)$ defined as:

$$f(t) * g(t) = \int_0^t f(t-\tau)g(\tau)d\tau = L^{-1}\{f(\tilde{s}) * g(\tilde{s}); t\} \ , \tag{36}$$

then term-by-term inversion gives:

$$T(t) = V_0 \sum_{n=0}^{\infty} \frac{(-1)^n}{n!} m^n t^{2(n+1)-1} E^{(n)}_{1,2+n}(-kt) \ , \tag{37}$$

where the two-parameter Mittag–Leffler function $E_{\alpha,\beta}(z)$ (see [26]) is defined as:

$$E_{\alpha,\beta}(z) = \sum_{n=0}^{\infty} \frac{z^n}{\Gamma[\alpha n + \beta]} \tag{38}$$

and the $k$th derivative of the two-parameter Mittag–Leffler function is defined as:

$$E^{(k)}_{\alpha,\beta}(z) = \sum_{j=0}^{\infty} \frac{(j+k)! z^j}{j! \Gamma[\alpha j + \alpha k + \beta]} \ . \tag{39}$$

Use the special function $1F1$, which is the Hypergeometric1F1$[a,b,c]$ function called the Kummer confluent hypergeometric function $1F1(a;b;c)$. It is related to the convergent function $e^{-z}$ by the relation $1F1(1,1,-z) = e^{-z}$; for more details about the relation between the Kummer confluent hypergeometric function and the Mittag–Leffler function, see [27,28]. Equation (37) can be written as:

$$T(t) = V_0 \sum_{n=0}^{\infty} (-1)^n \, t^{1+2n} \, \frac{1F1[1+n, 2+2n, -t]}{\Gamma[2+2n]} \ . \tag{40}$$

Finally, the analytic convergent solution in terms of the special functions, $1F1$ and $D_m(x)$, reads:

$$u(x,t) = V_0 \sum_{m=0}^{\infty} \sum_{n=0}^{\infty} A_m \, (-1)^n \, t^{1+2n} \, \frac{1F1[1+n, 2+2n, -t]}{\Gamma[2+2n]} \, D_m(\sqrt{\frac{b}{a}} x) \, e^{-\frac{bx^2}{4a}} \ , \tag{41}$$

In what follows, we derive the stationary solution of the discussed model (1), i.e., the solution as $t \to \infty$. This solution is derived from Equation (1) by omitting the dependence on the time variable $t$ as:

$$a \frac{d^2 u(x)}{dx^2} + \frac{d}{dx}(bx \, u(x,t)) = 0 \ . \tag{42}$$

The solution of this equation is $u(x) = c \, e^{-\frac{bx^2}{2a}}$. In the section of the numerical results, we give a numerical comparison of the above-defined special functions.

## 4. The Analytical Solution of the Time–Fractional Forced-Wave Equation with the Fractional Damping Term

For $\gamma = 2,\ 0 < \beta < 2$, and $0 < \alpha < 1$, Equation (5) can be written as:

$$\underset{t\ *}{D^{\beta}} u(x,t) + k \underset{t\ *}{D^{\alpha}} u(x,t) = L_{FP} u(x,t) \ , \tag{43}$$

where $L_{FP}$ is the general Fokker–Planck Equation (2). To find the analytic solution of Equation (43), apply the separation of variables method. To obtain the same ordinary differential Equation (28), for the independent variable $x$, and the following ordinary differential equation for $t$:

$$\underset{t\ *}{D^{\beta}} T + k \underset{t\ *}{D^{\alpha}} T + mT = 0 \ . \tag{44}$$

This equation represents the time-fractional harmonic oscillator in a fractional resisting medium. Now, apply the Laplace transformation to both sides taking into consideration its dependence on the initial condition (8) (see [3,9]) to obtain:

$$(s^{\beta} + ks^{\alpha} + m)\tilde{T}(s) = s^{\beta-1} + ks^{\alpha-1} \,. \tag{45}$$

Again, rewrite Equation (45) as:

$$\tilde{T}(s) = \frac{s^{\beta-1} + ks^{\alpha-1}}{(s^{\beta} + ks^{\alpha} + m)} = \tilde{G_3}(s)\, \tilde{P}(s) \,, \tag{46}$$

where $\tilde{G_3}(s)$ is the Laplace transform of the Green function of the three-term time-fractional Equation (44), defined as:

$$\tilde{G_3}(s) = \frac{1}{s^{\beta} + ks^{\alpha} + m} \,, \tag{47}$$

and:

$$\tilde{P}(s) = s^{\beta-1} + ks^{\alpha-1} \,. \tag{48}$$

Now, rearrange the terms of $\tilde{G_3}(s)$ as:

$$\tilde{G_3}(s) = \frac{s^{-\beta}}{1 + \frac{k}{s^{\beta-\alpha}}} \frac{1}{1 - \frac{-ms^{-\beta}}{1+\frac{k}{s^{\beta-\alpha}}}} \,, \tag{49}$$

and it can be rewritten as the sum of infinite series:

$$\tilde{G_3}(s) = \frac{s^{-\beta}}{1 - \frac{k}{s^{\beta-\alpha}}} \sum_{n=0}^{\infty} (-1)^n \Big(\frac{ms^{-\beta}}{1 + \frac{k}{s^{\beta-\alpha}}}\Big)^n \,. \tag{50}$$

The term-by-term inversion is based on the general expansion theorem for the Laplace transform (see [9,29]); we obtain:

$$G_3(t) = \sum_{n=0}^{\infty} (-1)^n \frac{m^n}{n!} t^{\beta(n+1)-1} E^{(n)}_{\beta-\alpha,\beta+\alpha n}(-kt^{\beta-\alpha}) \,, \tag{51}$$

where $E^{(n)}_{\alpha,\beta}$ is the $n$th derivative of $E_{\alpha,\beta}$. The inverse Laplace transform of $\tilde{P}(s)$ gives:

$$P(t) = \frac{t^{-\beta}}{\Gamma[1-\beta]} + \frac{kt^{-\alpha}}{\Gamma[1-\alpha]} \,. \tag{52}$$

Now, to find the solution $T(t)$ of Equation (44), the convolution property (36) is used to obtain:

$$T(t) = \frac{1}{\Gamma[1-\beta]} \int_0^t (t - t')^{-\beta} G_3(t')dt' + \frac{k}{\Gamma[1-\alpha]} \int_0^t (t - t')^{-\alpha} G_3(t')dt' \,. \tag{53}$$

$T(t)$ is obtained by using the convolution property (36) as:

$$T(t) = \sum_{n=0}^{\infty}\sum_{j=0}^{\infty} (-1)^{n+j} m^n k^j \frac{(j+n)!}{n!j!\Gamma[\beta(n+j+1) - j\alpha]} \int_0^t \Big(\frac{(t-t')^{-\beta}}{\Gamma(1-\beta)} + \frac{k(t-t')^{-\alpha}}{\Gamma(1-\alpha)}\Big) t'^{\beta(j+n+1)-1-\alpha j} dt' \,. \tag{54}$$

For the purpose of computing these integrals by Mathematica, it is better to rewrite Equation (54) as:

$$T(t) = \sum_{n=0}^{\infty}\sum_{j=0}^{\infty}(-1)^{n+j}m^n k^j \frac{(j+n)!}{n!j!\Gamma[\beta(n+j+1)-j\alpha]}$$
$$\left(\int_0^t \frac{(t-t')^{-\beta}}{\Gamma(1-\beta)} t'^{\beta(j+n+1)-1-\alpha j}\, dt' + \frac{k(t-t')^{-\alpha}}{\Gamma(1-\alpha)} t'^{\beta(j+n+1)-1-\alpha j}\, dt'\right) , \quad (55)$$

These integrations are valid under the conditions:

$$Re[\beta] < 1, Re[\alpha] < 1, t > 0, Re[-j\alpha + \beta(1+j+n)] > 0 .$$

Since $1 < \beta < 2$, then the first integral is omitted because it is divergent. The final computed form of $T(t)$ is written as:

$$T(t) = \sum_{n=0}^{\infty}\sum_{j=0}^{\infty}(-1)^{n+j}m^n k^j \frac{(j+n)!}{n!j!}\left(\frac{t^{-(1+j)\alpha+(1+j+n)\beta}}{\Gamma[1-(1+j)\alpha+(1+j+n)\beta]}\right) . \quad (56)$$

Now, substitute $T(t)$ defined in Equation (56) in Equation (53) to find the general solution $T(t)$ as:

$$T(t) = \sum_{n=0}^{\infty}\sum_{j=0}^{\infty}(-1)^{n+j}m^n k^j \frac{(j+n)!}{n!j!} t^{(\beta-\alpha)+j(\beta-\alpha)+n\beta}$$
$$\left(\frac{1}{\Gamma[1+(\beta-\alpha)+j(\beta-\alpha)+n\beta]}\right) . \quad (57)$$

Now, by using the definition of the $k$th derivative of the Mittag–Leffler, $E^{(k)}_{\alpha,\beta}(z)$, defined in (39), we obtain the following elegant form of $T$ as:

$$T(t) = \sum_{n=0}^{\infty}(-1)^n \frac{m^n}{n!} t^{n\beta+\beta-\alpha}\, E^{(n)}_{(1+\beta-\alpha),(1+n\beta)}(-kt^{(\beta-\alpha)}) . \quad (58)$$

Finally, to find the general solution (44), substitute from Equation (58) Equation (29), and after some minor mathematical manipulations, we obtain:

$$u(x,t) = \sum_{m=0}^{\infty}\sum_{n=0}^{\infty}(-1)^n A_m D_m(x) \frac{m^n}{n!} t^{n\beta+\beta-\alpha}\, E^{(n)}_{(1+\beta-\alpha),(1+n\beta)}(-kt^{(\beta-\alpha)}) , \quad (59)$$

where the constant $A_m$ is obtained by applying Equation (32). This is the general solution of the time-fractional forced wave equation with the fractional damping term. Finally, the stationary solution of Equation (43) is obtained by takingthe dependence on the time of Equation (43) to obtain the same Equation (42) and, consequently, the same solution. In other words, the classical and time-fractional multiterm wave equations have the same stationarity.

Another equation that has great interest among mathematicians and physicists is the time-fractional diffusion Fokker–Planck equation. The Fokker–Planck equation was numerically and analytically studied by Abdel-Rehim [25]. The studied version of the time-fractional Fokker–Planck equation can be obtained from Equation (43) by putting $0 < \alpha = \beta < 1$ and $\phi(x,t) = 0$ to obtain:

$${}_{t\,*}D^{\beta}\, u(x,t) = \frac{a}{1+k}\frac{\partial^2 u(x,t)}{\partial x^2} + \frac{b}{1+k}\frac{\partial}{\partial x}(x\, u(x,t)) , \quad (60)$$

where $\frac{a}{1+k} \geq 0$ is the constant of diffusion and $\frac{b}{1+k} \geq 0$ is the drift constant. The simulation of Equation (60) has the same stationary solution as the same studied models here.

Equation (5) has only a solution in the Laplace–Fourier domain, and it is hard to invert it to a unique solution. Therefore, it is better to seek convergent approximate solutions instead of the analytic solutions that are given in terms of special functions.

## 5. Approximate Solutions

In this section, we implement the common finite difference tools besides the Grünwald–Letnikov scheme to find the approximate solutions of the spacetime-fractional differential Equation (5). We begin with the discrete scheme of the Riesz–Feller operator. The Riesz space-fractional operator $\underset{0\ x}{D^{\gamma}}$ is a pseudo-differential and a symmetric differential operator for the fractional order $0 < \gamma \leq 2$ and is defined as:

$$I_0^{\gamma}\Phi(x) = \frac{1}{2\Gamma(\gamma)cos(\gamma\pi/2)} \int_{-\infty}^{\infty} |x-\xi|^{\gamma-1}\Phi(\xi)d\xi \,. \tag{61}$$

This definition was extended by Feller [30] and Samko [31] to introduce the inverse Riesz potential operator in the whole range $0 < \alpha \leq 2$ as:

$$\underset{0\ x}{D^{\gamma}} = \frac{-1}{2cos(\gamma\pi/2)} \left[I_+^{-\gamma} + I_-^{-\gamma}\right] , 0 < \gamma \leq 2\,,\ \gamma \neq 1\,, \tag{62}$$

where $I_{\pm}^{-\alpha}$ are the inverse of the operators $I_{\pm}^{\alpha}$, and its Fourier transform reads:

$$\widehat{\underset{0\ x}{D^{\gamma}}\Phi(x)} = -|\kappa|^{\gamma}\hat{\Phi(\kappa)} \,.$$

Since the Laplace operator $\Delta$ in one dimension, namely $\Delta = \frac{\partial^2 u(x,t)}{\partial x^2}$, is a symmetric differential operator and its Fourier image is $\widehat{\Delta^2\Phi(x)} = -|\kappa|^2\hat{\Phi(\kappa)}$, then we can simply write $\underset{0\ x}{D^{\gamma}} = -(-\Delta)^{\gamma/2}$; see for more details [30–33]. That is the reason for calling $\underset{0\ x}{D^{\gamma}}$ the Riesz–Feller space-fractional operator.

Now, to derive the approximate solutions of the discussed models, one has to define the grid point $(x_j, t_n)$:

$$x_j = jh,\ h > 0,\ j \in \mathbb{N}\,, \tag{63}$$

where $j \in [-R, R]$, $h = \frac{1}{2R+1}$, and $R \in \mathbb{N}$, while:

$$t_n = n\tau,\ \tau > 0,\ n \in \mathbb{N}_0\,. \tag{64}$$

Introduce the clump $y^{(n)}$ as an approximation to $u(x,t)$ as:

$$y^{(n)} = \{y_{-R}^{(n)}, y_{-R+1}^{(n)}, \cdots, y_0^{(n)}, \cdots, y_{R-1}^{(n)}, y_R^{(n)}\}^T\,. \tag{65}$$

Taking into consideration Equation (62), we have to distinguish the discrete scheme of $\underset{0\ x}{D^{\gamma}}$ according to the values of $\gamma$.

$$\underset{h\,\pm}{I}^{-\alpha} y_j(t_n) = \frac{1}{h^{\gamma}} \sum_{i=0}^{\infty} (-1)^i \binom{\gamma}{i} y_{j\mp i}\,,\ 0 < \gamma < 1\,, \tag{66}$$

while:

$$\underset{h\,\pm}{I}^{-\alpha} y_j(t_n) = \frac{1}{h^{\gamma}} \sum_{i=0}^{\infty} (-1)^i \binom{\gamma}{i} y_{j\pm 1\mp i}\,,\ 1 < \gamma \leq 2 \tag{67}$$

The case as $\gamma = 1$ is related to the Cauchy distribution, and one cannot use the Grünwald–Letnikov scheme for discretizing $\underset{0}{D^1}$ because the dominator $c_{\pm} \to 0$ in Equation (62) is undefined for $\gamma = 1$. Instead of the Grünwald–Letnikov scheme, we use the discretization introduced in [34] and successfully numerically applied by Abdel-Rehim [18]. In these references, the discretization of $\underset{0}{D^1}$ was deduced from the Cauchy density $p_1(x,0) = \frac{1}{\pi}\frac{1}{1+x^2}$, and the discrete scheme reads:

$$\underset{h\pm}{I}^{-1} y_j(t_n) = \frac{-2}{\pi h} y_j(t_n) + \frac{1}{h}\sum_{i=1}^{\infty}(-1)^i \frac{1}{\pi h i(i+1)} y_{j\mp i}(t_n)\,, \tag{68}$$

where:

$$\sum_{i=0}^{\infty} \frac{1}{i(i+1)} < \infty\,. \tag{69}$$

The Grünwald–Letnikov scheme of the Caputo time-fractional operator of order $0 < \beta \le 2$, defined in Equation (7), reads:

$$\underset{t\ *}{D^{\beta}}\, u(x,t) = \sum_{s=0}^{n+1} (-1)^s \binom{\beta}{s} \frac{y_j^{(n+1-s)} - y_j^{(0)}}{\tau^{\beta}} \quad , 0 < \beta \le 2\,. \tag{70}$$

Combining the above schemes, one obtains the discrete scheme of (5) for $a(x) = D$ and $b(x) = -bx$ for $1 < \gamma < 2$ as:

$$\begin{aligned}
&\tau^{-\beta}\Big(y_j^{(n+1)} - \beta y_j^{(n)} - \sum_{m=2}^{n+1}(-1)^m \binom{\beta}{m} y_j^{(n+1-m)} - \sum_{m=0}^{n+1}(-1)^m \binom{\beta}{m} y_j^{(0)}\Big) \\
&+ k\tau^{-\alpha}\Big(y_j^{(n+1)} - \alpha y_j^{(n)} - \sum_{m=2}^{n+1}(-1)^m \binom{\alpha}{m} y_j^{(n+1-m)} - \sum_{m=0}^{n+1}(-1)^m \binom{\alpha}{m} y_j^{(0)}\Big) \\
&= \frac{-h^{-\gamma}}{2\cos\frac{\gamma\pi}{2}} \sum_{i\in\mathbb{Z}} (-1)^i \binom{\gamma}{i} \{y_{j+1-i}(t_n) + y_{j-1+i}(t_n)\} + \frac{b}{2}\Big((j+1)y_{j+1}^{(n)} - (j-1)y_{j-1}^{(n)}\Big)\,.
\end{aligned} \tag{71}$$

Let $\frac{2}{b} = r$ and solve for $y^{n+1}$ to obtain:

$$\begin{aligned}
y^{(n+1)} = \\
&\frac{-1}{(\tau^{-\beta} + k\tau^{-\alpha})} \frac{h^{-\gamma}}{2\cos\frac{\gamma\pi}{2}} \sum_{i\in\mathbb{Z}} (-1)^i \binom{\gamma}{i} \{y_{j+1-i}^{(n)} + y_{j-1+i}^{(n)}\} \\
&+ \frac{1}{(\tau^{-\beta} + k\tau^{-\alpha})} \Big((\beta\tau^{-\beta} + k\alpha\tau^{-\alpha})y_j^{(n)} + \frac{j+1}{r} y_{j+1}^{(n)} - \frac{j-1}{r} y_{j-1}^{(n)}\Big) \\
&+ \frac{1}{(\tau^{-\beta} + k\tau^{-\alpha})} \Big(\tau^{-\beta}\sum_{m=2}^{n+1}(-1)^m \binom{\beta}{m} + k\tau^{-\alpha}\sum_{m=2}^{n+1}(-1)^m\binom{\alpha}{m}\Big) y_j^{(n+1-m)} \\
&+ \frac{1}{(\tau^{-\beta} + k\tau^{-\alpha})} \Big(\tau^{-\beta}\sum_{m=0}^{n+1}(-1)^m \binom{\beta}{m} + k\tau^{-\alpha}\sum_{m=0}^{n+1}(-1)^m\binom{\alpha}{m}\Big) y_j^{(0))}\,.
\end{aligned} \tag{72}$$

This scheme is stable, and henceforth, the approximate solution is convergent if the following condition is satisfied:

$$\frac{\beta + k\tau^{\beta-\alpha}}{h^{\gamma}} + \frac{2\gamma}{\cos\frac{\gamma\pi}{2}} \ge 0\,, \tag{73}$$

where $0 < k \le 1$; see [35]. For $0 < \gamma < 1$, we have:

$$\underset{h\pm}{I}^{-\gamma} y_j(t_n) = \frac{1}{h^{\gamma}} \sum_{i=0}^{\infty} (-1)^i \binom{\gamma}{i} y_{j\mp i}\,, \tag{74}$$

and to find the approximate solution of Equation (5) corresponding to this case, combine the discrete scheme of the Caputo time-fractional operator (70) with (66) to obtain:

$$
\begin{aligned}
y^{(n+1)} = & \\
& \frac{-1}{(\tau^{-\beta}+k\tau^{-\alpha})}\frac{h^{-\gamma}}{2cos\frac{\gamma\pi}{2}}\sum_{i\in\mathbb{Z}}(-1)^i\binom{\gamma}{i}\{y_{j+i}^{(n)}+y_{j-i}^{(n)}\} \\
& +\frac{1}{(\tau^{-\beta}+k\tau^{-\alpha})}\left((\beta\tau^{-\beta}+k\alpha\tau^{-\alpha})y_j^{(n)}+\frac{j+1}{r}y_{j+1}^{(n)}-\frac{j-1}{r}y_{j-1}^{(n)}\right) \\
& +\frac{1}{(\tau^{-\beta}+k\tau^{-\alpha})}\left(\tau^{-\beta}\sum_{m=2}^{n+1}(-1)^m\binom{\beta}{m}+k\tau^{-\alpha}\sum_{m=2}^{n+1}(-1)^m\binom{\alpha}{m}\right)y_j^{(n+1-m)} \\
& +\frac{1}{(\tau^{-\beta}+k\tau^{-\alpha})}\left(\tau^{-\beta}\sum_{m=0}^{n+1}(-1)^m\binom{\beta}{m}+k\tau^{-\alpha}\sum_{m=0}^{n+1}(-1)^m\binom{\alpha}{m}\right)y_j^{(0))}\,,
\end{aligned}
\tag{75}
$$

where this scheme is also satisfied if the condition (73) is satisfied, but with $0<\gamma<1$. Finally, the discrete scheme for the singular case as $\gamma=1$ reads:

$$
\begin{aligned}
y^{(n+1)} = & \\
& \frac{-1}{(\tau^{-\beta}+k\tau^{-\alpha})}\left(\frac{-2}{\pi h}y_j^{(n)}+\frac{1}{h}\sum_{i=1}^{\infty}(-1)^i\frac{1}{\pi hi(i+1)}(y_{j+i}^{(n)}+y_{j-i}^{(n)})\right) \\
& +\frac{1}{(\tau^{-\beta}+k\tau^{-\alpha})}\left((\beta\tau^{-\beta}+k\alpha\tau^{-\alpha})y_j^{(n)}+\frac{j+1}{r}y_{j+1}^{(n)}-\frac{j-1}{r}y_{j-1}^{(n)}\right) \\
& +\frac{1}{(\tau^{-\beta}+k\tau^{-\alpha})}\left(\tau^{-\beta}\sum_{m=2}^{n+1}(-1)^m\binom{\beta}{m}+k\tau^{-\alpha}\sum_{m=2}^{n+1}(-1)^m\binom{\alpha}{m}\right)y_j^{(n+1-m)} \\
& +\frac{1}{(\tau^{-\beta}+k\tau^{-\alpha})}\left(\tau^{-\beta}\sum_{m=0}^{n+1}(-1)^m\binom{\beta}{m}+k\tau^{-\alpha}\sum_{m=0}^{n+1}(-1)^m\binom{\alpha}{m}\right)y_j^{(0))}\,,
\end{aligned}
\tag{76}
$$

where this discrete scheme is stable and its corresponding approximate solution is convergent if the following condition is satisfied:

$$\beta+k\alpha\tau^{\beta-\alpha}+\frac{2\tau\beta}{\pi h}\geq 0\,. \tag{77}$$

In the following section, we give the simulation of the time evolution of the approximate solution $y^{(n)}$ discussed here for different values of the fractional orders $\alpha,\beta$, and $\gamma$ and for different values of the initial condition $f(x)$.

## 6. Numerical Results

To computationally prove that the analytic solutions in terms of the Mittag–Leffler function are convergent, we give a brief review of its asymptotic behaviors; see [35] and the references therein. The short and long time behaviors of the Mittag–Leffler function are computed from the following special forms:

$$E_\beta(-t^\beta)\ \sim\ \sum_{n=0}^{\infty}(-1)^n\frac{t^{n\beta}}{\Gamma(n\beta+1)}\ \text{as } t\geq 0\,. \tag{78}$$

This form is valid only for the short time. To deal with the long time, we have to compute the following function:

$$E_\beta(-t^\beta)\ \sim\ \frac{sin\,\beta\pi}{\pi}\frac{\Gamma(\beta)}{t^\beta}\ \text{as } t\to\infty\,, \tag{79}$$

and another useful form of the Mittag–Leffler function, namely:

$$E_\beta(-t^\beta)\ \sim\ exp(\frac{-t^\beta}{\Gamma[1+\beta]})\,, \tag{80}$$

where this form is called the stretched exponential function. Substituting in this function with $\beta = 1$, we obtain the fastest convergent function $e^{-t}$. Figures 1 and 2 show the asymptotic behaviors of the Mittag–Leffler function for the short and long time. The Hypergeometric1F1$[1+n, 2+n, -t]$ function is plotted in Figure 3 and is called the Kummer confluent hypergeometric function. It is known that $1F1$ is related to the convergent function $e^{-z}$ by the relation $1F1(1,1,-z) = e^{-z}$, for more details see [27,28]. Their time evolution is plotted in Figure 4. The simulation of these special functions indicates that the obtained analytic solutions are convergent as $t \to \infty$.

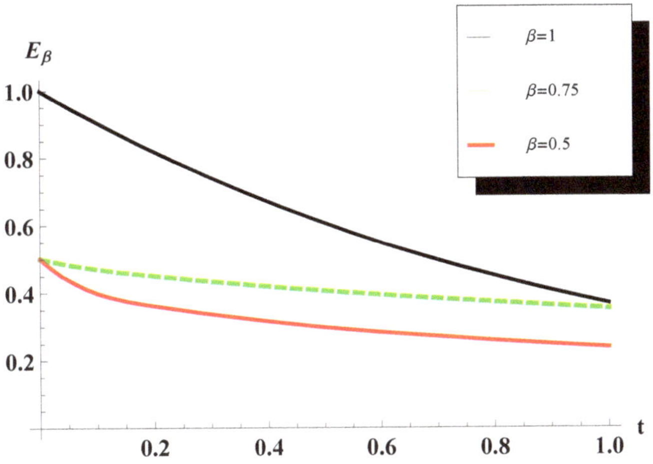


**Figure 1.** The simulation of the Mittag–Leffler as $t : 0 \to 1$, for different values of $\beta$.

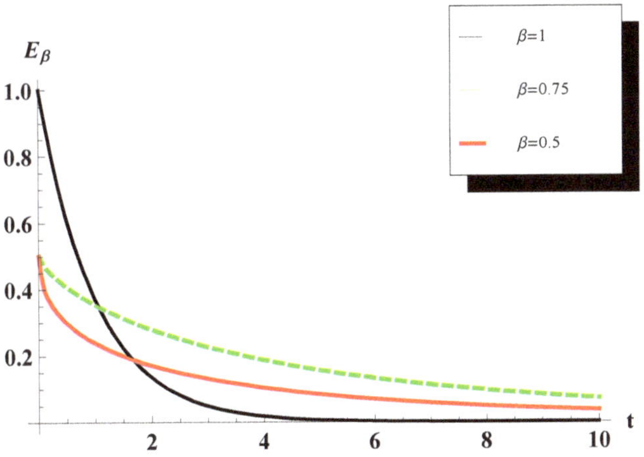


**Figure 2.** The simulation of the Mittag–Leffler as $t : 0 \to 10$, for different values of $\beta$.

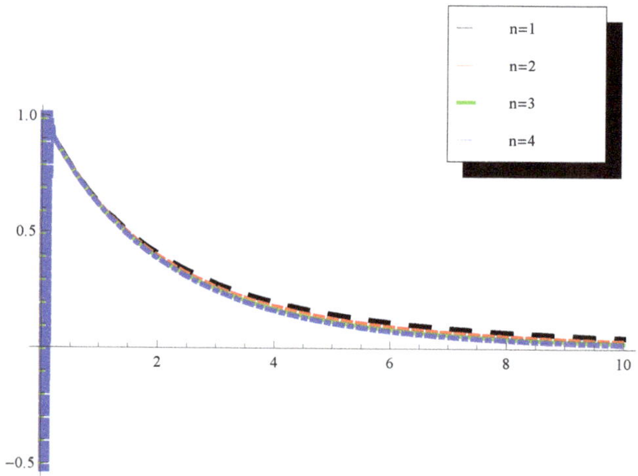


**Figure 3.** Hypergeometric1F1$[1+n, 2+n, -t]$.

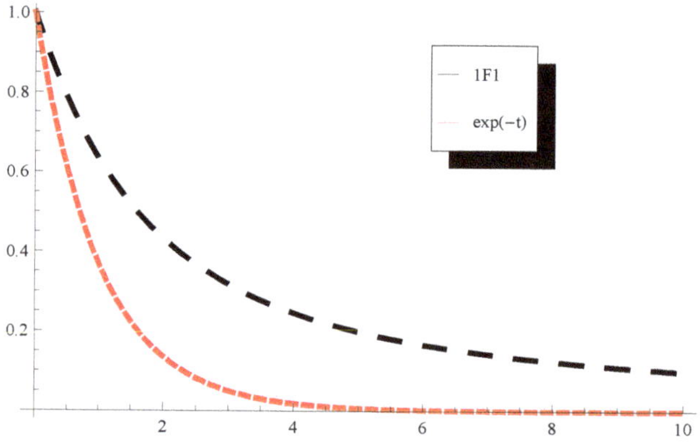


**Figure 4.** Hypergeometric1F1$[1, 2, -t]$.

The time evolution of the approximate solution of the classical Equation (5), i.e., as $\gamma = 2, \alpha = 1, \beta = 2, a(x) = 1, b(x) = -x$ and $f(x) = \sin\frac{\pi x}{L}$, is plotted in Figures 5–8.

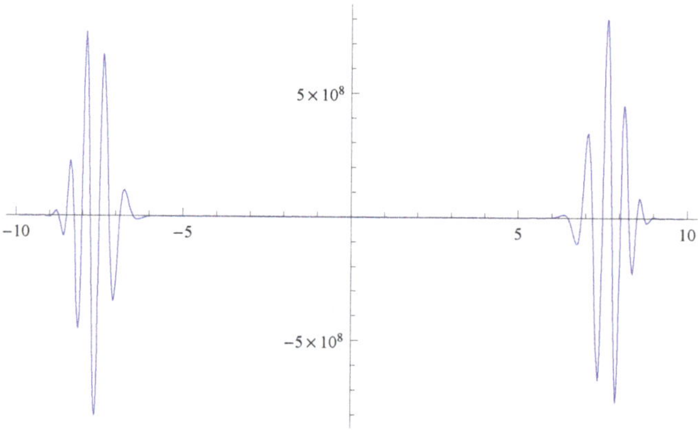


**Figure 5.** $t = 2$.

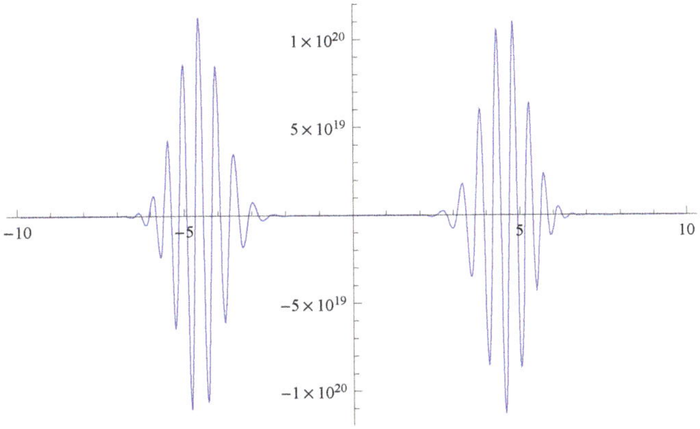


**Figure 6.** $t = 5$.

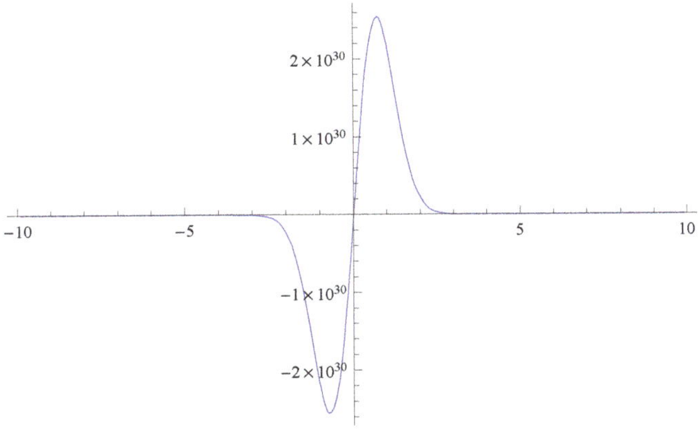


**Figure 7.** $t = 10$.

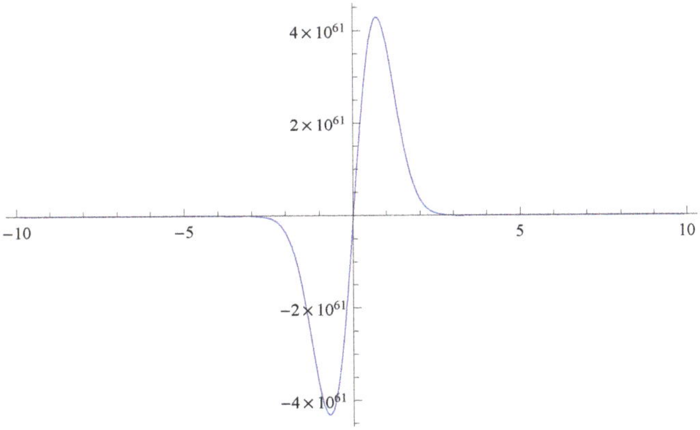


**Figure 8.** $t = 20$.

The time evolution of the approximate solution of Equation (5) is as $a(x) = a = 1$, $b(x) = -bx = -x$, $k = 1$, $\gamma = 2$, $\beta = 1.7$, $\alpha = 0.7$, $r = 100$, and $f(x) = \sin \frac{\pi x}{2r+1}$ is plotted in Figures 9–12. The figures shows that the approximate solution reaches its stationary solution very fast.

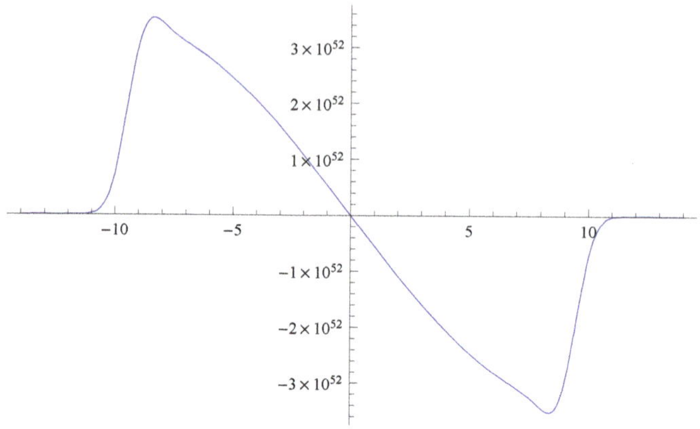


**Figure 9.** $t = 5$.

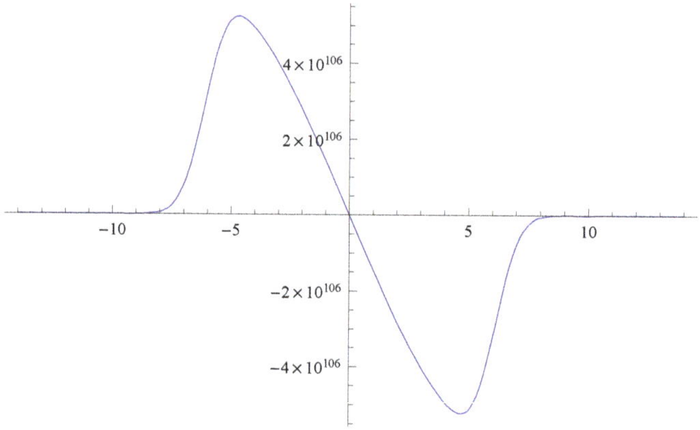


**Figure 10.** $t = 10$.

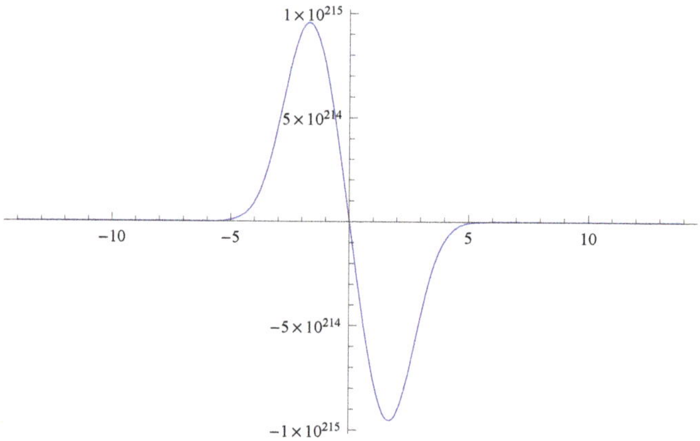


**Figure 11.** $t = 20$.

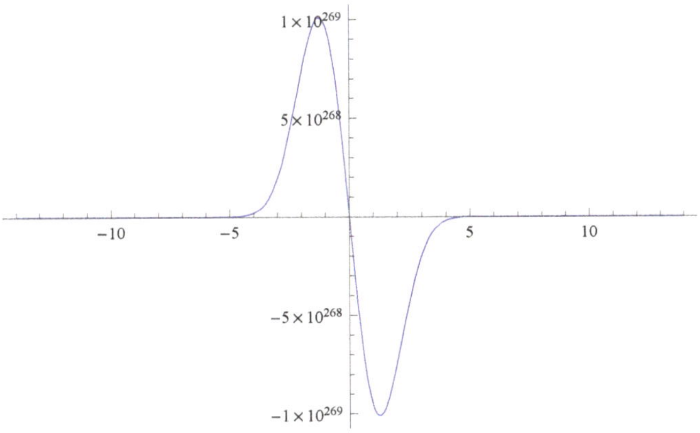


**Figure 12.** $t = 25$.

The time evolution of the approximate solution of Equation (5) for $a(x) = a = 1$, $b(x) = -bx$, $\gamma = 0.8$, $\beta = 1.7$, $\alpha = 1$, $k = 0.7$ and $f(x) = \delta(x)$ is plotted in Figures 13–16.

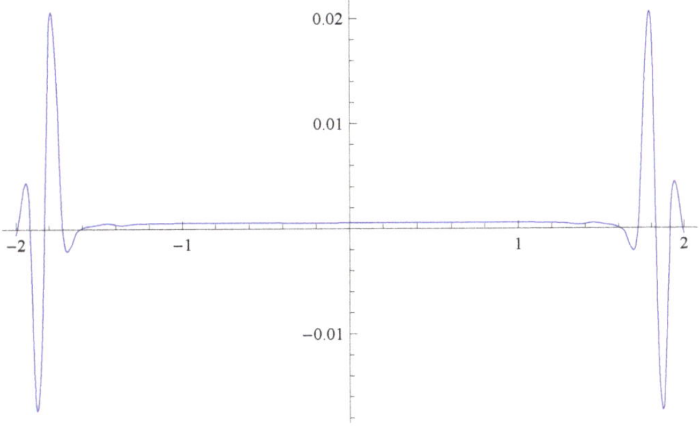


**Figure 13.** $t = 2$.

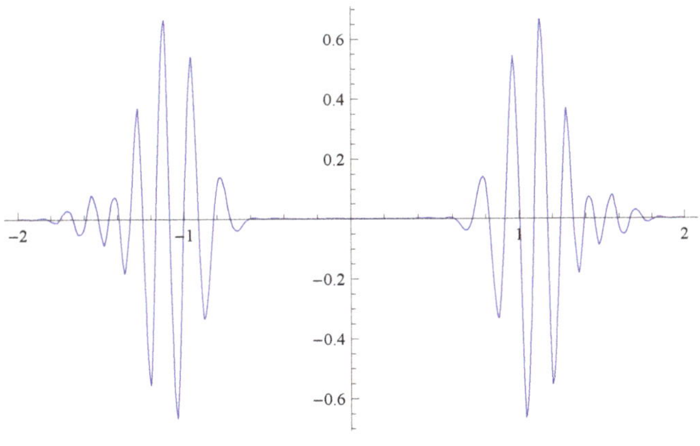


**Figure 14.** $t = 5$.

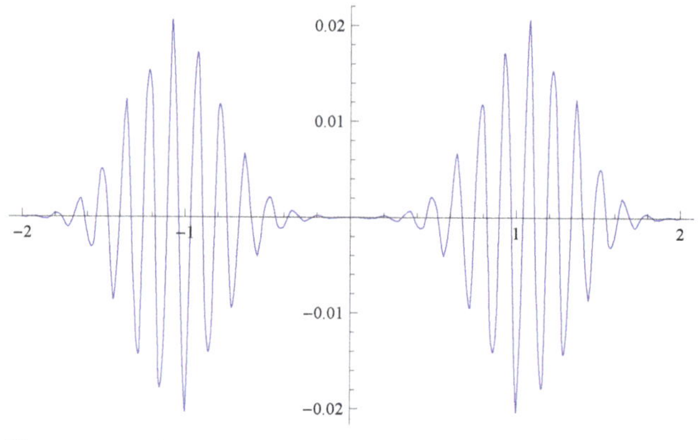


**Figure 15.** $t = 10$.

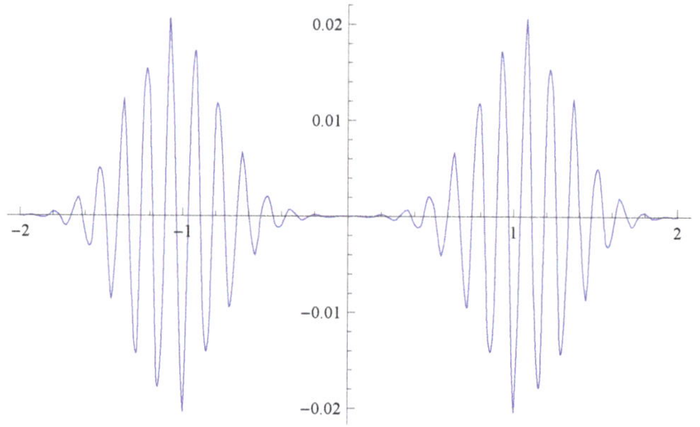


**Figure 16.** $t = 20$.

The time evolution of $y^{(n)}$ of the same equation, but corresponding to $\gamma = 1$, $\beta = 1.7$, $\alpha = 1$, and $f(x) = \sin \frac{\pi x}{L}$, is plotted Figures 17–20. These simulations show that the approximate solution reaches its stationary solution at $t = 20$, and it does not change even if we increase the number of iterations till we reach $t = 60$. This is a necessary property of any stochastic process.

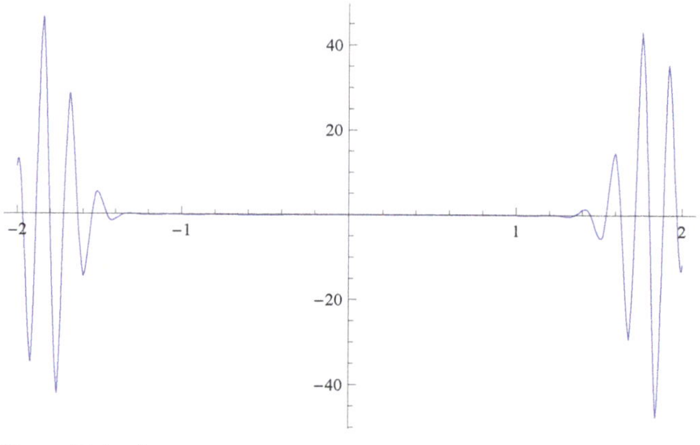


**Figure 17.** $t = 5$.

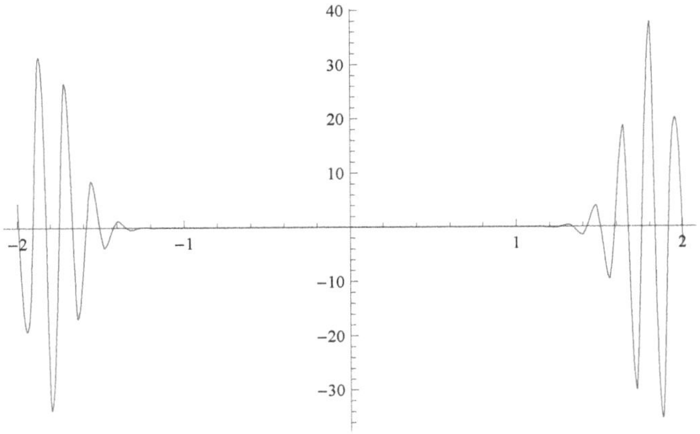

**Figure 18.** $t = 20$.

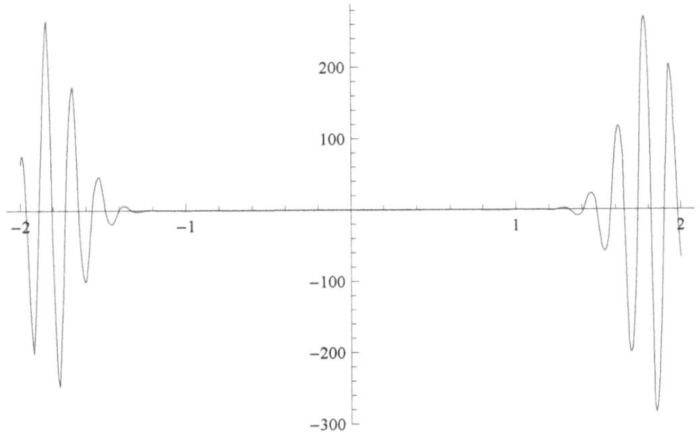

**Figure 19.** $t = 40$.

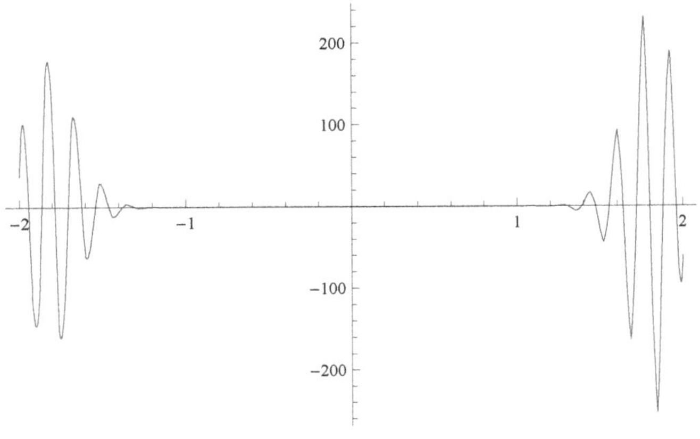

**Figure 20.** $t = 60$.

## 7. Conclusions

In this paper, we studied the classical wave equation with the damped term and associated with the stochastic Fokker–Planck operator. Two physical and biological models were studied as direct applications to this partial differential equation. The need to extend the time first-order derivative to the Caputo time-fractional operator was discussed. The need for the space-fractional operator was also discussed. The analytic solutions for the classical models were studied to illustrate that the special functions are very necessary, besides proving that the analytic solutions are not unique. The Laplace transform was implemented to obtain the solution of the time-fractional differential equation of three terms. The solution was given in terms of the Mittag–Leffler function and its $n$th derivative.

The explicit finite difference rules besides the Grünwald–Letnikov scheme were implemented to obtain the approximate solutions of the studied models. The simulation of the approximate solutions of the classical case and the space-time-fractional equations with different values of the fractional orders were presented. As stochastic processes, the approximate solutions do not change after reaching the stationary solution.

**Funding:** This research received no external funding.

**Institutional Review Board Statement:** Not applicable.

**Informed Consent Statement:** Not applicable.

**Conflicts of Interest:** There is no funders to have a role in the design of the study; in the collection, analyses, or interpretation of data; in the writing of the manuscript, or in the decision to publish the results.

## References

1. Risken, H. *The Fokker–Planck Equation (Methods of Solution and Applications)*, 2nd ed.; Springer: Berlin/Heidelberg, Germany, 1989.
2. Cascaval, R.C.; Eckstein, E.C.; Forta, C.L.; Goldstein, J.A. Fractional Telegraph Equations. *J. Math. Anal. Appl.* **2002**, *276*, 145–159. [CrossRef]
3. Kilbas, A.; Srivastava, H.; Trujillo, J. *Theory and Applications of Fractional Differential Equations*; Elsevier: Amsterdam, The Netherlands, 2006.
4. Liebler, M.; Ginter, S.; Dreyer, T.; Riedlinger, R.E. Full wave modeling of therapeutic ultrasound: Efficient time-domaint. implemetation of the frequency power-law attenuation. *J. Acoust. Soc. Am.* **2004**, *116*, 2742–2750. [CrossRef]
5. Szabo, T.L. Time domain wave equation for lossy media obeying a frequency power law. *J. Acoust. Soc. Am.* **1994**, *96*, 491–500. [CrossRef]
6. Gazit, Y.; Baish, J.W.; Safabakhsh, N.; Leunig, M.; Baxter, L.T.; Jain, R.K. Fractal Characteristics of tumor vascular architecture during tumor growth and regression. *Microcirculation* **1997**, *4*, 395–402. [CrossRef]
7. Duck, F.A. *Physicl Properties of Tissue: A Comperhensive Reference Book*; Academic Press: Boston, MA, USA, 1990.
8. Wang, J.; Li, H. Surpassing the fractional derivative: Concept of the memory-dependent derivative. *J. Comput. Math. Appl.* **2011**, *62*, 1562–1567. [CrossRef]
9. Podlubny, I. *Fractional Differential Equations*; Academic Press: San Diego, CA, USA; New York, NY, USA, 1999.
10. Caputo, M. Linear models of dissipation whose Q is almost independent II. *Geophy. J. R. Astron. Soc.* **1967**, *13*, 529–539. [CrossRef]
11. Luchko, Y. Multi–dimensional fractional wave equation and some properties of its fundamental solution. *Commun. Appl. Ind. CIAM* **2014**, *3*, e485. [CrossRef]
12. Gorenflo, R. Stochastic Processes related to time-fractional diffusion wave equation. *Comm. Appl. Ind. CIAM* **2015**, *6*, e531.
13. Anh, V.; Leonenko, N. Harmonic analysis of random fractional diffusion–wave equations. *Appl. Math. Comput.* **2003**, *141*, 77–85. [CrossRef]
14. Chen, J.; Liu, F.; Anh, V.; Turner, I. Methods of separating variables for the time-fractional telegraph equation. *J. Math. Anal. Appl.* **2008**, *338*, 1364–1377. [CrossRef]
15. Wyss, W. The fractional diffusion equation. *J. Math. Phys.* **1986**, *27*, 2782–2785. [CrossRef]
16. Abdel-Rehim, E.A.; El-Sayed, A.M.A.; Hashem, A.S. Simulation of the Approximate Solutions of the Time-Fractional Multi–Term Wave Equations. *J. Comp. Math. Appl.* **2017**, *73*, 1134–1154. [CrossRef]
17. El-Sayed, A.M.A.; Abdel-Rehim, E.A.; Hashem, A.S. Time evolution of the approximate and stationary solution of the time-fractional forced–damped–wave equation. *Tbil. Math. J.* **2017**, *10*, 127–144. [CrossRef]
18. Abdel-Rehim, E.A. From Power Laws to Fractional Diffusion Processes with and without External Forces, the Non Direct Way. *J. Fract. Calc. Appl. Anal.* **2019**, *22*, 60–77. [CrossRef]
19. Sarvestani, F.S.; Heydari, M.H.; Niknam, A.; Avazzadeh, Z. A wavelet approach for the multi–term time-fractional diffusion–wave equation. *Int. J. Comp. Math.* **2019**, *96*, 640–661. [CrossRef]
20. Mainardi, F.; Giusti, A. *Advances Mathematical Methods: Theory and Applications*; MDPI: Basel, Switzerland, 2020.
21. Codling, E.A.; Planck, M.J.; Benhamau, S. Random walk models in biology. *J. R. Soc. Interface* **2008**, *5*, 813–834. [CrossRef]

22. Prabhu, N.U. *Stochastic Processes (Basic Theory and its Applications)*; The Macmillan Company: New York, NY, USA; Collier-Macmillan Limited: London, UK, 1965.
23. Bharucha-Reid, A.T. *Elements of the theory of Markov Processes and Their Applications*; McGRAW-HILL Book Company: New York, NY, USA, 1960.
24. Smith, G.D. *Numerical Solution of Partial Differential Equations with Exercises and Worked Solutions*; London Oxford University Press: New York, NY, USA; Toronto, ON, Canada, 1965.
25. Abdel-Rehim, E.A. From the Ehrenfest Model to Time- Fractional Stochastic Processes. *J. Comput. Appl. Math.* **2009**, *233*, 197–207. [CrossRef]
26. Gorenflo, R.; Kilbas, A.A.; Mainardi, F.; Rogosin, S.V. *Mittage-Leffler Function, Related Topics and Applications*; Springer Monographs in Mathematics: Berlin, Germany, 2014.
27. Erdélyi, A.; Wilhelm, M.; Oberhettinger, F.; Tricomi, F.G. *Higher Ttanscendential Functions*; Mc Graw-Hill: New York, NY, USA, 1953 and 1955; Volume 1–3.
28. Fox, C. The asymptotic expansion of generalized hypergeometric functions. *Proc. Lond. Math. Soc.* **1928**, *27*, 389–400. [CrossRef]
29. Doetsch, G. *Anleitung zum Praktischen Gebraauch der Laplace-Transformation, Oldenbourg, Munich, 1956*; Fizmatgiz: Moscow, Russia, 1958.
30. Feller, W. On a generalization of Marcel Riesz'potentials and the semi-groups generated by them. In *Meddelanden Lunds Universitetes Matematiska Seminarium (Comm. Sém. Mathém. Université de Lund)*; Tome Suppl. Dédié a M. Riesz: Lund, Sweden, 1952; pp. 73–81.
31. Samko, S.G.; Kilbas, A.A.; Marichev, O.I. *Fractional Integrals and Derivatives (Theory and Applications)*; OPA: Amsterdam, The Netherlands, 1993.
32. Gorenflo, R.; Mainardi, F. Random walks model for space-fractional diffusion processes. *J. Fract. Calc. Appl. Analy.* **1998**, *1*, 167–191.
33. Gorenflo, R.; Mainardi, F. Fractional calculus: Integral and differential equations of fractional order. In *Fractals and Fractional Calculus in Continuum Mechanics*; Carpinteri, A., Mainardi, F., Eds.; Springer: Wien, Austria; New York, NY, USA, 1997; pp. 223–276.
34. Gorenflo, R.; Mainardi, F. Approximation of Lévy-Feller diffusion by random walk. *J. Anal. Appl. (ZAA)* **1999**, *18*, 231–146. [CrossRef]
35. Gorenflo, R.; Abdel-Rehim, E.A. Discrete models of time-fractional diffusion in a potential well. *J. Fract. Calc. Appl. Anal.* **2005**, *8*, 173–200.

axioms

MDPI

Article

# Forecasting Economic Growth of the Group of Seven via Fractional-Order Gradient Descent Approach

Xiaoling Wang [1], Michal Fečkan [2,3] and JinRong Wang [1,*]

1 Department of Mathematics, Guizhou University, Guiyang 550025, China; xlwangmath@126.com
2 Department of Mathematical Analysis and Numerical Mathematics, Comenius University in Bratislava, Mlynská dolina, 842 48 Bratislava, Slovakia; michal.feckan@fmph.uniba.sk
3 Mathematical Institute of Slovak Academy of Sciences, Štefánikova 49, 814 73 Bratislava, Slovakia
* Correspondence: jrwang@gzu.edu.cn

**Abstract:** This paper establishes a model of economic growth for all the G7 countries from 1973 to 2016, in which the gross domestic product (GDP) is related to land area, arable land, population, school attendance, gross capital formation, exports of goods and services, general government, final consumer spending and broad money. The fractional-order gradient descent and integer-order gradient descent are used to estimate the model parameters to fit the GDP and forecast GDP from 2017 to 2019. The results show that the convergence rate of the fractional-order gradient descent is faster and has a better fitting accuracy and prediction effect.

**Keywords:** fractional derivative; gradient descent; economic growth; group of seven

**MSC:** 26A33

**Citation:** Wang, X.; Fečkan, M.; Wang, J. Forecasting Economic Growth of the Group of Seven via Fractional-Order Gradient Descent Approach. *Axioms* **2021**, *10*, 257. https://doi.org/10.3390/axioms10040257

Academic Editor: Jorge E. Macías Díaz

Received: 29 August 2021
Accepted: 11 October 2021
Published: 15 October 2021



## 1. Introduction

In recent years, fractional model has become a research hotspot because of its advantages. Fractional calculus has developed rapidly in academic circles, and its achievements in the fields include [1–10].

Gradient descent is generally used as a method of solving the unconstrained optimization problems, and is widely used in evaluation and in other aspects. The rise in fractional calculus provides a new idea for advances in the gradient descent method. Although numerous achievements have been made in the two fields of fractional calculus and gradient descent, the research results combining the two are still in their infancy. Recently, ref. [11] applied the fractional order gradient descent to image processing and solved the problem of blurring image edges and texture details using a traditional denoising method, based on integer order. Next, ref. [12] improved the fractional-order gradient descent method and used it to identify the parameters of the discrete deterministic system in advance. Thereafter, ref. [13] applied the fractional-order gradient descent to the training of neural networks' backpropagation (BP), which proves the monotony and convergence of the method.

Compared with the traditional integer-order gradient descent, the combination of fractional calculus and gradient descent provides more freedom of order; adjusting the order can provide new possibilities for the algorithm. In this paper, economic growth models of seven countries are established, and their cost functions are trained by gradient descent (fractional- and integer-order). To compare the performance of fractional- and integer-order gradient descent, we visualize the rate of convergence of the cost function, evaluate the model with $MSE$, $MAD$ and $R^2$ indicators and predict the GDP of the seven countries in 2017–2019 according to the trained parameters.

*The Group of Seven (G7)*

The G6 was set up by France after western countries were hit by the first oil shock. In 1976, Canada's accession marked the birth of the G7, whose members are the United States, the United Kingdom, France, Germany, Japan, Italy and Canada seven developed countries. The annual summit mechanism of the G7 focuses on major issues of common interest, such as inclusive economic growth, world peace and security, climate change and oceans, which have had a profound impact on global, economic and political governance. In addition to the G7 members, there are a number of developing countries with large economies, such as China, India and Brazil. In the context of economic globalization, the study of G7 economic trends and economic-related factors can provide a useful reference for these countries' development.

The economic crisis broke out in western countries in 1973, so the data in this paper cover the period from 1973 to 2016, and data for the seven countries are available since then. Some G7 members (France, Germany, Italy and the United States) were members of the European Union (EU) during this period, so this paper also establishes the economic growth model of the EU. Data for this article are from the World Bank.

## 2. Model Describes

The prediction of variables generally uses time series models [14] (for example, ARIMA and SARIMA), or artificial neural networks [15,16], which have been very popular in recent years. The time series model mainly predicts the future trend in variables, but it is difficult to reflect the change in unexpected factors in the model. Additionally, the neural network model needs to adjust more parameters, the network structure selection is too large, the training efficiency is not high enough, and easy to overfit.

Although the linear model is simple in form and easy to model, its weight can intuitively express the importance of each attribute, so the linear model has a good explanatory ability. It is reasonable to build a linear regression model of economic growth, which can clearly learn which factors have an impact on the economy.

Next, we chose eight explanatory variables to describe the economic growth in this paper. The explained variable is $y$, where $y$ refers to GDP and is a function. The expression for $y$ is as follows:

$$y(t) = \sum_{j=1,2,3,4,5,6,7,8} \theta_j x_j(t) + \theta_0 + \epsilon, \tag{1}$$

where $t$ is year ($t = 44$), $\theta_0$ is the intercept. $\epsilon$ is an unobservable term of random error. $\theta_j$ represents the weight of each variable. The eight explanatory variables are:

$x_1$: land area (km$^2$)
$x_2$: arable land (hm$^2$)
$x_3$: population
$x_4$: school attendance (years)
$x_5$: gross capital formation (in 2010 US$)
$x_6$: exports of goods and services (in 2010 US$)
$x_7$: general government final consumer spending (in 2010 US$)
$x_8$: broad money (in 2010 US$)

## 3. Fractional-Order Derivative

Due to the differing conditions, there are different forms of fractional calculus definition, the most common of which are Grünwald–Letnikov, Riemann–Liouville, and Caputo. In this article, we chose the definition of fractional-order derivative in terms of the Caputo form. Given the function $f(t)$, the Caputo fractional-order derivative of order $\alpha$ is defined as follows:

$$^{Caputo}{}_{c}D_t^{\alpha} f(t) = \frac{1}{\Gamma(1-\alpha)} \int_c^t (t-\tau)^{-\alpha} f'(\tau) d\tau,$$

where ${}^{Caputo}{}_{c}D_{t}^{\alpha}$ is the Caputo derivative operator. $\alpha$ is the fractional order, and the interval is $\alpha \in (0,1)$. $\Gamma(\cdot)$ is the gamma function. $c$ is the initial value. For simplicity, ${}_{c}D_{t}^{\alpha}$ is used in this paper to represent the Caputo fractional derivative operator instead ${}^{Caputo}{}_{c}D_{t}^{\alpha}$.

Caputo fractional differential has good properties. For example, we provide the Laplace transform of Caputo operator as follows:

$$L\{D^{\alpha}f(t)\} = s^{\alpha}F(s) - \sum_{k=0}^{n-1} f^{(k)}(0)s^{\alpha-k-1},$$

where $F(s)$ is a generalized integral with a complex parameter $s$, $F(s) = \int_{0}^{\infty} f(t)e^{-st}dt$. $n =: [\alpha]$ is the $\alpha$ rounded up to the nearest integer. It can be seen from the Laplace transform that the definition of the initial value of Caputo differentiation is consistent with that of integer-order differential equations and has a definite physical meaning. Therefore, Caputo fractional differentiation has a wide range of applications.

## 4. Gradient Descent Method

### 4.1. The Cost Function

The cost function (also known as the loss function) is essential for a majority of algorithms in machine learning. The model's optimization is the process of training the cost function, and the partial derivative of the cost function with respect to each parameter is the gradient mentioned in gradient descent. To select the appropriate parameters $\theta$ for the model (1) and minimize the modeling error, we introduce the cost function:

$$C(\theta) = \frac{1}{2m}\sum_{i=1}^{m}(h_{\theta}(x^{(i)}) - y^{(i)})^2, \tag{2}$$

where $h_{\theta}(x^{(i)})$ is a modification of model (1), $h_{\theta}(x) = \theta_0 + \theta_1 x_1 + \cdots + \theta_j x_j$, which represents the output value of the model. $x^{(i)}$ are the sample features. $y^{(i)}$ is the true data, and $t$ represents the number of samples ($m = 44$).

### 4.2. The Integer-Order Gradient Descent

The first step of the integer-order gradient descent is to take the partial derivative of the cost function $C(\theta)$:

$$\frac{\partial C(\theta)}{\partial \theta_j} = \frac{1}{m}\sum_{i=1}^{m}(h_{\theta}(x^{(i)}) - y^{(i)})x_j^{(i)}, \qquad j = 1,2,\ldots,8, \tag{3}$$

and the update function is as follows:

$$\theta_{j+1} = \theta_j - \eta\frac{1}{m}\sum_{i=1}^{m}(h_{\theta}(x^{(i)}) - y^{(i)})x_j^{(i)}, \tag{4}$$

where $\eta$ is learning rate, $\eta > 0$.

### 4.3. The Fractional-Order Gradient Descent

The first step of fractional-order gradient descent is to find the fractional derivative of the cost function $C(\theta)$. According to Caputo's definition of fractional derivative, from [17] we know that if $g(h(t))$ is a compound function of $t$, then the fractional derivation of $\alpha$ with respect to $t$ is

$${}_{c}D_{t}^{\alpha}\, g(h) = \frac{\partial(g(h))}{\partial h} \cdot {}_{c}D_{t}^{\alpha}\, h(t). \tag{5}$$

It can be known from (5) that the fractional derivative of a composite function can be expressed as the product of integral and fractional derivatives. Therefore, the calculation for ${}_cD^{\alpha}_{\theta_j}C(\theta)$ is as follows:

$$\begin{aligned}
{}_cD^{\alpha}_{\theta_j}C(\theta) &= \frac{1}{m}\sum_{i=1}^{m}(h_\theta(x^{(i)}) - y^{(i)})\Gamma(1-\alpha)\int_c^{\theta_j}(\theta_j - \tau)^{-\alpha}\frac{\partial[h_\theta(x^{(i)}) - y^{(i)}]}{\partial\theta_j}d\tau \\
&= \frac{1}{m}\sum_{i=1}^{m}(h_\theta(x^{(i)}) - y^{(i)})x_j^{(i)}\Gamma(1-\alpha)\int_c^{\theta_j}(\theta_j - \tau)^{-\alpha}d\tau \\
&= \frac{1}{m(1-\alpha)\Gamma(1-\alpha)}(\theta_j - c)^{(1-\alpha)}\sum_{i=1}^{m}(h_\theta(x^{(i)}) - y^{(i)})x_j^{(i)},
\end{aligned}$$

and the update function is as follows:

$$\theta_{j+1} = \theta_j - \eta\frac{1}{m(1-\alpha)\Gamma(1-\alpha)}(\theta_j - c)^{(1-\alpha)}\sum_{i=1}^{m}(h_\theta(x^{(i)}) - y^{(i)})x_j^{(i)}, \qquad j = 1,2,\ldots,8 \quad (6)$$

where $\eta$ is the learning rate, $\eta > 0$. $\alpha$ is the fractional order, $0 < \alpha < 1$. $c$ is the initial value of Caputo's fractional derivative, and $c < \min\{\theta_j\}$.

## 5. Model Evaluation Indexes

We use the absolute relative error ($ARE$) to measure the prediction error:

$$ARE_i = \frac{|y_i - \hat{y}_i|}{y_i}.$$

To evaluate the fitting quality of gradient descent on the model, the following three indicators can be calculated:

The mean square error ($MSE$):

$$MSE = \frac{1}{n}\sum_{i=1}^{n}(y_i - \hat{y}_i)^2.$$

The coefficient of determination ($R^2$):

$$R^2 = 1 - \frac{\sum_{i=1}^{n}(y_i - \hat{y}_i)^2}{\sum_{i=1}^{n}(y_i - \bar{y}_i)^2}.$$

The mean absolute deviation ($MAD$):

$$MAD = \frac{\sum_{i=1}^{n}|y_i - \hat{y}_i|}{n}.$$

In these formulas, $n$ is the number of years ($n = 44$). $y_i$ and $\hat{y}_i$ are the real value and the model output, respectively. $\bar{y}_i$ is the mean of the GDP.

## 6. Main Results

In this article, we standardize the data for each country before running the algorithm, and each iteration to update $\theta$ uses m samples. The grid search method was used to select the appropriate learning rate and initial weight interval, and the effects of different fractional orders are compared to select the best order (see Table 1).The learning rate and the initial weight interval are applicable to both fractional-order gradient descent and integer-order gradient descent.

**Table 1.** Parameters for different countries.

| Country | $\alpha$ | Learning Rate | Initial Interval |
|---|---|---|---|
| Canada | 0.8 | 0.03 | $(-0.5, 0.5)$ |
| France | 0.8 | 0.03 | $(-0.8, 0.8)$ |
| Germany | 0.8 | 0.03 | $(-0.1, 0.1)$ |
| Italy | 0.8 | 0.03 | $(-0.5, 0.5)$ |
| Japan | 0.8 | 0.03 | $(-0.1, 0.1)$ |
| The United Kingdom | 0.8 | 0.03 | $(-0.5, 0.5)$ |
| The United States | 0.8 | 0.03 | $(-0.1, 0.1)$ |
| European Union | 0.8 | 0.03 | $(-0.5, 0.5)$ |

### *6.1. Comparison of Convergence Rate of Fractional and Integer Order Gradient Descent*

In order to facilitate visual comparison, (4) and (6) are iterated 50 times, respectively, as well as their convergence rates (see Figure 1).

As shown in Figure 1, for each dataset, after the same number of iterations, the convergence rate of fractional-order gradient descent is faster than that of integer-order gradient descent, which indicates that the method combining fractional-order and gradient descent is better than the traditional integer-order gradient descent in the convergence rate of update equation.

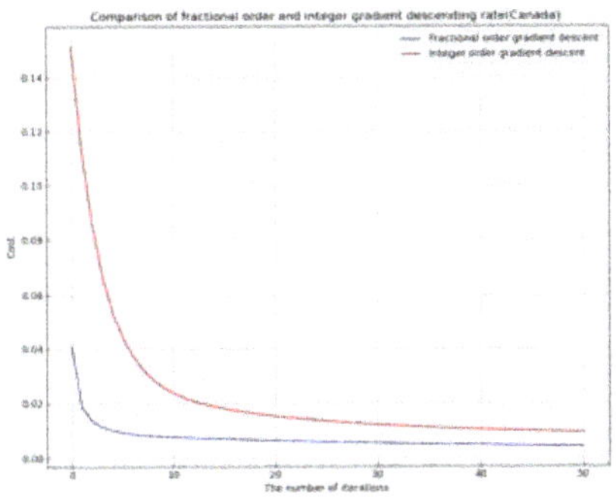


(**a**)

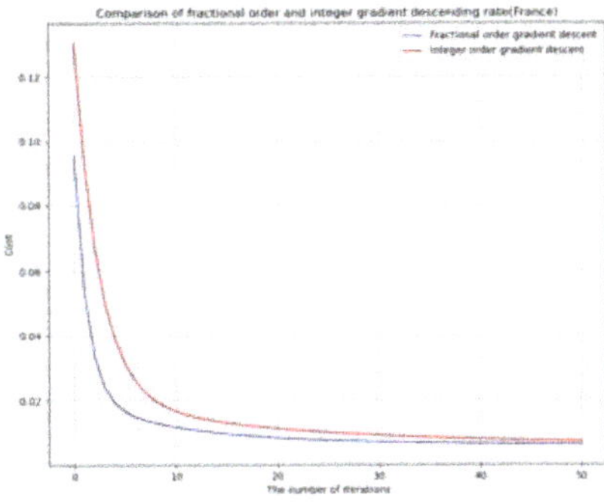


(**b**)

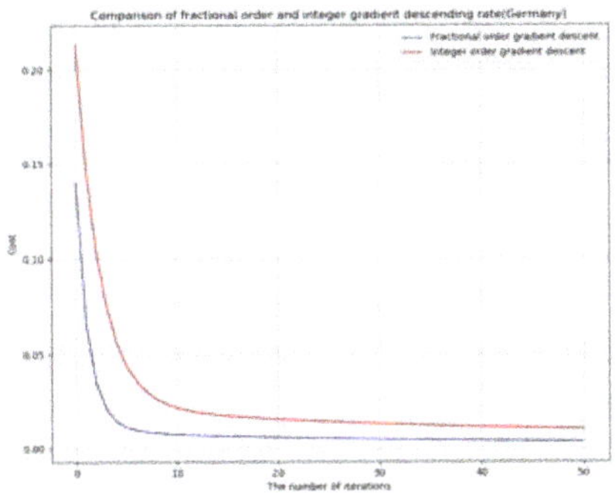


(**c**)

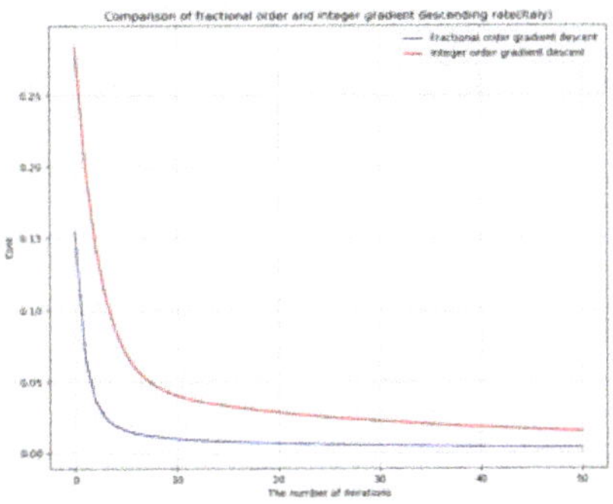


(**d**)

**Figure 1.** *Cont.*

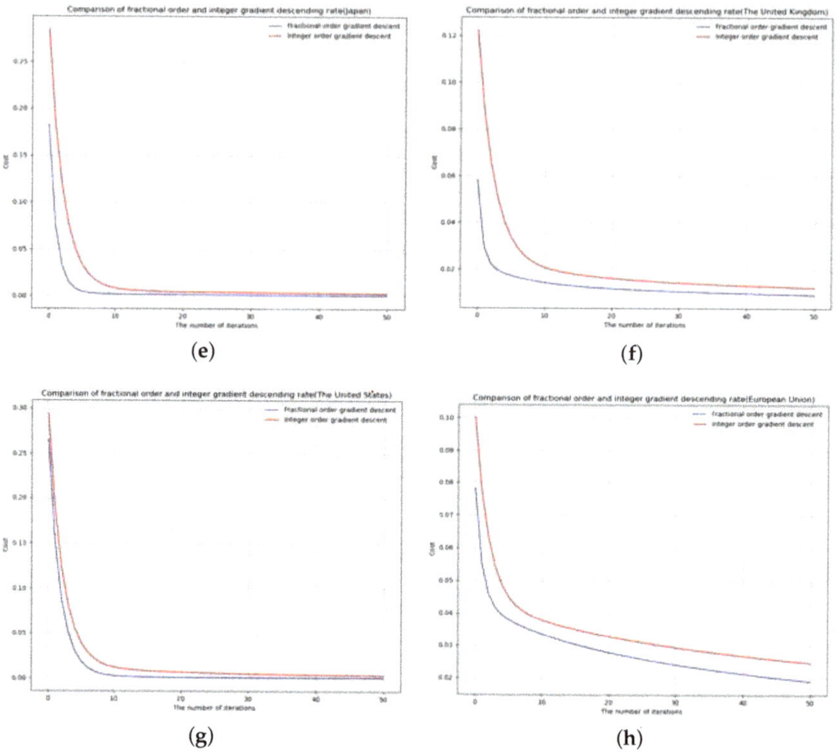


**Figure 1.** Comparison of convergence rate and fitting error between fractional- and integer-order gradient descent: (**a**) Canada (**b**) France (**c**) Germany (**d**) Italy (**e**) Japan (**f**) The United Kingdom (**g**) The United States (**h**) European Union.

### *6.2. Fitting Result*

Then, we fit GDP with integer-order gradient descent and fractional-order gradient descent, respectively. Start by setting a threshold and stop iterating when the gradient is less than this threshold. The fitting effect diagram is shown in Figure 2, and the performance evaluation of the model is shown in Table 2.

**Table 2.** Performance of integer order and fractional order gradient descent.

| | Canada | | France | | Germany | | Italy | |
|---|---|---|---|---|---|---|---|---|
| Index | Integer (4) | Fractional (6) | Integer (4) | Fractional (6) | Integer (4) | Fractional (6) | Integer (4) | Fractional (6) |
| $MSE\,(\times 10^{20})$ | 2.2548 | 1.5689 | 7.3396 | 4.3851 | 7.6262 | 6.8976 | 3.2521 | 2.701 |
| $R^2$ | 0.9984 | 0.9989 | 0.9971 | 0.9983 | 0.9981 | 0.9983 | 0.9974 | 0.9978 |
| $MAD\,(\times 10^{10})$ | 1.1015 | 0.9066 | 2.2076 | 1.68 | 2.2824 | 2.0203 | 1.4947 | 1.3146 |
| | Japan | | The United Kingdom | | The United States | | European Union | |
| Index | Integer (4) | Fractional (6) | Integer (4) | Fractional (6) | Integer (4) | Fractional (6) | Integer (4) | Fractional (6) |
| $MSE\,(\times 10^{20})$ | 19.9103 | 16.6656 | 15.2421 | 13.7876 | 98.4201 | 60.7402 | 197.9143 | 90.5717 |
| $R^2$ | 0.9986 | 0.9989 | 0.9946 | 0.9951 | 0.9993 | 0.9995 | 0.9983 | 0.9992 |
| $MAD\,(\times 10^{10})$ | 3.8663 | 3.2745 | 3.1182 | 2.9489 | 7.8593 | 5.714 | 11.8393 | 7.2684 |

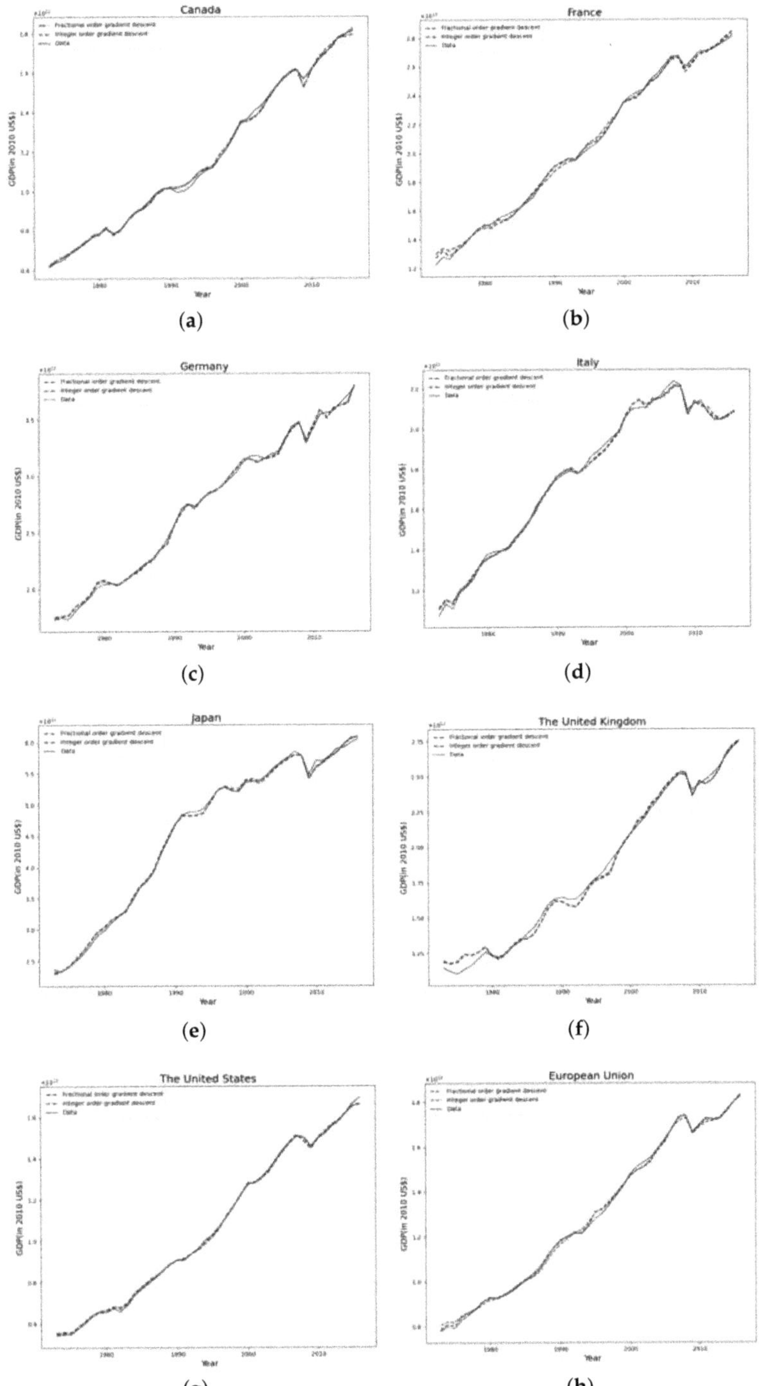


**Figure 2.** Fitting of GDP of the G7 countries by fractional-order gradient descent method: (**a**) Canada (**b**) France (**c**) Germany (**d**) Italy (**e**) Japan (**f**) The United Kingdom (**g**) The United States (**h**) European Union.

It can be seen from Table 2 that the $MSE$, $R^2$ and $MAD$ results of GDP fitted by fractional-order gradient descent are better than that fitted by integer-order gradient descent, which indicates that, under the same iteration number, learning rate and initial weight interval, the fitting performance of the data fitted by fractional-order gradient descent is better than that of integer-order.

### 6.3. Predicted Results

Finally, in order to test the prediction effect of fractional- and integer-order gradient descent on GDP, we forecast the GDP from 2017 to 2019, and used the $ARE$ index to measure the prediction error (see Table 3).

**Table 3.** Integer-order and fractional-order gradient descent for G7 countries' GDP data from 2017 to 2019.

| Country | Year | Actual Value | Predicted Value | | $ARE$ | |
|---|---|---|---|---|---|---|
| | | | Integer | Fractional | Integer | Fractional |
| Canada | 2017 | 1869939124387.55 | 1851176120948 | 1865471720455.36 | 0.01003 | 0.00239 |
| | 2018 | 1907592951375.51 | 1885635961969.18 | 1897212921116.78 | 0.01151 | 0.00544 |
| | 2019 | 1939183469806.34 | 1913183323405.81 | 1924536620147.11 | 0.01341 | 0.00755 |
| France | 2017 | 2876185347152.35 | 2945583296625 | 2913853765393.87 | 0.02313 | 0.01211 |
| | 2018 | 2927751436718.37 | 2987173241226.19 | 2955215192748.21 | 0.0193 | 0.0084 |
| | 2019 | 2971919320115.83 | 3052414282679.98 | 3007640733954.07 | 0.02608 | 0.01103 |
| Germany | 2017 | 3873475897139.37 | 3992089822476.93 | 3987473981388.45 | 0.03062 | 0.02943 |
| | 2018 | 3922591386837.48 | 4035516755191.92 | 4019973502352.35 | 0.02879 | 0.02483 |
| | 2019 | 3944379455526.15 | 4007551577032.44 | 3942199462068.09 | 0.01602 | 0.00055 |
| Italy | 2017 | 2124019926800.66 | 2152553322306.66 | 2148504123256.22 | 0.01343 | 0.01053 |
| | 2018 | 2144072575240.17 | 2184791916115.44 | 2178336024841.51 | 0.01899 | 0.01598 |
| | 2019 | 2151420719257.08 | 1694388219398.54 | 1946816137097.53 | 0.21243 | 0.0951 |
| Japan | 2017 | 6150456276847.65 | 6246751221623.44 | 6217262375879.73 | 0.01566 | 0.01086 |
| | 2018 | 6170335002849.18 | 6302599251651.13 | 6266099914852.53 | 0.02144 | 0.01552 |
| | 2019 | 6210698351093.34 | 6274298653661.42 | 6272342082178.18 | 0.01411 | 0.01379 |
| The United Kingdom | 2017 | 2841238185971.41 | 2714332507299.13 | 2737032647202.61 | 0.04467 | 0.03668 |
| | 2018 | 2879331251695.23 | 2735833239476.11 | 2760916583838.65 | 0.04984 | 0.041126 |
| | 2019 | 2921446026408.24 | 2784137398857.08 | 2812534141119.14 | 0.047 | 0.03728 |
| The United States | 2017 | 17403783207186.7 | 17154216039682.2 | 17344565695242.3 | 0.01434 | 0.0034 |
| | 2018 | 17913248631409.5 | 17681187933498.6 | 17835485270334.4 | 0.01725 | 0.00434 |
| | 2019 | 18300385513295.6 | 18004286468803.1 | 18168502346487.9 | 0.01618 | 0.00721 |
| European Union | 2017 | 16012037378199.3 | 17983491434848.4 | 18072460558164 | 0.04479 | 0.04006 |
| | 2018 | 16351210756244.2 | 18105516308926.6 | 18296349316535.8 | 0.05715 | 0.04272 |
| | 2019 | 16605351894524 | 18828265531889.1 | 19241290506759 | 0.03446 | 0.01328 |

## 7. Conclusions

In this paper, the gradient descent method is used to study the linear model problems which is different from [18,19]. The results show that, in addition to the least square estimation, the gradient descent method can also solve the regression analysis problem by iterating the cost function, and obtain good results, a without complicating the model. It also improves the interpretability of explanatory variables. We apply the fractional differential to gradient descent, and compare the performance of fractional-order gradient descent with that of integer-order gradient descent. It was found that the fractional-order has a faster convergence rate, higher fitting accuracy and lower prediction error than the integer-order. This provides an alternative method for fitting and forecasting GDP and has a certain reference value.

**Author Contributions:** J.W. supervised and led the planning and execution of this research, proposed the research idea of combining fractional calculus with gradient descent, formed the overall research objective, and reviewed, evaluated and revised the manuscript. According to this research goal, X.W. collected data of economic indicators and applied statistics to create a model and used Python software to write codes to analyze data and optimize the model, and finally wrote the first draft. M.F. reviewed, evaluated and revised the manuscript. All authors have read and agreed to the published version of the manuscript.

**Funding:** This work is partially supported by Training Object of High Level and Innovative Talents of Guizhou Province ((2016)4006), Major Research Project of Innovative Group in Guizhou Education Department ([2018]012), the Slovak Research and Development Agency under the contract No. APVV-18-0308 and by the Slovak Grant Agency VEGA No. 1/0358/20 and No. 2/0127/20.

**Institutional Review Board Statement:** Not applicable.

**Informed Consent Statement:** Not applicable.

**Data Availability Statement:** https://data.worldbank.org.cn/.

**Acknowledgments:** The authors are grateful to the referees for their careful reading of the manuscript and valuable comments. The authors thank the help from the editor too.

**Conflicts of Interest:** The authors declare no conflict of interest.

## References

1. Wang, J.; Ahmed, G.; O'Regan, D. Topological structure of the solution set for fractional non-instantaneous impulsive evolution inclusions. *J. Fixed Point Theory Appl.* **2018**, *20*, 1–25. [CrossRef]
2. Li, M.; Wang, J. Representation of solution of a Riemann-Liouville fractional differential equation with pure delay. *Appl. Math. Lett.* **2018**, *85*, 118–124. [CrossRef]
3. Yang, D.; Wang, J.; O'Regan, D. On the orbital Hausdorff dependence of differential equations with non-instantaneous impulses. *C. R. Acad. Sci. Paris, Ser. I* **2018**, *356*, 150–171. [CrossRef]
4. You, Z.; Fečkan, M.; Wang, J. Relative controllability of fractional-order differential equations with delay. *J. Comput Appl. Math.* **2020**, *378*, 112939. [CrossRef]
5. Wang, J.; Fečkan, M.; Zhou, Y. A Survey on impulsive fractional differential equations. *Frac. Calc. Appl. Anal.* **2016**, *19*, 806–831. [CrossRef]
6. Victor, S.; Malti, R.; Garnier, H.; Outstaloup, A. Parameter and differentiation order estimation in fractional models. *Automatica* **2013**, *49*, 926–935. [CrossRef]
7. Tang, Y.; Zhen, Y.; Fang, B. Nonlinear vibration analysis of a fractional dynamic model for the viscoelastic pipe conveying fluid. *Appl. Math. Model.* **2018**, *56*, 123–136. [CrossRef]
8. Li, W.; Ning, J.; Zhao, G.; Du, B. Ship course keeping control based on fractional order sliding mode. *J. Shanghai Marit. Univ.* **2020**, *41*, 25–30.
9. Yasin, F.; Ali, A.; Kiavash, F.; Rohollah, M.; Ami, R. A fractional-order model for chronic lymphocytic leukemia and immune system interactions. *Math. Methods Appl. Sci.* **2020**, *44*, 391–406.
10. Chen, L.; Altaf, M.; Abdon, A.; Sunil, K. A new financial chaotic model in Atangana-Baleanu stochastic fractional differential equations. *Alex. Eng.* **2021**, *60*, 5193–5204.
11. Pu, Y.; Zhang, N.; Zhang, Y.; Zhou, J. A texture image denoising approach based on fractional developmental mathematics. *Pattern Anal. Appl.* **2016**, *19*, 427–445. [CrossRef]
12. Cui, R.; Wei, Y.; Chen, Y. An innovative parameter estimation for fractional-order systems in the presence of outliers. *Nonlinear Dyn.* **2017**, *89*, 453–463. [CrossRef]
13. Wang, J.; Wen, Y.; Gou, Y.; Ye, Z.; Chen, H. Fractional-order gradient descent learning of BP neural networks with Caputo derivative. *Neural Netw.* **2017**, *89*, 19–30. [CrossRef] [PubMed]
14. Guo, J.; Dong, B. International rice price forecast based on SARIMA model. *Price Theory Pract.* **2019**, *1*, 79–82
15. Xu, Y.; Chen, Y. Comparison between seasonal ARIMA model and LSTM neural network forecast. *Stat. Decis.* **2021**, *2*, 46–50
16. Wang, X.; Wang, J.; Fečkan, M. BP neural network calculus in economic growth modeling of the Group of Seven. *Mathematics* **2020**, *8*, 37. [CrossRef]
17. Boroomand, A.; Menhaj, M. Fractional-order Hopfield neural networks. In *Advances in Neuro-Information Processing, ICONIP 2008*; Lecture Notes in Computer Science; Springer: Berlin/Heidelberg, Germany, 2009; Volume 5506, pp. 883–890.
18. Tejado, I.; Pérez, E.; Valério, D. Fractional calculus in economics growth modeling of the Group of Seven. *Fract. Calc. Appl. Anal.* **2019**, *22*, 139–157. [CrossRef]
19. Ming, H.; Wang, J.; Fečkan, M. The application of fractional calculus in Chinese economic growth models. *Mathematics* **2019**, *7*, 665. [CrossRef]

*axioms*

MDPI

*Article*

# GPU Based Modelling and Analysis for Parallel Fractional Order Derivative Model of the Spiral-Plate Heat Exchanger

**Guanqiang Dong and Mingcong Deng ***

The Graduate School of Engineering, Tokyo University of Agriculture and Technology, Tokyo 184-8588, Japan; guanqiangdong@gmail.com
* Correspondence: deng@cc.tuat.ac.jp

**Abstract:** Heat exchangers are commonly used in various industries. A spiral-plate heat exchanger with two fluids is a compact plant that only requires a small space and is excellent in high heat transfer efficiency. However, the spiral-plate heat exchanger is a nonlinear plant with uncertainties, considering the difference between the heat fluid, the heated fluid, and other complex factors. The fractional order derivation model is more accurate than the traditional integer order model. In this paper, a parallel fractional order derivation model is proposed by considering the merit of the graphics processing unit (GPU). Then, the parallel fractional order derivation model for the spiral-plate heat exchanger is constructed. Simulations show the relationships between the output temperature of heated fluid and the orders of fractional order derivatives with two directional fluids impacted by complex factors, namely, the volume flow rate in hot fluid, and the volume flow rate in cold fluid, respectively.

**Keywords:** fractional order derivative model; GPU; a spiral-plate heat exchanger; parallel model; heat transfer; nonlinear system

**Citation:** Dong, G.; Deng, M. GPU Based Modelling and Analysis for Parallel Fractional Order Derivative Model of the Spiral-Plate Heat Exchanger. *Axioms* **2021**, *10*, 344. https://doi.org/10.3390/axioms10040344

Academic Editor: Jorge E. Macías Díaz

Received: 23 November 2021
Accepted: 10 December 2021
Published: 16 December 2021



## 1. Introduction

A heat exchanger is most often used in industries such as space heating, refrigeration, air conditioning, power stations, chemical plants, petrochemical plants, petroleum refineries, natural-gas processing, and sewage treatment. It uses the principle of heat transfer between two or more fluids to transfer the heat energy of the high temperature heat fluid to the low temperature heat fluid in order to heating the low temperature fluid or cooling the high temperature heat fluid, which has the idea of energy saving [1]. A spiral-plate heat exchanger is a compact plant that only requires a small space for installation compared to traditional heat exchanger solutions and has excellent in high heat transfer efficiency (See [2–4]). However, the spiral-plate heat exchanger is a nonlinear plant with uncertainties, considering the difference between the heat medium, the heated medium and the other factors. In some applications, the output temperature heated or cooled for the heat exchanger must be controlled accurately. Because the heat transfer coefficient of the heat exchanger is impacted by various factors such as fluid flow, condition pressure, the uncertainties, the error of the mathematical model, and a long-time delay, etc., so it is difficult to be accurately modelled and controlled. In the past few years, the research of heat exchangers has mainly focused on the design of heat exchangers [5–7]. In some papers (Such as [8,9]), an effective internal fluid mathematical model is established by using the heat balance law between the two fluids. Only the effect of the flow velocity on the heat transfer coefficient, but not the effect of the two fluid flows velocity on the heat transfer time is considered.

Fractional order calculus and derivative is a old topic of a more than 300 years since a letter written by Leibniz to L'Hopital in 1695 [10]. Fractional order calculus is an extension from traditional integer calculus. The research of the theory and applications of fractional order calculus and derivatives (such as in solution of fractional order calculus and derivative [11,12] and stability [13–15]) expanded greatly over the 20th and 21st centuries.

In recent years, fractional order calculus and derivatives have been used in various fields such as engineering, physics, chemistry, and hydrology etc. The references in [10,16], give some knowledges about fractional order calculus and derivative. The fractional order PID controller was introduced by Podlubny in 1994 [10]. Fractional order controllers were being used extensively by many researchers to achieve the better robust performance in both the linear and the nonlinear systems. In [17], nonlinear thermoelastic fractional-order model of nonlocal plates is studied. The reference [18] proposed a fractional nonlocal elasticity model. They show elasticity model described by fractional order derivative is more accurate than the traditional system described by integer order in theory and application [19]. In control systems, modelling, stability, controllability, observability is very important for performance. In fractional order system, these need to be considered in [20–22], too. Nowadays, fractional order calculus and derivative are still the absence of solution method and rapid computing algorithm [23].

GPU (That is graphics processing unit), which provides more computing units and high data bandwidth in a limited area [24]. It is originally developed for graphics applications, now, it has been increasingly applied to do parallel computing in scientific and engineering. GPU has higher execution efficiency for parallel data, and the more data parallelism, the higher the execution efficiency. CUDA is a software and hardware system that can make GPU work as a device for data parallel computing [25].

References [20,26–28] show elasticity model described by fractional order derivative is more accurate than the traditional system described by integer order in theory and application. Fractional order derivative equation is more suitable to describe thermoelastic model than integer order equation. Heat transfer for the heat exchanger is thermoelastic model. Therefore, it is motivated by the above references. Traditionally, a spiral-plate heat exchanger mathematical model is constructed by integer order derivative equation. A spiral-plate heat exchanger mathematical model constructed by fractional order derivative equation is more accurate than conventional method. So, a parallel fractional order derivative model is proposed by considering the merits of GPU and fractional order derivative. Further, parallel fractional order derivation model for the spiral heat exchanger is constructed. The parallel fractional order derivation model for the spiral-plate heat exchanger executes faster than traditional model and can quickly reply to disturbance. In the future, we will study operator-based robust nolinear control system for the spiral heat exchanger by using the proposed parallel model [29–31].

The rest of this paper is constructed as follows. In Section 2, Preliminaries and Problem Statement, a parallel fractional order derivative model is proposed, and the problem statement is presented. A mathematic fractional order derivative model for the spiral-plate heat exchanger is derived in Section 3, Mathematics Analysis. The proposed parallel model for the spiral-plate heat exchanger with both the counter-flow type and the parallel-flow type and implementation on GPU are given in Section 4. Then, Section 5 compares the relationships between the output temperature of the heated flow fluid and the orders of the fractional order derivative with the two directional fluids, the volume flow rate of cold fluid, and the volume flow rate of hot fluid, respectively. Finally, in Section 6, a conclusion is given.

## 2. Preliminaries and Problem Statement

### *2.1. Parallel Fractional Order Derivative Model*

In reference [32], parallel fractional order derivative model is not complete only modelling of a spiral heat exchanger with counter-type by using fractional order equation and without theory support. It is richened to derive this paper.

According to the definition of the fractional order derivative (see Appendix A), the fractional order derivative Equation (1) are given as follows.

$$\begin{cases} D_t^q f(\Delta h) = & -(\Delta h)^{-q}\frac{\Gamma(q+1)}{\Gamma(2)\Gamma(q)}f(0) + (\Delta h)^{-q}f(\Delta h) \\ D_t^q f(2(\Delta h)) = (\Delta h)^{-q}\frac{\Gamma(q+1)}{\Gamma(3)\Gamma(q-1)}f(0) - (\Delta h)^{-q}\frac{\Gamma(q+1)}{\Gamma(2)\Gamma(q)}f(\Delta h) + (\Delta h)^{-q}f(2(\Delta h)) \\ D_t^q f(3(\Delta h)) = -(\Delta h)^{-q}\frac{-\Gamma(q+1)}{\Gamma(4)\Gamma(q-2)}f(0) + (\Delta h)^{-q}\frac{\Gamma(q+1)}{\Gamma(3)\Gamma(q-1)}f(\Delta h) \\ \qquad -(\Delta h)^{-q}\frac{\Gamma(q+1)}{\Gamma(2)\Gamma(q)}f(2(\Delta h)) + (\Delta h)^{-q}f(3(\Delta h)) \\ \vdots \\ D_t^q f(N(\Delta h)) = (\Delta h)^{-q}\sum_{j=1}^{N}(-1)^j\frac{\Gamma(q+1)}{\Gamma(j+1)\Gamma(q-j+1)}f(t-j(\Delta h)) + (\Delta h)^{-q}f(N(\Delta h)) \end{cases} \tag{1}$$

From (1), a parallel fractional order derivative model is described by the matrix, as follow.

$$F_k = (\Delta h)^q D_{frac} + BF_{k-1} \tag{2}$$

where $F_k$, $F_{k-1}$, $D_{frac} \in R^N$, and $B \in R^{N\times N}$

$$F_k = \begin{pmatrix} f(\Delta h) \\ f(2(\Delta h)) \\ \vdots \\ f(N(\Delta h)) \end{pmatrix} \tag{3}$$

$$D_{frac} = \begin{pmatrix} D_t^q f(\Delta h) \\ D_t^q f(2(\Delta h)) \\ \vdots \\ D_t^q f(N(\Delta h)) \end{pmatrix} \tag{4}$$

$$B = \begin{pmatrix} \frac{-\Gamma(q+1)}{\Gamma(2)\Gamma(q)} & 0 & \cdots & 0 \\ \frac{\Gamma(q+1)}{\Gamma(3)\Gamma(q-1)} & \frac{-\Gamma(q+1)}{\Gamma(2)\Gamma(q)} & \cdots & 0 \\ \vdots & \vdots & \vdots & \vdots \\ \frac{(-1)^N\Gamma(q+1)}{\Gamma(N+1)\Gamma(q-N+1)} & \frac{(-1)^{(N-1)}\Gamma(q+1)}{\Gamma(N)\Gamma((q-N+1)} & \cdots & \frac{-\Gamma(q+1)}{\Gamma(2)\Gamma(q)} \end{pmatrix} \tag{5}$$

$$F_{k-1} = \begin{pmatrix} f(0) \\ f(\Delta h) \\ \vdots \\ f((N-1)(\Delta h)) \end{pmatrix} \tag{6}$$

### 2.2. Problem Statement

Traditionally, a spiral-plate heat exchanger mathematical model is constructed described by the integer order derivative equation. The spiral-plate heat exchanger mathematical model described by the fractional order derivative is more accurate than the traditional method. So, a fractional order derivation model is considered to describe a spiral-plate heat exchanger plant. Further, parallel fractional order derivative model is proposed by considering the merit of GPU. The proposed parallel model executes faster than traditional model and can quickly reply to disturbance. Further, we get the parallel fractional order derivative model for the spiral heat exchanger by mathematics analysis.

## 3. Mathematics Analysis

### 3.1. A Spiral-Plate Heat Exchanger Plant

A spiral-plate heat exchanger is shown in Figure 1. The spiral-plate heat exchanger is used for its many merits, such as high-efficient heat transfer, small-size in comparison to the other heat exchangers, and self-cleaning due to the special spiral structure.

**Figure 1.** A spiral-plate heat exchanger plant.

The spiral-plate heat exchanger is an excellent process equipment, but it is difficult to obtain an accurate model due to a complex inner structure. The conventional method, such as logarithmic mean temperature difference method, could not obtain good control results. The other approach was conducted, but the obtained model was too complex. It is difficult to design a model based controller. Therefore, we consider a novel spiral-plate heat exchanger's fractional order derivative model. Figure 2 gives the cross-section inner structure of the spiral-plate heat exchanger. Where $\delta_h$ , $\delta_c$ $\delta_s$ is the width of hot fluid, the width of cold fluid and the width of solid wall, respectively. In this study, the cross-section inner structure as shown in Figure 2 is divided into a micro volume in cold fluid. The fractional order derivative model is constructed by considering the heat balance of the hot fluid and cold fluid, respectively.

$$r = b + a \cdot \theta, \theta \in [0, 11\pi] \tag{7}$$

Geometric parameters of the spiral-plate heat exchanger are denoted in Table 1.

**Table 1.** Parameters of the spiral heat exchanger.

| Meaning | Symbol | Value |
|---|---|---|
| Geometric parameter of a spiral function | a | $0.005/\pi$ m/rad |
| Initial radius of hot fluid side | b | 0.08 m |
| The width of hot flow channel | $\delta_h$ | 0.005 m |
| The width of cold flow channel | $\delta_c$ | 0.005 m |
| The width of solid wall | $\delta_s$ | 0.0018 m |
| The height of the spiral-plate heat exchanger | Z | 0.011 m |

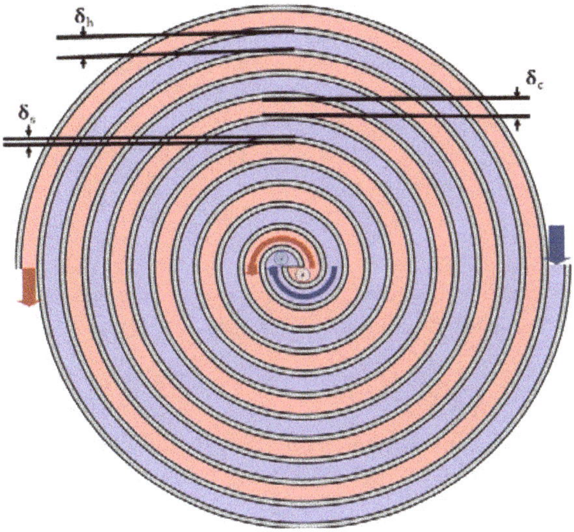


**Figure 2.** The cross-section inner structure of the spiral heat exchanger.

The heat exchanger is typically classified into the parallel-flow type and the count-flow type by arrangement [33]. The parallel-flow type is that both the input and the output of the two directional fluids (one is a hot fluid, the other is cold fluid) are in the same directions. If both the hot fluid and the cold fluid are in the opposite directions, then it is the counter-flow type heat exchanger. First, fractional order derivative model for the spiral-plate heat exchanger with the counter-flow type is considered.

### 3.2. *Fractional Order Derivative Model for the Spiral-Plate Counter-Flow Heat Exchanger*

In this section, the spiral-plate heat exchanger with the counter-flow type is analysed here. First, we consider the temperature variable in cold fluid, that is divided into a micro volume as shown in Figure 3. Here, $v_h$ is the flow rate in hot fluid. $v_c$ is the flow rate in cold fluid. The directions of $v_h$, and $v_c$ are opposite. $\Delta V$ is a micro volume in cold fluid. $\Delta m_1$ is the heat flux transferring from the inside $T_h(x)$. $\Delta m_2$ is the heat flux transferring from the outside $T_h(x + C)$, C is the length to the angle of $2\pi$.

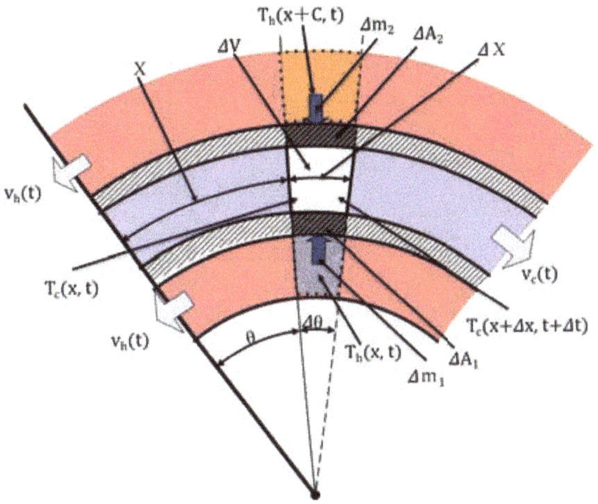


**Figure 3.** The principle of heat transfer for the spiral heat exchanger.

As seen in Figure 3, it denotes the heat transferring between the two fluids for the spiral-plate counter-flow heat exchanger.

Therefore, according to the heat energy balance law and heat transfer theory [34], the equations are derived as follows.

$$c_c\rho_c(\Delta V)\frac{\Delta T_c(x,t)}{\Delta t} = \Delta m_1 + \Delta m_2 \tag{8}$$

$$\frac{\Delta T_c(x,t)}{\Delta t} = T_c(x+\Delta x, t+\Delta t) - T_c(x,t) \tag{9}$$

where $c_c$, $\rho_c$, $\Delta V$, $k$ is the specific heat capacity of cold fluid, the density of cold fluid, a micro volume, the heat transfer coefficient of the spiral-plate heat exchanger, respectively. According to the Newton's law of cooling.

$$k = \frac{1}{h_h} + \frac{\delta_s}{\lambda} + \frac{1}{h_c} \tag{10}$$

where $h_h$, $h_c$, $\delta_s$, and $\lambda$ is the heat transfer coefficient of hot fluid, the heat transfer coefficient of cold fluid, the width of wall, thermal conductivity, respectively.

$$\Delta m_1 = k\cdot(T_h(x,t) - T_c(x,t))\cdot(\Delta A_1) \tag{11}$$

$\Delta m_1$ is the heat flux transferring from $T_h(x,t)$ to $T_c(x,t)$. Where $\Delta A_1$ is the heat transfer suface area $T_h(x,t)$ to $T_c(x,t)$.

$$\Delta m_2 = k\cdot(T_h(x+C,t) - T_c(x,t))\cdot(\Delta A_2) \tag{12}$$

$\Delta m_2$ is the heat flux transferring from $T_h(x+C,t)$ to $T_c(x,t)$. Where $\Delta A_2$ is the heat transfer surface area $T_h(x+C,t)$ to $T_c(x,t)$. Each element is of the length $\Delta x$ and the heat transfer surface area $\Delta A_1, \Delta A_2$, and $\Delta A_1 \approx \Delta A_2 = \Delta A = (\Delta x)\cdot Z$, $Z$ is the height of the spiral-plate heat exchanger, $\Delta x$ is the displacement of cold fluid that moves in time $\Delta t$, $\Delta V = (\Delta x)\cdot Z\cdot\delta_h$, $\Delta t = \frac{\Delta x}{v_c}$. So,

$$c_c\rho_c\delta_c v_c\frac{\Delta T_c(x,t)}{\Delta x} = k(T_h(x,t) + T_h(x+C,t) - 2T_c(x,t)) \tag{13}$$

Using the thought of differential theory, the relationship between the length in the differential arc and the angle in differential arc is derived.

$$\Delta x = \sqrt{\Delta r^2 + (r(\Delta\theta))^2} \tag{14}$$

Applying the spiral function of the spiral-plate heat exchanger, $r = a\theta + b$, it is obtained from (14):

$$\Delta x = \sqrt{a^2 + (b+a\theta)^2}(\Delta\theta) \tag{15}$$

Substituting (15) into (13), the differential equation in cold fluid is obtained as follow.

$$c_c\rho_c\delta_c v_c\frac{\Delta T_c(\theta,t)}{\Delta\theta} = k\sqrt{a^2+(b+a\theta)^2}(T_h(\theta,t) + T_h(\theta+2\pi,t) - 2T_c(\theta,t)), \theta \in [0, 11\pi) \tag{16}$$

Because (16) is complex. we simplify (17) as follows.

$$c_c\rho_c\delta_c v_c\frac{\Delta T_c(\theta,t)}{\Delta\theta} = Fk\sqrt{a^2+(b+a\theta)^2}(T_h(\theta,t) - T_c(\theta,t)), \theta \in [0, 11\pi) \tag{17}$$

where $F$ is the constant between 1 and 2 relation to the shape of the heat exchanger. According to the thought of fractional order derivative [10] (17) is extended from the integer order derivative to the fractional order derivative, we derive fractional order derivative equation in cold fluid for the spiral-plate counter-flow heat exchanger as follows. Fractional order of (18) is impacted by complex factors, it is difficult to derive by theory method.

$$c_c\rho_c\delta_c v_c D_\theta^{q_2} T_c(\theta,t) = Fk\sqrt{a^2+(b+a\theta)^2}(T_h(\theta,t)-T_c(\theta,t)), \theta \in [0, 11\pi) \tag{18}$$

With the same principle, the fractional order derivative equation in hot fluid is derived as follows.

$$c_h\rho_h\delta_h v_h D_\theta^{q_1} T_h(\theta,t) = Fk\sqrt{a^2+(b+a\theta)^2}(T_c(\theta,t)-T_h(\theta,t)), \theta \in [0, 11\pi) \tag{19}$$

$$A = \sqrt{a^2+(b+a\theta)^2} \tag{20}$$

Nonlinear fractional order derivative equations for the spiral-plate counter-flow heat exchanger are given as follows.

$$\begin{cases} D_\theta^{q_1} T_h(\theta,t) = \dfrac{kFA}{v_h c_h \rho_h \delta_h}((T_c(\theta,t)-T_h(\theta,t)) \\ D_\theta^{q_2} T_c(\theta,t) = \dfrac{kFA}{v_c c_c \rho_c \delta_c}((T_h(\theta,t)-T_c(\theta,t)) \\ \theta \in [0, 11\pi] \end{cases} \tag{21}$$

where $v_h(t)$ and $v_c(t)$ is the input flow rate of time $t$ in hot fluid, the input flow rate of time $t$ in cold fluid side, respectively.

$$\begin{cases} QL_1 = \delta_h Z v_h \\ QL_2 = \delta_c Z v_c \end{cases} \tag{22}$$

where $QL_1$ and $QL_2$ is the input volume flow rate in hot fluid side and the input volume flow rate in cold fluid side, respectively. Substituting (22) into (21), fractional order derivative model for the spiral-plate counter-flow heat exchanger is described as follows.

$$\begin{cases} D_\theta^{q_1} T_h(\theta,t) = \dfrac{kFAZ}{QL_1 c_h \rho_h}((T_c(\theta,t)-T_h(\theta,t)) \\ D_\theta^{q_2} T_c(\theta,t) = \dfrac{kFAZ}{QL_2 c_c \rho_c}((T_h(\theta,t)-T_c(\theta,t)) \\ \theta \in [0, 11\pi] \end{cases} \tag{23}$$

Considering initial conditions, $T_h(11\pi,t)$ and $T_c(0,t)$ is the input temperature of time $t$ in hot fluid, the input temperature of time $t$ in cold fluid, respectively.

### 3.3. Fractional Order Derivative Model for the Spiral-Plate Parallel-Flow Heat Exchanger

With the same method, the fractional order derivative model for the spiral-plate parallel-flow heat exchanger is derived as follows.

$$\begin{cases} D_\theta^{q_1} T_h(\theta,t) = \dfrac{kFAZ}{QL_1 c_h \rho_h}((T_c(\theta,t)-T_h(\theta,t)) \\ D_\theta^{q_2} T_c(\theta,t) = \dfrac{kFAZ}{QL_2 c_c \rho_c}((T_h(\theta,t)-T_c(\theta,t)) \\ \theta \in [0, 11\pi] \end{cases} \tag{24}$$

Considering initial conditions, $T_h(0,t)$ and $T_c(0,t)$ is the input temperature of time $t$ in hot fluid, the input temperature of time $t$ in cold fluid side, respectively.

The fractional order derivation equations for the spiral-plate parallel-flow heat exchanger are similar to that with the spiral-plate counter-flow heat exchanger, but the boundary conditions are different.

## 4. Parallel Fractional Order Derivative Model for the Spiral-Plate Heat Exchanger and Implementation on GPU

### *4.1. Parallel Fractional Order Derivative Model for the Spiral-Plate Heat Exchanger*

#### 4.1.1. Parallel Model for the Spiral-Plate Counter-Flow Heat Exchanger

Applying (1)–(6) into (23), parallel fractional order derivative model for the spiral-plate counter-flow heat exchanger is described as follows.

$$\begin{cases} T_{hk} = (\Delta\theta)^{q_1} D_{hfrac} + B_h T_{hk-1} \\ T_{ck} = (\Delta\theta)^{q_2} D_{cfrac} + B_c T_{ck-1} \end{cases} \tag{25}$$

where $T_{hk}, T_{hk-1}, D_{hfrac} \in R^N$, and $B_h \in R^{N\times N}$ $T_{ck}, T_{ck-1}, D_{cfrac} \in R^N$, and $B_c \in R^{N\times N}$

$$T_{hk} = \begin{pmatrix} T_h(\Delta\theta) \\ T_h(2(\Delta\theta)) \\ \vdots \\ T_h(N(\Delta\theta)) \end{pmatrix} \tag{26}$$

$$B_h = \begin{pmatrix} \frac{-\Gamma(q_1+1)}{\Gamma(2)\Gamma(q_1)} & 0 & \cdots & 0 \\ \frac{\Gamma(q_1+1)}{\Gamma(3)\Gamma(q_1-1)} & \frac{-\Gamma(q_1+1)}{\Gamma(2)\Gamma(q_1)} & \cdots & 0 \\ \vdots & \vdots & \vdots & \vdots \\ \frac{(-1)^N\Gamma(q_1+1)}{\Gamma(N+1)\Gamma(q_1-N+1)} & \frac{(-1)^{(N-1)}\Gamma(q_1+1)}{\Gamma(N)\Gamma((q_1-N+1)} & \cdots & \frac{-\Gamma(q_1+1)}{\Gamma(2)\Gamma(q_1)} \end{pmatrix} \tag{27}$$

$$T_{hk-1} = \begin{pmatrix} T_h(0) \\ T_h(\Delta\theta) \\ \vdots \\ T_h((N-1)(\Delta\theta)) \end{pmatrix} \tag{28}$$

$$B_c = \begin{pmatrix} frac{-}\Gamma(q_2+1)\Gamma(2)\Gamma(q_2) & 0 & \cdots & 0 \\ \frac{\Gamma(q_2+1)}{\Gamma(3)\Gamma(q_2-1)} & \frac{-\Gamma(q_2+1)}{\Gamma(2)\Gamma(q_2)} & \cdots & 0 \\ \vdots & \vdots & \vdots & \vdots \\ \frac{(-1)^N\Gamma(q_2+1)}{\Gamma(N+1)\Gamma(q_2-N+1)} & \frac{(-1)^{(N-1)}\Gamma(q_2+1)}{\Gamma(N)\Gamma((q_2-N+1)} & \cdots & \frac{-\Gamma(q_2+1)}{\Gamma(2)\Gamma(q_2)} \end{pmatrix} \tag{29}$$

$$T_{ck} = \begin{pmatrix} T_c(\Delta\theta) \\ T_c(2\Delta\theta) \\ \vdots \\ T_c(N(\Delta\theta)) \end{pmatrix} \tag{30}$$

$$T_{ck-1} = \begin{pmatrix} T_c(0) \\ T_c(\Delta\theta) \\ \vdots \\ T_c((N-1)(\Delta\theta)) \end{pmatrix} \tag{31}$$

So, the parallel fractional order derivative model for the spiral-plate counter-flow heat exchanger is obtained.

$$\begin{cases} T_{hk} = (\Delta\theta)^{q_1} \dfrac{FkZA}{QL_1 c_h \rho_h}(HT_{cK-1} - T_{hK-1}) + B_h T_{hk-1} \\ T_{ck} = (\Delta\theta)^{q_2} \dfrac{FkZA}{QL_2 c_c \rho_c}(HT_{hK-1} - T_{cK-1}) + B_c T_{ck-1} \\ T_{cout} = CT_{ck} \end{cases} \tag{32}$$

$$\begin{cases} D_{hfrac} = \dfrac{FkZA}{QL_1 c_h \rho_h}(HT_{cK-1} - T_{hK-1}) \\ D_{cfrac} = \dfrac{FkZA}{QL_2 c_c \rho_c}(HT_{hK-1} - T_{cK-1}) \end{cases} \tag{33}$$

$$\begin{cases} T_{hk} = (\Delta\theta)^{q_1} D_{hfrac} + B_h T_{hk-1} \\ T_{ck} = (\Delta\theta)^{q_2} D_{cfrac} + B_c T_{ck-1} \end{cases} \tag{34}$$

where

$$H = \begin{pmatrix} 0 & 0 & 0 & \dots & 0 & 1 \\ 0 & 0 & 0 & \dots & 1 & 0 \\ \vdots & \vdots & \vdots & \vdots & \vdots & \vdots \\ 1 & 0 & 0 & \dots & 0 & 0 \end{pmatrix} \tag{35}$$

$$C = \begin{pmatrix} 0 & 0 & 0 & 0 & \dots & 1 \end{pmatrix} \tag{36}$$

where $C \in R^{1\times N} and H \in R^{N\times N}$. The parallel fractional order derivative model for the spiral-plate counter-flow heat exchanger is a model with the parallel input data. It has high efficiency executed on GPU. The proposed parallel model is implemented on GPU by using MATLAB and CUDA [25].

#### 4.1.2. The Proposed Parallel Model for the Spiral-Plate Parallel-Flow Heat Exchanger

The parallel fractional derivation model for the spiral-plate parallel-flow heat exchanger is obtained by the same method with the spiral-plate counter-flow heat exchanger presented as above.

From (23) with the same method, the parallel fractional order derivative equations for the spiral-plate parallel-flow heat exchanger are described as follows.

$$\begin{cases} T_{hk} = (\Delta\theta)^{q_1} \dfrac{FkZA}{QL_1 c_1 \rho_h}(T_{cK-1} - T_{hK-1}) + B_h T_{hk-1} \\ T_{ck} = (\Delta\theta)^{q_2} \dfrac{FkZA}{QL_2 c_c \rho_c}(T_{hK-1} - T_{cK-1}) + B_c T_{ck-1} \\ T_{cout} = CT_{ck} \end{cases} \tag{37}$$

$$\begin{cases} D_{hfrac} = \dfrac{FkZA}{QL_1 c_h \rho_h}(T_{cK-1} - T_{hK-1}) \\ D_{cfrac} = \dfrac{FkZA}{QL_2 c_c \rho_c}(T_{hK-1} - T_{cK-1}) \end{cases} \tag{38}$$

The parallel fractional order derivative model for the spiral-plate parallel-flow heat exchanger is described as follow.

$$\begin{cases} T_{hk} = (\Delta\theta)^{q_1} D_{hfrac} + B_h T_{hk-1} \\ T_{ck} = (\Delta\theta)^{q_2} D_{cfrac} + B_c T_{ck-1} \end{cases} \tag{39}$$

where $T_{hk}, T_{hk-1}, D_{hfrac} \in R^N$, and $B_h \in R^{N\times N}$ $T_{ck}, T_{ck-1}, D_{cfrac} \in R^N$, and $B_c \in R^{N\times N}$.

### *4.2. Implementation on GPU for the Proposed Parallel Model*

In this section, implementation on GPU of the proposed parallel model for the spiral-plate heat exchanger is presented. The parallel model with the parallel data has faster efficiency executed on GPU than on CPU. The thread blocks of the proposed parallel model are given in Table 2.

**Table 2.** The thread blocks of the proposed parallel model implemented on GPU.

| Figure No. | Description |
|---|---|
| Figure 4 | The thread block of the proposed parallel model |
| Figure 5 | That of cold fluid for the counter-flow heat exchanger |
| Figure 6 | That of hot fluid side for the counter-flow heat exchanger |
| Figure 7 | That of cold fluid side for the parallel-flow heat exchanger |
| Figure 8 | That of hot fluid side for the parallel-flow heat exchanger |

The thread blocks of the proposed parallel model (2) implemented on GPU are shown in Figure 4.
where

$$F_k = \begin{pmatrix} f_1 \\ f_2 \\ \vdots \\ f_N \end{pmatrix} = \begin{pmatrix} f(\Delta h) \\ f(2(\Delta h)) \\ \vdots \\ f(N(\Delta h)) \end{pmatrix} \tag{40}$$

$$B = \begin{pmatrix} b_0 \\ b_1 \\ b_2 \\ \vdots \\ b_{N-1} \end{pmatrix} = \begin{pmatrix} \frac{-\Gamma(q+1)}{\Gamma(2)\Gamma(q)} & 0 & \dots & 0 \\ \frac{\Gamma(q+1)}{\Gamma(3)\Gamma(q-1)} & \frac{-\Gamma(q+1)}{\Gamma(2)\Gamma(q)} & \dots & 0 \\ \vdots & \vdots & \vdots & \vdots \\ \frac{(-1)^N\Gamma(q+1)}{\Gamma(N+1)\Gamma(q-N+1)} & \frac{(-1)^{(N-1)}\Gamma(q+1)}{\Gamma(N)\Gamma((q-N+1))} & \dots & \frac{-\Gamma(q+1)}{\Gamma(2)\Gamma(q)} \end{pmatrix} \tag{41}$$

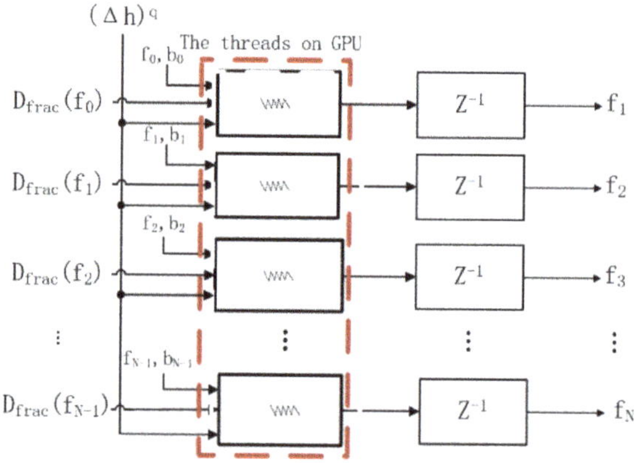


**Figure 4.** The thread blocks of the proposed parallel model.

$$D_{frac} = \begin{pmatrix} Df_0 \\ Df_1 \\ \vdots \\ Df_{N-1} \end{pmatrix} = \begin{pmatrix} D_t^q f(\Delta h) \\ D_t^q f(2(\Delta h)) \\ \vdots \\ D_t^q f(N(\Delta h)) \end{pmatrix} \tag{42}$$

$$F_{k-1} = \begin{pmatrix} f_0 \\ f_1 \\ f_2 \\ \vdots \\ f_{N-1} \end{pmatrix} = \begin{pmatrix} f(0) \\ f(\Delta h) \\ \vdots \\ f((N-1)(\Delta h)) \end{pmatrix} \tag{43}$$

where $F_{k-1}$ is a parallel input data, $D_{frac}$ is a parallel input derivation data, $B$ is a matrix relation to the order of fractional order derivation, $F_k$ is a parallel output data.

The thread blocks of the proposed parallel model for the spiral-plate counter-flow exchanger (32)–(34) are as shown in Figures 5 and 6.

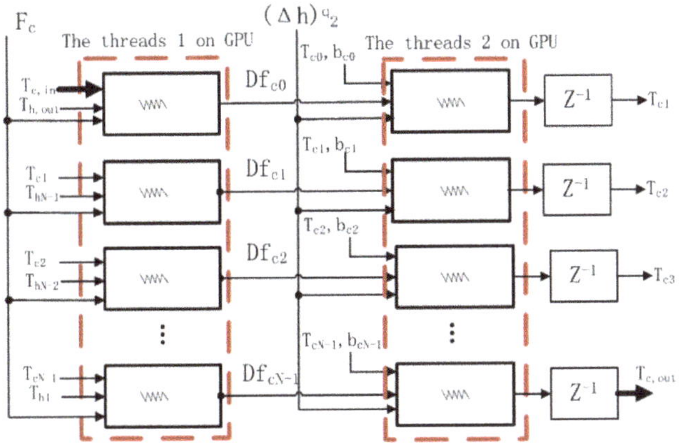


**Figure 5.** The thread blocks of the proposed parallel model in cold fluid for the counter-flow heat exchanger .

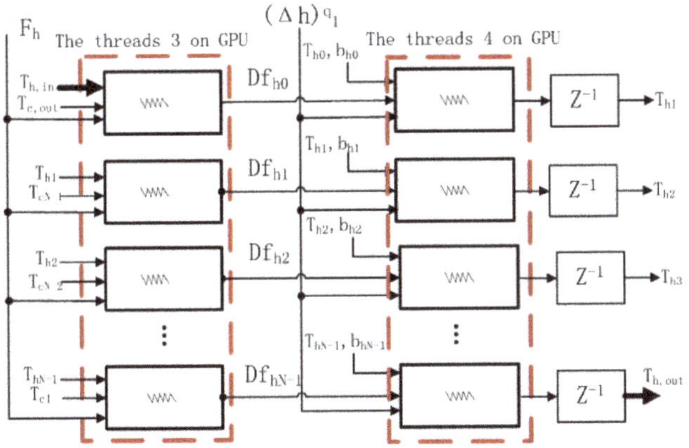


**Figure 6.** The thread blocks of the proposed parallel model in hot fluid for the counter-flow heat exchanger.

Here:

$$T_{ck-1} = \begin{pmatrix} T_c(0) \\ T_c(\Delta\theta) \\ \vdots \\ T_c((N-1)\Delta\theta) \end{pmatrix} = \begin{pmatrix} T_{c,in} \\ T_{c1} \\ \vdots \\ T_{cN-1} \end{pmatrix} \tag{44}$$

$$\tilde{T}_{hk-1} = HT_{hk-1} = \begin{pmatrix} T_{hN} \\ T_{hN-1} \\ \vdots \\ T_{h1} \end{pmatrix} = \begin{pmatrix} T_{h,out} \\ T_{hN-1} \\ \vdots \\ T_{h1} \end{pmatrix} \tag{45}$$

$$T_{ck} = \begin{pmatrix} T_c(\Delta\theta) \\ T_c(2(\Delta\theta)) \\ \vdots \\ T_c(N(\Delta\theta)) \end{pmatrix} = \begin{pmatrix} T_{c1} \\ T_{c2} \\ \vdots \\ T_{h,out} \end{pmatrix} \tag{46}$$

In Figure 5, $\tilde{T}_{hk-1}$ and $T_{ck-1}$ is parallel input data, respectively. $T_{ck}$ is a parallel output data.

$$T_{hk-1} = \begin{pmatrix} T_h(0) \\ T_h(\Delta\theta) \\ \vdots \\ T_h((N-1)\Delta\theta) \end{pmatrix} = \begin{pmatrix} T_{h,in} \\ T_{h1} \\ \vdots \\ T_{hN-1} \end{pmatrix} \tag{47}$$

$$\tilde{T}_{ck-1} = HT_{ck-1} = \begin{pmatrix} T_{cN} \\ T_{cN-1} \\ \vdots \\ T_{c1} \end{pmatrix} = \begin{pmatrix} T_{c,out} \\ T_{cN-1} \\ \vdots \\ T_{c1} \end{pmatrix} \tag{48}$$

$$T_{hk} = \begin{pmatrix} T_h(\Delta\theta) \\ T_h(2(\Delta\theta)) \\ \vdots \\ T_h(N(\Delta\theta)) \end{pmatrix} = \begin{pmatrix} T_{h1} \\ T_{h2} \\ \vdots \\ T_{c,out} \end{pmatrix} \tag{49}$$

In Figure 6, $\tilde{T}_{ck-1}$ and $T_{hk-1}$ is parallel input data, $T_{hk}$ is a parallel output data.

The thread blocks of proposed parallel model for the spiral-plate counter-flow exchanger (37)–(39) are as shown in Figures 7 and 8.

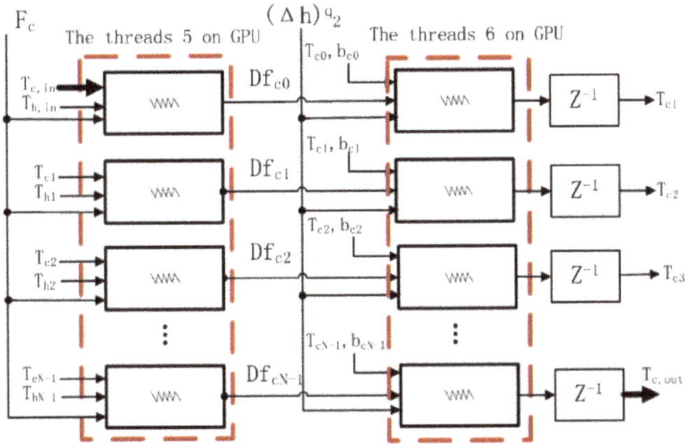


**Figure 7.** The thread blocks of the proposed parallel model in cold fluid for the parallel-flow heat exchanger.

Here:

$$T_{hk-1} = \begin{pmatrix} T_h(0) \\ T_h(\Delta\theta) \\ \vdots \\ T_h((N-1)(\Delta\theta)) \end{pmatrix} = \begin{pmatrix} T_{h,in} \\ T_{h1} \\ \vdots \\ T_{hN-1} \end{pmatrix} \tag{50}$$

$$T_{ck-1} = \begin{pmatrix} T_c(0) \\ T_c(\Delta\theta) \\ \vdots \\ T_c((N-1)\Delta\theta) \end{pmatrix} = \begin{pmatrix} T_{c,in} \\ T_{c1} \\ \vdots \\ T_{cN-1} \end{pmatrix} \tag{51}$$

$$T_{ck} = \begin{pmatrix} T_c(\Delta\theta) \\ T_c(2(\Delta\theta)) \\ \vdots \\ T_c(N(\Delta\theta)) \end{pmatrix} = \begin{pmatrix} T_{c1} \\ T_{c2} \\ \vdots \\ T_{h,out} \end{pmatrix} \tag{52}$$

$$T_{hk} = \begin{pmatrix} T_h(\Delta\theta) \\ T_h(2(\Delta\theta)) \\ \vdots \\ T_h(N(\Delta\theta)) \end{pmatrix} = \begin{pmatrix} T_{h1} \\ T_{h2} \\ \vdots \\ T_{c,out} \end{pmatrix} \tag{53}$$

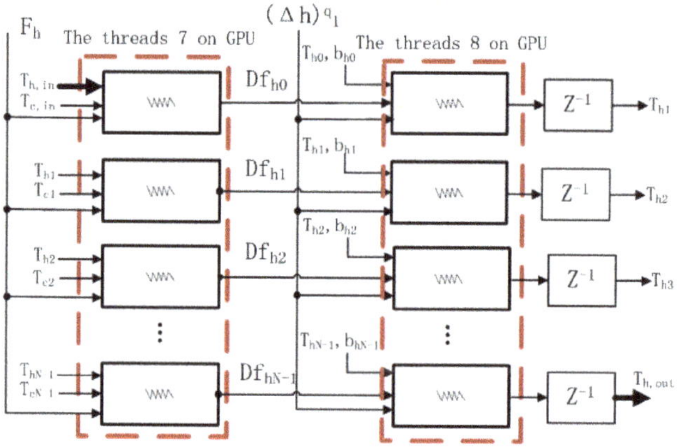


**Figure 8.** The thread blocks of the proposed parallel model in hot fluid for the parallel-flow heat exchanger.

In Figure 7, $T_{hk-1}$ and $T_{ck-1}$ is a parallel input data, respectively. $T_{ck}$ is a parallel output data. In Figure 8, $T_{ck-1}$ and $T_{hk-1}$ is a parallel input data, respectively. $T_{hk}$ is a parallel output data. $F_h = \dfrac{FZkA}{QL_1 c_h \rho_h}$, $F_c = \dfrac{FZkA}{QL_2 c_c \rho_c}$, $T_{c,in}$, $T_{c,out}$, $T_{h,in}$, and $T_{h,out}$ is the input temperature and output temperature in cold fluid, the input temperature and the output temperature in hot fluid, respectively. $Z^{-1}$ is a sampling delay time.

$$B_h = \begin{pmatrix} b_{h0} \\ b_{h1} \\ \vdots \\ b_{hN-1} \end{pmatrix} \tag{54}$$

$$B_c = \begin{pmatrix} b_{c0} \\ b_{c1} \\ \vdots \\ b_{cN-1} \end{pmatrix} \tag{55}$$

Therefore, parallel fractional order derivative model for the spiral-plate heat exchanger is a parallel model with the parallel input and output data. It has high execution efficiency implemented on GPU as shown Figures 4–8.

### 4.3. The Comparison of Execution Time for the Proposed Parallel Model on CPU and GPU

The proposed parallel model is implemented on CPU and GPU. Here, GPU (Gefore GTX 1080TI) is used to execute the proposed parallel model. In Figure 9, the comparison of execution time for the proposed parallel model on CPU and GPU is given. where $\Delta\theta$ is discretisation angle for the proposed parallel model. N is Discrete total. It shows that as the N increases, the execution time on the CPU increases, but the execution time on the GPU changes little.

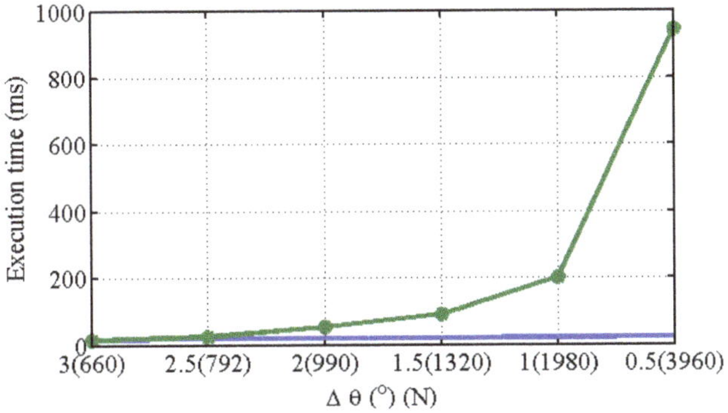


**Figure 9.** The comparison of execution time for the proposed parallel model on CPU and GPU.

## 5. Simulation on the Proposed Parallel Model for the Spiral-Plate Heat Exchanger

In this section, it is analysed for the relationships between the output temperature in cold fluid and the fractional orders $q_1, q_2$ for the proposed parallel model for the spiral-plate heat exchanger, the volume flow rate in hot fluid and the volume flow rate in cold fluid.

### 5.1. Simulation Conditions

Simulation parameters of the spiral-plate heat exchanger are shown in Table 3.

**Table 3.** Simulation parameters of the spiral-plate heat exchanger.

| Meaning | Symbol | Value |
|---|---|---|
| The densities of the two fluids | $\rho_c, \rho_h$ | 1000 $Kg/m^3$ |
| The specific heat capacity of the two fluids | $c_c, c_h$ | 4.2 KJ/(Kg · °C) |
| The input temperature of cold fluid | $T_{c,in}$ | 20 °C |
| The input temperature of hot fluid | $T_{h,in}$ | 50 °C |
| Thermal conductivity of SUS304 | $\lambda$ | 16.7 W/(m °C) |
| Heat transfer coefficients of the two fluids | $h_h, h_c$ | 366 $w/m^2 \cdot K$ |
| The orders for fractional order derivative | $q_1, q_2$ | 0.9–1.02 |
| The volume flow rate of hot fluid | $QL_1$ | 1–7 L/min |
| The volume flow rate of cold fluid | $QL_2$ | 1–7 L/min |
| Correction factor | F | 1.8 |
| Simulation time | t | [0, 12] s |

### 5.2. Simulation on the Proposed Parallel Model for the Spiral-Plate Counter-Flow Heat Exchanger

The index of all figures for the relationships between the output temperature of cold fluid and the flow rates of hot fluid, cold fluid for the proposed parallel model of the spiral-plate counter-flow heat exchanger is shown in Table 4.

**Table 4.** The relationships between the output temperature of cold fluid and the volume flow rates of hot fluid, cold fluid for the proposed parallel model for the spiral-plate counter-flow heat exchanger.

| Figure No. | Descrption |
|---|---|
| Figure 10 | $q_1, q_2$ = 0.9, 0.92, 0.94, 0.96, 0.98, 1.0 |
| Figure 11 | $q_1, q_2$ = 1.004, 1.008, 1.01, 1.02 |
| Figure 12 | $QL_1$ = 1 L/min, $QL_2$ = 1, 3, 5, 7 L/min |
| Figure 13 | $QL_1$ = 3 L/min, $QL_2$ = 1, 3, 5, 7 L/min |
| Figure 14 | $QL_1$ = 5 L/min, $QL_2$ = 1, 3, 5, 7 L/min |
| Figure 15 | $QL_1$ = 7 L/min, $QL_2$ = 1, 3, 5, 7 L/min |
| Figure 16 | $QL_1$ = 1, 3, 5, 7 L/min, $QL_2$ = 1 L/min |
| Figure 17 | $QL_1$ = 1, 3, 5, 7 L/min, $QL_2$ = 3 L/min |
| Figure 18 | $QL_1$ = 1, 3, 5, 7 L/min, $QL_2$ = 5 L/min |
| Figure 19 | $QL_1$ = 1, 3, 5, 7 L/min, $QL_2$ = 7 L/min |

5.2.1. Simulation with the Different Fractional Orders as $q_1, q_2 \leq 1$

The relationships between the output temperature in cold fluid and the fractional orders as $q_1, q_2 \leq 1$ are shown in Figure 10. Those show that the output temperature increases with the fractional orders $q_1, q_2$ rises up as shown in Figure 10.

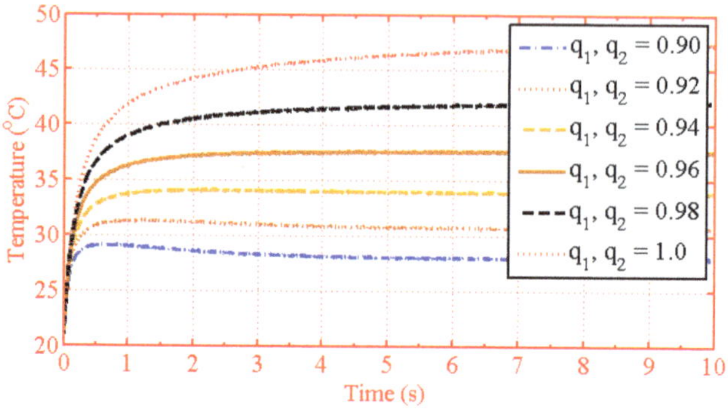


**Figure 10.** The output temperature in cold fluid as $q_1, q_2 \leq 1$.

5.2.2. Simulation with the Different Fractional Orders as $q_1, q_2 > 1$

The relationships between the output temperature in cold fluid and the different fractional orders as $q_1, q_2 > 1$ are shown in Figure 11. It shows when $q_1, q_2 = 1.025$, the output temperature in cold fluid is unstable.

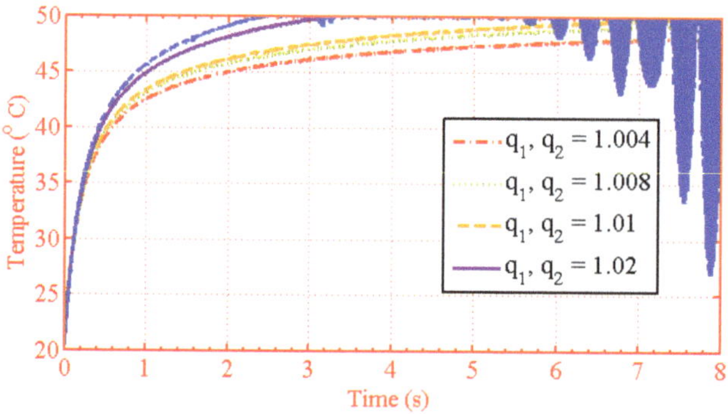


**Figure 11.** The output temperature in cold fluid as $q_1, q_2 > 1$.

5.2.3. The Relationships between the Output Temperature in Cold Fluid and the Different Volume Flow Rate of Hot Fluid

The relationships between the output temperature in cold fluid and the different volume flow rate of hot fluid are shown in Figures 12–15. Those figures show that the output temperature rises with the volume flow rate of hot fluid increases.

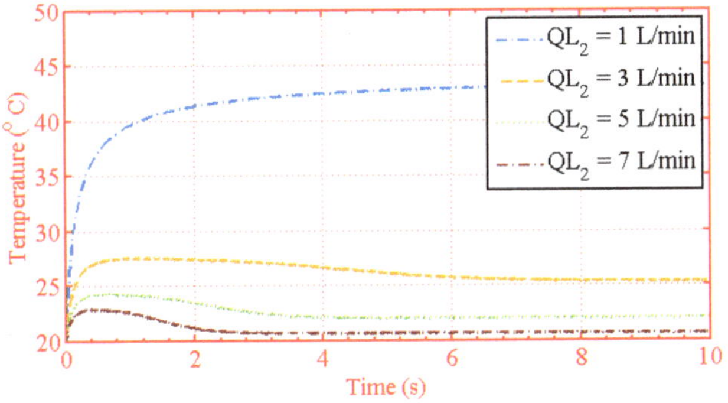


**Figure 12.** The output temperature in cold fluid with $QL_1 = 1$ L/min.

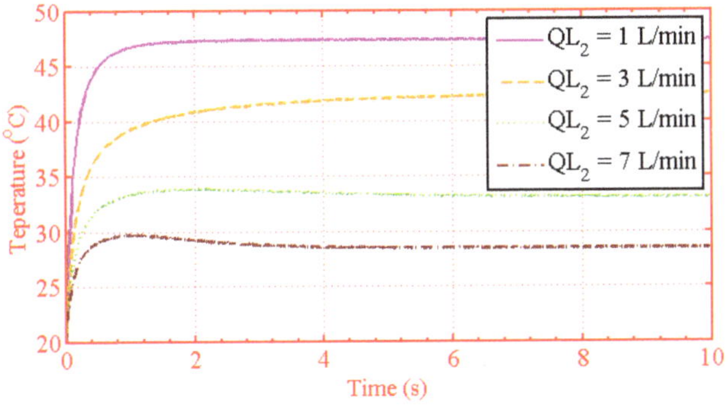


**Figure 13.** The output temperature in cold fluid with $QL_1 = 3$ L/min.

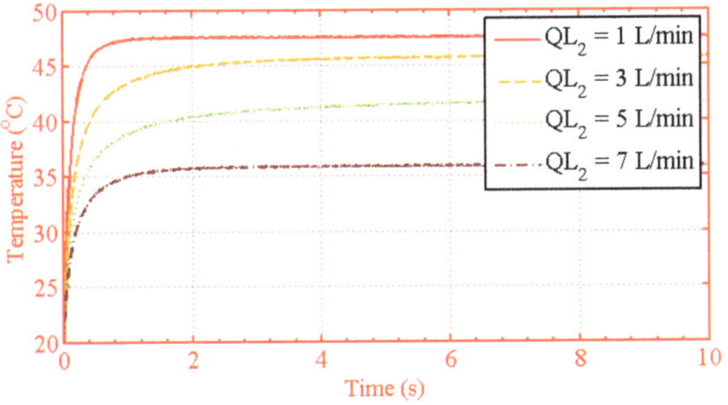


**Figure 14.** The output temperature in cold fluid with $QL_1 = 5$ L/min.

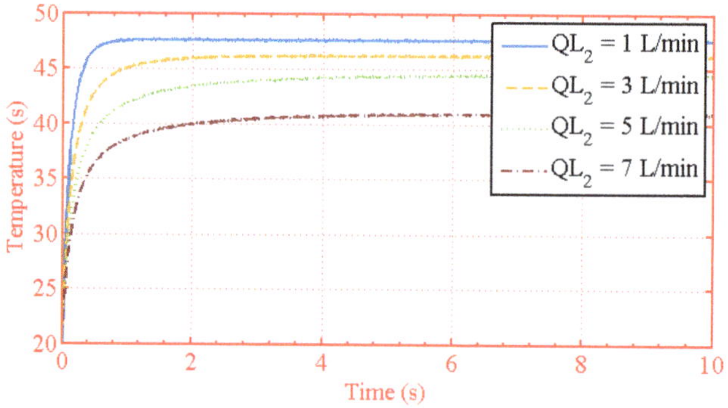


**Figure 15.** The output temperature in cold fluid with $QL_1 = 7$ L/min.

5.2.4. The Relationships between the Output Temperature in Cold Fluid and the Different Volume Flow Rate of Cold Fluid

The relationships between the output temperature in cold fluid and the different volume flow rate of cold fluid are shown in Figures 16–19. Those figures show that the output temperature in cold fluid goes down with the volume flow rate of cold fluid increases.

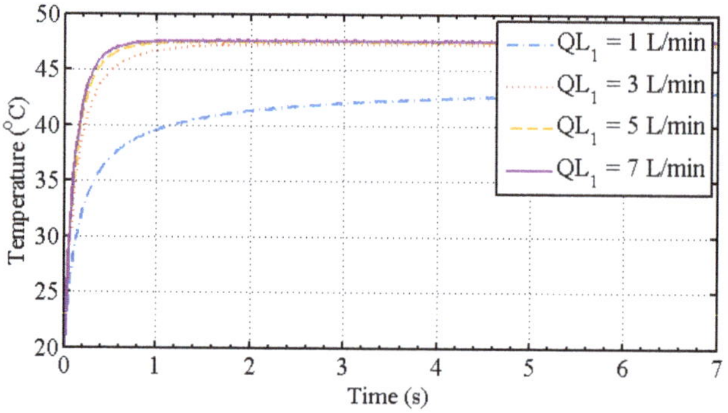


**Figure 16.** The output temperature in cold fluid with $QL_2 = 1$ L/min.

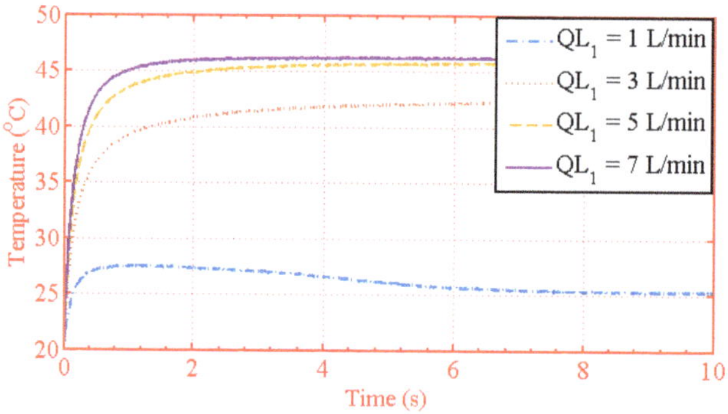


**Figure 17.** The output temperature in cold fluid with $QL_2 = 3$ L/min.

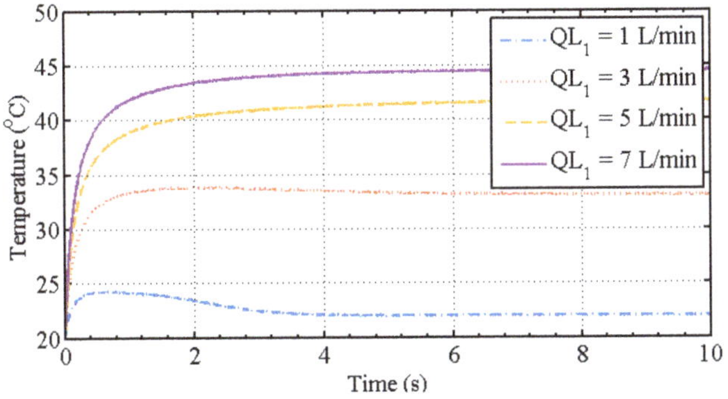


**Figure 18.** The output temperature in cold fluid with $QL_2 = 5$ L/min.

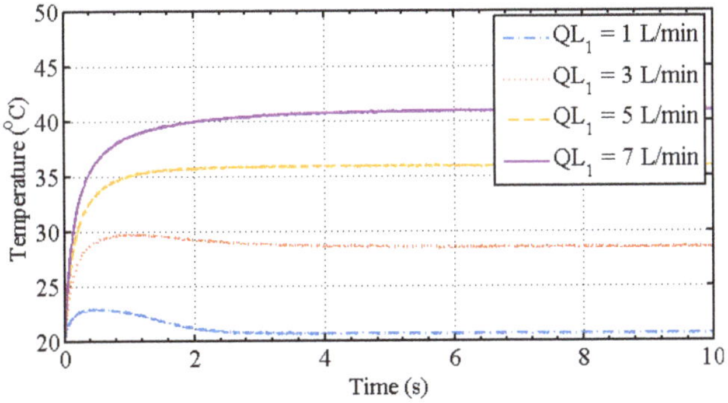


**Figure 19.** The output temperature in cold fluid with $QL_2 = 7$ L/min.

### 5.3. Simulation on the Proposed Parallel Model for the Spiral-Plate Parallel-Flow Heat Exchanger

The index of all figures for the relationships between the output temperature of cold fluid and the flow rates of hot fluid, cold fluid for the proposed parallel model of the spiral-plate parallel-flow heat exchanger is shown in Table 5.

**Table 5.** The relationships between the output temperature of cold fluid and the flow rates of hot fluid, cold fluid for the proposed parallel model of the spiral-plate parallel-flow heat exchanger.

| Figure No. | Descrption |
|---|---|
| Figure 20 | $q_1, q_2 = 0.9, 0.92, 0.94, 0.96, 0.98, 1.0$ |
| Figure 21 | $q_1, q_2 = 1.004, 1.008, 1.01, 1.02$ |
| Figure 22 | $QL_1$ =1 L/min, $QL_2 = 1, 3, 5, 7$ L/min |
| Figure 23 | $QL_1$ =3 L/min, $QL_2 = 1, 3, 5, 7$ L/min |
| Figure 24 | $QL_1$ =5 L/min, $QL_2 = 1, 3, 5, 7$ L/min |
| Figure 25 | $QL_1$ =7 L/min, $QL_2 = 1, 3, 5, 7$ L/min |
| Figure 26 | $QL_1 = 1, 3, 5, 7$ L/min, $QL_2 = 1$ L/min |
| Figure 27 | $QL_1 = 1, 3, 5, 7$ L/min, $QL_2 = 3$ L/min |
| Figure 28 | $QL_1 = 1, 3, 5, 7$ L/min, $QL_2 = 5$ L/min |
| Figure 29 | $QL_1 = 1, 3, 5, 7$ L/min, $QL_2 = 7$ L/min |

#### 5.3.1. Simulation with the Different Fractional Orders as $q_1, q_2 \leq 1$

The relationships between output temperature in cold fluid and the fractional orders as $q_1, q_2 \leq 1$ are shown in Figure 20. They show that the output temperature rises with the fractional orders $q_1, q_2$ increases as shown in Figure 20.

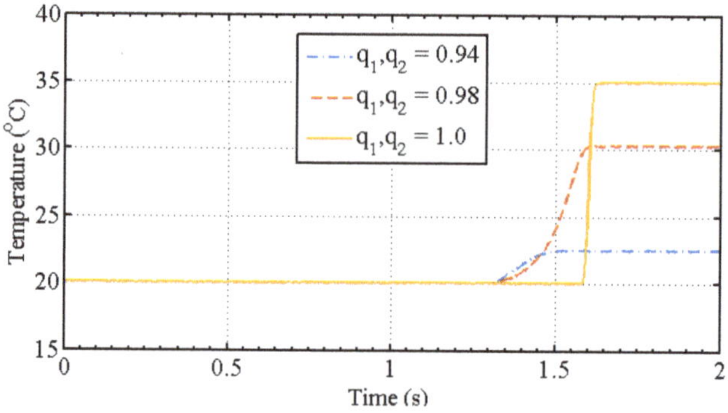


**Figure 20.** The output temperature in cold fluid as $q_1, q_2 \leq 1$.

#### 5.3.2. Simulation with the Different Fractional Orders as $q_1, q_2 > 1$

The relationships between the output temperature in cold fluid and the fractional orders as $q_1, q_2 > 1$ are shown in Figure 21. When $q_1, q_2$ is 1.025, the output temperature in cold fluid is unstable.

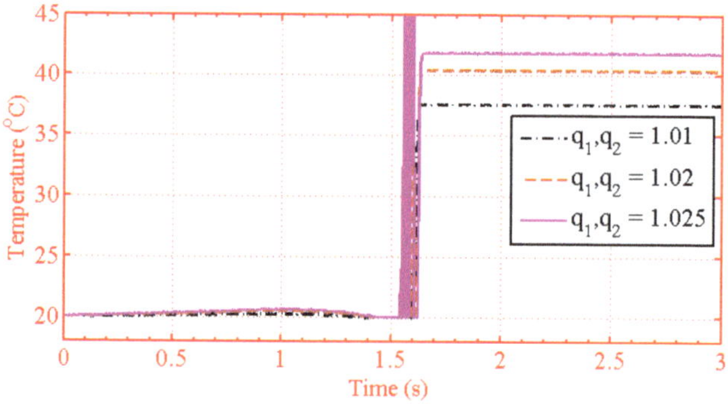


**Figure 21.** The output temperature in cold fluid as $q_1, q_2 > 1$.

#### 5.3.3. The Relationships between the Output Temperature of Cold Fluid and the Different Volume Flow Rate of Hot Fluid

The relationships between the output temperature in cold fluid and the different volume flow rate of hot fluid are shown in Figures 22–25. Those figures show that output temperature in cold fluid rises with the volume flow rate of hot fluid increases.

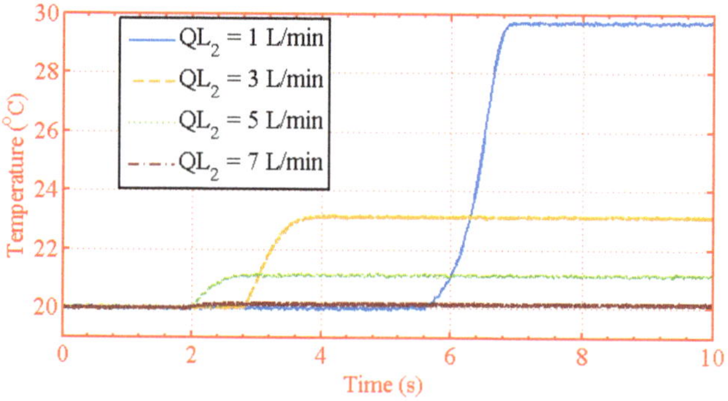


**Figure 22.** The output temperature in cold fluid with $QL_1$ = 1 L/min.

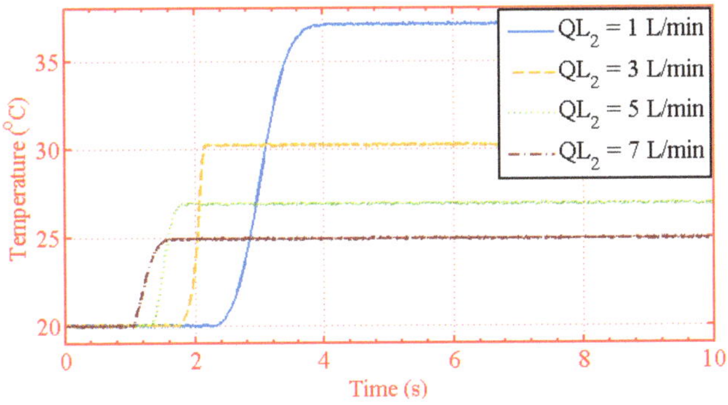


**Figure 23.** The output temperature in cold fluid with $QL_1 = 3$ L/min.

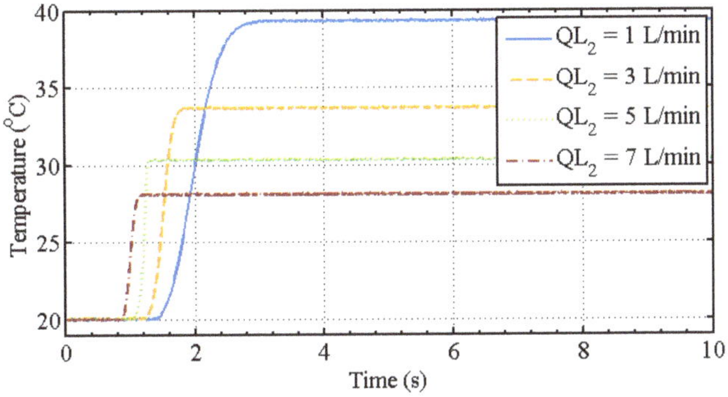


**Figure 24.** The output temperature in cold fluid with $QL_1 = 5$ L/min.

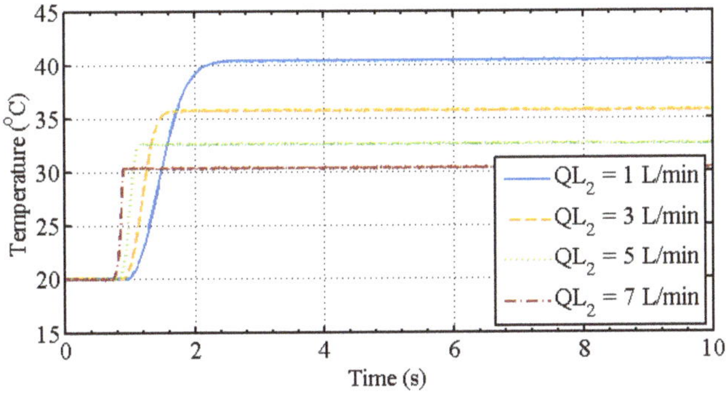


**Figure 25.** The output temperature in cold fluid with $QL_1 = 7$ L/min.

5.3.4. The Relationships between the Output Temperature of Cold Fluid and the Different Volume Flow Rate of Cold Fluid

The relationships between the output temperature in cold fluid and the different volume flow rate of cold fluid are shown in Figures 26–29. Those figures show that the output temperature in cold fluid drops down with the volume flow rate of cold fluid increases.

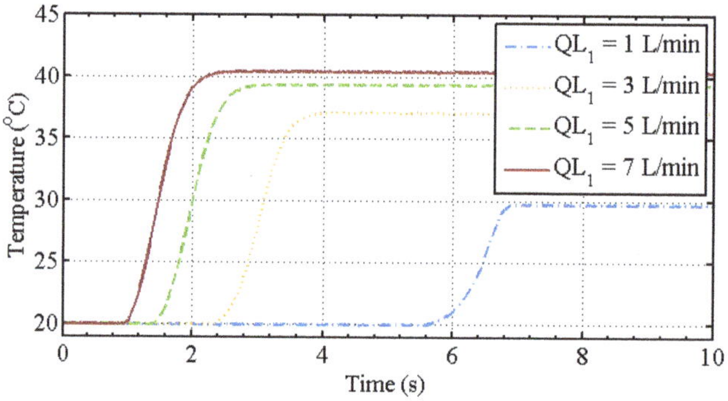


**Figure 26.** The output temperature in cold fluid with $QL_2 = 1$ L/min.

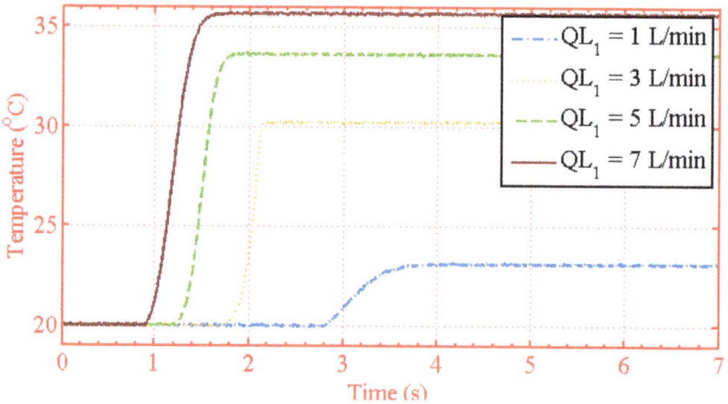


**Figure 27.** The output temperature in cold fluid with $QL_2 = 3$ L/min.

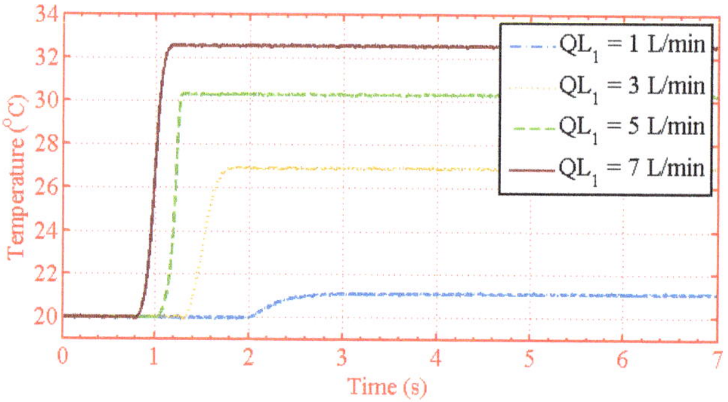


**Figure 28.** The output temperature in cold fluid with $QL_2 = 5$ L/min.

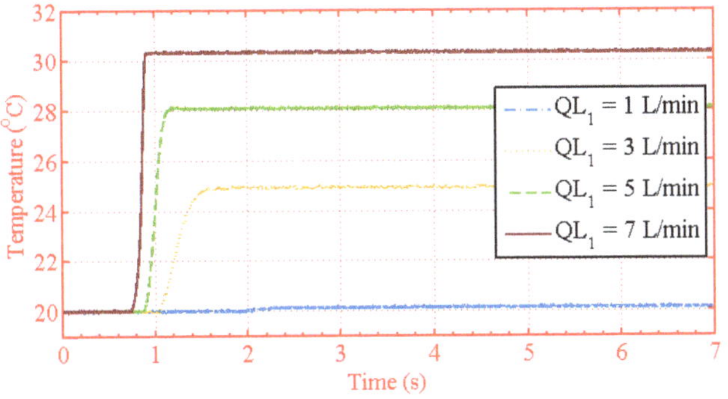


**Figure 29.** The output temperature in cold fluid with $QL_2 = 7$ L/min.

## 6. Conclusions

A parallel fractional order derivative model and the problem statement are introduced in this paper. Then, the fractional order derivative model for the spiral-plate heat exchanger is constructed by mathematic analysis and extending from classical integer order derivative. Further, the parallel fractional order derivative model for the spiral-plate heat exchanger is constructed by considering the merit of GPU. Finally, the parallel fractional order derivative model for the spiral-plate heat exchanger is simulated. Simulations show the relationships between the output temperature of heated fluid and the fractional orders of the two fluids, the input volume flow rate of cold fluid, and the input volume flow rate of cold fluid, respectively.

**Author Contributions:** M.D. supervised the work; G.D. finished the simulation, and wrote the rest of the work. All authors have read and agreed to the published version of the manuscript.

**Funding:** This research received no external funding.

**Institutional Review Board Statement:** Not applicable.

**Informed Consent Statement:** Not applicable.

**Data Availability Statement:** Not applicable.

**Conflicts of Interest:** The authors declare no conflict of interest.

## Appendix A

**Definition A1** ([10]). *(the Caputo's fractional order derivative)*

$$ {}_a^C D_t^q f(t) = \begin{cases} \frac{1}{\Gamma(n-q)} \int_a^t \frac{f^{(n)}(t)}{(t-\tau)^{n-q-1}} d\tau, & n-1 < q < n \\ \frac{d^n f(t)}{dt^n}, & q = n \end{cases} \tag{A1} $$

*where* $\Gamma(\cdot)$ *is gamma function defined by* $\Gamma(x) = \int_0^\infty e^{-t} t^{x-1}$ *and n is a positive integer number.*

**Definition A2** ([10]). *(the Grunwald-Letnikov's fractional order derivative)*

$$ {}_a^{GL} D_t^q f(t) = \lim_{\Delta h \to 0} (\Delta h)^{-q} \sum_{j=0}^{\left[\frac{t-a}{\Delta h}\right]} (-1)^j \frac{\Gamma(q+1)}{\Gamma(j+1)\Gamma(q-j+1)} f(t - j(\Delta h)) \tag{A2} $$

*where* $[\cdot]$ *means the integer part.*

(A1) *and* (A2) *are equivalent if* $f(\cdot)$ *is differentiable.* (A1) *is a continues type definition of fractional order derivative.* (A2) *is a non-continues type definition of fractional order derivative.*

(A2) *is implemented easily on computer.* (A2) *is used in this paper.* (A1) *is easy to analyse system performance such as stability, tracking, etc. for the fractional order control system.*

*If* $\Delta h \approx 0$ *then*

$$ {}_{0}^{GL}D_{t}^{q}f(t) \approx (\Delta h)^{-q}\sum_{j=0}^{N}(-1)^{j}\frac{\Gamma(q+1)}{\Gamma(j+1)\Gamma(q-j+1)}f(t-j(\Delta h)) \tag{A3} $$

*where* $N$ *is* $[\frac{t-a}{\Delta h}]$.

## References


1. Tapre, R.W.; Kaware, J.P. Review on heat transfer in spiral heat exchanger. *Int. J. Sci. Res.* **2015**, *5*, 1–5.
2. Sathiyan, S.; Rangarajan, M. An experimental study of spiral-plate heat exchanger for nitrobenzene-water two-phase system. *Bulg. Chem. Commun.* **2010**, *42*, 205–209.
3. Khorshidi, J.; Heidari, S. Design and construction of a spiral heat exchanger. *Adv. Chem. Eng. Sci.* **2016**, *6*, 201–298. [CrossRef]
4. Memon, S.; Gadhe, P.; Kulkarni, S. Design and testing of a spiral plate heat exchanger for textile industry. *Int. J. Sci. Eng. Res.* **2019**, *10*, 149–157.
5. Metta, V.R.; Konijeti, R.; Dasore, A. Thermal design of spiral plate heat exchanger through numerical modelling. *Int. J. Mech. Eng. Technol.* **2018**, *9*, 736–745.
6. Gomadam, P.M.; White, R.E.; Weidner, J.W. Modeling heat conduction in spiral geometries. *J. Electrochem. Soc.* **2003**, *150*, A1339–A1345. [CrossRef]
7. Bidabadi, M.; Sadaghiani, A.K.; Azad, A.V. Spiral heat exchanger optimization using genetic algorithm. *Sci. Iran. B* **2013**, *20*, 1445–1454.
8. Wen, S.; Deng, M. Operator-based robust nonlinear control and fault detection for a Peltier actuated thermal process. *Math. Comput. Model.* **2012**, *57*, 16–29. [CrossRef]
9. Fujii, R.; Deng, M.; Wakitani, S. Nonlinear remote temperature control of a spiral plate heat exchanger. In Proceedings of the 2015 International Conference on Advanced Mechatronic Systems, Beijing, China, 22–24 August 2015; pp. 533–537.
10. Podlubny, I. *Fractional Differential Equations*; Academic Press: Cambridge, MA, USA, 1999.
11. Jafari, H.; Khalique, C.M.; Nazari, M. An algorithm for the numerical solution of nonlinear fractional-order Van der Pol oscillator equation. *Math. Comput. Model.* **2012**, *55*, 1782–1786. [CrossRef]
12. Ibrahim, R.W.; Darus, M. On a new solution of factional differential equation using complex transform in the unit disk. *Math. Comput. Appl.* **2014**, *19*, 152–160.
13. Qian, D.; Li, C.; Agarwal, R.P. Stability analysis of fractional differential system with Riemann–Liouville derivative. *Math. Comput. Model.* **2010**, *52*, 862–874.
14. Baranowski, J.; Zagorowska, M.; Bauer, W.; Dziwinski, T.; Piatek, P. Applications of Direct Lyapunov Method in Caputo Non-Integer Order Systems. *Elektron. Elektrotechnika* **2015**, *21*, 10–13. [CrossRef]
15. Li, Y.; Chen, Y.; Podlubny, I. Mittag–Leffler stability of fractional order nonlinear dynamic systems. *Automatica* **2009**, *45*, 1965–1969. [CrossRef]
16. Caponetto, R.; Dongola, G.; Fortuna, L.; Petras, I. *Fractional Order Systems: Modeling and Control Applications*; World Scientific: Singapore, 2010.
17. Patnaik, S.; Sidhardh, S.; Semperlotti, F. Nonlinear thermoelastic fractional-order model of nonlocal plates: Application to postbuckling and bending response. *Thin-Walled Struct.* **2021**, *164*, 107809. [CrossRef]
18. Challamel, N.; Zorica, D.; Atanacković, T.M.; Spasić, D.T. On the fractional generalization of Eringen's nonlocal elasticity for wave propagation. *Comptes Rendus Mécanique* **2013**, *341*, 298–303. [CrossRef]
19. Sidhardh, S.; Patnaik, S.; Semperlotti, F. Thermodynamics of fractional-order nonlocal continua and its application to the thermoelastic response of beams. *Eur. J. Mech. A/Solids* **2021**, *88*, 104238. [CrossRef]
20. Monje, C.A.; Chen, Y.; Vinagre, B.M.; Xue, D.; Feliu, V. *Fractional Order Systems and Controls: Fundamentals and Applications*; Springer: Berlin/Heidelberg, Germany, 2010.
21. Oldham, K.B.; Spanier, J. *The Fractional Calculus: Theory and Applications of Differentiation and Integration to Arbitrary Order*; Dover Publications: Mineola, NY, USA, 2006.
22. Magin, R.L.; Ovadia, M. Modeling the cardiac tissue electrode interface using fractional calculus. *J. Vib. Control* **2008**, *14*, 1431–1442. [CrossRef]
23. Padovan, J. Computational algorithms for FE formulations involving fractional operator. *Comput. Mech.* **1987**, *2*, 271–287. [CrossRef]
24. Zhong, L. Comparative analysis of GPU and CPU. *Technol. Mark.* **2009**, *9*, 13–14.
25. Liu, S.; Liu, M.; Zhang, G. Model of accelerating MATLAB computation based on CUDA. *Appl. Res. Comput.* **2010**, *6*, 2140–2143.
26. Povstenko, Y. *Fractional Thermoelasticity*; Springer International Publishing: Berlin/Heidelberg, Germany, 2015.

27. Challamel, N.; Grazide, C.; Picandet, V.; Perrot, A.; Zhang, Y. A nonlocal Fourier's law and its application to the heat conduction of one-dimensional and two-dimensional thermal. *Comptes Rendus Mécanique* **2016**, *344*, 388–401. [CrossRef]
28. Sumelka, W. Thermoelasticity in the Framework of the Fractional Continuum Mechanics. *J. Therm. Stress.* **2014**, *37*, 678–706. [CrossRef]
29. Deng, M.; Wen, S.; Inoue, A. Operator-based robust nonlinear control for a Peltier actuated process. *Meas. Control. J. Inst. Meas. Control.* **2011**, *44*, 116–120. [CrossRef]
30. Bi, S.; Deng, M.; Xiao, Y. Robust Stability and Tracking for Operator-Based Nonlinear Uncertain Systems. *IEEE Trans. Autom. Sci. Eng.* **2015**, *12*, 1059–1066. [CrossRef]
31. Deng, M.; Kawashima, T. Adaptive Nonlinear Sensorless Control for an Uncertain Miniature Pneumatic Curling Rubber Actuator Using Passivity and Robust Right Coprime Factorization. *IEEE Trans. Control Syst. Technol.* **2016**, *24*, 318–324. [CrossRef]
32. Dong, G.; Deng, M. Modeling of a spiral heat exchanger using fractional order equation and GPU. In Proceedings of the 2019 International Conference on Advanced Mechatronic Systems (ICAMechS), Kusatsu, Japan, 26–28 August 2019; pp. 108–113.
33. Magadum, A.; Pawar, A.; Patil, R.; Phadtare, R.; Mestri, T.C. Review of experimental analysis of parallel and counter flow heat exchanger. *Int. J. Eng. Res. Technol.* **2016**, *5*, 395–397.
34. Bergman, T.; Lavine, A.; Incropera, F.; Dewitt, D. *Faundamentals of Heat and Mass Transfer*, 8th ed.; Wiley: Hoboken, NJ, USA, 2017.

axioms

MDPI

*Article*

# Design, Analysis and Comparison of a Nonstandard Computational Method for the Solution of a General Stochastic Fractional Epidemic Model

**Nauman Ahmed [1], Jorge E. Macías-Díaz [2,3,*], Ali Raza [4], Dumitru Baleanu [5,6], Muhammad Rafiq [7], Zafar Iqbal [1] and Muhammad Ozair Ahmad [1]**

1 Department of Mathematics and Statistics, The University of Lahore, Lahore 54000, Pakistan; nauman.ahmed@math.uol.edu.pk (N.A.); zafar.iqbal@math.uol.edu.pk (Z.I.); ozair@uet.edu.pk (M.O.A.)
2 Department of Mathematics, School of Digital Technologies, Tallinn University, 10120 Tallinn, Estonia
3 Departamento de Matemáticas y Física, Universidad Autónoma de Aguascalientes, Avenida Universidad 940, Ciudad Universitaria, Aguascalientes 20130, Mexico
4 Department of Mathematics, Govt. Mulana Zafar Ali Khan Graduate College Wazirabad, Gujranwala 52250, Pakistan; alimustasamcheema@gmail.com
5 Department of Mathematics, Cankaya University, Ankara 06530, Turkey; dumitru@cankaya.edu.tr
6 Institute of Space Sciences, 06530 Bucharest, Romania
7 Department of Mathematics, Faculty of Sciences, University of Central Punjab, Lahore 54000, Pakistan; m.rafiq@ucp.edu.pk
* Correspondence: jemacias@correo.uaa.mx; Tel.: +52-449-9108400

**Abstract:** Malaria is a deadly human disease that is still a major cause of casualties worldwide. In this work, we consider the fractional-order system of malaria pestilence. Further, the essential traits of the model are investigated carefully. To this end, the stability of the model at equilibrium points is investigated by applying the Jacobian matrix technique. The contribution of the basic reproduction number, $R_0$, in the infection dynamics and stability analysis is elucidated. The results indicate that the given system is locally asymptotically stable at the disease-free steady-state solution when $R_0 < 1$. A similar result is obtained for the endemic equilibrium when $R_0 > 1$. The underlying system shows global stability at both steady states. The fractional-order system is converted into a stochastic model. For a more realistic study of the disease dynamics, the non-parametric perturbation version of the stochastic epidemic model is developed and studied numerically. The general stochastic fractional Euler method, Runge–Kutta method, and a proposed numerical method are applied to solve the model. The standard techniques fail to preserve the positivity property of the continuous system. Meanwhile, the proposed stochastic fractional nonstandard finite-difference method preserves the positivity. For the boundedness of the nonstandard finite-difference scheme, a result is established. All the analytical results are verified by numerical simulations. A comparison of the numerical techniques is carried out graphically. The conclusions of the study are discussed as a closing note.

**Keywords:** stochastic epidemic model; malaria infection; stochastic generalized Euler; nonstandard finite-difference method; positivity; boundedness

**MSC:** 65M06; 65M12; 35K15; 35K55; 35K57

**Citation:** Ahmed, N.; Macías-Díaz, J.E.; Raza, A.; Baleanu, D.; Rafiq, M.; Iqbal, Z.; Ahmad, M.O. Design, Analysis and Comparison of a Nonstandard Computational Method for the Solution of a General Stochastic Fractional Epidemic Model. *Axioms* **2022**, *11*, 10. https://doi.org/10.3390/axioms11010010

Academic Editors: Carlos Lizama and Chris Goodrich

Received: 19 October 2021
Accepted: 21 December 2021
Published: 24 December 2021



## 1. Introduction

Malaria is a Latin word which means "foul air". Biologically, malaria is an ailment due to the microorganism plasmodium, which is a bug found in the mosquito. It is also observed that not all mosquitoes transmit malaria; only the female mosquito Anopheles can inject this plasmodium into the human body, causing the fatal malaria disease. Its incubation period varies from 7 to 30 days, and research shows that five types of malarial parasites are found, namely, *P. malarie*, *P. ovale*, *P. vivax*, *P. falciparum* and *P. knowles*. In particular, *P. falciparum* is extremely dangerous and fatal, causing a wide range of physical symptoms, such as fever, flu, severe chills, vomiting, muscle aches, headache, nausea, diarrhea, tiredness, low blood pressure, respiratory disorder, cerebral disorder, and hemoglobin in the urine, with some cases showing jaundice and anemia.

Physicians knew about this disease at least 2000 years ago, and noted that it is very common in marshy areas, where stagnant water is found frequently. It was assumed that water and malaria have some relation, and some volunteers at that time drank from pond water but they did not show any symptoms. A treatment for malaria was discovered accidentally in the seventeenth century, when Americans started to use the bark of the plant Quina to cure this disease in America. In 1880, the name plasmodium was given to this parasite because it resembled the multinucleated cells of the sludge type. Nowadays, the vaccine of malaria is used to prevent it, but it is not so effective due to the fact that plasmodium has a very complicated life cycle. Trials and experiments are still in progress. Currently, the vaccine RTSS is used, but it is still rather inefficient.

In America, about 2000 cases of malaria are diagnosed every year. According to the World Health Organization, 2.29 billion cases of malaria were reported in 2019, and 2.28 billion cases were reported in 2018. In 2019, there were 409,000 deaths. In 2018, 411,000 causalities were recorded, worldwide. In 2019, 23% of deaths were calculated in Nigeria, 11% in Congo, 5% in Tanzania, and 45% in Niger. The only region in the world which is free of malaria in northern Australia. In total, 94% of cases were reported in Africa which was the highest ratio in the world. Children under the age of 5 years are at high risk; about 67% of children died worldwide in 2019. In Pakistan, during the monsoon season, the ratio of malarial patients remains at its peak. It is calculated that about 300,000 cases are reported every year in Pakistan. Some cautions are taken to control malaria, such as wearing full clothes during summer, using different mosquito-repellent lotions, using a net on windows and doors, having a proper sanitation system for water, using nets at night while sleeping, using different medicated body oils, etc.

In 2020, Cristhian et al. proposed a SIR model to inhibit malaria [1]. In 2020, Olaniyi et al. presented an SEIR mathematical model to control malaria among travelers [2]. In 2020, Kim et al. modulated an SEI model to save Korean people from Plasmodium vivax [3]. Ibrahim et al. introduced an SEIR model to control the transmission of malaria disease using awareness techniques [4]. In 2020, Baihaqi et al. proposed an SEIRS p-model to investigate how malaria disease spreads among humans [5]. In 2020, Traore et al. proposed an ELPN model by describing different stages of mosquitoes that are involved in malaria transmission [6]. Djidjou et al. formulated an SEIR model to study the effects of weather conditions for spreading malaria disease [7]. That year, Pandey presented a mathematical model to describe how domestic and industrial effluents play a major role in malaria spreading [8]. In 2019, Song et al. introduced a malaria-dynamics mathematical model [9]. In turn, Ogunmiloro presented a model to simulate the infectivity of plasmodium and toxoplasma [10]; Koutou et al. proposed an ELPA model to study the relationship of malaria with mosquito population [11]; and Bakary et al. suggested a model to analyze the impact of frequent biting of mosquitoes and blood transfusions [12].

Beretta et al. studied mathematically the mortality in children and adults caused by malaria [13]. Rafia et al. observed the consequences of vaccination on the dynamics of malaria [14]. In 2017, Traoré et al. presented a model to estimate the variation in the intensity of malaria epidemic by considering the seasonal effects and frequent bite rate of mosquitoes [15]. In 2017, Mojeeb et al. presented an SEIR model to investigate the ways to control the mosquito population and eradication of malaria outbreaks [16]. Olaniyi suggested a system to demonstrate the non-linearity in malarial propagation [17]. In 2011, Mandal et al. projected a system to understand the propagation of malaria disease [18], Chitnis developed an SEIR model to check the propagation of malaria by infectious mosquitoes [19] and Smith et al. presented a scientific design to predict the presence of malaria in a human population [20]. The purpose of this work is to propose a stochastic compartmental system using fractional operators to model the spreading of more general epidemics in a human population. Our scheme will be able to preserve various important properties of the solutions [21–25].

## 2. Mathematical Models

In this section, we introduce the extended stochastic fractional epidemic model [26]. To start with, we quote some basic definitions of fractional calculus.

**Definition 1.** *The Riemann–Liouville fractional derivative of $\psi : \mathbb{R} \to \mathbb{R}$ of order $\alpha > 0$ is defined as*

$$_{RL}D_0^\alpha \psi(t) = \frac{1}{\Gamma(k-\alpha)} \frac{d^k}{dt^k} \int_0^t \frac{\psi(s)}{(t-s)^{k-\alpha-1}} ds, \quad \forall t \in \mathbb{R}, \tag{1}$$

*where $k = [\alpha] + 1$, $k - 1 < \alpha < k$ and $\Gamma$ is the gamma function. Meanwhile, the respective Caputo fractional derivative of order $\alpha$ is given by*

$$_0^C D_t^\alpha \psi(t) = \frac{1}{\Gamma(k-\alpha)} \int_0^t (t-s)^{k-\alpha-1} \frac{d^k}{dt^k} \mathcal{F}(s) ds \tag{2}$$

To start with, let us consider the following compartmental epidemic model studied in [26]:

$$\frac{dS_h(t)}{dt_1} = \mu_h N_h(t) - \beta_h S_h(t) \left( \frac{I_v(t)}{N_v(t)} \right) - \alpha_h S_h(t), \tag{3}$$

$$\frac{dI_h(t)}{dt_1} = \beta_h S(t)_h I_v(t) - (\delta_h + \alpha_h + \gamma_h) I_h(t), \tag{4}$$

$$\frac{dR_h(t)}{dt_1} = \gamma_h I_h(t) - \alpha_h R_h(t), \tag{5}$$

$$\frac{dS_v(t)}{dt_1} = \mu_V N_v(t) - \beta_v S_v(t) \frac{I_h(t)}{N_h(t)} - \alpha_v S_v(t), \tag{6}$$

$$\frac{dI_v(t)}{dt_1} = \beta_v S_v \frac{I_h(t)}{N_h(t)} - \alpha_v I_v(t). \tag{7}$$

In the above system, $S_h(t)$ describes the susceptible population at time $t$, $I_h(t)$ is the infected population, $R_h(t)$ is the number of recovered individuals, $S_v(t)$ is the susceptible mosquitoes, $I_v(t)$ is the number of infected mosquitoes, $N_h(t)$ is the population size, and $Nv(t)$ is the total mosquito population. Meanwhile, $\mu_h$ is the per capita birth rate of human individuals $[time^{-1}]$, $\alpha_h$ is the per capita natural death rate for human individuals $[time^{-1}]$, $\delta_h$ denotes the per capita disease-induced death rate for human population $[time^{-1}]$, $\beta_h$ is the contact rate of human population $[time^{-1}]$, $\gamma_h$ represents the per capita recovery rate of humans $[time^{-1}]$, $\mu_v$ denotes the per capita birth rate of mosquitoes $[time^{-1}]$, $\alpha_v$ is the per capita natural death rate of mosquitoes $[time^{-1}]$, and $\beta_v$ is the mosquito contact rate $[time^{-1}]$.

To generalize systems (3)–(7), we use fractional operators by a scaling of the model. From (3),

$$\frac{1}{\mu_h N_h} \frac{dS_h}{dt_1} = \frac{\mu_h N_h}{\mu_h N_h} - \frac{\beta_h}{\mu_h} \left( \frac{S_h}{N_h} \right) \left( \frac{I_v}{N_v} \right) - \left( \frac{\alpha_h}{\mu_h} \right) \left( \frac{S_h}{N_h} \right), \tag{8}$$

which leads to the equation

$$\frac{ds_h}{dt} = 1 - \beta s_h i_v - \alpha_1 s_h, \tag{9}$$

where $s_h = \frac{S_h}{N_h}$, $i_v = \frac{I_v}{N_v}$, $\alpha_1 = \frac{\alpha_h}{\mu_h}$, $\beta = \frac{\beta_h}{\mu_h}$ and $t = t_1 \mu_h$. Similarly,

$$\frac{di_h}{dt} = \beta s_h i_v - (\gamma + \alpha_1) i_h, \tag{10}$$

$$\frac{di_v}{dt} = v(1 - i_v) - \delta i_v. \tag{11}$$

Here, $\gamma = \frac{\delta_h + \gamma_h}{\mu_h}$, $v = \frac{\beta_v}{N_v}$, $\delta = \frac{\alpha_v}{\mu_v}$, $R_h = N_h - S_h - I_h$, and $S_v = N_v - I_v$. Finally, the following time-fractional system results:

$$D_t^\alpha s_h = 1 - \beta^\alpha s_h(t) i_v(t) - \alpha_1^\alpha s_h(t), \tag{12}$$

$$D_t^\alpha i_h = \beta^\alpha s_h(t) i_v(t) - (\alpha_1^\alpha + \gamma^\alpha) i_h(t), \tag{13}$$

$$D_t^\alpha i_v = v^\alpha (1 - i_v(t)) i_h(t) - \delta^\alpha i_v(t). \tag{14}$$

In this system, we convey that $D_t^\alpha = {}_0^C D_t^\alpha$ and, for simplicity, the birth rate and death are same. Moreover, the solution region for systems (12)–(14) is $\Omega = \{(s_h, i_h, i_v) : s_h + i_h + i_v \leq 1, s_h \geq 0, i_h \geq 0, i_v \geq 0\}$.

Finally, we investigate a stochastic extension of the fractional epidemic models (12)–(14) following various stochastic approaches available in the literature [27–30]. More precisely, we consider the following system of stochastic differential equations, which extends our fractional epidemic model:

$$\begin{cases} D_t^\alpha s_h(t) = 1 - \beta^\alpha s_h(t) i_v(t) - \alpha_1^\alpha s_h(t) + \sigma_1 s_h(t) dB_1(t), \\ D_t^\alpha i_h(t) = \beta^\alpha s_h(t) i_v(t) - (\alpha_1^\alpha + \gamma^\alpha) i_h(t) + \sigma_2 i_h(t) dB_2(t), \\ D_t^\alpha i_v(t) = v^\alpha (1 - i_v) i_h(t) - \delta^\alpha i_v(t) + \sigma_3 i_v(t) dB_3(t). \end{cases} \tag{15}$$

Here, $\sigma_1, \sigma_2$, and $\sigma_3$ are stochastic perturbations of each state variable and $B_m(t)$ is the autonomous Brownian motion for each $m = 1, 2, 3$.

## 3. Mathematical Analysis

This part is devoted to obtain the equilibrium points of steady states and stability analysis of systems (12)–(14). To that end, we set $D_t^\alpha s_h(t) = D_t^\alpha i_h(t) = D_t^\alpha i_v(t) = 0$. Then, there are two equilibria of the epidemic models (12)–(14), which are the disease-free $E_0 = (s_{h_0}, i_{h_0}, i_{v_0}) = (1, 0, 0)$, and the disease-existing steady state $E_1 = (s_h^*, i_h^*, i_v^*)$. It is easy to check algebraically that

$$i_v^* = \frac{v^\alpha i_h^*}{v^\alpha i_h^* + \delta^\alpha}, \tag{16}$$

$$s_h^* = \frac{(\alpha_1^\alpha + \gamma^\alpha)(v^\alpha i_h^* + \delta^\alpha)}{\beta^\alpha v^\alpha}, \tag{17}$$

$$i_h^* = \frac{\beta^\alpha v^\alpha - \alpha_1^\alpha (\alpha_1^\alpha + \gamma^\alpha) \delta^\alpha}{v^\alpha (\alpha_1^\alpha + \gamma^\alpha)(\beta^\alpha + \alpha_1^\alpha)}. \tag{18}$$

On the other hand, to obtain the basic reproductive number, we apply the next generation approach. This method assures that the following identity is satisfied:

$$\begin{bmatrix} i_h^* \\ i_v^* \end{bmatrix} = F \begin{bmatrix} i_h \\ i_v \end{bmatrix} - V \begin{bmatrix} i_h \\ i_v \end{bmatrix}, \tag{19}$$

where

$$F = \begin{bmatrix} 0 & \beta^\alpha s_h \\ 0 & 0 \end{bmatrix}, \qquad V = \begin{bmatrix} (\alpha_1^\alpha + \gamma^\alpha) & 0 \\ -v^\alpha & \delta^\alpha \end{bmatrix}. \tag{20}$$

As a consequence,

$$FV^{-1} = \frac{1}{\delta^\alpha(\alpha_1^\alpha + \gamma^\alpha)} \begin{bmatrix} \beta^\alpha s_h v^\alpha & \beta^\alpha s_h \alpha^\alpha + v^\alpha \\ 0 & 0 \end{bmatrix} \tag{21}$$

We conclude that the basic reproductive number is

$$R_0 = \frac{\beta^\alpha v^\alpha}{\delta^\alpha(\alpha_1^\alpha + \gamma^\alpha)}. \tag{22}$$

In what follows, we require the Jacobian associated to ouR system fractional differential equations. Its determination is a straightforward task, and it can be readily checked that it is given by

$$J(s_h, i_h, i_v) = \begin{bmatrix} -\beta^\alpha i_v - \alpha_1^\alpha & 0 & -\beta^\alpha s_h \\ \beta^\alpha i_v & -(\alpha_1^\alpha + \gamma^\alpha) & \beta^\alpha s_h \\ 0 & v^\alpha(1 - i_v) & -v^\alpha i_h - \delta^\alpha \end{bmatrix} \tag{23}$$

**Theorem 1.** *The disease-free steady-state $E_0$ is locally asymptotically stable when $R_0 < 1$.*

**Proof.** Let $I_3$ represent the identity matrix of size $3 \times 3$. In order to study the stability at the point $E_0(1,0,0)$, observe firstly that

$$|J(1,0,0) - \lambda I_3| = \begin{vmatrix} -\alpha_1^\alpha - \lambda & 0 & -\beta^\alpha \\ 0 & -(\alpha_1^\alpha + \gamma^\alpha) - \lambda & \beta^\alpha \\ 0 & v & -\delta^\alpha - \lambda \end{vmatrix} = 0, \tag{24}$$

if and only if $\lambda$ satisfies $\lambda = -\alpha_1^\alpha$ or the quadratic equation

$$\lambda^2 + (\alpha_1^\alpha + \gamma^\alpha + \delta^\alpha)\lambda + \delta^\alpha \alpha_1^\alpha + \delta^\alpha \gamma^\alpha - v^\alpha \beta^\alpha = 0. \tag{25}$$

By using Routh–Hurwitz criteria for second-order polynomials, we conclude that the system is locally asymptotically stable at $E_0$ if $R_0 < 1$. □

**Theorem 2.** *If $R_0 > 1$, then the system is locally asymptotically stable at $E_1$.*

**Proof.** Proceeding as in the previous theorem, it follows that the characteristic equation associated to the Jacobian matrix at the equilibrium point is given by

$$\lambda^3 + \lambda^2(-A - D - G) + \lambda(AD + AG + DG - EF) - ADG - BCF + AEF = 0, \tag{26}$$

where $A = -\beta^\alpha i_v - \alpha_1^\alpha$, $B = -\beta^\alpha s_h$, $C = \beta^\alpha i_v$, $D = -(\alpha_1^\alpha + \gamma)$, $E = \beta^\alpha s_h$, $F = v^\alpha(1 - i_v)$ and $G = -v^\alpha i_h - \delta^\alpha$. The conclusion readily follows now from the Routh–Hurwitz criterion for cubic polynomials. □

The following lemma is provided to improve the global stability analysis of the system (12)–(14).

**Lemma 1** (Leon [31]). *Let $x : [0, \infty) \to \mathbb{R}^+$ be a continuous function, and let $t_0 \geq 0$. Then, for any time $t \geq t_0$, $\alpha \in (0,1)$ and $x^* \in \mathbb{R}^+$, the following inequality holds:*

$$D^\alpha \left[ x(t) - x^* - x^* ln \frac{x(t)}{x^*} \right] \leq \left( 1 - \frac{x^*}{x(t)} \right) D^\alpha x(t). \tag{27}$$

We tackle now the global asymptotic stability of the system (12)–(14) at the equilibrium points.

**Theorem 3.** *If $R_0 < 1$, then the system is globally asymptotically stable at $E_0$.*

**Proof.** Firstly, let us define the Lyapunov functional

$$G = \left(s_h + (i_h + i_v) - s_{h_0} - s_{h_0} log \frac{s_h}{s_{h_0}}\right) = \left(s_h - s_{h_0} - s_{h_0} log \frac{s_h}{s_{h_0}}\right) + i_h + i_v. \quad (28)$$

Using Lemma 1 now, we obtain that

$$\begin{aligned} D_t^\alpha G &\leq \left(\frac{s_h - s_{h_0}}{s_h}\right) D_t^\alpha s_h + D_t^\alpha i_h + D_t^\alpha i_h \\ &= \left(\frac{s_h - s_{h_0}}{s_h}\right)(1 - \beta^\alpha s_h i_v - \alpha_1^\alpha s_h) + \beta^\alpha s_h i_v - (\alpha_1^\alpha + \gamma^\alpha) i_h + v(1 - i_v) i_h - \delta^\alpha i_v \\ &= \frac{-(s_h - s_{h_0})^2}{s_h s_{h_0}} - (\alpha_1^\alpha + \gamma^\alpha)\left(i_h - \frac{\beta^\alpha s_h i_v}{\alpha_1^\alpha + \gamma^\alpha}\right) - \delta^\alpha \left(i_v - \frac{v^\alpha (1 - i_v) i_h}{\delta^\alpha}\right). \end{aligned} \quad (29)$$

Clearly, $D_t^\alpha G < 0$ if $R_0 < 1$. Meanwhile, $D_t^\alpha G = 0$ if $s_h = 1$, $i_h = 0$ and $i_v = 0$. We conclude that the system is globally asymptotically stable at the disease-free equilibrium point when $R_0 < 1$. □

**Theorem 4.** *The system (12)–(14) is globally asymptotically stable at $E_1$ when $R_0 > 1$.*

**Proof.** The proof is similar to that of the previous theorem. In this case, we construct the Lyapunov functional at $E_1$ as

$$G = \left(s_h - s_h^* - s_h^* log \frac{s_h}{s_h^*}\right) + \left(i_h - i_h^* - i_h^* log \frac{i_h}{i_h^*}\right) + \left(i_v - i_v^* - i_v^* log \frac{i_v}{i_v^*}\right). \quad (30)$$

Using Lemma 1 and proceeding as in the proof of the preceding theorem, it follows that

$$\begin{aligned} D_t^\alpha G &\leq \left(\frac{s_h - s_h^*}{s_h}\right) D_t^\alpha s_h + \left(\frac{i_h - i_h^*}{i_h}\right) D_t^\alpha i_h + \left(\frac{i_v - i_v^*}{i_v}\right) D_t^\alpha i_v \\ &= -\frac{(s_h - s_h^*)^2}{(s_h s_h^*)} - \frac{\beta^\alpha s_h i_v (i_h - i_h^*)^2}{(i_h i_h^*)} - \frac{v i_h (i_v - i_v^*)^2}{i_v i_v^*}. \end{aligned} \quad (31)$$

Observe that $D_t^\alpha G \leq 0$ when $R_0 > 1$. Moreover, $D_t^\alpha G = 0$ if $s_h = s_h^*$, $i_h = i_h^*$ and $i_v = i_v^*$, which means that the system is globally asymptotically stable at the endemic equilibrium solution. □

Before closing this section, we investigate the sensitivity of the parameters of the fractional epidemic model. To that end, we employ the derivative based local method to take the partial derivatives of outputs with respect to inputs. Let

$$R_0 = \frac{\beta v}{(\alpha_1 + \gamma)\delta}. \quad (32)$$

Observe that the following are satisfied:

$$A_\beta = \frac{\beta}{R_0} \times \frac{\partial R_0}{\partial \beta} = 1 > 0, \quad (33)$$

$$A_v = \frac{v}{R_0} \times \frac{\partial R_0}{\partial v} = 1 > 0, \quad (34)$$

$$A_{\alpha_1} = \frac{\alpha_1}{R_0} \times \frac{\partial R_0}{\partial \alpha_1} = -\left(\frac{\alpha_1}{\alpha_1 + \gamma}\right) < 0, \quad (35)$$

$$A_\delta = \frac{\delta}{R_0} \times \frac{\partial R_0}{\partial \delta} = -1 < 0, \quad (36)$$

$$A_\gamma = \frac{\gamma}{R_0} \times \frac{\partial R_0}{\partial \gamma} = -\frac{\gamma}{(\alpha_1 + \gamma)} < 0. \quad (37)$$

As a conclusion, $\beta$ and $v$ are sensitive, and all the remaining parameters concerning the reproduction number are not sensitive.

## 4. Numerical Model

We present three generalized stochastic fractional techniques to solve the stochastic fractional-order system (15), namely, Euler, Runge–Kutta and a nonstandard finite-difference (NSFD) scheme. The first two are already standard techniques which are well known in the literature [32,33]. The third model is a new technique which is constructed using a non-local approach [34]. Throughout, $\Delta t$ representS the temporal step-size.

*Stochastic Euler method:*

$$\begin{cases} s_h^{n+1} = s_h^n + \dfrac{(\Delta t)^\alpha}{\Gamma(\alpha+1)}[1 - \beta^\alpha s_h^n i_v^n - \alpha_1^\alpha s_h^n + \sigma_1 \Delta B_1 s_h^n], \\ i_h^{n+1} = i_h^n + \dfrac{(\Delta t)^\alpha}{\Gamma(\alpha+1)}[\beta^\alpha s_h^n i_v^n - (\alpha_1^\alpha + \gamma^\alpha) i_h^n + \sigma_2 \Delta B_2 i_h^n], \\ i_v^{n+1} = i_v^n + \dfrac{(\Delta t)^\alpha}{\Gamma(\alpha+1)}[v^\alpha (1 - i_v^n) i_h^n - \delta^\alpha i_v^n + \sigma_3 \Delta B_3 i_v^n]. \end{cases} \tag{38}$$

*Stochastic Runge–Kutta method:*

$$\begin{cases} \omega^{n+1} = \omega^n + \dfrac{1}{6}[M_1 + 2M_2 + 2M_3 + M_4], \\ M_1 = (\Delta t)\phi(t^n, \omega^n) + (\Delta t)\sigma \Delta B \psi(t^n, \omega^n), \\ M_2 = (\Delta t)\phi\left(t^n + \dfrac{1}{2}\Delta t, \omega^n + \dfrac{1}{2}M_1\right) + (\Delta t)\sigma \Delta B \psi\left(t^n \dfrac{1}{2}\Delta t, \omega^n, \dfrac{1}{2}M_1\right), \\ M_3 = (\Delta t)\phi\left(t^n + \dfrac{1}{2}\Delta t, \omega^n + \dfrac{1}{2}M_2\right) + (\Delta t)\sigma \Delta B \psi\left(t^n \dfrac{1}{2}\Delta t, \omega^n, \dfrac{1}{2}M_2\right), \\ M_4 = (\Delta t)\phi(t^n + \hbar, \omega^n + M_3) + (\Delta t)\sigma \Delta B \psi(t^n \hbar, \omega^n, M_3). \end{cases} \tag{39}$$

*NSFD method:*

$$\begin{cases} s_h^{n+1} = \dfrac{s_h^n + \frac{(\Delta t)^\alpha}{\Gamma(\alpha+1)}[1 + \sigma_1 \Delta B_1 s_h^n]}{1 + \frac{h^\alpha}{\Gamma(\alpha+1)}(\beta^\alpha i_v^n + \alpha_1^\alpha)}, \\ i_h^{n+1} = \dfrac{i_h^n + \frac{(\Delta t)^\alpha}{\Gamma(\alpha+1)}[\beta^\alpha s_h^n i_v^n + \sigma_2 \Delta B_2 i_h^n]}{1 + \frac{h^\alpha}{\Gamma(\alpha+1)}(\alpha_1^\alpha + \gamma^\alpha)}, \\ i_v^{n+1} = \dfrac{i_v^n + \frac{(\Delta t)^\alpha}{\Gamma(\alpha+1)}[v^\alpha i_h^n + \sigma_3 \Delta B_3 i_v^n]}{1 + \frac{h^\alpha}{\Gamma(\alpha+1)}(v^\alpha i_h^n + \delta^\alpha)}. \end{cases} \tag{40}$$

Next, we establish the most important properties of the NSFD method.

**Theorem 5** (Positivity). *The deterministic form of system (40) preserves the non-negativity of the solution.*

**Proof.** All the equations in the system (40) contain no negative term. So, if the initial conditions are non-negative, then the numerical solutions remain non-negative, as desired. □

**Theorem 6** (Boundedness). *Suppose that the initial data of (40) are nonnegative. Then, there exists a constant $K(n, \alpha) \geq 0$, such that $s_h^n, i_h^n, i_v^n \in [0, K(n, \alpha)]$, for each $n \in \mathbb{N}$.*

**Proof.** By adding and rearranging the equations of the numerical model (40), we readily check that

$$
\begin{aligned}
& s_h^{n+1} + i_h^{n+1} + i_v^{n+1} \\
& \leq s_h^{n+1}\left[1 + \frac{(\Delta t)^\alpha(\beta^\alpha i_v^n + \alpha_1^\alpha)}{\Gamma(\alpha+1)}\right] + i_h^{n+1}\left[1 + \frac{(\Delta t)^\alpha(\alpha_1^\alpha + \gamma^\alpha)}{\Gamma(\alpha+1)}\right] + i_v^{n+1}\left[1 + \frac{(\Delta t)^\alpha(v^\alpha i_h^n + \delta^\alpha)}{\Gamma(\alpha+1)}\right] \\
& = (s_h^n + i_h^n + i_v^n) + \frac{(\Delta t)^\alpha}{\Gamma(\alpha+1)}[1 + \sigma_1 \Delta B_1 s_h^n + \beta^\alpha s_h^n i_v^n + \sigma_2 \Delta B_2 i_h^n + v^\alpha i_h^n + \sigma_3 \Delta B_3 i_v^n].
\end{aligned} \tag{41}
$$

The proof is established using mathematical induction, letting $K(n+1,\alpha)$ be the right end of this chain of identities and inequalities. □

Next, we examine the stability of the NSFD system (40).

**Definition 2** (Arenas et al. [21]). *The discrete system* (40) *is* asymptotically stable *if there exist constants* $\mathcal{K}_1$, $\mathcal{K}_2$ *and* $\mathcal{K}_3$ *with the property that* $s_h^{n+1} \leq \mathcal{K}_1$, $i_h^{n+1} \leq \mathcal{K}_2$ *and* $i_v^{n+1} \leq \mathcal{K}_3$ *as* $\alpha \to 1^-$.

**Theorem 7.** *Under the hypotheses of Theorem 6, the system* (40) *is asymptotically stable.*

**Proof.** The conclusion of this result is a direct consequence of Theorem 6. □

Before closing this section, we provide some numerical simulations for the stochastic fractional-order epidemic model (15). To that end, we fix the model parameters as given by Table 1 (see [26]). To start with, Figure 1 depicts the convergence behavior of each compartment of the model at the endemic equilibrium (EE). The behavior of the graphs is investigated for various values of $\alpha$. Each graph adopts a random path to reach the EE at the temporal step-size $h = 0.1$. When the step-size is increased, the infected population may diverge at each value of the non-integer parameter. We conclude from this that the generalized stochastic Euler method fails to illustrate the actual behavior of the disease dynamics.

**Table 1.** Model parameters employed in the simulations of this work. Here, DFE stands for disease-free equilibrium, and EE for endemic equilibrium.

| Parameters | Values |
|---|---|
| $\delta^\alpha$ | 0.6 |
| $\alpha_1^\alpha$ | 1 |
| $\beta^\alpha$ (DFE) | 3 |
| $\beta^\alpha$ (EE) | 3.5 |
| $\gamma^\alpha$ | 0.6 |
| $v^\alpha$ | 0.3 |
| $\sigma_1$ | 0.09 |
| $\sigma_2$ | 0.008 |
| $\sigma_3$ | 0.007 |

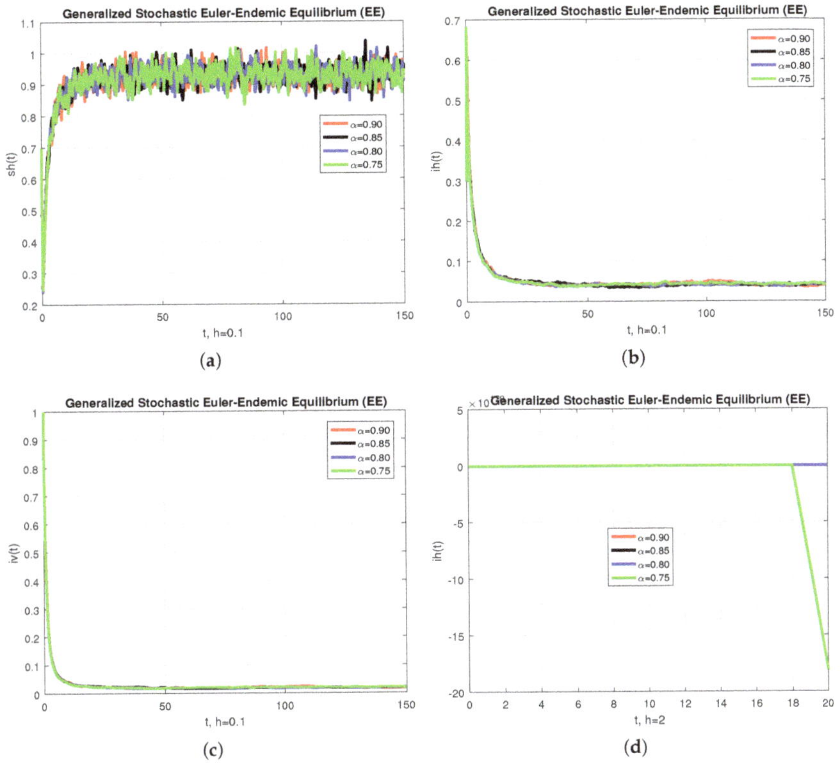


**Figure 1.** The graphical behavior of each sub-population is presented in the (**a**) numerical solution of $s_h$, (**b**) numerical solution of $i_h$, (**c**) numerical solution of $i_v$ and (**d**) numerical solution of $i_h$, with different values of $\alpha$, using the generalized fractional stochastic Euler method.

In a second experiment, we used the generalized stochastic Runge–Kutta method to solve the same problem of the last paragraph. The results are shown in Figure 2, which provides the convergence behavior of each compartment of the model at endemic equilibrium (EE) for various values of $\alpha$. When the step-size is increased above $\Delta t = 0.1$, the infected population may diverge at each value of $\alpha$. Again, we conclude that this method is not a reliable tool to reflect the actual behavior of the model. On the contrary, Figure 3 provides two runs (left and right columns) obtained by means of the generalized stochastic NSFD. The results show that this technique converges to the equilibrium solution for each of the values of $\alpha$ considered, using steps of sizes between $\Delta t = 0.1$ and $\Delta t = 100$, and at a low computational cost. In that sense, this method is more robust and reliable than the standard approaches used for comparison purposes.

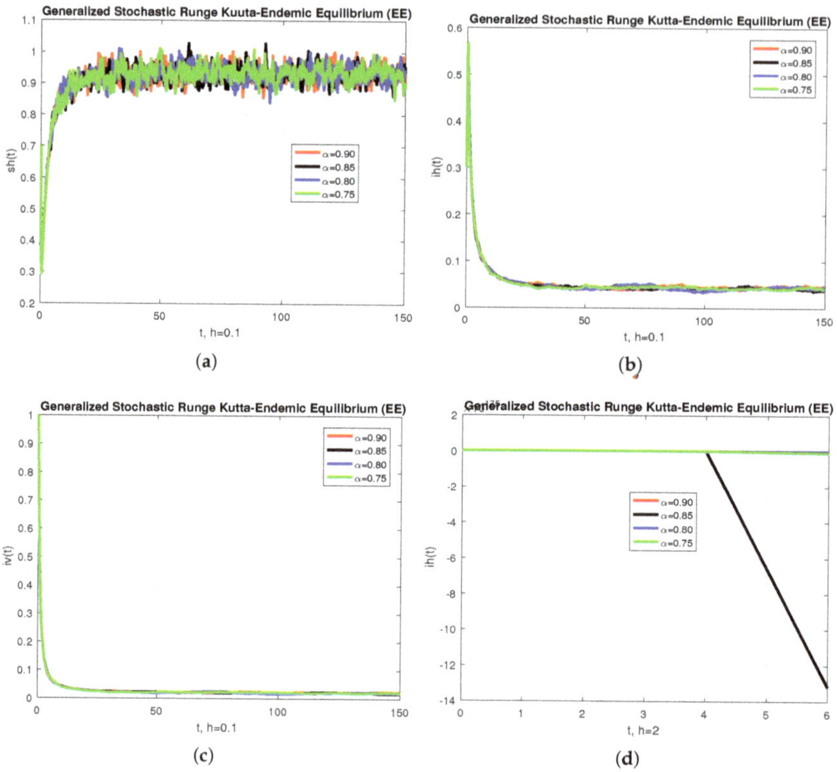


**Figure 2.** The graphical performance of each sub-population is presented in the (**a**) numerical solution of $s_h$, (**b**) numerical solution of $i_h$, (**c**) numerical solution of $i_v$ and (**d**) numerical solution of $i_h$, with different value of $\alpha$, using the generalized fractional stochastic Runge–Kutta method.

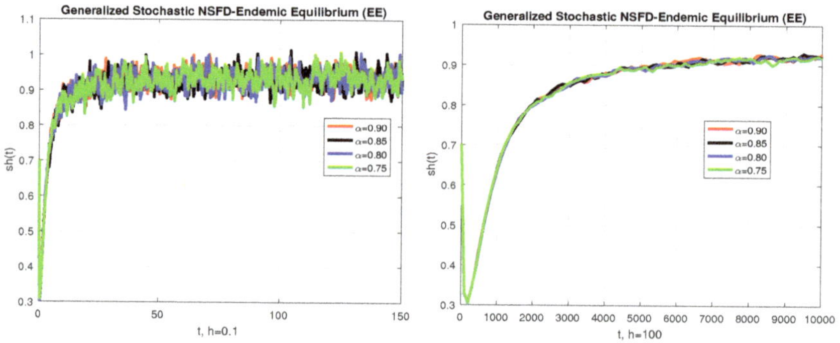


(**a**) Numerical solution of $s_h$

(**b**) Numerical solution of $s_h$

**Figure 3.** *Cont.*

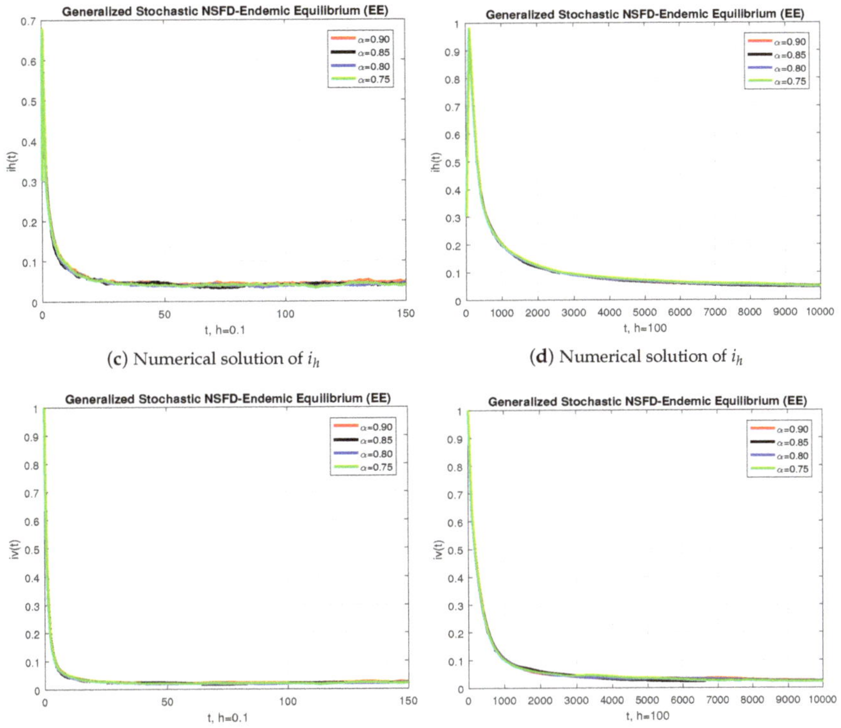


(**c**) Numerical solution of $i_h$

(**d**) Numerical solution of $i_h$

(**e**) Numerical solution of $i_v$

(**f**) Numerical solution of $i_v$

**Figure 3.** The graphical behavior of each sub-population is presented for two sets of numerical experiments (left and right columns) with different values of $\alpha$, using the generalized fractional stochastic NSFD.

## 5. Conclusions

In this work, we departed from a fractional-order disease model and transformed it into a non-parametric perturbation stochastic model. A generalized stochastic fractional NSFD method was proposed and applied to solve the epidemic model under study. The proposed scheme preserves the positivity of the numerical solutions at each temporal step. The generalized stochastic fractional NSFD is also capable of preserving the boundedness of the approximations. We proved that the given system has two steady states, namely, a disease-free and an endemic steady state. Furthermore, the constraints under which the given system is locally and globally asymptotically stable were investigated. It is concluded that the system attains the local and global stability when the disease is absent if $R_0 < 1$. In the same way, the role of $R_0$ when $R_0 > 1$ was studied for the endemic equilibrium. Two other methods (a generalized fractional Euler method and a generalized Runge–Kutta method) were also applied to compare the obtained results. The simulations showed that the proposed scheme is superior in terms of its capability to identify correctly the equilibrium solutions, in that sense our present report investigated a structure-preserving technique [35–37] to solve a mathematical system in epidemiology. As a final comment, we would like to point out that the investigation of the stochastic system is justified by the fact that solutions exist for that model. Indeed, notice that the drift functions of this model are locally Lipschitz continuous, which implies that the solutions exist locally. The global existence follows an argument similar to that in [38]. We do not provide the details, as such a study is outside the scope of the present work.

**Author Contributions:** Conceptualization, N.A., J.E.M.-D., A.R., D.B., M.R., Z.I. and M.O.A.; data curation, N.A., J.E.M.-D., A.R., D.B., Z.I. and M.O.A.; formal analysis, N.A., J.E.M.-D., A.R., D.B. and M.R.; funding acquisition, J.E.M.-D.; investigation, N.A., J.E.M.-D., A.R., D.B., M.R. and Z.I.; methodology, N.A., J.E.M.-D., A.R., D.B., M.R. and M.O.A.; project administration, N.A. and J.E.M.-D.; resources, N.A., J.E.M.-D., A.R., D.B. and M.R.; software, N.A., J.E.M.-D., A.R., D.B. and Z.I.; supervision, N.A., J.E.M.-D., A.R., D.B., M.R. and M.O.A.; validation, N.A., J.E.M.-D., A.R., D.B., M.R., Z.I. and M.O.A.; visualization, N.A., J.E.M.-D. and D.B.; writing—original draft, N.A., J.E.M.-D., A.R., D.B., M.R., Z.I. and M.O.A.; writing—review and editing, N.A., J.E.M.-D., A.R., D.B., M.R., Z.I. and M.O.A. All authors have read and agreed to the published version of the manuscript.

**Funding:** The corresponding author wishes to acknowledge the financial support from the National Council for Science and Technology of Mexico (CONACYT) through grant A1-S-45928.

**Data Availability Statement:** The data presented in this study are available on request from the corresponding author.

**Acknowledgments:** The authors wish to thank the guest editors for their kind invitation to submit a paper to the special issue of *Axioms MDPI* on "Fractional Calculus—Theory and Applications". They also wish to thank the anonymous reviewers for their comments and criticisms. All of their comments were taken into account in the revised version of the paper, resulting in a substantial improvement with respect to the original submission.

**Conflicts of Interest:** The authors declare no potential conflict of interest.

## References

1. Montoya, C.; Romero-Leiton, J.P. Analysis and optimal control of a malaria mathematical model under resistance and population movement. *arXiv* **2020**, arXiv:2002.00070.
2. Olaniyi, S.; Okosun, K.O.; Adesanya, S.O.; Lebelo, R.S. Modelling malaria dynamics with partial immunity and protected travellers: Optimal control and cost-effectiveness analysis. *J. Biol. Dyn.* **2020**, *14*, 90–115. [CrossRef]
3. Kim, S.; Byun, J.H.; Park, A.; Jung, I.H. A mathematical model for assessing the effectiveness of controlling relapse in *Plasmodium vivax* malaria endemic in the Republic of Korea. *PLoS ONE* **2020**, *15*, e0227919. [CrossRef]
4. Ibrahim, M.M.; Kamran, M.A.; Naeem, Mannan, M.M.; Kim, S.; Jung, I.H. Impact of Awareness to Control Malaria Disease: A Mathematical Modeling Approach. *Complexity* **2020**, *2020*, 1–13. [CrossRef]
5. Baihaqi, M.A.; Adi-Kusumo, F. Modelling malaria transmission in a population with $SEIRS_p$ method. In *AIP Conference Proceedings*; AIP Publishing LLC: Melville, NY, USA, 2020; Volume 2264, pp. 1–13.
6. Traoré, B.; Koutou, O.; Sangaré, B. A global mathematical model of malaria transmission dynamics with structured mosquito population and temperature variations. *Nonlinear Anal. Real World Appl.* **2020**, *53*, 103081. [CrossRef]
7. Djidjou-Demasse, R.; Abiodun, G.J.; Adeola, A.M.; Botai, J.O. Development and analysis of a malaria transmission mathematical model with seasonal mosquito life-history traits. *Stud. Appl. Math.* **2020**, *144*, 389–411. [CrossRef]
8. Pandey, R. Mathematical Model for Malaria Transmission and Chemical Control with Human-Related Activities. *Natl. Acad. Sci. Lett.* **2020**, *43*, 59–65. [CrossRef]
9. Song, T.; Wang, C.; Tian, B. Mathematical models for within-host competition of malaria parasites. *Math. Biosci. Eng.* **2020**, *16*, 6623–6653. [CrossRef] [PubMed]
10. Ogunmiloro, O.M. Mathematical Modeling of the Coinfection Dynamics of Malaria-Toxoplasmosis in the Tropics. *Biom. Lett.* **2019**, *56*, 139–163. [CrossRef]
11. Koutou, O.; Traoré, B.; Sangaré, B. Mathematical modeling of malaria transmission global dynamics: Taking into account the immature stages of the vectors. *Adv. Differ. Equ.* **2018**, *2018*, 1–34. [CrossRef]
12. Bakary, T.; Boureima, S.; Sado, T. A mathematical model of malaria transmission in a periodic environment. *J. Biol. Dyn.* **2018**, *12*, 400–432. [CrossRef]
13. Beretta, E.; Capasso, V.; Garao, D.G. A mathematical model for malaria transmission with asymptomatic carriers and two age groups in the human population. *Math. Biosci.* **2018**, *300*, 87–101. [CrossRef]
14. Rafia, G.; He, J.; Sana, D.; Ebrahim, A.S. A Simple SIR Mathematical Model of Malaria Transmission with the Efficacy of the Vaccine. In Proceedings of the 2018 2nd International Conference on Computational Biology and Bioinformatics, Bari, Italy, 26–28 December 2018; Volume 1145, pp. 6–11.
15. Traoré, B.; Sangaré, B.; Traoré, S. A mathematical model of malaria transmission with structured vector population and seasonality. *J. Appl. Math.* **2017**, *2017*, 1–15. [CrossRef]
16. Mojeeb, A.L.; Adu, I.K. Simple mathematical model for malaria transmission. *J. Adv. Math. Comput. Sci.* **2017**, *25*, 1–24.
17. Olaniyi, S.; Obabiyi, O.S. Mathematical model for malaria transmission dynamics in human and mosquito populations with nonlinear forces of infection. *Int. J. Pure Appl. Math.* **2013**, *88*, 125–156. [CrossRef]
18. Mandal, S.; Sarkar, R.R.; Sinha, S. Mathematical models of malaria—A review. *Malar. J.* **2011**, *10*, 1–19. [CrossRef] [PubMed]

19. Chitnis, N.; Cushing, J.M.; Hyman, J.M. Bifurcation analysis of a mathematical model for malaria transmission. *SIAM J. Appl. Math.* **2006**, *67*, 24–45. [CrossRef]
20. Smith, T.; Killeen, G.F.; Maire, N.; Ross, A.; Molineaux, L.; Tediosi, F.; Tanner, M. Mathematical modeling of the impact of malaria vaccines on the clinical epidemiology and natural history of Plasmodium falciparum malaria: Overview. *Am. J. Trop. Med. Hyg.* **2006**, *75*, 1–10. [CrossRef] [PubMed]
21. Arenas, A.J.; González-Parra, G.; Chen-Charpentier, B.M. Construction of nonstandard finite difference schemes for the SI and SIR epidemic models of fractional order. *Math. Comput. Simul.* **2015**, *121*, 48–63. [CrossRef]
22. Iqbal, Z.; Ahmad, N.; Baleanu, D.; Adel, W.; Rqfiq, M.; Rehman, M.A.; Alshomrani, A.S. Positivity and boundedness preserving numerical algorithm for the solution of fractional nonlinear epidemic model of HIV/AIDS transmission. *Chaos Solitons Fractals* **2020**, *134*, 109706. [CrossRef]
23. Iqbal, Z.; Ahmad, N.; Baleanu, D.; Rqfiq, M.; Iqbal, M.S.; Rehman, M.A. Structure preserving computational technique for fractional order Schnakenberg model. *Comput. Appl. Math.* **2020**, *39*, 61. [CrossRef]
24. Macías-Dxixaz, J.E.; Hendy, A.S.; Markov, N.S. A bounded numerical solver for a fractional FitzHugh-Nagumo equation and its high-performance implementation. *Eng. Comput.* **2021**, *37*, 1593–1609. [CrossRef]
25. Iqbal, Z.; Rehman, M.A.; Baleanu, D.; Ahmed, N.; Raza, A.; Rafiq, M. Mathematical and numerical investigations of the fractional-order epidemic model with constant vaccination strategy. *Rom. Rep. Phys.* **2021**, *73*, 112.
26. Gebremeskel, A.A.; Krogstad, H.E. Mathematical modelling of endemic malaria transmission. *Am. J. Appl. Math.* **2015**, *3*, 36–46. [CrossRef]
27. Sweilam, N.H.; Al-Mekhlafi, S.M.; Baleanu, D. A hybrid stochastic fractional order Coronavirus (2019-nCov) mathematical model. *Chaos Solitons Fractals* **2021**, *145*, 110762. [CrossRef]
28. Omar, O.A.M.; Elbarkouky, R.A.; Ahmed, H.M. Fractional stochastic models for COVID-19: Case study of Egypt. *Results Phys.* **2021**, *23*, 104018. [CrossRef] [PubMed]
29. Alkahtani, B.S.T.; Koca, I. Fractional stochastic sir model. *Results Phys.* **2021**, *24*, 104124. [CrossRef]
30. Akinlar, M.A.; Inc, M.; Gómez-Aguilar, J.F.; Boutarfa, B. Solutions of a disease model with fractional white noise. *Chaos Solitons Fractals* **2020**, *137*, 109840. [CrossRef]
31. Leon, C.V. Volterra Lyapunov functions for fractional-order epidemic systems. *Commun. Nonlinear Sci. Numer. Simul.* **2015**, *24*, 75–85. [CrossRef]
32. Milici, C.; Machado, J.T.; Draganescu, G. Application of the Euler and Runge-Kutta generalized methods for FDE and symbolic packages in the analysis of some fractional attractors. *Int. J. Nonlinear Sci. Numer. Simul.* **2019**, *21*, 159–170. [CrossRef]
33. Sweilama, N.H.; Al-Mekhlafi, S.M.; Almutairi, A.; Baleanu, D. A hybrid fractional COVID-19 model with general population mask use. *Numer. Treat. Alex. Eng. J.* **2021**, *60*, 3219–3232. [CrossRef]
34. Mickens, R.E. *Nonstandard Finite Difference Models of Differential Equations*; World Scientific: Singapore, 1994.
35. Macías-Díaz, J.E.; Puri, A. A numerical method for computing radially symmetric solutions of a dissipative nonlinear modified Klein-Gordon equation. *Numer. Methods Partial Differ. Equ. Int. J.* **2005**, *21*, 998–1015. [CrossRef]
36. Macías-Díaz, J.E.; Anna, S. Existence and uniqueness of monotone and bounded solutions for a finite-difference discretization à la Mickens of the generalized Burgers–Huxley equation. *J. Differ. Equ. Appl.* **2014**, *20*, 989–1004. [CrossRef]
37. Macías-Díaz, J.E.; González, A.E. A convergent and dynamically consistent finite-difference method to approximate the positive and bounded solutions of the classical Burgers–Fisher equation. *J. Comput. Appl. Math.* **2017**, *318*, 604–615. [CrossRef]
38. Din, A.; Khan, T.; Li, Y.; Tahir, H.; Khan, A.; Ali Khan, W. Mathematical analysis of dengue stochastic epidemic model. *Results Phys.* **2021**, *20*, 103719. [CrossRef]

MDPI
St. Alban-Anlage 66
4052 Basel
Switzerland
Tel. +41 61 683 77 34
Fax +41 61 302 89 18
www.mdpi.com

*Axioms* Editorial Office
E-mail: axioms@mdpi.com
www.mdpi.com/journal/axioms

www.ingramcontent.com/pod-product-compliance
Lightning Source LLC
LaVergne TN
LVHW070720100526
838202LV00013B/1134
*9783036532622*